COMMUNITY POLICING AND PROBLEM SOLVING

Sixth Edition

COMMUNITY POLICING AND PROBLEM SOLVING

STRATEGIES AND PRACTICES

Kenneth J. Peak
University of Nevada, Reno

Ronald W. Glensor
Reno, Nevada, Police Department (Ret'd)

PEARSON

Boston   Columbus   Indianapolis   New York   San Francisco   Upper Saddle River
Amsterdam   Cape Town   Dubai   London   Madrid   Milan Munich   Paris   Montreal   Toronto
Delhi   Mexico City   Sao Paulo   Sydney   Hong Kong   Seoul   Singapore   Taipei   Tokyo

Vice President and Executive Publisher: Vernon Anthony
Senior Acquisitions Editor: Eric Krassow
Editorial Assistant: Lynda Cramer
Media Project Manager: Karen Bretz
Director of Marketing: David Gesell
Marketing Manager: Cyndi Eller
Senior Marketing Coordinator: Alicia Wozniak
Production Manager: Holly Shufeldt
Creative Director: Jayne Conte
Cover Designe: Karen Salzbach
Cover Illustration/Photo: Fotolia
Image Permission Coordinator: Karen Sanatar
Full-Service Project Management/Composition: Nitin Agarwal/Aptara®, Inc.
Printer/Binder: R.R. Donnelley & Sons

Credits and acknowledgments borrowed from other sources and reproduced, with permission, in this textbook appear on appropriate page within text.

Library of Congress Cataloging-in-Publication Data

Peak, Kenneth J.
    Community policing and problem solving : strategies and practices/Kenneth J. Peak, Ronald W. Glensor.—6th ed.
        p.   cm.
    Includes bibliographical references and index.
    ISBN-13: 978-0-13-512086-6 (alk. paper)
    ISBN-10: 0-13-512086-1 (alk. paper)
    1. Community policing.   2. Crime prevention—United States—Citizen participation.   3. Police administration.
4. Police-community relations.   5. Community policing—United States.   6. Police administration—United States.
I. Glensor, Ronald W.   II. Title.
    HV7936.C83P43 2012
    363.2'3—dc23

                                                                                    2011027619

10 9 8 7 6 5 4 3 2 1

ISBN-10:   0-13-512086-1
ISBN-13: 978-0-13-512086-6

For Emma, Oli, and Nic, all best wishes for great things and happy lives; and to Jen, in recognition of her recent achievement of graduate degree status.

–K.J.P.

To my wonderful and supportive family: my wife Kristy, daughter and son Breanne and Ronnie, son and daughter-in-law Derek and Katie, and grandchildren Addison and Chloe

–R.W.G.

BRIEF CONTENTS

CONTENTS

NEW TOPICS IN THIS SIXTH EDITION

In addition to updated information throughout and a myriad of new examples of "what works" with COPPS initiatives throughout the text, following are other substantively new topics that have been added:

Chapter 1: Language of policing; an "information age"

Chapter 2: Sense of community; effects of economy (i.e., housing and mortgage crisis); community governance; community justice; influence of immigration (and the Arizona controversy); shifting and sharing responsibility for addressing crime and disorder

Chapter 3: Considerations when planning/conducting problem analysis; tools for problem solving

Chapter 4: Officers' and victims' roles in crime prevention; managing publicity campaigns

Chapter 5: Establishing an IT framework; intelligence-gathering process; intelligence-led policing; predictive policing; social networking and crime analysis

Chapter 6: Transforming organizations from "good" to "great"; value-laden leadership; Level 5 leader; "moments of truth"; officer recruitment; the Millennial generation

Chapter 7: Effects of the economy on planning; two hands-on exercises (implementing a transition to COPPS, opening a POP project); using force field analysis; Gantt chart

Chapter 8: Rationales for knowing "what works" in criminal justice; assessment vis-à-vis evaluation; methods and challenges of performing empirical/impact evaluations of COPPS; the Community Policing Self-Assessment Tool (CP-SAT); two examples of empirical studies of COPPS

Chapter 9: Adult learning for Millennials; mentoring as a training tool; e-learning; online training

Chapter 10: Contagious shootings; recruiting toolkit; legal aspects of hate crimes; a federal hate crimes act; the federal Community Relations Service; new model biased-policing training curricula

Chapter 11: The "shake and bake" production method of methamphetamines; what works with street-level drug enforcement"; prescription drug abuse and "pharming parties"; gang facts from the National Gang Intelligence Center; the Gang Prevention Network; new approaches to graffiti; gun and youth violence; cyberbullying

Chapter 12: New and/or updated information concerning best practices for addressing identity theft, problems involving the mentally ill, the homeless, domestic violence, neighborhood disorder, stalking, and Internet crimes

Chapter 13: New and/or updated information concerning: COPPS initiatives in Charlotte-Mecklenburg, North Carolina; Chicago, Illinois; Minneapolis, Minnesota; San Diego, California; Hawaii County, Hawaii; Lincoln, Nebraska; Oxnard, California; Arroyo Grande, California; progressive stages of community policing; U.S. Department of Homeland Security's online

PREFACE

This book is about policing at its most important and challenging levels—in neighborhoods and in communities across the nation and in foreign venues. It is about the evolution of the latest era in policing that began in the mid-70s, one that centers on collaborating with the community and other agencies and organizations that are responsible for community safety. It is a philosophy and style of policing that requires officers to obtain new knowledge and tools such as problem solving, and it is grounded in strategic thinking and planning to enable agencies to keep up with the rapid societal changes such as homeland defense. This policing style also allows agencies to make the necessary organizational and administrative adjustments to maintain a capable and motivated workforce.

This sixth edition is premised on the assumption that the reader is most likely an undergraduate or graduate student studying criminal justice or policing, or perhaps the reader is a police practitioner with a fundamental knowledge of police history and operations or is working in a government agency outside policing and is interested in learning about community policing and problem solving. Citizens who are collaborating with police to resolve neighborhood problems in innovative ways can also be well served by reading this book.

The book also imparts some of the major underpinnings, prominent names, theories, practices (with myriad examples), and processes that are being implemented under community oriented policing and problem solving (COPPS) to control and prevent crime, disorder, and fear. A considerable number of textbooks have already been written about community policing. Most of them, however, emphasize its philosophy and provide little information about its practical aspects—putting the philosophy into daily practice. The application of community policing and problem solving is the primary focus of this book, as indicated in its title.

While some fundamental components of COPPS contribute to its success, no one single model exists; there is no cookie-cutter approach that can guarantee success. COPPS is an individualized, long-term process that involves fundamental institutional change, going beyond such simple tactics as foot and bicycle patrols or neighborhood police stations. It redefines the role of the officer on the street from crime fighter to problem solver. It forces a cultural transformation of the entire police agency, involving changes in recruiting, training, awards systems, evaluations, and promotions.

It has been said that problem solving is not new in policing and that police officers have always tried to solve problems in their daily work.

As is demonstrated throughout this text, however, problem solving is not the same as solving problems. Problem solving in the context of COPPS is very different and considerably more complex. It requires that officers identify and examine the underlying causes of recurring incidents of crime and disorder. Such policing thus seeks to make "street criminologists" of police officers, teaching them to expand their focus on offenders to include crime settings and victims. Such an approach presents great challenges for those patrol officers who are engaged in analytical work.

We emphasize that this book is not a call to ignore or discard policing's past methods, nor do we espouse an altogether new philosophy of policing in its place. Instead, we recommend that the police borrow from the wisdom of the past and adopt a holistic approach to the way police organizations are learning to address public safety more successfully. This book describes how many agencies should and are actively going about the process of revolutionizing their philosophy and operations.

ORGANIZATION AND CONTENTS OF THE BOOK

Like its five predecessors, this book is distinguished by its applied approach. In doing so, it showcases more than 50 exhibits and provides dozens of additional case studies and examples of problem solving in the field.

In that regard, the authors are enthusiastic about the addition of a new type of hands-on, pedagogical tool that has been added to this sixth edition—which we term "Learning by Doing"—and is found at the end of each chapter. This learning tool comports with the early 1900s teaching of famed educator John Dewey, who advocated the "learning by doing" approach to education, or problem-based learning. It also comports with the popular learning method espoused by Benjamin Bloom in 1956, known as "Bloom's Taxonomy," in which he called for "higher-order thinking skills"—critical and creative thinking that involves analysis, synthesis, and evaluation. These scenarios and activities will shift your attention from textbook-centered instruction and move the emphasis to student-centered projects. By being placed in these hypothetical situations, you can thus learn and apply some of the concepts covered in this chapter, develop skills in communication and self-management, at times become a problem solver, and learn about/address current community issues.

We also showcase in this edition the advancements and applications of information technologies (IT) in policing and the changing role of the crime analyst to support COPPS. In addition, chapter sections concerning major issues and problems as drugs, gangs, youth, computer crime, crime prevention, changing agency culture, evaluating COPPS initiatives, cyber-bullying, and special populations (e.g., the mentally ill, the homeless, the younger generation of police officers), and the future have been added or received major revisions.

To understand the methods and challenges of community policing and problem solving, we first need to look at the big picture. Thus, in the first three chapters we discuss (1) the history of policing and the major transformations over time that led to the present community policing era; (2) the need for, and means of, engaging the community in all components of the criminal justice system (included is a look at our nation's economic struggles, demographics, and shifts in crime); and (3) a specific examination of COPPS (along with Chapters 4 and 5, Chapter 3 composes the heart and soul of the book). It is imperative that the reader have a firm grasp of these first five chapters prior to moving on to the remaining chapters. The following is a more comprehensive breakdown of the book's 15 chapters.

Chapter 1 begins with a brief discussion of Britain's and Sir Robert Peel's influence and the Metropolitan Police Act in England. Next we review the evolution of policing in America, followed by a look at police and change. Then we examine the community problem-solving era, including what its principal components are, why it emerged, and how it evolved to its current third generation. We also examine the language of policing as it concerns its current era, and the elevated importance and use of COPPS in homeland security.

Chapter 2 opens with an examination of what is meant by a sense of "community" and (as noted above) why the criminal justice system should partner with the public in making neighborhoods safer. Included is a review of the many rapid changes that are occurring in the United States, particularly concerning its economic challenges, demographics, and the changing nature of crime.

As mentioned above, another foundational chapter of the book is Chapter 3, which includes discussions of the development and methods of community policing and problem-oriented policing. We maintain throughout the book that these are complementary core components. The problem-solving process, known as S.A.R.A., is discussed as the primary tool for understanding crime and disorder. Included are the basic principles of police problem solving, the role of the street officer within it, some difficulties with problem solving, and some ways to tailor strategies to individual neighborhoods.

Crime prevention now involves much more than conducting "lock-it-or-lose-it" speeches and programs or distributing brochures. Chapter 4 looks at two important and contemporary components of crime prevention: crime prevention through environmental design (CPTED) and situational crime prevention. These approaches help officers understand how opportunities for crime can be blocked and how environments can be designed or changed to lessen a person's or location's vulnerability to crime. Included are discussions of the role of designing out crime, the use of second-generation CPTED, and the obstacles to adoption of CPTED. The chapter concludes by delineating what approaches work, what approaches do not appear to be successful, and what approaches hold promise for crime prevention.

Chapter 5—Technologies and Tools for the Task: Collecting and Analyzing Information— begins with a discussion of how to build an IT network, and then looks at tools available for crime analysis and other functions: computer-aided dispatch (CAD), mobile computing, records management system (RMS), geomapping, CompStat, intelligence-led and predictive policing, Global Positioning Systems (GPS), use of the Internet, and surveys. This chapter concludes with a discussion of counterterrorism and the changing role of the crime analyst.

In Chapter 6, we recognize that police agencies have a life and culture of their own, and we first present some basic theories and lessons learned about how police agencies go about modifying their culture, including their core values, in order to fully embrace COPPS. A new emphasis here is on how to move an organization from being "good" to being "great," as well as training future leaders (called succession planning) and recruiting quality officers for COPPS work. The separate roles and responsibilities of chief executives, middle managers, supervisors, and rank-and-file officers are included, as are some case studies of agencies that have modified their culture for adopting the COPPS approach.

Chapter 7 discusses how to plan and implement COPPS and stresses the need for police organizations to engage in strategic thinking and management. This chapter also explains the strategic planning process and how to assess local needs and develop a planning document as a road map. Then it shifts to the implementation of COPPS per se, considering some principal components. Included are several case studies that will challenge you to lead the transition to COPPS, and how to launch a COPPS initiative.

Although COPPS has been implemented and embraced by police agencies across our nation as well as in foreign venues, a challenge that remains is determining how to assess the success of this strategy. Chapter 8 confronts the issue of evaluation, beginning with the rationale for evaluating COPPS and social interventions generally, and then reviewing the different methods for evaluation—empirical as well as non-empirical—and some new methods that have been employed successful in this endeavor. Case studies of agencies and research are presented.

Another difficult challenge for those agencies involved in COPPS is the training and education of police officers and others, which are addressed in Chapter 9. First, we consider what is meant by a "learning organization," and ways in which adult and problem-based learning are infused into training programs that focus on problem solving. Next, we review why police officers comprise a unique and challenging learning audience as well as some means of and approaches to training. We also examine the current research concerning the role of higher education in COPPS and some ideas for a COPPS-based curriculum.

Chapter 10 examines the history of relations between minorities and the police and some ways COPPS can enhance those relations. Included are discussions of racial profiling and bias-based policing; police responses to hate crimes; cultural differences, customs, and problems;

selected federal, state, and local initiatives; diversity and recruiting in police organizations; and some scenarios.

Today's police struggle with an almost overwhelming array of gang-, drug-, and youth-related problems. Chapter 11 describes the application of COPPS to those problems. Topics covered in this chapter include methamphetamine and prescription drug abuse, drug labs, open-air drug markets, raves, gangs and graffiti, youth gun violence, disorderly youth, underage drinking, and school violence and cyberbullying.

Chapter 12 then addresses other selected issues and problems confronting the police, including identity theft, special populations (the mentally ill and the homeless), domestic violence, neighborhood disorder, and prostitution; we also briefly touch on stalking and other cybercrimes. Exhibits and case studies are included throughout this chapter and demonstrate the power of collaborative partnerships and problem solving.

Chapter 13 allows the reader to glean insight concerning COPPS by looking at agencies' COPPS initiatives across the U.S. Featured are brief discussions of COPPS in 19 domestic venues: 5 large (categorized as having more than 250,000 population), 10 medium-size (between 50,000 and 250,000 population), and 4 small (less than 50,000 population) jurisdictions. Brief descriptions of such initiatives also appear in several exhibits throughout the chapter.

COPPS functions internationally as well, and much can be learned from looking at the activities and approaches undertaken in foreign venues. So in Chapter 14, we "travel" to Canada, Japan, Australia, selected venues in Europe, and other locations. Several venues are also discussed in chapter exhibits.

Chapter 15 is nearly totally revised in this edition. It explores the future, with a look at those forces that may influence COPPS in years to come: the nature and types of crime, succession planning, debates concerning federalization and militarization of the police, and more on the language of policing.

An appendix provides a look at a model academic training curriculum for problem-oriented policing as espoused by the federal Office of Community Oriented Policing Services.

We believe that this book comprehensively lays out how COPPS is being embraced here and abroad. A major strength of this book lies in its many case studies and exhibits, which demonstrate how the concept is planned, implemented, operationalized, and evaluated. As Samuel Johnson wrote, "Example is always more efficacious than precept."

Ken Peak
Ron Glensor

ABOUT THE AUTHORS

Kenneth J. Peak, Ph.D., is a professor and former chairman of the criminal justice department at the University of Nevada, Reno. Beginning his career in Reno in 1983, he has been named "Teacher of the Year" by the University of Nevada, Reno, Honor Society, and served as acting director of public safety. He has authored or coauthored 22 textbooks on justice administration, general policing, community policing, women in law enforcement, and police supervision and management; he has published more than 60 journal articles and additional book chapters on a wide range of justice-related subjects. He has served as chairman of the Police Section, Academy of Criminal Justice Sciences, and is a past president of the Western and Pacific Association of Criminal Justice Educators. Dr. Peak entered municipal policing in Kansas in 1970 and subsequently held positions as criminal justice planner for southeast Kansas; director of the Four-State Technical Assistance Institute, Law Enforcement Assistance Administration; director of university police, Pittsburg State University; and assistant professor at Wichita State University. He received two gubernatorial appointments to statewide criminal justice committees while in Kansas and holds a doctorate from the University of Kansas.

    Ronald W. Glensor, Ph.D., is an assistant chief (retired) of the Reno, Nevada, Police Department (RPD). He has accumulated more than 36 years of police experience and commanded the department's patrol, administration, and detective divisions. In addition to being actively involved in RPD's implementation of community oriented policing and problem solving (COPPS) since 1987, he has provided COPPS training to thousands of officers, elected officials, and community members representing jurisdictions throughout the United States as well as Canada, Australia, and the United Kingdom. He is also a judge for the Herman Goldstein International Problem Oriented Policing Awards held annually throughout the nation. Dr. Glensor was the 1997 recipient of the prestigious Gary P. Hayes Award, conferred by the Police Executive Research Forum, recognizing his contributions and leadership in the policing field. Internationally, he is a frequent featured speaker on a variety of policing issues. He served a six-month fellowship as problem oriented policing coordinator with the Police Executive Research Forum in Washington, D.C., and received an Atlantic Fellowship in public policy, studying repeat victimization at the Home Office in London. He is the coauthor of *Police Supervision and Management in an Era of Community Policing* (third edition), with K. Peak and L. K. Gaines, and the coeditor of *Policing Communities: Understanding Crime and Solving Problems*, with M. Correia and K. Peak, and has published in several journals and trade magazines. Dr. Glensor is an adjunct criminal justice professor at the University of Nevada, Reno, and instructs at area police academies and criminal justice programs. He holds a doctorate in political science and a master's of public administration from the University of Nevada, Reno.

The Evolution of Policing
Past Wisdom and Future Directions

KEY TERMS AND CONCEPTS

Community oriented
  policing and problem
  solving (COPPS)
Community policing and
  problem solving
CompStat

Homeland security
Intelligence-led Policing
Language of policing
Metropolitan Police Act
Peel's Principles
Police-community relations

Political era
Predictive policing
Professional era
Reform of policing
Research findings
Wickersham Commission

LEARNING OBJECTIVES

As a result of reading this chapter, the student will:

■ Understand the evolution of policing from its nonprofessional origins in England to modern-day professional policing in the United States

■ Have a foundation in community oriented policing and problem solving (COPPS)

■ Know how research studies of policing resulted in major changes in methods and approaches

■ Be able to distinguish between the three primary eras of policing, including the primary focus of each

■ Know the three generations of community policing and problem solving

■ Understand some of the authors' concerns with the language being used in policing in general, how it relates to a delineation of the eras of policing, and the contemporary use of three management tools: CompStat, intelligence-led policing, predictive policing

■ Know how Harvard University's Kennedy School of Government is affecting policing in general, and COPPS in specific

When we pull back the layers of government services,
the most fundamental and indispensable virtues
are public safety and social order.

—Hon. David A. Hardy, Washoe County
District Court, Reno, Nevada

To understand what is, we must know what has been, and what
it tends to become.

—Oliver Wendell Holmes

INTRODUCTION

It is difficult to accurately establish the beginning of community-oriented policing in America. This is possibly because the notion of community policing is not altogether new; parts of it are as old as policing itself, emanating (as will be seen later) from concerns about policing that were indicated in the early nineteenth century.

We also must mention at the outset of this book that community-oriented policing and problem solving (COPPS) is not a unitary concept but rather a collection of related ideas. Several prominent individuals, movements, studies, and experiments have brought policing to where it is today. In this chapter, we examine the principal activities involving the police for more than a century and a half—activities which led to the development of **community policing and problem solving**.

This historical examination of policing begins with a brief discussion of Britain's and Sir Robert Peel's influence and the Metropolitan Police Act in England. Then we review the evolution of policing in America, including the emergence of the political era and attempts at reform through the professional crime fighter model. Next we look at police and change, including how "sacred cow" policing methods have been debunked by research, demonstrated the actual nature of police work, and shown the need for a new approach.

Following is an examination of the community problem-solving era, including what the principles of this new model are, why it emerged, and how it evolved. In this connection, we discuss how local police departments and sheriff's offices have evolved and rewritten their agency's history by adopting the COPPS strategy. Included in this chapter section are some brief comments concerning the **language of policing** in general, which leads into a discussion of some relatively new police management tools—**CompStat**, **intelligence-led policing**, and **predictive policing**—and how they are currently being viewed by some as constituting a new "era" of policing. We respectfully disagree with that line of thought, and offer a rationale for that belief. Next is a brief discussion of how COPPS can enhance the nation's defense and homeland security. Then, after considering how Executive Sessions at Harvard University's Kennedy School of Government have affected COPPS, the chapter concludes with a summary, review questions, and several scenarios and activities that provide opportunities for you to "learn by doing" (these are explained more below).

BRITISH CONTRIBUTIONS

The population of England doubled between 1700 and 1800. Parliament, however, took no measures to help solve the problems that arose from the accompanying social change.[1] London, awash in crime, had whole districts become criminal haunts, and thieves became very bold. In the face of this situation, Henry Fielding began to experiment with possible solutions. Fielding, appointed in 1748 as London's chief magistrate of Bow Street, argued against the severity of the English penal code, which applied the death penalty to a large number of offenses. He felt the country should reform the criminal code in order to deal more with the origins of crime. In 1750 Fielding made the pursuit of criminals more systematic by creating a small group of "thief-takers."[2] When Fielding died in 1754, his half-brother John Fielding succeeded him as Bow Street magistrate. By 1785, his thief-takers had evolved into the Bow Street Runners—some of the most famous policemen in English history.

Later, Robert Peel, a wealthy member of Parliament, felt strongly that London's population and crime problem merited a full-time professional police force, but many English people and other politicians objected to the idea, fearing possible restraint of their liberty. They also feared a strong police organization because the criminal law was already quite harsh (by the early nineteenth century, there were 223 crimes in England for which a person could be hanged). Indeed, Peel's efforts to gain support for full-time paid police officers failed for seven years.[3]

Peel finally succeeded in 1829. His bill to Parliament, titled "An Act for Improving the Police in and Near the Metropolis," succeeded and became known as the **Metropolitan Police Act** of 1829. The *General Instructions* of the new force stressed its preventive nature, saying that "the principal object to be attained is 'the prevention of crime.' The security of persons and property will thus be better effected, than by the detection and punishment of the offender after he has succeeded in committing the crime."[4] It was decided that constables would don a uniform (blue coat, blue pants, and black top hat) and would arm themselves with a short baton (known as a truncheon) and a rattle (for raising an alarm); each constable was to wear his individual number on his collar where it could be easily seen.[5]

Peel proved very farsighted and keenly aware of the needs of a community-oriented police force as well as the need of the public who would be asked to maintain it. Indeed, Peel perceived that the poor quality of policing was a contributing factor to the social disorder. Accordingly, he drafted several guidelines for the force, many of which focused on improving the relationship between the police and the public. He wrote that the power of the police to fulfill their duties depended on public approval of their actions; that as public cooperation increased, the need for physical force by the police decreased; that the officers needed to display absolutely impartial service to law; and that force should be employed by the police only when the attempt at persuasion and warning had failed and only the minimal degree of force possible should be used. Peel's statement that "The police are the public, and the public are the police" emphasized his belief that the police are first and foremost members of the larger society.[6]

Peel's attempts to appease the public were well-grounded; during the first three years of his reform effort, he encountered strong opposition. Peel was denounced as a potential dictator; the *London Times* urged revolt, and *Blackwood's Magazine* referred to the bobbies as "general spies" and "finished tools of corruption." A national secret body was organized to combat the police, who were nicknamed the "Blue Devils" and the "Raw Lobsters." Also during this initial five-year period, Peel endured one of the largest police turnover rates in history. Estimates range widely, but it is probably accurate to accept the figure of 1,341 constables resigning from London's Metropolitan Police from 1829 to 1834.[7]

Peel drafted what have become known as **Peel's Principles** of policing, most (if not all) of which are still apropos to today's police community. They are presented in Box 1–1.

BOX 1–1
Peel's Principles of Policing

Look at these

1. The basic mission for which the police exist is to prevent crime and disorder as an alternative to the repression of crime and disorder by military force and severity of legal punishment.

2. The ability of the police to perform their duties is dependent upon public approval of police existence, actions, behavior, and the ability of the police to secure and maintain public respect.

3. The police must secure the willing cooperation of the public in voluntary observance of the law to be able to secure and maintain public respect.

4. The degree of cooperation of the public that can be secured diminishes, proportionately, the necessity for the use of physical force and compulsion in achieving police objectives.

5. The police seek and preserve public favor, not by catering to public opinion, but by constantly demonstrating absolutely impartial service to the law, in complete independence of policy, and without regard to the justice or injustice of the substance of individual laws; by ready offering of individual service and friendship to all members of the society without regard to their race or social standing; by ready exercise of courtesy and friendly good humor; and by ready offering of individual sacrifice in protecting and preserving life.

6. The police should use physical force to the extent necessary to secure observance of the law or to restore order only when the exercise of persuasion, advice, and warning is found to be insufficient to achieve police objectives; and police should use only the minimum degree of physical force which is necessary on any particular occasion for achieving a police objective.

7. The police at all times should maintain a relationship with the public that gives reality to the historic tradition that the police are the public and that the public are the police; the police are the only members of the public who are paid to give full-time attention to duties which are incumbent on every citizen in the interest of the community welfare.

8. The police should always direct their actions toward their functions and never appear to usurp the powers of the judiciary by avenging individuals or the state, or authoritatively judging guilt or punishing the guilty.

9. The test of police efficiency is the absence of crime and disorder, not the visible evidence of police action in dealing with them.

Source: W. L. Melville Lee, *A History of Police in England* (London: Methuen, 1901), Chapter 12.

POLICING IN AMERICA: THE POLITICAL ERA

Early Beginnings

THE NEW YORK MODEL. Americans meanwhile were observing Peel's overall successful experiment with the bobbies on the patrol beat. Industrialization and social upheaval had not reached the proportions that they had in England, however, so there was not the urgency for full-time policing that had been experienced in England. Yet by the 1840s, when industrialization began in earnest in America, U.S. officials were watching the police reform movement in England more closely.

To comprehend the blundering, inefficiency, and confusion that surrounded nineteenth-century police in what would be called the **political era** of policing, we must remember that this was an age when the best forensic techniques could not clearly distinguish the blood of a pig from that of a human and the art of criminal detection was little more than divination. Steamboats blew up, trains regularly mutilated and killed pedestrians, children got run over by wagons, injury very often meant death, and doctors resisted the germ theory of disease. In the midst of all this, the police would be patrolling—the police being men who at best had been trained by reading pathetic little rule books that provided them little or no guidance in the face of human distress and disorder.[8]

New York Police Department officers initially refused to wear uniforms because they did not want to appear as "liveried lackeys." A blue frock coat with brass buttons was adopted in 1853.
Courtesy NYPD Photo Unit.

The movement to initiate policing in America began in New York City. (Philadelphia, with a private bequeath of $33,000, actually began a paid daytime police force in 1833; however, it was disbanded in three years.) In 1844, New York's state legislature passed a law establishing a full-time preventive police force for New York City. This new body was very different from that adopted from Europe, deliberately placed under the control of the city government and city politicians. The mayor chose the recruits from a list of names submitted by the aldermen and tax assessors of each ward; the mayor then submitted his choices to the city council for approval. Politicians were seldom concerned about selecting the best people for the job; instead, the system allowed and even encouraged political patronage and rewards for friends.[9]

The police link to neighborhoods and politicians was so tight that the police of this era have been considered virtual adjuncts to political machines.[10] The relationship was often reciprocal: Political machines recruited and maintained police in office and on the beat while police helped ward leaders maintain their political offices by encouraging citizens to vote for certain candidates. Soon other cities adopted the New York model. New Orleans and Cincinnati adopted plans for a new police in 1852; Boston and Philadelphia followed in 1854, Chicago in 1855, and Baltimore and Newark in 1857.[11] By 1880, virtually every major American city had a police force based on Peel's model, pioneered in New York City.

FROM THE EAST TO THE WILD, WILD WEST. These new police were born of conflict and violence. An unprecedented wave of civil disorder swept the nation from the 1840s until the 1870s.

Few cities escaped serious rioting, caused by ethnic and racial conflicts, economic disorder, and public outrage about such things as brothels and medical school experiments. These occurrences often made for hostile interaction between citizens and the police, who were essentially a reactive force. Riots in many major cities actually led to the creation of the "new police." The use of the baton to quell riots, known as the "baton charge," was not uncommon.[12]

Furthermore, while large cities in the east were struggling to overcome social problems and establish preventive police forces, the western half of America was anything but passive. When people left the wagon trains and their relatively law-abiding ways, they attempted to live together in communities. Many different ethnic groups—Anglo-Americans, Mexicans, Chinese, Indians, freed blacks, Australians, Scandinavians, and others—competed for often-scarce resources and fought one another violently, often with mob attacks. Economic conflicts were frequent between cattlemen and sheep herders, often leading to major range wars. There was constant labor strife in the mines. The bitterness of the slavery issue remained, and many men with firearms skills learned during the Civil War turned to outlawry after leaving the service (Jesse James was one such person).[13]

Despite these difficulties, westerners established peace by relying on a combination of four groups who assumed responsibility for law enforcement: private citizens, U.S. marshals, businessmen, and town police officers.[14] Private citizens usually helped to enforce the law by use of posses or through individual efforts, such as vigilante committees.[15] While it is true that they occasionally hanged outlaws, they also performed valuable work by ridding their communities of dangerous criminals.

Federal marshals were created by congressional legislation in 1789. As they began to appear on the frontier, the vigilantes tended to disappear. U.S. marshals enforced federal laws, so they only had jurisdiction over federal offenses, such as theft of mail, crimes against railroad property, and murder on federal lands. Their primary responsibility was in civil matters arising from federal court decisions. Finally, when a territory became a state, the primary law enforcement functions usually fell to local sheriffs and marshals. Sheriffs quickly became important officials, but they spent more time collecting taxes, inspecting cattle brands, maintaining jails, and serving civil papers than they did actually dealing with outlaws.[16]

Politics and Corruption

During the late nineteenth century, large cities gradually became more orderly. American cities absorbed millions of newcomers after 1900 without the social strains that attended the Irish immigration of the 1830s to 1850s.[17]

Partly because of their closeness to politicians, police during this era provided a wide array of services to citizens. Many police departments were involved in crime prevention and order maintenance as well as a variety of social services. In some cities, they operated soup lines, helped find lost children, and found jobs and temporary lodging for newly arrived immigrants.[18] Police organizations were typically quite decentralized, with cities being divided into precincts and run like small-scale departments—hiring, firing, managing, and assigning personnel as necessary. Officers were often recruited from the same ethnic stock as the dominant groups in the neighborhoods; they lived in the beats they patrolled and were given considerable discretion in handling their individual beats. Decentralization encouraged foot patrol, even after call boxes and automobiles became available. Detectives operated from a caseload of "persons" rather than offenses, relying on their caseload to inform on other criminals.[19]

The strengths of the political era centered on the fact that police were integrated into neighborhoods. This strategy proved useful as it helped contain riots and the police assisted

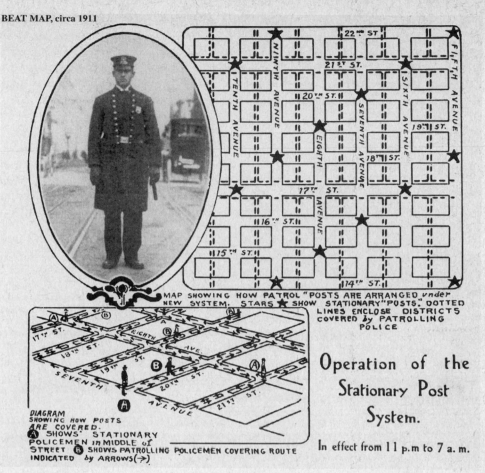

Foot patrol was the primary strategy for policing neighborhoods during the early 1900s.
Courtesy NYPD Photo Unit.

immigrants in establishing themselves in communities and finding jobs. There were weaknesses as well: The intimacy with the community, the closeness to politicians, and a decentralized organizational structure (and its inability to provide supervision of officers) also led to police corruption. The close identification of police with neighborhoods also resulted in discrimination against strangers, especially minority ethnic and racial groups. Police often ruled their beats with the "end of their nightsticks" and practiced "curbside justice."[20] The lack of organizational control over officers also caused some inefficiencies and disorganization; thus the image of Keystone Cops—bungling police—was widespread.

Emergence of Professionalism

In summary, the nineteenth-century police officer was essentially a political operative rather than a modern-style professional committed to public service. Because the police were essentially a political institution and perceived as such by the citizenry, they did not enjoy widespread acceptance by the public. As political appointees, officers enjoyed little job security, and salaries were determined by local political factors. Primitive communications technology of the era meant that police chiefs were unable to supervise their captains at the precinct level; thus, policy was greatly influenced by the prevailing political and social mores of the neighborhoods. As a consequence police behavior was very much influenced by the interaction between individual officers and individual citizens. The nature of that interaction, later termed the problem of **police-community relations**, was perhaps even more complex and ambiguous in the nineteenth century than in the late twentieth century.[21]

THE PROFESSIONAL ERA

Movement Toward Reform

The idea of policing as a profession, however, began to emerge slowly in the latter part of the nineteenth century. Reform ideas first appeared as a reaction to the corrupt and politicized state of the police. Reformers agreed that partisan politics was the heart of the problem. Even reformers in the National Prison Association bemoaned the partisan politics that hindered the improvement of the police. Slowly the idea of policing as a higher calling (higher than the concerns of local politics, that is), as a profession committed to public service, began to gain ground. Two other ideas about the proper role of the police in society also appeared. One emphasized improvement in the role of police with respect to scientific techniques of crime detection. The other idea was that police could play more of a social work role; by intervening in the lives of individuals, police officers could reform society by preventing crime and keeping people out of the justice system. These reformers were closely tied to the emerging rehabilitative ideal in correctional circles in what is termed the **professional era**.[22]

New Developments and Calls for Reform

There were several important developments in the **reform of policing** during the late 1800s. Policing realized the beginning of a body of literature. Most authors were closely tied to the police and thus painted an inaccurate picture in some respects (e.g., the corruption that existed in many police departments), but their writings were also very illuminating. They provided glimpses into the informal processes that governed police departments and focused on the individual officer, a focus that would be lost in the later professionalization movement with its emphasis on impersonal bureaucratic standards. Furthermore, the late 1800s witnessed improvements in the areas of testing and training. The physical and mental qualifications of police officers concerned new police commissioners, and formal schools of instruction were developed (the best being Cincinnati's, which required a total of 72 hours of instruction) During the late 1800s, there was also the appearance of police conventions, such as the National Police Chiefs Union (later named the International Association of Chiefs of Police [IACP]) and fraternal and benefit societies.[23]

August Vollmer, pioneer of police professionalism from 1905 to 1932, rallied police executives around the idea of reform during the 1920s and 1930s, emerging as the leading national spokesman for police professionalism. What is often overlooked among the abundance of Vollmer's contributions to policing was his articulate advocacy of the idea that the police should function as social workers. The belief that police officers should do more than merely arrest offenders, that they should actively seek to prevent crime by "saving" potential or actual offenders, was an important theme in police reform. It was an essential ingredient in the notion of professionalism. Indeed, in a series of addresses to the IACP, Vollmer advanced his ideas in "The Policeman as a Social Worker" (1918) and "Predelinquency" (1921). He began by arguing that the "old methods of dealing with crime must be changed, and newer ones adopted."[24]

August Vollmer, a national spokesman for and early pioneer of police professionalism, established one of the first fingerprint bureaus and formal police schools while he was chief of police in Berkeley, California.
Courtesy Samuel G. Chapman.

Vollmer's views were very prescient for today, especially given the contemporary movement toward community policing. Vollmer felt that traditional institutions and practices were no longer adequate for a modern and complex industrial society. He believed that the police should intervene and be involved with people before they entered lives of crime, and he suggested that police work closely with existing social welfare agencies and become advocates of additional reform proposals. Vollmer also suggested that police inform voters about overcrowded schools and support the expansion of recreational facilities, community social centers, and antidelinquency agencies. Basically, he was suggesting that the police play an active part in the political life of the community, yet the major thrust of police professionalization had been to insulate the police from politics. This contradiction illustrated one of the fundamental ambiguities of the whole notion of professionalism.[25]

Other reformers continued to reject political involvement by police, and civil service systems were created to eliminate patronage and ward influences in hiring and firing police officers. In some cities, officers could not live in the same beat they patrolled, to isolate them as completely as possible from political influences. Police departments, needing to be removed from political influence, became one of the most autonomous agencies in urban government.[26] However, policing also became a matter viewed as best left to the discretion of police executives to address. Police organizations became law enforcement agencies, with the sole goal of controlling crime. Any non-crime activities they were required to do were "social work." The "professional model" of policing was in full bloom.

The scientific theory of administration was adopted, as advocated by Frederick Taylor during the early twentieth century. Taylor had studied the work process, breaking down jobs into their basic steps and emphasizing time and motion studies, all with an eye toward maximizing production. From this emphasis on production and unity of control flowed the notion that police officers were best managed by a hierarchical pyramid of control. Police leaders routinized and standardized police work; officers were to enforce laws and make arrests whenever possible. Discretion was limited to the extent possible. When special problems arose, special units (e.g., vice, juvenile, drugs, tactical) were created rather than assigning problems to patrol officers.

Crime Commissions and Early Police Studies

The early 1900s also became the age of the crime commission, including the **Wickersham Commission** reports in 1931. President Herbert Hoover, concerned with the lax enforcement of prohibition and other forms of police corruption, created the National Commission on Law Observance and Enforcement—popularly known as the Wickersham Commission after its chairman, former U.S. Attorney General George W. Wickersham. This commission completed the first national study of crime and criminal justice, issuing 14 reports and recommending that the corrupting influence of politics be removed from policing, police chief executives be selected on merit, patrol officers be tested and meet minimal physical standards, police salaries and working conditions be decent, and policewomen be used in juvenile and female cases. Many of these recommendations represented what progressive police reformers had been wanting over the previous 40 years; unfortunately, President Hoover and his administration could do little more than report the Wickersham Commission's recommendations before leaving office.

The most important change in policing during this decade was the advent of the automobile and its accompanying radio. Gradually the patrol car replaced foot patrol, expanding geographic beats and further removing people from neighborhoods. There was also Prohibition (which affected the police very little in a long-term way), a bloody wave of racial violence in American cities, and the rise and defeat of police unionism and strikes. The impact of two-way radios was also felt, as supervisors were able to maintain a far closer supervision of patrol officers, and the radio and telephone made it possible for citizens to make heavier demands for police service. The result was not merely a greater burden on the police but also an important qualitative redefinition of the police role.[27]

The 1930s marked an important turning point in the history of police reform. The first genuine empirical studies of police work began to appear, and O. W. Wilson emerged as the leading authority on police administration. The major development of this decade was a redefinition of the police role and the ascendancy of the crime fighter image. Wilson, who took guidance from J. Edgar Hoover's transformation of the Federal Bureau of Investigation (FBI) into an agency of high prestige, became the principal architect of the police reform strategy.[28] Hoover, appointed FBI director in 1924, had raised eligibility and training standards of recruits, giving FBI agents stature as upstanding moral crusaders and developing an incorruptible crime-fighting organization. He also developed impressive public relations programs that presented the bureau in the most favorable light. Municipal police found Hoover's path a compelling one. Following Wilson's writings on police administration, they began to shape an organizational strategy for urban police that was analogous to that pursued by the FBI.

Also by the 1930s, the policewomen's movement, begun in the early 1900s, had begun losing ground. Professionalism came to mean a combination of managerial efficiency, technological sophistication, and an emphasis on crime fighting. The social work aspects of policing—the idea of rehabilitative work, which had been central to the policewomen's movement—were almost totally eclipsed. The result was a severe identity crisis for policewomen: They were caught between a social work orientation and a law enforcement ideology. Later, by the 1960s, women would occupy an extremely marginal place in American policing.[29]

In sum, under the reform era's professional model of policing, officers were to remain in their "rolling fortresses," going from one call to the next with all due haste. As Mark Moore and George Kelling observed, "In professionalizing crime fighting, the 'volunteers,' citizens on whom so much used to depend, [were] removed from the fight. If anything has been learned from the history of American policing, it is that, whatever the benefits of professionalization (e.g., reduced corruption, due process, serious police training), the reforms . . . ignored, even attacked, some features that once made the police powerful institutions in maintaining a sense of community security."[30]

Professional Crime Fighter

EMPHASIS ON EFFICIENCY AND CONTROL.   The decade of the 1930s ended the first phase in the history of police professionalization. From the 1940s through the early 1960s, police reform continued along the lines that were already well established. Police professionalism was defined almost exclusively in terms of managerial efficiency, and administrators sought to further strengthen their hand in controlling rank-and-file officers; however, many of the old problems, such as racial unrest and an unclear definition of the police role, persisted. Nonetheless, by the late 1930s and early 1940s, there was a clear sense of mission for the police, a commitment to public service where one had not existed before.[31] Also, policing had begun to develop its own sense of professional autonomy. And, ironically perhaps, the most articulate groups and the most creative thinking were to be found in nonpolice groups: the National Prison Association, the social work profession, and the field of public administration. The efforts by reformers to remove political influence over police, though not entirely successful, were beginning to take hold as police boards and powerful police chiefs met their demise. Police unions reappeared, however, and the emergence of careerism among police officers significantly altered their attitudes toward the job and the public they served.

The professional model demanded an impartial law enforcer who related to citizens in professionally neutral and distant terms, personified by television's Sgt. Friday on "Dragnet": "Just the facts, ma'am." The emphasis on professionalization also shaped the role of citizens in crime control. Like physicians caring for health problems, teachers for educational problems, and social workers for social adjustment problems, the police would be responsible for crime problems. Citizens became relatively passive in crime control, mere recipients of professional crime control services. Citizens' responsibility in crime control was limited to calling police and serving as witnesses when asked to do so. Police were the "thin blue line." The community's need for rapid response to calls for service (CFS) was sold as efficacious in crime control. Foot patrol, when demanded by citizens, was rejected as an outmoded, expensive frill. Professionalism in law enforcement was often identified in terms of firearms expertise, and the popularity of firearms put the police firmly in the anti-gun control camp.[32]

Citizens were no longer encouraged to go to "their" neighborhood police officers or districts. Officers were to drive marked cars randomly through streets, to develop a feeling of police omnipresence. The "person" approach ended and was replaced by the case approach. Officers were judged by the numbers of arrests they made or by the number of miles they drove during a shift. The crime rate became the primary indicator of police effectiveness.

REESTABLISHMENT OF COMMUNICATION: POLICE-COMMUNITY RELATIONS.   While much of the country was engaged in "practicing" and "selling" police reform embodied in the professional

FBI agents practice shooting from vehicle in the 1930s.
Courtesy FBI

model of policing, a movement was beginning in Michigan to bring the police and community closer together. Louis Radelet served on the executive staff of the National Conference of Christians and Jews (NCCJ) from 1951 to 1963, when he became a professor in what was then the School of Police Administration and Public Safety at Michigan State University (MSU). In 1955 Radelet, having conducted many NCCJ workshops dedicated to reducing tensions between elements of the community, founded the National Institute on Police and Community Relations (NIPCR) at MSU; he served as institute director from 1955 to 1969 and was also coordinator of the university's National Center on Police and Community Relations, created to conduct a national survey on police-community relations, from 1965 to 1973.[33]

The institute held 5-day conferences each May during its 15-year existence, bringing together teams of police officers and other community leaders to discuss common problems. In peak years, more than 600 participants came from as many as 165 communities and 30 states as well as several foreign countries. As a result of the institute's work, such programs proliferated rapidly across the nation. We believe the stated purposes of the many programs initiated during this period are still applicable today and are listed here[34]:

1. To encourage police-citizen partnership in the cause of crime prevention
2. To foster and improve communications and mutual understanding between the police and the total community
3. To promote interprofessional approaches to the solution of community problems and to stress the principle that the administration of justice is a total community responsibility
4. To enhance cooperation among the police, the prosecution, the courts, and the corrections

5. To assist the police and other community leaders to achieve an understanding of the nature and causes of complex problems in people-to-people relations and especially to improve police-minority relationships
6. To strengthen implementation of equal protection under the law for all persons

The NIPCR was discontinued at the end of 1969. Radelet wrote that its demise was "a commentary on the evolution of issues and social forces pertinent to the field. The purposes, assumptions, and institute design of past years may have been relevant in their time. But it became imperative now to think about police-community relations programs in different terms, with more precise purposes that could be better measured."[35]

Problems with the Professional Model

Several problems with the professional model of policing began to arise during the late 1960s.

Crime began to rise, and research suggested that conventional police methods were not effective. The 1960s was a time of explosion and turbulence. Inner-city residents rioted in several major cities; protestors denounced military involvement in Vietnam; and assassins ended the lives of President John F. Kennedy, Robert F. Kennedy, and civil rights leader Rev. Martin Luther King, Jr. The country was witnessing tremendous upheaval, and such incidents as the so-called police riot at the 1968 Democratic National Convention in Chicago raised many questions about the police and their function and role. Largely as a result of this turmoil, five national studies, each with a different focus, looked into police practices during the 1960s and 1970s: the President's Commission on Law Enforcement and the Administration of Justice (termed the "President's Crime Commission" [1967]), the National Advisory Commission on Civil Disorders (1968), the National Commission on the Causes and Prevention of Violence (1968), the President's Commission on Campus Unrest (1970), and the National Advisory Commission on Criminal Justice Standards and Goals (1973). Of particular note was the aforementioned President's Crime Commission of 1967, charged by President Lyndon Johnson to find solutions to America's internal crime problems. Among the commission's recommendations for the police were hiring more minorities as police officers to improve police-community relations, upgrading the quality of police officers through better-educated officers, and using better applicant screening and intensive preservice training.[36]

The President's Crime Commission brought policing full circle, restating several of the same principles that were laid out by Sir Robert Peel in 1829: that the police should be close to the public, that poor quality of policing contributed to social disorder, and that the police should focus on community relations.

Police administrators became more willing to challenge traditional assumptions and beliefs and to open the door to researchers and their **research findings**. That willingness to allow researchers to examine traditional methods led to the growth and development of two important policing research organizations: the Police Foundation and the Police Executive Research Forum (PERF).

Fear rose. Citizens abandoned parks, public transportation, neighborhood shopping centers, churches, and entire neighborhoods. What puzzled police and researchers was that levels of fear and crime did not always correspond: Crime levels were low in some areas, but fear was high, and vice versa. Researchers found that fear is more closely associated with disorder than with crime. Ironically, order maintenance was one of the functions that police had been downplaying over the years.

1965 Selma-to-Montgomery Voting Rights March

Never Lose Sight of Freedom

Three Selma-to-Montgomery (Alabama) marches in 1965 marked the peak of the American civil rights movement, growing out of the voting rights movement launched by African-Americans. The first march took place on March 7, 1965—"Bloody Sunday"—when 600 civil rights marchers were attacked by state and local police with batons and tear gas.

Many minority citizens did not perceive their treatment as equitable or adequate. They protested not only police mistreatment but lack of treatment—despite attempts by most police departments to provide impartial policing to all citizens.

The antiwar and civil rights movements challenged police. The legitimacy of the police was questioned: Students resisted police, minorities rioted against them for what they represented, and the public (for the first time at this level) questioned police tactics. Moreover, minorities and women insisted that they be represented in policing if the police were to be legitimate.

Some of the myths on which the reform era was founded—that police officers use little or no discretion and that their primary duty is law enforcement—could no longer be sustained. Over and over, research underscored that the use of discretion was needed at all levels and that law enforcement composed but a small portion of police officers' activities.[37] Other research findings shook the foundations of old assumptions about policing; for example, two-person patrol cars are neither more effective nor safer than one-person cars in reducing crime or catching criminals.[38] Other "sacred cows" of policing that were debunked by research are discussed below.

Although managers had tried to professionalize policing, line officers continued to have low status. Police work continued to be routinized; petty rules governed officer behavior. Meanwhile, line officers received little guidance in the use of discretion and had little opportunity for providing input concerning their work. As a result, many departments witnessed the rise of militant unionism.

The police lost a significant portion of their financial support. Many police departments were reduced in size, demonstrating an erosion of public confidence.

Police began to acquire competition: private security and the community crime control movement. Businesses, industries, and private citizens began to seek alternative means of protecting themselves and their property, further suggesting a declining confidence in the capability of police to provide the level of services that citizens desired. Indeed, today there are more than 1.5 million private police personnel employed in the United States—two to three times more personnel than there are in all federal, state, and municipal police agencies combined.[39] The social upheaval of the 1960s and 1970s obviously changed the face of policing in America. Not to be overlooked is the impact of the courts during this period as well. A number of major landmark Supreme Court decisions curtailed the actions of police and, concurrently, expanded the rights of the accused.

Changing Wisdom of Policing: More Recent Studies of Police Work

As a result of the problems mentioned earlier and the civil unrest that occurred during the professional era of policing, research evolved a new "common wisdom" of policing. As will be shown, much of this research shook the foundation of policing and rationalized the changes in methods we offer in later chapters. We discuss what might be termed the two primary clusters of police research that illuminated where policing has been and what officers actually do.

The first cluster of research actually began in the 1950s and would ultimately involve seven empirical studies of the police: the early work of sociologist William Westley concerning the culture of policing,[40] the ambitious studies of the American Bar Foundation,[41] the field observations of Jerome Skolnick,[42] the work of Egon Bittner analyzing the police function on skid row,[43] Raymond Parnas's study of the police response to domestic disturbances,[44] James Q. Wilson's analysis of different policing styles,[45] and the studies of police-citizen contact by Albert Reiss.[46] These studies collectively provided a "new realism" about policing[47]:

- Informal arrangements for handling incidents and behavioral problems were found to be more common than was compliance with formally established procedures.
- Workload, public pressures, and interagency pressures as well as the interests and personal predilections of functionaries in the criminal justice system were found in many instances to have more influence on how the police and the rest of the criminal justice system operated than the Constitution, state statutes, or city ordinances.
- Arrest, commonly viewed as the first step in the criminal process, had come to be used by the police to achieve a whole range of objectives in addition to that of prosecuting wrongdoers (e.g., to investigate, harass, punish, or provide safekeeping).
- A great variety of informal methods outside the criminal justice system had been adopted by the police to fulfill their formal responsibilities and to dispose of the endless array of situations that the public—rightly or wrongly—expected them to handle.
- Individual police officers were found to be routinely exercising a great deal of discretion in deciding how to handle the tremendous variety of circumstances with which they were confronted.

These findings also underscored that the police had, in the past, depended too much on the criminal law in order to get their job done; that they were not autonomous but rather were accountable, through the political process, to the community; and that dealing with fear and enforcing public order are appropriate functions for the police.[48] Other early studies indicated that less than 50 percent of an officer's time was committed to CFS, and of those calls handled, over 80 percent were noncriminal incidents.[49]

The five national studies of policing practices during the riots and the Vietnam War of the 1960s and 1970s (discussed in the previous section) began a quest for new directions. Later, a second cluster of police research occurred that provided further knowledge about police methods. The Kansas City Preventive Patrol Experiment of 1973 questioned the usefulness of random patrol in police vehicles.[50] Other studies showed that officers and detectives are limited in their abilities to successfully investigate crimes[51] and that detectives need not follow up every reported unsolved crime.[52] In short, most serious crimes were unaffected by the standard police actions designed to control them.

Since the 1970s, additional studies have dispelled many assumptions commonly held by police about their efficiency and effectiveness. For example, preventive patrol has been shown to be costly, producing only minimal results in the reduction of crime.[53] Rapid response to calls has been shown to be less effective at catching criminals than educating the public to call the police sooner after a crime is committed.[54] We now know that police response time is largely unrelated to the probability of making an arrest or locating a witness. The time it takes to report a crime is the major determining factor of whether an on-scene arrest takes place and whether witnesses are located.[55] Despite their best efforts, police have had little impact on preventing crime.[56]

Box 1–2 shows examples of substantive studies and experiments that were undertaken in policing from 1972 to 2008. Many of them were related to COPPS initiatives and initiated through funding by the National Institute of Justice.

BOX 1–2
Police Studies and Experiments, 1972–2008

Year	Subject	Focus
2008	Major funding emphases placed on solving cold cases and assisting forensics laboratories	Solving "cold cases" (definitions vary) and to reduce forensic lab backlogs (more than 500 projects funded)
2007	Smart Police Deployment: Evaluating the Use of Automated Vehicle Locator Technologies in Policing	Using a global positioning device for monitoring police vehicle location across real time/space, for CompStat and other directed patrol strategies (e.g., hot spots policing)
2006	Evaluation of Gang Hot-Spots Policing in Chicago	Stopping shootings and killings through outreach, public education, and community mobilization.
2005	Identity Theft: Assessing Offenders' Strategies and Perceptions of Risk	Determine traits of persons engaged in identity theft
2003	National Institute of Justice use of biometrics and face and iris recognition technologies in prisons and schools	Security and criminal justice
2002	National Institute of Justice study of less lethal weapons aboard commercial aircraft	Focus on thwarting onboard attacks
2001	National Institute of Justice onsite assistance for terrorist attacks	Post 9-11 search-and-rescue tools and technology, protective gear
2000	COPS Program—National Evaluation	Federal Office of Community Oriented Policing Services (COPS) grants
2000	National Evaluation of the Problem Solving Partnerships Project for federal COPS office	Success of 447 police agencies receiving problem-solving grants
1999	National Evaluation of Project Weed and Seed (discussed in Chapter 12)	Proactive drug enforcement and prevention
1998	National Evaluation of Youth Firearms Violence	Approaches to reduce firearms related violence
1998	Information Systems Technology Enhancement Project	Technology uses for COPPS
1997	Federal Study of Crime Prevention Programs	Broad range of programs
1995	Repeat Victimization	Prevention of revictimization
1995	Integrated Criminal Apprehension Program	Crime analysis–based deployment
1993	"Tipping Point" Studies	Examination of crime epidemics

BOX 1–2
(continued)

Year	Subject	Focus
1992	Crime Prevention Through Environmental Design	Use of designing out crime
1992	Situational Crime Prevention	Reduction of crime opportunities
1991	Quality Policing in Madison, Wisconsin	Quality management study
1990	Minneapolis "Hot Spot" Patrolling	Intensive patrol of problem areas
1988	Police Decoy Operations	Criminal targeting tactic
1987	Problem Oriented Policing, Newport News, Virginia	Crime problem-solving model
1987	Houston and Newark Fear of Crime Studies	Fear reduction study
1985	Repeat Offender Programs	Focus on career criminals
1984	Minneapolis Domestic Violence Experiment	Analysis of effective police action
1983	Differential Police Response Field Test	Call priority and alternative reporting
1982	Directed Patrol National Survey	Survey of patrol strategies
1981	Newark Foot Patrol Experiment	Cost benefits of foot patrol
1977	Split Force Patrol Experiment, Wilmington, Delaware	Patrol deployment study
1977	Patrol Staffing in San Diego	One- vs. two-officer cars
1975	RAND Study of Investigations	Detective and patrol effectiveness
1974	Kansas City Preventive Patrol Experiment	Effectiveness of random patrol
1973	Team Policing Experiment in Seven U.S. Cities	Team vs. traditional policing
1973	Police-Community Relations	Study of organizational orientation
1972	Policewomen on Patrol	Evaluation of women on patrol

Source: Adapted from Annual Reports of the U.S. Department of Justice, National Institute of Justice; see, for example, http://www.ncjrs.gov/pdffiles1/nij/227725.pdf (Accessed July 8, 2010).

Viewing "Sacred Cow" Methods with Caution

What did the studies mentioned previously mean for the police? Was the professional model of policing (discussed earlier) completely off base? No, in fact it can have a positive impact on a police agency's organization, efficiency, and control. However, these studies do show that the police erred in doggedly investing so much of their resources in a limited number of practices that were based on a rather naive and simplistic concept of the police role.[57] Furthermore, as we noted above, the police got caught up in the "means over ends" syndrome, measuring their success by the numbers of arrests, quickness of responses, and so on (the means) while often neglecting the outcome of their work (the ends).

As we have seen, the "We've always done it this way" mentality, still pervading policing to a large extent, may be not only an ineffective means of organizing and administering a police agency but also a costly squandering of valuable human and financial resources. For many police agencies today operating under the traditional incident-driven style of policing, the *beat* (rather than the *neighborhood*) is, to borrow a term from research methodology, the "unit of analysis." Under this timeworn model, officers have been glued to their police radios, flitting like pinballs from one call for service to the next as rapidly as possible. Furthermore, police officers seldom leave their vehicles to address incidents except when answering a CFS. They know very little about the underlying causes of problems in the neighborhoods on their beats.

The results of employing conventional police methods have been inglorious. Problems have persisted or been allowed to go unnoticed and grow while neighborhoods deteriorated. Officers became frustrated after they repeatedly handled similar calls, with no sign of progress. Petty offenses contributed to this decline and drove stable community members away once the message went out to offenders and vandals that no one cares about the neighborhood. Yet many in the police field are unaware of or refuse to accept that the old ways are open to serious challenge.

Time for a New Approach

We believe it is clear from all we've discussed thus far that police agencies must change their daily activities, their management practices, and even their view of their work in order to confront the changes that are occurring. We maintain that given the current levels of violence and the public's fear of it, the disorder found in countless American neighborhoods, the poor police-community relations in many cities, and the rapidly changing landscape of crime and demographics in America, the police need to seriously consider whether a bureaucratic overhaul is needed to meet the demands of the future.

Police research also demonstrated the need for agencies to evaluate the effectiveness of their responses. Both quantitative and qualitative data should be used as a basis for evaluation and change. Departments need to know more about what their officers are doing. Agencies are struggling to find enough resources for performing crime trend analyses; most also do not conduct proper workload analyses to know what uncommitted time is possessed by their officers.

Research has also provided the realization that policing consists of developing the most effective means for dealing with a multitude of troublesome situations. For example, problem solving is a whole new way of thinking about policing and carries the potential to reshape the way in which police services are delivered.[58]

One of several things the police must do to accomplish their mission is to reacquaint themselves with members of the community by involving citizens in the resolution of neighborhood problems. Simply stated, police must view the public as well as other government and social services organizations as "a part of," as opposed to "apart from," their efforts. This change in conventional thinking advocates efficiency with effectiveness and quality over quantity, and it encourages collaborative problem solving and creative resolutions to crime and disorder.

THE COMMUNITY PROBLEM-SOLVING ERA

Team Policing, Foot Patrol, and Shattered Myths

In the early 1970s, it was suggested that the performance of patrol officers would improve more by using job redesign based on "motivators."[59] This suggestion later evolved into a concept known as "team policing," which sought to restructure police departments, improve police-community relations, enhance police officer morale, and facilitate change within the police organization. Its primary element was a decentralized neighborhood focus to the delivery of police services. Officers were to be generalists, trained to investigate crimes and basically attend to all of the problems in their area, with a team of officers being assigned to a particular neighborhood and responsible for all police services in that area—the **community problem- solving era**.

Teen policing in the 70s

(In the end, however, team policing failed for several reasons. Most of the experiments were poorly planned and hastily implemented, resulting in street officers not understanding what they were supposed to do. Many midmanagement personnel felt threatened by team policing; as a result, some sabotaged the experiment. Furthermore, team policing did not represent a completely different view of policing. As Samuel Walker observed, "It was essentially a different *organizational approach* to traditional policing: responding to calls for service (CFS), deterring crime through patrol, and apprehending criminals" (emphasis in original).[60])

There were other developments for the police during the late 1970s and early 1980s. Foot patrol became more popular, and many jurisdictions (such as Newark, New Jersey; Boston, Massachusetts; and Flint, Michigan) even demanded it. In Newark, an evaluation found that foot patrol was readily perceived by residents and that it produced a significant increase in the level of satisfaction with police service, led to a significant reduction of perceived crime problems, and resulted in a significant increase in the perceived level of safety of the neighborhood.[61] Flint researchers reported that the crime rate in the target areas declined slightly; CFS in these areas dropped by 43 percent. Furthermore, citizens indicated satisfaction with the program, suggesting that it had improved relations with the police.[62]

These findings and others discussed below shattered several long-held myths about measures of police effectiveness. In addition, research conducted during the 1970s suggested that *information* could help police improve their ability to deal with crime. These studies, along with those of foot patrol and fear reduction, created new opportunities for the police to understand the increasing concerns of citizens' groups about disorder (e.g., gangs, prostitutes) and to work with citizens to do something about it. Police discovered that when they asked citizens about their priorities, citizens appreciated their asking and often provided useful information.

The Community Patrol Officer Program (CPOP), instituted by the New York City Police Department in 1984, was similar in many respects to the Flint foot patrol program. Officers involved in this program were responsible for getting to know the residents, merchants, and service providers in their beat area; identifying the principal crime and order maintenance problems confronting the people within their beat; and devising strategies for dealing with the identified problems.[63]

Principles of the New COPPS Model

Simultaneously, Herman Goldstein's problem-oriented approach to policing was being tested in Madison, Wisconsin; Baltimore County, Maryland; and Newport News, Virginia. These studies found that police officers enjoy operating with a holistic approach to their work, have the capacity to do problem solving successfully, and can work with citizens and other agencies to solve problems. Also, citizens seemed to appreciate working with police. Moreover, this approach was a rethinking of earlier strategies of handling CFS: Officers were given more autonomy and trained to analyze the underlying causes of problems and to find creative solutions. These findings were similar to those of the foot patrol experiments and fear reduction experiments.

Community oriented policing and problem solving (COPPS) requires not only new police strategies but a new organizational approach as well. There is a renewed emphasis on community collaboration for many police tasks. Crime control remains an important function, but equal emphasis is given to *prevention*. Police officers return to their wide use of discretion under this model and move away from routinization and standardization in addressing their tasks. This discretion pushes operational and tactical decision making to the lower levels of the organization.

Participative management is greatly increased, and fewer levels of authority are required to administer the organization; middle management layers are reduced. Concurrently, many cities

Police storefronts and substations provide convenience and improved customer service to neighborhoods.
Courtesy Huntington Beach, California, Police Department.

have developed what are, in effect, "demarketing" programs, attempting to rescind programs (such as the area of rapid response to CFS and to 911 calls except for dire emergencies) that had been actively sold earlier.

Community problem solving has helped to explain what went wrong with team policing in the 1960s and 1970s. It was a strategy that innovators mistakenly approached as a tactic. Team policing also competed with traditional policing in the same departments, and they were incompatible with one another. A police department might have a small team policing unit or conduct a team policing experiment, but the traditional professional model of policing was still "business as usual."

The classical theory of police organization that continues to dominate many agencies is likewise alien to the community problem-solving strategy. The new strategy will not accommodate the classical theory of traditional policing; the latter denies too much of the real nature of police work, continues old methods of supervision and administration, and creates too much cynicism in officers attempting to do creative problem solving.

Box 1–3 displays the three elements of COPPS—community partnerships (discussed more thoroughly in Chapter 2), problem solving (see Chapter 3), and organizational transformation (see Chapter 4)—as we envision its contemporary fundamental structure. This is a very important framework for you to comprehend because, in addition to framing and explaining the construction of COPPS, it essentially underlies and guides all other chapters that are contained in this book.

Why the Emergence of COPPS?

Although we will discuss COPPS in greater detail in Chapters 2, 3, and 4, following is a summary of the factors that set the stage for the emergence of COPPS:

- Narrowing of the police mission to crime fighting
- Increased cultural diversity in our society and heightened concern with police violation of minority civil rights

BOX 1–3

A Framework for COPPS Elements and Principles

Community Partnerships	Problem Solving	Organizational Transformation
Collaborative partnerships between the law enforcement agency and the individuals and organizations they serve, and anyone with a stake in the community.	The process and effect of problem solving should be assessed at each stage of the problem-solving process.	1. Leadership and administration • Policies and procedures • Management approach • Information management • Planning/program evaluation • Resources and finances
1. Agency has multi-disciplinary partnerships with community partners, including other government agencies, nonprofit and community groups, businesses, the media, and individuals.	1. General problem-solving approach 2. Problem-solving processes: • Scanning • Analysis • Response • Assessment	2. Human resources • Recruiting, selection, training • Performance evaluation/promotion • Honors and awards • Discipline • Labor Relation
2. Existing partnerships bring appropriate resources and level of commitment to community policing activities.	3. General skill in problem solving	3. Field operations • Call prioritization • Alternative reporting • Beat boundaries • Permanent shifts • Reduced specialization
3. Level of interaction between the law enforcement agency and community partners.		4. External relations • Community, media, businesses, local government service providers

Source: Adapted from Gayle Fisher-Stewart, *Community Policing Explained: A Guide for Local Governments* (Washington, D.C.: U. S. Department of Justice, Office of Community Oriented Policing Services, and the International City/County Management Association, July 2007), p. 5, http://www.cops.usdoj.gov/files/ric/Publications/cp_explained.pdf (Accessed July 8, 2010).

- Detachment of patrol officers in patrol vehicles and of administration from officer and community input
- Increased violence in our society
- Downturn in the economy and, subsequently, a "do more with less" philosophy regarding the police
- Increased dependence on high-technology equipment rather than contact with the public
- Emphasis on organizational change, including decentralization and greater officer discretion
- Desire for greater personalization of government services
- Burgeoning attempts by the police to adequately reach the community through crime prevention, team policing, and police-community relations

Most of these elements contain a common theme: the isolation of the police from the public. In sum, the police got caught up in the "means over ends" syndrome, wherein they measured their success by the numbers of arrests, quickness of responses, and so on. They often neglected the outcome of their work—the ends. For many decades, this isolation often resulted in an "us versus them" mentality on the part of both the police and the citizenry. The notion of community policing therefore "rose like a phoenix from the ashes of burned cities, embattled campuses, and crime-riddled neighborhoods."[64]

Well Entrenched: Three Generations of COPPS

COPPS is the established paradigm of contemporary policing, both at home and abroad (see Chapter 14); it enjoys a large degree of public acceptance[65] and receives widespread attention by academicians who have published a growing number of journal articles and doctoral dissertations on the topic.[66] Furthermore, it has now moved through three generations or eras, according to Willard Oliver: innovation, diffusion, and institutionalization[67]:

1. The first generation of COPPS, *innovation,* spans from 1979 through 1986, beginning with the seminal work of Herman Goldstein concerning needed improvement of policing,[68] coupled with the "broken windows" theory by James Wilson and George Kelling.[69] Early concepts of community policing during this generation were often called "experiments," "test sites," and "demonstration projects," and were often restricted to larger metropolitan cities. The style of policing that was employed was predominately narrow in focus (e.g., foot patrols, problem-solving methods, and community substations). These small-scale test sites provided a source of innovative ideas for others to consider.

2. The second generation, *diffusion,* spans from 1987 through 1994. The concepts and philosophy of community policing and problem solving spread rapidly among police agencies through a variety of communication means within the policing subculture. Adoption of the strategy was fast becoming a reality during this generation, as evidenced by the fact that in 1985 slightly more than 300 police agencies had adopted some form of community policing,[70] whereas by 1994 it had spread to more than 8,000 agencies.[71] The practice of community policing during this generation was still generally limited to large- and medium-size cities, and the style of policing during this generation was much broader than the first, being more involved with neighborhood and quality-of-life issues. The strategies normally targeted drug use and fear of crime issues while improving police-community relationships. Much more emphasis was placed on evaluating outcomes through the use of appropriate research methodologies.

3. The third generation, *institutionalization,* spans from 1995 to the present and has seen widespread implementation of community policing and problem solving across the United States: Today nearly 7 in 10 (68 percent) of the nation's 17,000 local police agencies, *employing 90 percent of all officers,* have adopted this strategy.[72] This generation has seen COPPS become deeply entrenched within the political process and has featuring federal grant money through the Violent Crime Control and Law Enforcement Act of 1994. This act authorized $8.8 billion over six years to create the Office of Community Oriented Policing Services (COPS) in the U.S. Department of Justice. By July 2009, the COPS office had funded approximately 117,000 additional officers to more than 13,000 of the nation's 17,000 law enforcement agencies, in small and large jurisdictions alike. Nearly 500,000 law enforcement personnel, community members, and government leaders had been trained through COPS Office-funded training organizations. And, as of 2009, the COPS Office had distributed more than 2 million publications, training curricula, white papers, and resource CDs.[73] Table 1–1 shows the history of funded programs and personnel of the COPS office, from 1994 to 2010.

TABLE 1–1	History of the Federal Office of Community-Oriented Policing Services and Its Significant Funding Initiatives

2010

COPS allocates $302 million, which it uses to allocate grants for law enforcement technology ($170 million) and $40 million each to meth initiatives and for Indian Country.

2009

The COPS office receives $284 million in funding, which—as with FY 2008—it uses to primarily fund law enforcement technology ($187 million) and meth initiatives ($39 million).

2008

Congress awards the COPS office a $335 million budget, which it uses primarily to fund law enforcement technology ($205 million) and meth initiatives ($61 million).

2007

COPS announces $49.5 million in grants to fight methamphetamine and awards $159 million to establish integrated voice and data communication networks in 37 metropolitan statistical areas in 25 states; $14.7 million is awarded in support of tribal law enforcement initiatives, as well as $14.8 million in grants to 152 local law enforcement agencies to enhance school safety. COPS distributes its millionth technical assistance publication to the law enforcement field.

2006

- COPS awards $14.8 million to 174 local law enforcement agencies to enhance school safety and more than $12 million to support tribal law enforcement initiatives. It also announces $8.8 million to enhance interoperable communication networks.

2005

- COPS awards more than $193 million to support tribal law enforcement agencies and community court initiatives, and announces $10.2 million to fund the hiring of 65 community policing officers and 44 school resource officers; $14.7 million is awarded to 187 local law enforcement agencies through the Secure Our Schools program, and $92.7 million to 26 law enforcement agencies to develop interoperable data and communication networks.

2004

COPS awards $47.2 million in grants through the Universal Hiring Program (UHP) to 178 law enforcement agencies to hire 905 community policing officers; $4.6 million is allocated to 19 jurisdictions to combat methamphetamine use and to develop and enhance eradication strategies. More than $82 million in grants is awarded to 23 communities in 17 states to develop interoperable communications networks.

2003

COPS launches the Homeland Security Overtime Program (HSOP) and awards $59.6 million to 294 law enforcement agencies. The Interoperable Communications Technology Program is created, with $66.5 million awarded to 14 communities to develop integrated communications networks among emergency response agencies. COPS awards over $41 million in CIS grants.

2002

COPS awards more than $70 million through the Methamphetamine Program and more than $154 million through the Technology Program, and announces $128 million in UHP grants that allow 367 agencies to hire 1,750 community policing professionals.

2001

COPS launches two new series of publications: COPS Innovations and Problem-Oriented Policing Guides; it also awards $600,000 through its Justice-Based After School (JBAS) program to seven law enforcement agencies. COPS supports the NYPD and Arlington County Police Department as they respond to the September 11 attacks.

TABLE 1–1   *(continued)*

2000

COPS launches its Police as Problem-Solvers and Peacemakers program, through which it awards $1 million to five law enforcement agencies. The JBAS and Value-Based Initiatives (VBI) programs are announced, and $12 million is awarded to 41 state law enforcement agencies for the purchase of 2,900 in-car cameras.

1999

The COPS in Schools (CIS) grant program is initiated, and the 100,000th community police officer is funded; the Tribal Resources Grant Program (TRGP) is announced.

1998

COPS has now funded 75,000 new community policing officers nationwide. Three new programs are introduced: Distressed Neighborhoods Pilot Project, Police Corps Program, and Small Communities Grant Program. COPS launches the Methamphetamine Program, through which it awards $34 million throughout the fiscal year, and awards a total of $38 million through its Technology Program.

1997

COPS publishes *Police Integrity: Public Service with Honor*, and its funding establishes a nationwide network of Regional Community Policing Institutes (RCPIs).

1996

COPS funds more than 52,000 community policing officers and announces its Anti-Gang Initiative, domestic violence, and Problem-Solving Partnership initiatives.

1995

COPS funds 25,000 more officers; the Universal Hiring Program (UHP) is announced, which incorporates the Accelerated Hiring, Education and Deployment (AHEAD) and Funding Accelerated for Smaller Towns (FAST) programs. Grants totaling $10 million are awarded through the Youth Firearms Violence Initiative.

1994

The Violent Crime Control & Law Enforcement Act is enacted, authorizing an $8.8 billion in expenditures over six years. COPS is created to distribute and monitor these funds. COPS launches AHEAD, FAST, and Making Officer Redeployment Effective (MORE). COPS awards $200 million to 392 agencies for 2,700 additional community policing professionals.

Source: U.S. Department of Justice, Office of Community Oriented Policing Services, *Community Policing Dispatch,* "FY 2010 COPS Budget Highlights," http://www.cops.usdoj.gov/html/dispatch/January_2010/FY2010.htm (Accessed September 16, 2010); "COPS History," http://www.cops.usdoj.gov/Default.asp?Item=44#2005 (Accessed May 19, 2010).

The style of policing under this generation has extended to such programs as youth firearms violence, gangs, and domestic violence, while extending into geo-mapping software and crime prevention through environmental design (CPTED, discussed in Chapter 5).

COPPS has obviously become the culture of many police organizations, affecting and permeating their hiring processes, recruit academies, in-service training, promotional examinations, and strategic plans. COPPS is also having an impact in the form of community-oriented government and in the criminal justice system.

Having discussed the three primary eras of policing, we show them in Table 1–2.

TABLE 1-2	The Three Eras of Policing		
	Political Era (1840s to 1930s)	Reform Era (1930s to 1980s)	Community Era (1980s to Present)
Authorization	Politics and law	Law and professionalism	Community support (political), law, and professionalism
Function	Broad social services	Crime control	Broad provision of services
Organizational design	Decentralized	Centralized and classical	Decentralized using task forces and matrices
Relationship to community	Intimate	Professional and remote	Intimate
Tactics and technology	Foot patrol	Preventive patrol and rapid response to calls	Foot patrol, problem solving, and public relations
Outcome	Citizen and political satisfaction	Crime control	Quality of life and citizen satisfaction

Source: Adapted from George L. Kelling and Mark H. Moore, *The Evolving Strategies of Policing* (Washington, D.C.: U.S. Department of Justice, National Institute of Justice Perspectives on Policing, November 1988).

EMERGING MANAGEMENT PROCESSES AND TOOLS: IMPORTANT— BUT AN "ERA" THEY DO NOT MAKE

The Language of Policing, Generally

There are some in policing who now contend that in the late 2000s policing left the community era and entered a new one—a so-called "information era," which includes CompStat, intelligence-led policing (ILP), and predictive policing (PP) (both of these concepts are discussed more fully in later chapters). We believe that we are in an information "age," but not an era.

First, throughout its history policing has had a tendency to label everything anew; as Chris Braiden, former police superintendent in Edmonton, Canada, observed:

> The problem with cliché policing is that it waters down the Purpose. Over time the Purpose fades into the background as clichés proliferate. No need for clichés. The latest cliché? Intelligence-led policing, which says something itself about policing's past. Since the early 1970s we've had Zone, Team, Hard, Soft, Problem-Oriented, Reactive, Proactive, and Community Policing. Cliché policing started the growth of specialized centralized sub-units, each of which fixates on its own function in isolation from all others.[74]

This is not a minor issue for the field. Indeed, a long-standing criticism of policing has been what Braiden mentions above: the tendency of policing to quickly and, at times, blithely put new labels on different strategies and tactics—labels that are not altogether accurate. This criticism has even been applied to community policing, because in the past some police executives failed to properly articulate, grasp, and implement the strategy; too often, agencies merely created a peripheral "unit" or merely put an officer on a bicycle or foot patrol and then anointed theirs a "community policing organization."

Still Around, Acclaimed and Aggressive

In mid-2009, George Kelling, who has been at the core of most innovations in modern policing, said regarding the aforementioned desire by some to call community policing by some other name:

> My fear is that there is always the constant search for something sexier than community policing, because community policing sounds kind of soft, a little bit like community relations. But as a matter of fact, people don't realize how intrusive and aggressive community policing is. When you decide to take the community policing model and *prevent* crime, it means you're intervening *before* things happen. And that's really aggressive.[75]

Kelling added that community policing is needed now more than ever:

> Tough economic times are exactly when community policing is needed most, because the recession is going to hit poor communities the worst. I get a lot of calls from the news media, and they say, "We've talked to Department X, we've talked to Department Y, and they're losing a certain percentage of their budgets, so they say they're going to go back to basic policing." I'm afraid this means that departments think they can eliminate community policing and go back [to reactive policing]."[76]

An Information "Age"

We believe policing needs to "jettison the jargon." As stated above, we acknowledge that policing exists in an information *age*, but not in a new *era*. Problem-solving policing is information driven. Training in homeland security must involve the community and the identification of threats. Technologies involve reaching out to the community, and giving citizens the ability (through police agency Web sites and even social networking sites such as Twitter and Facebook) to assist with preventing crime and addressing disorder.

However, we believe these are all *tools* that simply provide a new evolution for better doing the work of community policing and problem solving in an information *age*. Furthermore, the role of the community in addressing and preventing crime and disorder must not be overlooked; it would be sheer folly to go back to one of the worst aspects of the reform era: when the police were driven—and judged—primarily by data (i.e., numbers of arrests, response times, calls for service) and primarily seen by citizens as they raced from call to call in their rolling fortresses.

COPPS AND HOMELAND SECURITY

New Threats and New Measures

Unquestionably, historians of the future will maintain that terrorist acts of the early twenty-first century changed forever the nature of policing efforts in the area of **homeland security** in the United States. Words are almost inadequate to describe how the events of September 11, 2001, forever modified and heightened the fears and concerns of all Americans—and the police—with regard to domestic security and the methods necessary for securing the general public.

Police have several means to address domestic terrorism. First, and perhaps the most fruitful, is military support of law enforcement. The Posse Comitatus Act of 1878 prohibits using the military to generally execute the laws; the military may be called on, however, to provide personnel and equipment for certain special support activities, such as domestic terrorism events involving weapons of mass destruction.[77]

To further combat terrorism, the U.S. Department of Homeland Security (DHS) was formed in 2002. [78]

Role of COPPS

What can COPPS contribute to the goal of maintaining our nation's defense? As an overarching answer to that question, 9–11 taught all Americans that we—the police and citizens—must work together to ensure our collective safety; the responsibility of responding to terrorist threats falls directly on the shoulders of state and local law enforcement and their government and community partners. Furthermore, the philosophy underlying COPPS can be directed toward trying to prevent terrorist activities before they occur. A task force report put it thusly:

> Most of the real frontlines of homeland security are outside of Washington, D.C. Likely terrorists are encountered, and the targets they might attack are protected, by local officials—a cop hearing a complaint from a landlord, an airport official who hears about a plane some pilot trainee left on the runway, an FBI agent puzzled by an odd flight school student, or an emergency room resident trying to treat patients stricken by an unusual illness.[79]

Beat officers are also a vital part of our safety. They know their neighborhoods, provide community policing, track identity theft and fraud, and develop trusted local sources. As one policy analyst put it, "They are in the best position to 'collect' the dots that federal agencies need to 'connect' to forecast the next attack."[80]

Terrorism is obviously a local issue, and homeland security and COPPS have much in common. Homeland security requires a shift in the culture of law enforcement agencies that involves the creation of external partnerships, citizen involvement, problem solving, and transformation of the organization. COPPS serves as a solid framework for the development of an effective prevention strategy for homeland security by local law enforcement agencies.[81]

Certainly crime-mapping systems, data collection and analysis protocols, and other kinds of COPPS technologies that are discussed in Chapter 5 may be used as platforms for gathering intelligence to assess terrorism vulnerability and to implement preparedness plans. As examples, agencies that use geographic information systems (GIS) to conduct crime mapping and analysis can also use GIS to conduct terrorism target mapping and analysis; agencies that use their Web site to disseminate crime prevention information can use it to disseminate homeland security information.

Certainly ILP, discussed above, and crime analysis can help in these endeavors. Crime analysts keep their fingers on the pulse of crime in the jurisdiction: which crime trends are up, which ones are down, where the hot spots are, what type of property is being stolen, and so on. Intelligence analysts, on the other hand, are likely to be more aware of the specific *people* and groups who are responsible for crime in the jurisdiction: who they are, where they live, what they do, who they associate with, and so on. Unifying and utilizing both of these functions—crime analysis and intelligence analysis—is essential for obtaining a comprehensive grasp of the crime picture. In other words, *crime analysis* allows police to understand the what, when, and where, while *intelligence analysis* provides an understanding of who is involved—crime networks and individuals.

We also believe it is important for the police to establish and maintain partnerships and lines of communication with immigrant communities, although there may be cultural, language, and other barriers to overcome. These groups may be in the best position to provide information that could lead to the prevention of a terror attack because they often possess information that is unknown outside of what are often insular communities.

The terrorist attacks on New York's World Trade Center linked forever the concepts of community policing, problem solving, and homeland security.
AP Wide World Photos

In sum, factors associated with the COPPS philosophy and the implementation of homeland security strategies are highly correlated. COPPS also involves intergovernmental and interagency collaborations with state and federal agencies that are essential for the collection and exchange of intelligence and the sharing of resources in the event of an attack.[82]

HARVARD'S KENNEDY SCHOOL OF GOVERNMENT AND COPPS: THE INFLUENCE ON POLICING OF TWO EXECUTIVE SESSIONS

Executive Sessions Defined

In the early 1980s, Harvard University's John F. Kennedy School of Government and The Program in Criminal Justice Policy and Management developed a series of Executive Sessions with the general purpose of allowing practitioners and academics to meet, confer, and search for effective means of addressing important public problems.

More specifically, these Executive Sessions constitute:

1. a "sustained conversation,"
2. among a "core group of members selected for their ability to provide leadership to a practice field," which
3. produces "learning and transformation in a practice field through continuing dialogue, digestible publications, and education."[83]

The basic model of an Executive Session is a series of five or six 3-day meetings, usually held over a period of three years, in which 25 to 30 high-level practitioners and academics engage in a creative dialogue with a view to redefining, and proposing solutions for, substantive policy issues.[84]

The First Executive Session

In 1983, the first Executive Session on Policing, jointly sponsored by the National Institute of Justice (NIJ) and the Kennedy School of Government, convened to consider policy recommendations that would guide policing for the next two decades. The overarching strategy that evolved from this first Session was community policing, the strategy that became the dominant paradigm for policing across the nation and around the world.

Papers were published following this Session in a series called *Perspectives on Policing*; these papers would become essential reading in thousands of departments and executive offices across the country. Among those notable publications were the following[85]:

- George L. Kelling, *Police and Communities: The Quiet Revolution*, June 1988, available at: http://www.ncjrs.gov/pdffiles1/nij/109955.pdf
- George L. Kelling and Mark H. Moore, *The Evolving Strategy of Policing*, November 1988, available at: http://www.ncjrs.gov/pdffiles1/nij/114213.pdf.
- Mark H. Moore and Robert C. Trojanowicz, *Corporate Strategies for Policing*, November 1988, available at: http://www.ncjrs.gov/pdffiles1/nij/114215.pdf.
- Malcolm K. Sparrow, *Implementing Community Policing*, November 1988, available at: http://www.ncjrs.gov/pdffiles1/nij/114217.pdf.
- Edwin Meese III, *Community Policing and the Police Officer*, January 1993, available at: http://www.ncjrs.gov/pdffiles1/nij/139164.pdf.

A Second Executive Session

Of course, as mentioned earlier in this chapter, policing has changed tremendously since September 11, 2001. Therefore, to better understand how policing will change in the future, the NIJ and Harvard's Kennedy School of Government are now collaborating on a "Executive Session on Policing and Public Safety." This second Session was convened from 2008 to 2010; like its predecessor, this session has high ambitions and will result in a new series of papers—to be called *New Perspectives in Policing*—that hope to influence the field in the way the earlier series did.[86] The second Executive Session on Policing and Public Safety will examine:

- How police can manage the challenges of the coming years, including community relations, terrorism, and the rising costs of public policing.
- New challenges and opportunities made possible by fast-changing technologies.
- The impact of the growing internationalization of crime.[87]

Given the impact of the first Session, we can only wait anxiously for the results of this second session—the likely discussion topics for which include:

- Police-community relations and the legitimacy of law enforcement in minority communities
- The federal role in policing
- The impact of international crime and terrorism
- The changing face of technology
- The effects of mass incarceration on relationships between police and their communities
- The role of detectives, forensic scientists, and other police professionals
- The media's role in driving police action and focus
- Professional development of police officers and leaders.[88]

Summary

This chapter has shown the evolution of policing in America, up through and including its contemporary community era and its emphasis on homeland defense. Problems with some of the old methods, as well as the willingness of police leaders to rethink their basic role and develop new strategies, led us to community oriented policing and problem solving (COPPS). It is much more than simply "a return to the basics" but is instead a retooling of the basics, coming full circle.

The incorporation of past wisdom and the use of new tools, methods, and strategies via COPPS offer the most promise for detecting and preventing crime,

addressing crime and disorder, and improving relations with the public. These partnerships are essential for addressing the "broken windows" phenomenon[89] (an influential theory asserting that once the process of physical decay begins, its effects multiply until some corrective action is taken). The lesson, Wilson and Kelling argued, was that we should redirect our thinking toward improving police handling of "little" problems. In short, the police need to be thinking like what might be termed "street-level criminologists," examining the underlying causes of crime rather than functioning like bureaucrats. This theme will be echoed at various points throughout the book.

Items for Review

1. Describe the British contributions to American policing.
2. Explain when and where modern-day policing first came to America and what its primary challenges were.
3. List and briefly explain the three eras of policing, focusing on their primary differences and foci.
4. Explain what is meant by the new "common wisdom" of policing, and discuss the major research findings of the latter half of the 1900s regarding policing methods.
5. Describe the three generations of COPPS.
6. Delineate some of the major accomplishments and funding initiatives of the federal Office of Community Oriented Policing Services since its inception.
7. Explain the authors' concerns about the language of policing in general, and why they believe policing still remains in the community era and not in a so-called "information era."
8. Provide an overview of how the Executive Sessions at Harvard's Kennedy School of Government have influenced COPPS and policing in general.

Learn by Doing

As indicated in the Preface, the "Scenarios and Activities: `Learning by Doing'" section here and at the ends of all the other chapters of the book comports with the early 1900s

teaching of famed educator John Dewey, who advocated the "learning by doing" approach to education, or problem-based learning. It also comports with the popular learning method espoused by Benjamin Bloom in 1956, known as "Bloom's Taxonomy," in which he called for "higher-order thinking skills"—critical and creative thinking that involves analysis, synthesis, and evaluation.[90] The following scenarios and activities will shift your attention from textbook-centered instruction and move the emphasis to student-centered projects. By being placed in these hypothetical situations, you can thus learn and apply some of the concepts covered in this chapter, develop skills in communication and self-management, at times become a problem solver, and learn about or address current community issues.

1. As part of a criminal justice honor society poster presentation at a forthcoming conference, you are assigned to present an overview of the history of policing in the United States, focusing on its three eras. How will you depict each era, and what will you emphasize for each on your poster(s)?

2. You have a friend who is a police officer and is instructing a class on COPPS at the Regional Police Academy. She knows of your academic background and asks that you assist this instruction, focusing on the differences between policing's professional (or reform) and community eras. What will be the content of this assignment?

3. Your criminal justice professor has assigned a group project in which you are to debate "the use of language in policing." Set forth what will be your major points, focusing on the debate concerning the eras, tactics, and tools of policing.

Notes

1. David R. Johnson, *American Law Enforcement History* (St. Louis, Mo.: Forum Press, 1981), p. 11.
2. Ibid., p. 13.
3. Ibid., pp. 14–15.
4. Leon Radzinowicz, *A History of English Criminal Law and Its Administration from 1750, Vol. IV: Grappling for Control* (London: Stevens & Son, 1968), p. 163.
5. Johnson, *American Law Enforcement History*, pp. 19–20.
6. A. C. Germann, Frank D. Day, and Robert R. J. Gallati, *Introduction to Law Enforcement and Criminal Justice* (Springfield, Ill.: Charles C Thomas, 1962), p. 63.
7. Clive Emsley, *Policing and Its Context, 1750–1870* (New York: Schocken Books, 1983), p. 37.
8. Eric H. Monkkonen, *Police in Urban America, 1860–1920* (Cambridge, U.K.: Cambridge University Press, 1981), pp. 1–2.
9. Johnson, *American Law Enforcement History*, pp. 26–27.
10. See K. E. Jordan, *Ideology and the Coming of Professionalism: American Urban Police in the 1920s and 1930s* (Dissertation, Rutgers University, 1972); Robert M. Fogelson, *Big-City Police* (Cambridge, Mass.: Harvard University Press, 1977).
11. Johnson, *American Law Enforcement History*, p. 27.
12. James F. Richardson, *Urban Policing in the United States* (New York: Oxford University Press, 1970), p. 51.
13. Johnson, *American Law Enforcement History*, p. 92.
14. Ibid.
15. Ibid.
16. Ibid., pp. 96–98.
17. Ibid.
18. Monkkonen, *Police in Urban America, 1860–1920*, p. 158.
19. John E. Eck, *The Investigation of Burglary and Robbery* (Washington, D.C.: Police Executive Research Forum, 1984).
20. See George L. Kelling, "Juveniles and Police: The End of the Nightstick," in Francis X. Hartmann (ed.), *From Children to Citizens, Vol. II: The Role of the Juvenile Court* (New York: Springer-Verlag, 1987).
21. Samuel Walker, *A Critical History of Police Reform: The Emergence of Professionalism* (Lexington, Mass.: Lexington Books, 1977), pp. 8–9, 11.
22. Ibid., p. 33.
23. Ibid., pp. 33–34, 42, 47.
24. Ibid., p. 81.
25. Ibid., pp. 80–83.
26. Herman Goldstein, *Policing a Free Society* (Cambridge, Mass.: Ballinger, 1977).
27. Albert Reiss, *The Police and the Public* (New Haven, Conn.: Yale University Press, 1971).
28. See Orlando Wilson, *Police Administration* (New York: McGraw-Hill, 1950).
29. Walker, *A Critical History of Police Reform*, pp. 93–94.
30. Mark H. Moore and George L. Kelling, "'To Serve and Protect': Learning from Police History," *The Public Interest* 70 (Winter 1983):49–65.
31. Peter K. Manning, "The Police: Mandate, Strategies, and Appearances," in Jack D. Douglas (ed.), *Crime and Justice in American Society* (Indianapolis, Ind.: Bobbs-Merrill, 1971), pp. 149–163.

32. Walker, *A Critical History of Police Reform*, p. 161.

33. Louis Radelet, *The Police and the Community* (4th ed.) (New York: Macmillan, 1986), p. ix.

34. Ibid., p. 17.

35. Ibid., p. 21.

36. William G. Doerner, *Introduction to Law Enforcement: An Insider's View* (Englewood Cliffs, N.J.: Prentice Hall, 1992), pp. 21–23.

37. Mary Ann Wycoff, *The Role of Municipal Police Research as a Prelude to Changing It* (Washington, D.C.: Police Foundation, 1982).

38. Jerome H. Skolnick and David H. Bayley, *The New Blue Line: Police Innovation in Six American Cities* (New York: Free Press, 1986), p. 4.

39. William C. Cunningham, John J. Strauchs, and Clifford W. Van Meter, *The Hallcrest Report II: Private Security Trends, 1970–2000* (McLean, Va.: Hallcrest Systems, 1990).

40. William Westley, *Violence and the Police: A Sociological Study of Law, Custom, and Morality* (Cambridge, Mass.: MIT Press), 1970.

41. American Bar Foundation, *The Urban Police Function,* approved draft (Chicago: Author, 1973).

42. Jerome Skolnick, *Justice Without Trial: Law Enforcement in Democratic Society* (New York: John Wiley & Sons, 1966).

43. Egon Bittner, "The Police on Skid Row: A Study of Peace Keeping," *American Sociological Review* 32 (1967):699–715.

44. Raymond I. Parnas, "The Police Response to the Domestic Disturbance," *Wisconsin Law Review* 4 (1967):914–955.

45. James Q. Wilson, *Varieties of Police Behavior: The Management of Law and Order in Eight Communities* (Cambridge, Mass.: Harvard University Press, 1968).

46. Albert J. Reiss, Jr., *The Police and the Public* (New Haven, Conn.: Yale University Press, 1971).

47. Goldstein, *Policing a Free Society*, pp. 22–24.

48. Ibid., p. 11.

49. Elaine Cumming, Ian Cumming, and Laura Edell, "Policeman as Philosopher, Guide, and Friend," *Social Problems* 12 (1965):285; T. Bercal, "Calls for Police Assistance," *American Behavioral Scientist* 13 (1970):682; Reiss, *The Police and the Public.*

50. George Kelling, Tony Pate, Duane Dieckman, and Charles E. Brown, *The Kansas City Preventive Patrol Experiment: A Summary Report* (Washington, D.C.: Police Foundation, 1974).

51. Peter W. Greenwood, Joan Petersilia, and Jan Chaiken, *The Criminal Investigation Process* (Lexington, Mass.: D.C. Heath, 1977); John E. Eck, *Managing Case Assignments: The Burglary Investigation Decision Model Replication* (Washington, D.C.: Police Executive Research Forum, 1979).

52. Bernard Greenbert, S. Yu Oliver, and Karen Lang, *Enhancement of the Investigative Function, Vol. 1: Analysis and Conclusions, Final Report, Phase 1* (Springfield, Va.: National Technical Information Service, 1973).

53. Kelling, Pate, Dieckman, and Brown, *The Kansas City Preventive Patrol Experiment.*

54. Ibid.

55. Joan Petersilia, "The Influence of Research on Policing," in Roger C. Dunham and Geoffrey P. Alpert (eds.), *Critical Issues in Policing: Contemporary Readings* (Prospect Heights, Ill.: Waveland Press, 1989), pp. 230–247.

56. James Q. Wilson, *Thinking About Crime* (New York: Vintage Books, 1975).

57. Herman Goldstein, *Problem-Oriented Policing* (New York: McGraw-Hill, 1990), p. 13.

58. Ibid., p. 3.

59. Thomas J. Baker, "Designing the Job to Motivate," *FBI Law Enforcement Bulletin* 45 (1976):3–7.

60. Samuel Walker, *The Police in America: An Introduction* (2nd ed.) (New York: McGraw-Hill, 1992), p. 185.

61. Police Foundation, *The Newark Foot Patrol Experiment* (Washington, D.C.: Author, 1981).

62. Robert Trojanowicz, *An Evaluation of the Neighborhood Foot Patrol Program in Flint, Michigan* (East Lansing, Mich.: School of Criminal Justice, Michigan State University, 1982).

63. Michael J. Farrell, "The Development of the Community Patrol Officer Program: Community-Oriented Policing in the New York City Police Department," in Jack R. Greene and Stephen D. Mastrofski (eds.), *Community Policing: Rhetoric or Reality* (New York: Praeger, 1988), pp. 73–88.

64. Robert Trojanowicz and Bonnie Bucqueroux, *Community Policing: A Contemporary Perspective* (Cincinnati, Ohio: Anderson, 1990), p. 67.

65. George Gallup, *Community Policing Survey* (Wilmington, N.Y.: Scholarly Resources, 1996).

66. Willard M. Oliver, "The Third Generation of Community Policing: Moving Through Innovation, Diffusion, and Institutionalization," *Police Quarterly* 3 (December 2000):367–388.

67. Ibid.

68. Herman Goldstein, "Improving Policing: A Problem-Oriented Approach," *Crime and Delinquency* 25 (1979):236–258.

69. James Q. Wilson and George L. Kelling, "Broken Windows: The Police and Neighborhood Safety," *Atlantic Monthly* (March 1982):29–38.

70. Samuel Walker, *The Police in America: An Introduction* (New York: McGraw-Hill, 1985).

71. T. McEwen, *National Assessment Program: 1994 Survey Results* (Washington, D.C.: National Institute of Justice, 1995).

72. U.S. Department of Justice, Bureau of Justice Statistics, *Law Enforcement Management and Administrative Statistics: Local Police Departments 2000* (Washington, D.C.: Author, January 2003), p. iii.

73. U.S. Department of Justice, Office of Community Oriented Policing Services, "About COPS, http://www.cops.usdoj.gov/Default.asp?Item=35 (Accessed May 19, 2010).

74. Chris Braiden, "Cliché Policing: Answer Before Question," Unpublished paper, n.d.

75. George Kelling, quoted in "Don't Let Budget Cuts Damage Your Commitment to Community Policing," *Subject to Debate* 23 (June 2009): 3.

76. Ibid.

77. D. G. Bolgiano, "Military Support of Domestic Law Enforcement Operations: Working Within Posse Comitatus," *FBI Law Enforcement Bulletin* (December 2001):16–24.

78. See U.S. Department of Homeland Security, "Department Components and Subagencies," http://www.dhs.gov/xabout/structure/ (Accessed September 26, 2010).

79. U.S. Department of Justice, Office of Community Oriented Policing Services, "Community Partnerships: A Key Ingredient in an Effective Homeland Security Approach," *Community Policing Dispatch* 1(2) (February 2008), p. 2, http://www.cops.usdoj.gov/html/dispatch/february_2008/security.html (Accessed July 8, 2010).

80. Michael E. O'Hanlon, "Homeland Security: How Police Can Intervene," *The Washington Times*, August 18, 2004. http://www.brookings.edu/view/op-ed/ ohanlon/20040818.htm (Ac-cessed February 22, 2006), p. 2.

81. Jose Docobo, "Community Policing as the Primary Prevention Strategy for Homeland Security at the Local Law Enforcement Level," *Homeland Security Affairs* 1(1) (Summer 2005):1.

82. Ibid., p. 2.

83. Adapted from Mark H. Moore and Francis X. Hartmann, "On the Theory and Practice of Executive Sessions," http://www.hks.harvard.edu/var/ezp_site/storage/fckeditor/file/pdfs/centers-programs/programs/criminal-justice/exec_sessions_theory.pdf (Accessed September 27, 2010).

84. Harvard University, John F. Kennedy School of Government, The Program in Criminal Justice Policy and Management, "Research & Publications," http://www.hks.harvard.edu/programs/criminaljustice/research-publications (Accessed September 27, 2010).

85. Kelling, *Police and Communities,* National Institute of Justice, June 1988, http://www.ncjrs.gov/pdffiles1/nij/109955.pdf; Kelling and Moore, *The Evolving Strategy of Policing,* National Institute of Justice, November 1988, http://www.ncjrs.gov/pdffiles1/nij/114213.pdf; Moore and Trojanowicz, *Corporate Strategies for Policing,* National Institute of Justice, November 1988, http://www.ncjrs.gov/pdffiles1/nij/114215.pdf; Sparrow, *Implementing Community Policing,* National Institute of Justice, November 1988, http://www.ncjrs.gov/pdffiles1/nij/114217.pdf; and Meese III, *Community Policing and the Police Officer,* National Institute of Justice, January 1993, http://www.ncjrs.gov/pdffiles1/nij/139164.pdf (all were accessed on September 27, 2010).

86. Harvard University, Kennedy School of Government, "Executive Session on Policing and Public Safety (2008-2010)," http://www.hks.harvard.edu/programs/criminaljustice/research-publications/executive-sessions/executive-session-on-policing-and-public-safety-2008-2010; also see ibid., "Executive Session on Policing and Public Safety: Members," http://www.ojp.usdoj.gov/nij/topics/law-enforcement/administration/executive-sessions/members.htm (Accessed September 27, 2010).

87. National Institute of Justice, "Harvard Executive Session on Policing and Public Safety (2008-2010)."

88. Ibid.

89. Wilson and Kelling, "Broken Windows," pp. 29–38.

90. Benjamin S. Bloom, *Taxonomy of Educational Objectives, Handbook I: The Cognitive Domain* (New York: David McKay, 1956).

COPPS
Partnerships in a Changing Society

KEY TERMS AND CONCEPTS

Communitarianism

Community corrections

Community court

Community engagement

Community governance

Community justice

Community policing

Community prosecution

Community service center

Demographics

E-government

Restorative justice

"Second-generation" station house

Sense of community

Social capital

LEARNING OBJECTIVES

As a result of reading this chapter, the student will:

- Have a grasp of what is meant by "community" and the roles that communitarianism, social capital, and volunteerism play in it

- Know why it is essential for government and the police to view citizens and other organizations and agencies as invaluable partners in crime prevention and crime control

- Comprehend the meaning of community policing, and understand how it differs from traditional policing

- Understand the challenges posed to the police by our nation's shifting demographics, immigration patterns, and high technology

- Be familiar with the implications of an aging nation as well as the challenges posed by younger generations of people and the changing nature of crime

- Know what some jurisdictions are doing to make their police station houses more warm, open, and community-oriented

No problem can be solved by the same consciousness that
created it. We must learn to see the world anew.

—ALBERT EINSTEIN

> *When earth breaks up and heaven expands,*
> *How will the change strike me and you ...?*
> —ROBERT BROWNING

INTRODUCTION

What is a "community," and how do the police go about engaging and addressing problems within a changing community with its shifting types of crime? What are some of the changes that are occurring in our nation, with both its population and methods of crime? How must the police prepare to deal with them?

This chapter examines those questions, beginning with a look at some of the elements that compose a community. Included in this discussion, and to better understand how our nation and policing have evolved into the current community policing era, we emphasize one of the basic premises on which that strategy is founded: All agencies of government should view their citizens as invaluable customers and should understand the roles that community justice and governance, social capital, and volunteerism play in that view. Then we look at how courts and corrections agencies are also partnering with citizens through community and restorative justice; included here is a look at how units of government are reaching out with community service centers and e-government activities.

Then we discuss the point to which all of this has evolved: community-oriented policing. This portion of the chapter, together with Chapter 3, comprises the heart and soul of the book; we review community policing's basic principles and how this philosophy differs from traditional policing. Following that is a review of some of the challenges that exist today as police agencies attempt to engage this changing nation, with its demographics, its economic and immigration issues, its aging population, and its high technology, as well as how police must deal with violence and fear of crime.

The overarching theme of this chapter is that the police and the community must partner to engage in crime fighting (indeed, a national survey found that police agencies employing 73 percent of all police officers now include elements of community policing in their mission statements).[1] We do not examine problem-oriented policing and problem solving at length here; those discussions will follow later, primarily in Chapter 3. Furthermore, we discuss several other aspects of our changing society, such as challenges being posed by the new generation of Millennials, who are now entering the police workplace as baby boomers retire, in later chapters as well.

The chapter concludes with a summary, review questions, and several scenarios and activities that provide opportunities for you to "learn by doing."

WHAT *IS* COMMUNITY?

A Sense of Community

This chapter is essentially about community. But what is meant by the term "community," and how do the police interact with it? Those fundamental questions must be addressed before proceeding to discuss how this nation is changing.

First, it is important to note that today's notion of community, under COPPS, is quite different from the traditional view. The traditional community was homogeneous (as will be seen below); today most of us live with heterogeneity. Traditional communities experienced little change from one year to the next, commonly demanded a high degree of conformity, were often unfriendly to strangers, and could boast generations of history and continuity.

A **sense of community** is an intangible yet vital component of a healthy community. Many times a sense of community has deep historical roots, centered around a place, building, or event—a town square, church, holiday parades, sporting events, and so on. As well as good schools, clean air and water, and a low crime rate, a sense of community is increasingly a key factor in where people reside. Strong communities also connect the different groups within them, and their members to each other and to civic life. They find ways for people to connect and contribute within the entire spectrum of community life.[2]

John Gardner[3] delineated some key elements of a sense of community and what is needed to rebuild its sense of community in the future:

1. *Membership.* People become members of a community when they feel emotionally secure, personally invested, and a sense of belonging or identification in the community.
2. *Influence.* People who have a sense of community must feel that their opinion can have influence over what the group does.
3. *Integration and fulfillment of goals.* People are rewarded for their participation in the community, providing positive rewards and satisfying experiences.
4. *Shared emotional connection.* This final element seems to be the defining feature for people to experience a true emotional connection. There are many features of a community that facilitate people having such a connection, including a shared history or historical district, public places where they can socialize and interact, positive interactions between business owners and loyal customers, a nice blend between open spaces and buildings, and corridors that link cities and natural environment (rivers, biking trails).

A community's quality of life is obviously determined by its citizens[4]; therefore, it is important that the public be empowered by government to engage in the identification and resolution of neighborhood concerns. It is well established that people act more responsibly when they control their own environments than when they are controlled by others. Empowerment is an American tradition.[5] Citizens should understand their community's problems, and "good citizens make strong communities."[6]

Communitarianism

A concept that has application to policing is **communitarianism.** This term, promulgated by prominent sociologist Amitai Etzioni and other academics, argues that we have gone too far toward extending rights to our citizens and not far enough in asking them to fulfill responsibilities to the community as a whole. Focusing not so much on politics as on the process of government, "it is a mindset that says the whole community needs to take responsibility for itself. People need to actively participate, not just give their opinions ... but instead give time, energy, and money."[7]

In this view, communitarianism is an attempt to nurture an underlying structure of "civil society"—sound families, caring neighbors, the whole web of churches, Rotary clubs, block associations, and nonprofit organizations that give individuals their moral compass and communities their strength. Communitarians see our political culture as being in very bad shape, not just because elected officials have done a bad job but because citizens have not attended to what citizenship is all about.

Citizen surveys provide police departments with vital information about their performance and citizens' concerns.
Courtesy Reno, Nevada, PoliceDepartment.

As a result, communitarians support processes such as problem solving, where neighborhoods have taken matters into their own hands, closing off streets and creating other physical barriers to disrupt the drug trade, working to overcome problems of homelessness and panhandling, and so on. This is where communitarians overlap with the objectives of community problem solving: the recognition that many of the answers to community problems lie not with government but in the community at large.

Social Capital

Social capital concerns those "features of social organization such as networks, norms, and trust that facilitate cooperation or coordination for mutual benefits."[9] In other words, civic participation is essential within American communities. Building partnerships between citizens and police is part of a larger community-building movement that requires high levels of trust and **community engagement**. For example, as will be seen below, making city services more accessible, increasing citizen volunteers in government agencies, and developing neighborhood-based governing organizations have helped to increase problem-solving efforts.[10]

The first and most basic form of social capital is found among members of a family and between citizens within a community. Therefore, the importance of organizing a community cannot be overemphasized; doing so is the most effective way to work against often well-organized adversaries (criminals).

The second level of social capital consists of those social networks tying the individual to broader community institutions: churches, schools, civic and voluntary organizations. These informal associations with other citizens help build familiarity and trust among individuals and keep individuals engaged in communal affairs.

If communities lack strong social cohesion, citizens are not likely to engage in collective activities, and police agencies will have difficulty implementing initiatives that require long-term citizen participation.

Volunteerism

The current economic crisis has probably placed more need for, and emphasis on the use of volunteers than any other time in our history. And people have responded to the call: An estimated

Senior volunteers provide assistance to visitors in the downtown area of Reno, Nevada. They relieve police of many duties and patrol parks, schools, business districts, residential areas, and downtown.

Courtesy Reno Police Department.

63.4 million Americans now volunteer to help their communities—an increase of 1.6 million volunteers compared to 2008; volunteers also provide about 8.1 billion hours of service. Most volunteers participate in fundraising/selling activities (26.6 percent do this activity), followed closely by preparing or serving food (23.5 percent), providing labor or transportation (20.5 percent), or tutoring or teaching (19 percent). It is also known that as the rates of homeownership and employment decrease, the volunteer rate also tends to decrease; people with higher levels of education tend to volunteer more, while persons living in poverty volunteer less.[11]

The police have certainly taken advantage of this surge in volunteerism. Exhibit 2-1 provides an example of how several police agencies use, and benefit from, the public's interest in volunteerism.

PARTNERS IN COMMUNITY JUSTICE

In today's complex and diverse society, the police understand full well that community engagement is at the core of successful problem solving. Most police-community partnerships are informal, but some—even those involving regular meetings with neighborhood groups—go farther and have a formalized structure. Examples of the latter abound, but following are a few good illustrations:

- The New Rochelle, New York Police Department partnered with community leaders and clergy to develop a program to facilitate a mutually respectful relationship between the police and the community through open lines of communication and cooperation.
- In Boston, the police department developed the "Boston Re-Entry Initiative" in partnership with faith-based, community, and criminal justice agencies to help former prisoners adjust to life in their communities; it also works with clergy to make unofficial visits to the homes of troubled youth.
- The Pasadena, California, police partner with licensed clinical social workers through the Homeless Outreach Psychiatric Evaluation Unit to address long-term solutions for the homeless and those suffering from mental illness.[12]

Certainly, agencies of criminal justice other than the police—courts and corrections organizations as well—must partner with their communities. Next we examine some of the activities they employ in engaging the public, beginning with a relatively new concept known as restorative justice.

| Exhibit 2-1 | Volunteering in Police Services (VIPS): Some Examples |

Following are three examples of how the police can utilize volunteers; national awards are now available to police agencies for those efforts. A part of this initiative is the Volunteers in Police Service (VIPS) Program. Managed by the International Association of Chiefs of Police and the Bureau of Justice Assistance, Office of Justice Programs, U.S. Department of Justice, VIPS has the sole objective of enhancing the capacity of state and local law enforcement agencies to utilize volunteers.

▶ Any employee of the Bellevue, Washington, Police Department can request volunteer help with an event or program. The volunteer program coordinator writes a volunteer assignment description that outlines the volunteer's responsibilities, describes any special skills or abilities the volunteer should have, and sets the hours the volunteer will work. The volunteer program coordinator then finds the best available volunteer for the assignment. Volunteers in the program have served as archive managers, case assistants, bicycle registration and recovery specialists, fire lane parking enforcers, community projects administrators, quartermasters, and chaplains, to name just a few of the 30 or so roles they play.

▶ Volunteers assigned to VIPS Patrol in Vacaville, California, issue citations for all non-moving violations, direct traffic, service police vehicles, relieve school crossing guards, assist with searches for missing persons, report unlicensed businesses, and help enforce municipal codes involving neighborhood blight and reporting violations of all kinds. Volunteers also assist in the records section (releasing crash records, running citations for traffic court, providing customer service at the front counter), the property and evidence section (purging unneeded evidence, updating computer records), the K-9 unit (putting on the protective wear and standing in for the bad guy during training exercises), and the investigations division (coordinating the crime prevention program).

▶ The Hazelwood, Missouri, police department's Volunteer Services Unit first requires volunteers to have completed the citizens' police academy; they are then eligible to participate in the Citizen Observer Patrol, in which volunteers patrol designated areas of the city, in a marked car or on foot, watching for and reporting suspect activity; looking for disabled automobiles, injured persons, fires, and broken windows and open doors at homes and businesses; watching for teenagers who appear to be involved in mischief; and so on. Volunteers receive quarterly in-service training on such topics as traffic direction, radio procedures, first aid, and CPR.

Source: Adapted from Volunteers in Police Service, "VIPS Focus," pp. 1–3, http://www.policevolunteers.org/pdf/2007%20Award.pdf (Accessed July 9, 2010). Reprinted by permission.

Community Justice, Community Governance, and Restorative Justice

As indicated above, in addition to the police, courts and corrections organizations have also been compelled to change their strategies and approaches to a concept of community justice. **Community justice** is a new way of thinking about the criminal justice system; it is a systemic approach to public safety, emphasizing problem solving and focusing on community concerns.

TABLE 2-1	Comparison of Retributive and Restorative Justice

Old Retributive Justice	New Restorative Justice
Crime defined as a violation of the state	Crime defined as a violation of one person by another
Focus on blame, guilt, and the past	Focus on problem solving, liabilities, and future obligations
Adversarial relationships	Dialogue and negotiation
Imposition of pain to punish, the goal being deterrence/prevention	Restitution as a means of restoring both parties, the goal being restoration
The community as a passive observer represented by the state	The community as facilitator
A "debt" owed to society	A "debt" to the victim recognized

Source: Adapted from Michael Phillips, "The New Paradigm of Justice," *Government Technology (Special Report: Building Digital Government) in the 21st Century* (February 1, 2001), p. 41.

Increasingly, all segments of society as well as the nation's criminal justice system are realizing that the only viable approach to mediating their problems is community-wide participation and cooperation.[13]

The concept of **community governance** has also been evolving, having its roots in community policing. Indeed, the principles and practices of community policing can be used to address a host of issues confronted by any unit of local government. Community governance focuses on the quality of life of citizens and their satisfaction with local government services. And, as with community policing, the central component of community governance is the development of strong partnerships to foster trust and collaborative problem solving.[14]

Closely related to the concept of community justice is **restorative justice**, the elements of which include repairing harm (first taking care of the victim who suffered the harm prior to trying to help the offender become a better citizen), reducing risk (managing the offender in such a way that he or she will not commit another crime), and building community (taking responsibility for the behavior of community members and becoming involved in the resolution process, not just turning crime over to government to be dealt with). Table 2-1 compares the traditional standard of retributive justice with restorative justice, which concerns active involvement of victims and the community.

Community justice services aim to identify and solve the problems that foster crime and injustice. Next, though, we present some of the means by which the police, courts, and corrections components of the justice system have worked successfully to revitalize their communities.

Police

"FOUR R'S."   It is probably difficult for a police officer who was just kicked, bitten, scratched, and otherwise injured by a citizen to think in terms of collaboration with the public. Nonetheless, the fact remains that most of the people with whom the officer interacts do not conduct themselves in that manner. Moreover, citizens expect and deserve a public servant who is wearing the uniform to provide specific things. The "four R's" that citizens want from their police are:

- reliability
- responsiveness

- reassurance, and
- results.

Certainly the officer's providing excellent customer service, being a good listener, and using excellent communication skills will go far toward meeting those four desires.[15]

NOW MISSING IN SOME AREAS: "STATION HOUSE BLUES."   A relatively new and important way in which some police agencies are engaging in community building involves the design and amenities of their station houses. Generally, the public areas of most station houses are very stark, cold, unfriendly places. And, as with their dentist, few people go to their police station voluntarily. But some jurisdictions are hoping to change that.

In the Los Angeles Police Department's West Valley station, in Reseda, residents will find ATMs in the light-filled lobby, kitchen-equipped meeting rooms for public use, and even an inviting outdoor courtyard with barbecue facilities. Gone from such **"second-generation" station houses** are the small windows that were located high off the ground to deter drive-by shootings but that made the buildings look like bunkers and armed camps. Such police stations also typically offer more areas that are open to the public (such as cafeterias where officers and civilians can eat together), bigger lobbies where people can comfortably sit, and community rooms where people can hold meetings and training sessions.[16]

In a related vein, later in this chapter we discuss some police uses of the Internet to provide citizens with real-time information concerning officer responses to crimes and other calls for service.

The Los Angeles Police Department's West Valley "second-generation" station house.
Courtesy Los Angeles Police Department. Used with permission.

Courts

Community courts are now being launched in jurisdictions across the United States. Focused on bridging the gap between themselves and the neighborhoods they serve, community courts adapt the problem-solving approach (first tested by community policing) to the complex issues they face. They build new relationships and engage residents schools, churches, and other stakeholders. They combine punishment and help, requiring low-level offenders to pay back the community while addressing the issues that often underlie criminal behavior, like drug addiction and unemployment.[17]

Community prosecutors can also focus on criminal and civil problems in specific neighborhoods and develop a long-term proactive partnership between their office, police agencies, the community, and public and private organizations. The community prosecutor steps out of the traditional role (see Exhibit 2-2). Instead of reacting to a crime after it happens and a suspect is arrested, he or she uses such tools as nuisance abatement, drug-free and prostitute-free zones, restorative justice (discussed above), truancy abatement, and graffiti cleanup to improve neighborhood safety.[18]

Defense attorneys are also engaged in community justice. They know about their clients and the communities from which they come; the staff members see their communities as a series of interconnected family networks. Relatives often call the office out of concern for a person's safety as he or she entered the justice system. The program provides a deeper understanding of clients through continuity of representation and better investigation, better presentation of sentencing options through greater connection to community resources, and greater ability to represent residents' support for a less severe sentence.

A good example of a community court's activities is the Midtown Community Court in New York City.[19] This court targets quality-of-life offenses, such as prostitution, illegal vending, graffiti, shoplifting, fare beating, and vandalism in midtown Manhattan. Residents, businesses, and social service agencies collaborate with the court by supervising projects and by providing onsite services, including drug treatment, health care, and job training. Social services located in

---

Exhibit 2-2	Community Prosecution in Albany, New York

The Office of the Albany County District Attorney has made it a priority to implement a progressive philosophy of restorative justice under the auspices of community prosecution. This program involves a long-term, proactive partnership between the prosecutor's office, law enforcement, public and private organizations, and the community. Through these partnerships, the authority of the prosecutor's office is used to solve problems, improve public safety, and enhance the quality of life of community members. Community Prosecution Offices (CPOs) are staffed with a community prosecution coordinator, an assistant district attorney, a probation officer, and a community representative. CPOs interact with the community at the neighborhood level to recruit volunteers and to identify and solve problems that contribute to crime and pose hazards to public order and safety. CPOs also:

▶ maximize potential for successful reintegration of re-entering prison inmates.
▶ keep middle-school-aged kids out of the drug distribution economy.
▶ Make public safety services more responsive to the needs of the aging population.
▶ Foster and strengthen the Neighborhood Watch organizations.

Source: Adapted from Office of the Albany County District Attorney, "Community Prosecution: Action," http://www. albanycountyda.com/issues/comm_pros.html (Accessed July 9, 2010).

the court provide the judge with these services as well as a health education class for prostitutes and "johns," counseling for young offenders and mentally ill persons, and employment training. For offenders with lengthier records, the court offers a diversionary program. Many defendants return to court voluntarily to take advantage of these services, including English as a second language (ESL) and General Educational Development (GED) classes.

Other partnerships that can involve the courts and citizens include child care during trials for victims and witnesses, law-related education, and job training and referral for offenders and victims. A community-focused court can also practice restorative justice, emphasizing the ways in which disputes and crimes adversely affect relationships among community residents, treating parties to a dispute as real individuals rather than abstract legal entities, and using community resources in the adjudication of disputes.[20]

Corrections

Community corrections may be defined as non-prison sanctions that are imposed on convicted adults or adjudicated juveniles either by a court instead of a prison sentence or by a parole board following release from prison. Community corrections programs are usually operated by probation and parole agencies, and the programs can include general community supervision as well as day reporting centers, halfway houses and other residential facilities, work release, and other community programs. The multiple goals are: providing offender accountability, delivering rehabilitation services and surveillance, and achieving fiscal efficiency.[21]

At the core of a good community corrections program is the use of an objective risk and needs assessment. The "risk" part assesses risk of offenders to reoffend; the "need" portion of the assessment instrument identifies the segment of the offender population that will benefit from being in rehabilitation treatment programs.[22]

According to Joan Petersilia, a future trend of community corrections includes the use of technologies to monitor compliance with court-ordered conditions, such as drug testing, global positioning systems, alcohol breathalyzers, and so on. Another trend has to do with "wrap-around" services, where mental health, alcohol and drug abuse, housing, and medical services agencies are planning an offender's case management together.[23]

Exhibit 2-3	Corrections Partner with Others in Ohio

In Richland County, Ohio, a partnership exists between the county adult probation office, sheriff's office, police department (city of Mansfield), and state parole authority, with teams of community policing and community corrections officers conducting major joint operations. They engage in joint inspections of local bars, check for curfew violations, do fugitive surveillance, and perform joint visitations of probationers' and parolees' homes to seek out and question clients for possible violations. Community policing officers handle specific clients, which enhances their familiarity with supervised offenders; likewise, corrections officers supervise offenders in the police department's beat areas, which gives them greater knowledge of the neighborhoods in which their clients reside. Crime statistics reveal a much greater reduction in violent and property crimes in areas where these agencies work together.

Source: David Leitenberger, Pete Semenyna, and Jeffrey B. Spelman, "Community Corrections and Community Policing," *FBI Law Enforcement Bulletin* (November 2003):20–23.

Sentencing low-risk offenders to community work projects is one community-based corrections strategy.
Courtesy Washoe County, Nevada, Sheriff's Office.

Community Service Centers

Beginning in the mid-1980s, when community policing was becoming more widespread, police storefronts also became more popular. Today, however, cities are going beyond just using a storefront, instead providing a **community service center** where citizens can do "one-stop shopping" to access government services. In addition to filing police reports or obtaining information, following is a list of some other kinds of services being provided:

- Affordable housing listings
- Alarm permit applications
- Business licenses
- Bus schedules
- City job listings and applications
- Community event information
- Community maps and plans
- Crime prevention information
- Dockets of city council meetings
- Dog license applications
- Notary services
- Park and recreation class and event schedules

- Passport applications
- Permits
- Social service referrals
- Tax forms
- Water bill payments

Police neighborhood resource centers (PNRCs) are also helping to break down barriers between the police department and the community and now offer a wide range of services, such as the following[24]:

- ESL classes
- School district outreach services
- Mobile public library services
- Blood pressure screenings
- Computer classes
- Purchase of vehicle stickers

E-Government

The Internet is dramatically changing the way government operates—in terms of not only a greater ability of residents or businesses to interact with public agencies but also the manner in which government delivers services: **e-government** at work. Now obtaining information is literally just a click away. Exhibit 2-4 shows some of the kinds of services and information that may be obtained online from the city government in Clearwater, Florida, a community of about 108,000 on the state's west-central coast (see http://www.myclearwater.com/services/index.asp). The Clearwater Police Department uniquely provides an "Active Calls for Service" Web site whereby citizens can, in near real-time terms, see calls that are being dispatched to police officers. Exhibit 2-5 shows a display of that screen (it may be viewed at http://www.clearwaterpolice.org/cfs/ active.asp). Other Web-based functions are discussed in Chapter 5.

With such services available to them, constituents perceive government as a responsive entity, with greater convenience and ease of use, better and faster information, and a level of service that customers had come to expect only in the private sector.

WHERE ALL THESE ROADS HAVE LED: COMMUNITY POLICING

Basic Principles

As we noted in Chapter 1, Robert Peel emphasized the police and community working together in the 1820s when setting forth his principles of policing: "The police are the only members of the public who are paid to give full-time attention to duties which are incumbent on every citizen in the interest of the community welfare."[25]

Unfortunately, as Herman Goldstein posited, the police have erred in recent decades by pretending that they could take on, and successfully discharge, all of the responsibilities that are now theirs:

> It is simply not possible for a relatively small group of individuals, however powerful and efficient, to meet those expectations. A community must police itself. The police, at best, can only assist in that task. We are long overdue in recognizing this fact.[26]

Exhibit 2-4

Courtesy Clearwater Police Department.

Exhibit 2-5

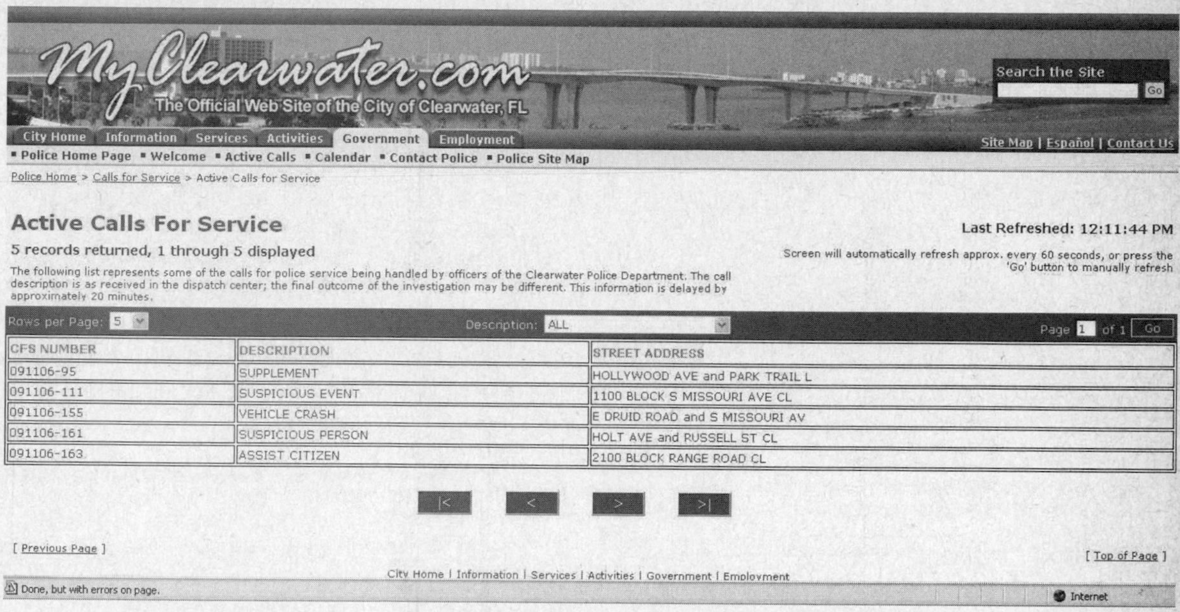
MyClearwater.com
The Official Web Site of the City of Clearwater, FL
Search the Site Go
City Home | Information | Services | Activities | Government | Employment
Site Map | Español | Contact Us
▪ Police Home Page ▪ Welcome ▪ Active Calls ▪ Calendar ▪ Contact Police ▪ Police Site Map
Police Home > Calls for Service > Active Calls for Service

Active Calls For Service

Last Refreshed: 12:11:44 PM

5 records returned, 1 through 5 displayed

Screen will automatically refresh approx. every 60 seconds, or press the 'Go' button to manually refresh

The following list represents some of the calls for police service being handled by officers of the Clearwater Police Department. The call description is as received in the dispatch center; the final outcome of the investigation may be different. This information is delayed by approximately 20 minutes.

Rows per Page: 5 Description: ALL Page 1 of 1 Go

CFS NUMBER	DESCRIPTION	STREET ADDRESS
091106-95	SUPPLEMENT	HOLLYWOOD AVE and PARK TRAIL L
091106-111	SUSPICIOUS EVENT	1100 BLOCK S MISSOURI AVE CL
091106-155	VEHICLE CRASH	E DRUID ROAD and S MISSOURI AV
091106-161	SUSPICIOUS PERSON	HOLT AVE and RUSSELL ST CL
091106-163	ASSIST CITIZEN	2100 BLOCK RANGE ROAD CL

|< < > >|

[Previous Page] [Top of Page]

City Home | Information | Services | Activities | Government | Employment

Done, but with errors on page. Internet

Courtesy Clearwater Police Department.

In the early 1980s, the notion of **community policing** emerged as the dominant direction for thinking about policing. It was designed to reunite the police with the community. "It is a philosophy and not a specific tactic; a proactive, decentralized approach, designed to reduce crime, disorder, and fear of crime, by involving the same officer in the same community for a long-term basis."[27] But no single program describes community policing. It has been applied in various forms by police agencies in the United States and abroad and differs according to the community needs, politics, and resources available.

Differences between Community Policing and Traditional Policing

It is important to understand where community policing departs from traditional policing; the major points of departure may be seen in Table 2-2. Note that the definition, role, priorities, and assessment of the police differ between the two models.

Many past and present practitioners have become staunch proponents of the concept. For example, former Atlanta, Houston, and New York City Chief of Police Lee P. Brown wrote:

> I believe that community policing—the building of problem-solving partnerships between the police and those they serve—is the future of American law enforcement. In essence, we are bringing back a modern version of the "cop on the beat." We need to *solve* community problems rather than just *react* to them. It is time to adopt new strategies to address the dramatic increases in crime and the fear of crime. I view community policing as a better, smarter and more cost-effective way of using police resources.[28]

TABLE 2-2	Traditional Versus Community Policing: Questions and Answers	
Question	**Traditional Policing**	**Community Policing**
Who are the police?	A government agency principally responsible for law enforcement.	Police are the public and the public are the police: The police officers are those who are paid to give full-time attention to the duties of every citizen.
What is the relationship of the police force to other public service departments?	Priorities often conflict.	The police are one department among many responsible for improving the quality of life.
What is the role of the police?	Focusing on solving crimes.	A broad problem-solving approach.
How is police efficiency measured?	By detection and arrest rates.	By the absence of crime and disorder.
What are the highest priorities?	Crimes that are high value (e.g., bank robberies) and those involving violence.	Whatever problems disturb the community most.
With what, specifically, do police deal?	Incidents.	Citizens' problems and concerns.
What determines the effectiveness of police?	Response times.	Public cooperation.
What view do police take of service calls?	Deal with them only if there is no real police work to do.	Vital function and great opportunity.
What is police professionalism?	Swift, effective response to serious crime.	Keeping close to the community.
What kind of intelligence is most important?	Crime intelligence (study of particular crimes or series of crimes).	Criminal intelligence (information about the activities of individuals or groups).
What is the essential nature of police accountability?	Highly centralized; governed by rules, regulations, and policy directives; accountable to the law.	Emphasis on local accountability to community needs.
What is the role of headquarters?	To provide the necessary rules and policy directives.	To preach organizational values.
What is the role of the press liaison department?	To keep the "heat" off operational officers so they can get on with the job.	To coordinate an essential channel of communication with the community.
How do the police regard prosecutions?	As an important goal.	As one tool among many.

Source: Malcolm K. Sparrow, *Implementing Community Policing* (Washington, D.C.: U.S. Department of Justice, National Institute of Justice: U.S. Government Printing Office, November 1988), pp. 8–9.

It should be emphasized, however, that community-oriented policing can be a long-term process in some tradition-bound agencies, and it involves fundamental institutional change. One scholar warned police managers that "if you approach community-oriented policing as a program, you will likely fail. Beware of the trap that seeks guaranteed, perfect, and immediate results."[29]

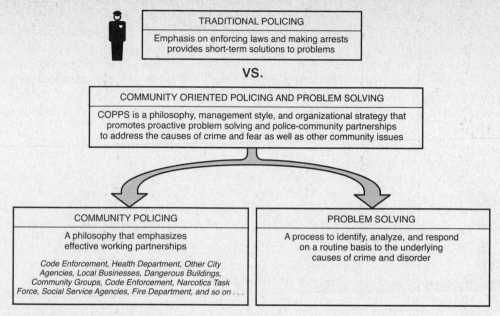

FIGURE 2-1   Traditional Policing Versus Community Oriented Policing, Problem Oriented Policing, and Neighborhood Police Officers.

Community policing goes beyond simply implementing foot and bicycle patrols or neighborhood stations. It redefines the role of the officer on the street, from crime fighter to problem solver and neighborhood ombudsman. It forces a cultural transformation of the entire department, including a decentralized organizational structure and changes in recruiting, training, awards systems, evaluations, promotions, and so forth. Furthermore, this philosophy asks officers to break away from the binds of incident-driven policing and to seek proactive and creative resolution to crime and disorder. See Figure 2-1.

UNIQUE CHALLENGES: ENGAGING A CHANGING NATION

Certainly the changing demographics and greater heterogeneity of today's America pose unique challenges for the police in terms of engaging the community (discussed above). In this section, we examine specifically how America is evolving in terms of its demographics, its aging population, its generational differences, and its technology.

Demographics: Who We Are

Although Chapter 10 specifically addresses how the police can engage a diverse society, here we briefly discuss how America is being transformed in terms of its **demographics**.

Although the results of the 2010 U.S. Census may change the nation's demographics considerably, today about 300 million people are believed to be legally residing in America. Approximately 80 percent of the population of the United States is white; nearly 13 percent is black; and nearly 7 percent is Asian, Pacific Islander, American Indian, or of two or more races. About one-fourth (26.4 percent) of all households are headed by one person. [30] The mean age of Americans is estimated to be 37.5 years; about one-fourth of the population (27.5 percent) is less than 19 years of age, while about 12.8 percent are over 65. [31]

There is an increasing number of fatherless children in this nation, children who are more often prone to delinquency and other social pathologies. Of the 72 million children under age 18 living in the United States, about a third (31.4 percent) live where there is either one parent or no parent present in the household (23 percent live with their mother only).[32] Many problems in crime control are strongly related to absence of a father: About 90 percent of all homeless and runaway youths are from fatherless homes, as are 71 percent of high school dropouts, 70 percent of youths in state institutions, 75 percent of adolescent patients in substance abuse centers, and 85 percent of rapists who were motivated by displaced anger.[33]

With the Asian and Hispanic populations being the fastest growing in the United States,[34] the face of America is indeed changing. Each year since 1990, between 600,000 and 1 million aliens have been lawfully admitted into this country for permanent residence.[35] The Hispanic population is projected to increase rapidly over the 1995 to 2025 period, accounting for 44 percent of the growth of the nation's population (32 million Hispanics out of a total of 72 million persons added to the nation's population).[36] Currently the nation's population is 14 percent Hispanic.[37]

The Influences and Challenges of Immigration

The influence of immigration to America and the growth of minority group populations in general cannot be overstated. There are now an estimated 11.5 million illegal immigrants in the United States, according to the Pew Hispanic Center—certainly a significant number, but still the lowest number in a decade and still declining. From 2000 to 2005, an average of 800,000 illegal immigrants entered the United States each year, but since then an average of 500,000 have arrived annually.[38]

The reasons for this decline are several. First, a new 700-mile fence along the southwestern border (that represents only about one-third of the U.S.-Mexican border, and that keeps no one out who is determined to enter illegally) and increased patrolling and enforcement have been crucial to this decrease. Also, the federal Immigration and Customs Enforcement (ICE) has been increasingly raiding U.S. businesses that employ illegal immigrants. And in the recession of the mid- and late-2000s, fewer immigrants were coming to the United States because jobs were disappearing. Furthermore, a number of states, counties, and cities are taking legal actions never before heard of. The most controversial and toughest was that enacted in Arizona in April 2010, which:

- made it a violation of state law to be in the country illegally, and requiring immigrants to have proof of their immigration status; repeat offenses were to be a felony.
- required police officers to "make a reasonable attempt" to determine the immigration status of a person if "reasonable suspicion" exists that he or she was an illegal immigrant.[39]

Legal reactions (as well as outcries by many civic groups) to Arizona's law came swiftly: first, in July 2010 the Justice Department filed a lawsuit to challenge the law, arguing that it would undermine the federal government's pursuit of terrorists, gang members, and other criminal immigrants.[40] Then, in July 2010, a federal judge issued a preliminary injunction against the most controversial provisions of the law—those that enabled police officers to check a person's immigration status while enforcing other laws, and required immigrants to prove that they were authorized to be in the United States or risk state charges. The court largely sided with legal arguments filed by the Obama administration—that the law interfered with long-standing federal authority over immigration and could lead to harassment of citizens and legal immigrants.[41]

Tens of thousands of people across the U.S. protested in 2010 against Arizona's controversial anti-immigration legislation.
Courtesy Shutterstock.

Following are some other examples of new legislation enacted in the states relating to immigration:

- In 2008, statehouses passed more than 200 laws relating to immigration, the majority of them clamping down on illegal immigrants and their employers; however, at the local level, such legal populism has not fared well; for example:
  - Columbia County, Oregon, imposed a $10,000 fine on anyone in the county who gave jobs to undocumented workers (in April 2009, a circuit court judge overturned the measure)
  - A city in Texas is fighting for the right to make all renters show proof of citizenship.[42]

For many aliens, however, their investment in the American dream is too great to leave; they also know that if they return to Mexico, given the enhanced enforcement, they probably will not be able to return.[43]

Certainly the police are caught in the middle of this politically and emotionally charged issue. Furthermore, they do not appear to know or agree as to the relationships between illegal immigrants and crime. A national survey by the Police Executive Research Forum found that there is a perception by many police chiefs that illegal immigration contributed to increased crime, while others believe illegal immigrants are *less* likely to commit crime because most are here to work, and they try to avoid coming to the attention of the police.[44] Perhaps the truth is more like that expressed by a Canadian police chief[45]:

> We're having problems with the second generation of immigration. The parents come in and they're hard-working, they want to succeed. But their kids are having a little bit of trouble integrating, and they're committing crime, and violent crime, disproportionately to their numbers.

A police officer works with Asian business owners to improve a shopping center that was run-down and was experiencing increased crime.
Courtesy Community Policing Consortium.

Graying of America: Implications and Concerns

As indicated above, we live in a "graying" country as well, with 12.4 percent of the total population being at least 65 years old.[46] The golden years for baby boomers represents a graying of the population. The first boomers reached age 50, or midlife, in 1996; soon they will command the aging agenda as they prepare for retirement in 2010 through 2030. The good news is the elderly are less likely than younger people to become victims of violence and are less likely to be injured during a violent crime; only about 2.1 violent crimes per 1,000 are committed against persons over 65 years of age.[47] However, elderly victims are more likely to have been killed during the commission of a felony. Furthermore, with brittle bones, when they are injured, their injuries are more severe and their victimization can be permanently disabling. Being on fixed income, they cannot receive the best medical care; most are female. They also have a high fear of crime but are less likely to take protective measures than younger people and more likely to report a crime. They can also be victimized in nursing homes and hospitals, and their relative isolation can lead to a high percentage of their victimization occurring in their homes. They are targeted more often for fraud involving finances than other people, which can lead to severe depression and other serious health problems.[48]

Certainly the police must become more adept at preventing and investigating those types of crimes that tend to target our seniors. Their susceptibility to fraudulent schemes, purse snatchings, theft of checks from the mail, and crimes in long-term care settings poses unique challenges for investigative personnel.

The police must maintain close contact with seniors to understand their needs and provide the best possible services.
Courtesy of Cedar City, Utah, Police Department.

High Technology

The world has rapidly become more technological; today more than 311 million English-speaking people as well as 500 million non-English-speaking people use the Internet.[49] The ability to produce and analyze information has become very important to our country economically in terms of a person's social standing or ability to get a job.

Yet there exists what can be termed a serious "digital divide". "Smokestack America" is largely gone; today there are fewer blue-collar jobs and more white-collar positions. The fastest-growing careers are those requiring more language, mathematics, and reasoning skills. In sum, today's economy is based on knowledge and the ability to process information; whereas employers in the past mostly wanted muscle, today more and more jobs presuppose skills, training, and education.

SHIFTS IN CRIME

As with challenges to the police that are caused by alterations in our demographics, so are the police being challenged by shifts in criminal behavior. While we will discuss in Chapters 11 and 12 how problems involving gangs, drugs, and other crimes are being addressed under COPPS, here we mention in more general terms the violent nature of our society and our fear of being victimized.

A Violent Venue

Although the nation's violent crime rate declined by 41 percent and the property crime rate fell by 32 percent from 1999 to 2008 (contributing factors, according to experts, including the overall aging of the population, longer prison sentences for habitual offenders, a relatively healthy economy, and the community-oriented policing and problem-solving strategy), ours is certainly a long way from being a "safe" venue in which to live. It would seem that John Bunyan understood the human capacity for violence in 1686 when in his *Book for Boys and Girls* he wrote:

Children become, while little, our delights,

When they grow bigger, they begin to fright's.

While juvenile crime has been declining, concern about youth crime and violence continues.
Courtesy Washoe County, Nevada, Sheriff's Office.

Their sinful Nature prompts them to rebel,

And to delight in Paths that lead to Hell.[50]

We still experience nearly 5 million violent crimes and 16.3 million property crimes each year.[51] A number of factors contribute to these victimizations: immediate access to firearms, alcohol and substance abuse, drug trafficking, poverty, racial discrimination, and cultural acceptance of violent behavior.

Federal, state, and local governments spend more than $200 billion per year for criminal justice activities (including law enforcement, courts, and corrections agencies).[52] Nearly half (about $99 billion) of this amount is for police protection, while about $47 billion is for the courts and about $67 billion is for corrections.[53] On any given day, about 7.3 million Americans are under some form of correctional supervision: 4.2 million are on probation, 2.3 million persons are incarcerated in prisons and jails, and 800,000 are on parole.[54]

Fear of Crime

Crime, fear, and disorder frighten Americans, with 42 percent of Americans describing the nation's crime problem today as either extremely serious or very serious.[55]

We know that neighborhood disorder affects a person's perception of safety as much as crime does. People express greater fear of strangers loitering near their homes than they do the threat of murder. They fear being bothered by people they view as sinister: panhandlers, drunks, addicts, rowdy teens, mental patients, and the homeless. They also fear physical disorder: litter, abandoned buildings, potholes, broken streetlights and windows, wrecked cars, and other indicators of neighborhood decline.

Thomas Hobbes wrote in 1651 that the "fundamental purpose of civil government is to establish order, protecting citizens from a fear of criminal attack that can make life nasty, brutish, and short."[56] It would appear that we have yet to reach the goal that Hobbes established for civil government.

After identifying that fear of crime exists—through community surveys and/or meetings, perhaps talking with key individuals such as postal carriers and business people, and looking for graffiti and other sources of fear—certainly there are many approaches the police can undertake to address the fear of crime, including the following—all of which are discussed in greater detail in later chapters:

- *Personalized policing*: using such strategies as following up on citizen complaints, engaging in reassurance efforts, and solving neighborhood problems
- *Community engagement*: volunteering in community programs, mentoring, forming community groups, conducting neighborhood cleanups, holding marches, scheduling regular beat meetings, and establishing citizen patrols
- *Environmental design*: enhancing lighting increasing natural or electronic surveillance
- Engaging in an overall problem-solving strategy[57]

Exhibit 2-6 describes another contemporary fear: how the return of prisoners to the community will affect public safety.

Exhibit 2-6	**Prisoner Re-entry into the Community: Hazards of Early Release**

During the recent recession, a number of states trimmed their prison populations by expanding parole programs and early releases. But the result—more convicted felons on the streets rather than behind bars—has often been disastrous in terms of public safety. For example, Oregon was forced to suspend its early-release program (touted to save $6 million) after a woman was attacked in her home by a registered sex offender; Illinois' early-release program was described as "a big mistake" after convicts committed violent crimes within a few weeks. Colorado's program, meant to save $19 million, was forced to scale back its releases after determining that many inmates were bad release risks. Similar programs in California and Michigan were challenged by victims' rights groups and prosecutors.

Several issues and challenges militate against the successful reintegration of inmates through early release jail and prison programs:

- ▶ *Mental illness* Sixteen percent of both jail inmates and state prisoners report a mental condition
- ▶ *Substance abuse and dependence* More than two-thirds of jail inmates were dependent on or abuse drugs or alcohol, with 69 percent being regular drug users.
- ▶ *Limited employability.* Forty-three percent of jail inmates did not hold full-time jobs at the time of their arrest.
- ▶ *Extensive criminal histories.* Three-fourths of jail inmates served a prior probation or incarceration sentence, and about a quarter served three or more prior sentences to incarceration.

Sources: Monica Davey, "Safety Is Issue as Budget Cuts Free Prisoners," *New York Times*, March 4, 2010, http://www.nytimes.com/2010/03/05/us/05parole.html?pagewanted=all (Accessed July 10, 2010); U.S. Department of Justice, Office of Community Oriented Policing Services, *Prisoner Reentry and Community Policing: Strategies for Enhancing Public Safety*, March 2006, pp. 8–9, http://www.cops.usdoj.gov/files/RIC/Publications/e12051219.pdf (Accessed July 10, 2010).

The homeless, inebriates, and panhandlers—many of whom have been sorely affected by the economy—can add to peoples' fear of crime as much as actual crimes do.
Courtesy Shutterstock.

IT'S THE ECONOMY

The Housing and Mortgage Crisis

There is an old saying among criminal justice planners: "There's a lot of crime prevention in a T-bone steak." Although historically that statement was likely to be more false than true—the commission of most crimes probably being much more closely associated with *greed* rather than *need*—there is little doubt that in today's recession there is a causal relationship between the economy and crime.

Certainly crime and disorder have been affected by the recent housing and foreclosure crisis. Police agencies must now take proactive measures to counteract increases in crimes involving mortgage-related issues. The incidence of mortgage fraud has increased over the past few years, as well as crimes against vacant properties, mortgage fraud, and metal theft. The public must be educated concerning these crimes and in the methods for preventing them. Furthermore, the police should be prepared for an increase in the incidence of domestic violence, because studies show that there is a connection between worsening economies and increases in such offenses.[58]

Agencies must now pay close attention to their crime statistics to see if the relationship between the economy and these and other crimes exists and, if so, in what neighborhoods; then, responses can be designed to address them and to mitigate the effects on crime that arise from economic distress.

Shifting and Sharing Responsibility for Addressing Crime and Disorder

For quite a few years, the police have been subtly coercing people to take greater responsibility for their property. Examples would include business owners being fined by units of government if they have excessive false burglary alarms (in fact, more than 90 percent of such alarms are false, triggered by malfunction, rodents, and so forth), and the refusal of the police to help citizens get into their locked vehicle or jump-starting or pushing disabled vehicles. The resulting effect on police workload and the potential for liability are simply too great. Police are also more often seeking reimbursement for the cost of rescue when someone's quest for adventure goes awry, or, say, a tavern or apartment complex has an inordinate volume of calls for service. Some agencies are even withholding services altogether, as when a self-service gas station has a high volume of drive-offs but has refused to install a prepayment system, or a restaurant has a poor system for monitoring customers and collecting payments.[59]

Now we find that the police are making even bolder formal attempts to coerce or persuade citizens to address crime and disorder problems. With the current economic recession, there is a growing tendency to ask, for example, who is really responsible for preventing and controlling retail theft? Is it the police? The business owner? The consumer? The insurance carrier? To a large extent, this is a political issue that comes down to who possesses the power to avoid accepting responsibility.[60]

Some agencies are even, as a last resort, resorting to publicly shaming delinquent parties. Public reputation is of great value to individuals and business owners; therefore, exposing, for example, the irresponsible practices of tavern or video arcade owners to local government or media outlets can serve to quickly quell a problem.[61]

Summary

This chapter, with its centerpiece being the partnership between the community and its police agency, has defined what is meant by "community," demonstrated several means by which the police and other justice organizations are partnering with this dynamic populace, and how and why COPPS evolved and offers the best hope for meeting the challenges posed. Also discussed were several means by which government entities are expanding their community building and customer service.

We also examined a number of changes that are occurring in America, particularly with respect to the nature of its people and their crimes—and some innovative means the police have adopted for dealing with them, including fines, public shaming, and withdrawal of services.

While violent crime has been declining of late, the years ahead certainly may not be tranquil. We cannot afford to hurtle into the future with our eyes fixed firmly on the rearview mirror. Social, political, and economic events of today will cause policing to change forever. A failure to anticipate and plan for what many people predict will be a turbulent and complex future could produce untenable consequences. "Business as usual" will probably not suffice.

Items for Review

1. Explain what is meant by "community," including its ingredients and the roles that communitarianism, social capital, and volunteerism play in it.
2. Describe why it is essential for the government and the police to view citizens as invaluable customers.
3. Compare the ways in which community policing differs from traditional policing.
4. Review the challenges posed to the police by our nation's shifting demographics, immigration patterns, and use of high technology.
5. Outline the implications of an aging nation as well as the challenges posed by younger generations of people and the changing nature of crime.
6. Explain the characteristics of a "second-generation" police station house that serve to make it more warm, open, and community-oriented.
7. Describe how the economy has changed the nature of crime, and some innovative ways by which the police are attempting to deal with it.

Learn by Doing

1. Assume that your state's governor is considering pros and cons of legislation such as that enacted in Arizona in mid-2010 that would give greater latitude to police officers for identifying and arresting illegal immigrants. As legislative liaison for your law enforcement agency, you've been asked to prepare a position paper on this legislation. What would you identify as being possible positive and negative aspects of such legislation?

2. You are a patrol sergeant and have been tasked to lecture to your agency's Citizens' Police Academy about police-community partnerships and working with stakeholders. Your chief informs you that the group has particular interest in the relatively new concepts of restorative justice, community courts, and community corrections initiatives. How would you explain each of these three concepts?

3. Each year your criminal justice faculty sponsor a "Career Day" program. The department chairperson requests that you participate by making a short presentation on policing recruitment and hiring—certainly topics of interest to your fellow students. What will you say about how the economy—particularly the housing and mortgage crisis—has affected policing, and some methods by which agencies are shifting and sharing responsibility for addressing crime and disorder?

Notes

1. U.S. Department of Justice, Bureau of Justice Statistics, *Local Police Departments, 2003*, April 2006, p. iii, http://bjs.ojp.usdoj.gov/index.cfm?ty=pbdetail&iid=1045 (Accessed July 9, 2010).

2. University of New Hampshire Cooperative Extension, *Community Building: Strengthening the Sense of Community*, http://extension.unh.edu/resources/representation/Resource000625_Rep647.pdf (Accessed July 9, 2010).

3. Adapted from John Gardner, "There Is More Than a Ray of Hope for America's Future: Rebuilding America's Sense of Community," http://www.world-trans.org/qual/Americancommunity.html (Accessed July 9, 2010).

4. David Couper and Sabine Lobitz, *Quality Policing: The Madison Experience* (Washington, D.C.: Police Executive Research Forum, 1991), p. 65.

5. David Osborne and Ted Gaebler, *Reinventing Government: How the Entrepreneurial Spirit Is Transforming the Public Sector* (Reading, Mass.: Addison-Wesley, 1992), p. 51.

6. Tom Dewar, quoted in David A. Lanegran, Cynthia Seelhammer, and Amy L. Walgrave (eds.), *The Saint Paul Experiment: Initiatives of the Latimer Administration* (St. Paul, Minn.: City of St. Paul, 1989), p. xxii.

7. Rob Gurwitt, "Communitarianism: You Can Try It at Home," *Governing* 6 (August 1993):33–39.

8. Ibid., 39.

9. R. Putnam, "Tuning in, Tuning Out: The Strange Disappearance of Social Capital in America," *Political Science and Politics* (December 1995):664–683.

10. Mark E. Correia, "Social Capital and Sense of Community Building: Building Social Cohesion," in Ronald W. Glensor, Mark E. Correia, and Kenneth J. Peak (eds.), *Policing Communities: Understanding Crime and Solving Problems* (Los Angeles: Roxbury, 2000), pp. 75–82.

11. Corporation for National & Community Service, "Volunteering in America 2010: National, State, and City Information," pp. 2-8, http://www.volunteeringinamerica.gov/assets/resources/IssueBriefFINALJune15.pdf (Accessed July 9, 2010).

12. Carlos Fields, *Award-Winning Community Policing Strategies 1999-2006* (U.S. Department of Justice, Office of Community Oriented Policing Services, September 2007, pp. 16–17, http://www2.gsu.edu/~crirxf/COPS-CP.pdf (Accessed July 9, 2010).

13. Laurie J. Wilson, "Placing Community-Oriented Policing in the Broader Realms of Community Cooperation," *The Police Chief* (April 1995):127.

14. U.S. Department of Justice, Office of Community Oriented Policing Services, "Community Policing Dispatch: From Community Policing to Community Governance," May 2008, http://www.cops.usdoj.gov/html/dispatch/may_2008/nugget.htm (Accessed July 9, 2010).

15. Gerald W. Garner, "Exceptional Customer Service," *Law and Order* (June 2003):103–106.

16. Sheila Muto, "Arresting Design: Police Stations Get a Lift," *The Wall Street Journal* (January 5, 2005), p. B-1.

17. U.S. Department of Justice, Office of Community Oriented Policing Services, "Community Policing Dispatch: Inspiring the Judiciary: Community Courts Adapt Community Policing Principles," February 2009, http://www.cops.usdoj.gov/html/dispatch/February_2009/courts_adapt.htm (Accessed July 9, 2010).

18. American Prosecutors Research Institute and the National District Attorneys Association, "What Is Community Prosecution?" http://www.ndaa-apri/programs/community_pros/whis_is_community_prosecution.html (Accessed March 3, 2006).

19. Ibid.

20. Ibid., pp. 46–51.

21. The Pew Center on the States, *What Works in Corrections: An Interview with Dr. Joan Petersilia,* November 2007, p. 1, http://www.pewtrusts.org/uploadedFiles/wwwpewtrustsorg/Reports/sentencing_and_corrections/QA_Community_Corrections.pdf (Accessed July 9, 2010).

22. Ibid., p. 2.

23. Quoted in ibid., p. 3.

24. See, for example, the Des Plaines, Illinois, Web site, http://www.desplaines.org/ Services/Police/PNRC.htm (Accessed March 3, 2006).

25. W. L. Melville Lee, *A History of Police in England* (London: Methuen, 1901), Chapter 12.

26. Herman Goldstein, "Toward Community-Oriented Policing: Potential, Basic Requirements, and Threshold Questions," *Crime and Delinquency* 33 (1987):17.

27. Robert Trojanowicz and Bonnie Bucqueroux, *Community Policing: A Contemporary Perspective* (Cincinnati, Ohio: Anderson, 1990), p. 154.

28. Lee P. Brown, "Community Policing: Its Time Has Come," *The Police Chief* 62 (September 1991):10.

29. Jerald R. Vaughn, *Community-Oriented Policing: You Can Make It Happen* (Clearwater, Fla.: National Law Enforcement Leadership Institute, no date), p. 8.

30. U.S. Census Bureau, "U.S. and World Population Clocks—POPClocks," http://www.census.gov//main/www/popclock.html (Accessed February 24, 2006); also see U.S. Census Bureau, "Population Projections for States by Age, Sex, Race, and Hispanic Origin: 1995–2025," http://www.census.gov/ population/www/projections/pp147.html (Accessed July 9, 2010).

31. Ibid.; also see U.S. Census Bureau, "United States—Fact Sheet—American FactFinder." http://factfinder.census.gov/servlet/ACSSAFFFacts?_event=&geo_id=01000US&_geo (Accessed July 9, 2010).

32. U.S. Census Bureau, *Population Profile of the United States: Living Arrangements of Children in 2002* (Washington, D.C.: Author, 2003), p. 1.

33. U.S. Census Bureau, *Statistics in Brief: Population and Vital Statistics* (Washington, D.C.: Author, 2000), pp. 13–16.

34. U.S. Citizenship and Immigration Services, "Immigrants," in *2003 Yearbook of Immigration Statistics,* http://uscis.gov/graphics/shared/aboutus/statistics/ IMM03yrbk/2003IMM.pdf (Accessed July 9, 2010).

35. Ibid., p. 6.

36. Pearson Education, Information Please Database, "Population of the United States by Race and Hispanic/Latino Origin, Census 2000 and July 1, 2004," http://www.infoplease.com/ipa/A0762156.html (Accessed February 23, 2006).

37. U.S. Census Bureau, "Population Projections for States by Age, Sex, Race, and Hispanic Origin."

38. Immigrants from Mexico decline to lowest in decade," *World News Network,* July 21, 2009, http://www.examiner.com/a-2130084~Immigrants_from_Mexico_decline_to_lowest_in_decade.html (Accessed August 1, 2009).

39. Adapted from Erin Kelly, "Immigration Measure may Spark Action in Other States, Congress," *Gannett Washington Bureau,* April 25, 2010, http://www.azcentral.com/news/articles/2010/04/24/20100424arizona-immigration-bill-federal-action.html (Accessed April 26, 2010); Kevin Johnson and Joan Biskupic, "Arizona Immigration Crackdown Raises Flags," *USA TODAY,* http://www.usatoday.com/news/nation/2010-04-29-arizona-immigration_N.htm (Accessed April 30, 2010).

40. Julia Preston, "Dept. Sues Arizona Over Its Immigration Law," http://www.nytimes.com/2010/07/07/us/07immig.html (Accessed July 9, 2010).

41. Randal C. Archibold, "Judge Blocks Arizona's Immigration Law" *New York Times,* July 28, 2010, www.nytimes.com/2010/07/29/us/29arizona.html (Accessed July 29, 2010).

42. "Court Overrules Oregon County's Anti-Immigrant Law," *Salem News.com,* http://www.salem-news.com/articles/april152009/immig_rights_4-15-09.php (Accessed August 1, 2009).

43. Nathan Thornburgh, "Undocumented and Undeterred," *Time,* April 20, 2009, p. 34.

44. Police Executive Research Forum, *Police Chiefs and Sheriffs Speak Out on Local Immigration Enforcement,* April 2008, p. 12, http://www.policeforum.org/upload/Immigration_6a_main%20text_596427705_6252010114851.pdf (Accessed July 9, 2010).

45. William Blair, quoted in Police Executive Research Forum, *Violent Crime in America: "A Tale of Two Cities"* November 2007, p. 15, http://www.policeforum.org/upload/VC%20Summit%2007_full_148192123_1272007111812.pdf (Accessed July 9, 2010).

46. U.S. Census Bureau, "USA Statistics in Brief: Population by Sex, Age, and Region," http://www.census.gov/statab/www/pop.html (Accessed February 22, 2006).

47. U.S. Department of Justice, Bureau of Justice Statistics, "Violent Victimization Rates by Age, 1973–2004," http://www.ojp.usdoj.gov/bjs/glance/tables/ vagetab.htm (Accessed February 25, 2006).

48. Andrew Karmen, *Crime Victims: An Introduction to Victimology* (6th ed.) (Belmont, Calif.: Wadsworth, 2006), p. 228.

49. "Internet World Stats: Usage and Population Statistics," http://www .internetworldstats.com/stats7.htm (Accessed February 23, 2006).

50. John Bunyan, *A Book for Boys and Girls: Or, Country Rhimes for Children* (London: N.P., 1686), pp. 71–73.

51. U.S. Department of Justice, Bureau of Justice Statistics, "Criminal Victimization, 2008," http://bjs.ojp.usdoj.gov/index.cfm?ty=pbdetail&iid=1975 (Accessed July 9, 2010).

52. U.S. Department of Justice, Bureau of Justice Statistics, "Direct Expenditure by Level of Government, 1982–2006," http://bjs.ojp.usdoj.gov/content/glance/tables/expgovtab.cfm (Accessed July 10, 2010).

53. U.S. Department of Justice, Bureau of Justice Statistics, "Direct Expenditures by Criminal Justice Function, 1982–2006," http://bjs.ojp.usdoj.gov/content/glance/tables/exptyptab.cfm (Accessed July 10, 2010).

54. U.S. Department of Justice, Bureau of Justice Statistics, "Correctional Populations," http://bjs.ojp.usdoj.gov/content/glance/tables/corr2tab.cfm (Accessed July 10, 2010).

55. Gallup, "U.S. Crime Problem Less Troubling to Americans," http://www.gallup.com/poll/13987/us-crime-problem-less-troubling-americans.aspx (Accessed July 10, 2010).

56. Thomas Hobbes, "Leviathan," in C. B. Macpherson (ed.), *Leviathan* (Baltimore, Md.: Pelican Books), p. 5.

57. Gary Cordner, *Reducing Fear of Crime: Strategies for Police*, U.S. Department of Justice, Office of Community Oriented Policing Services, January 2010, pp. 45–52. http://www.saferhastings.co.uk/pdfs/reassurance%20pdf's/COPS_guide_ReducingFear.pdf (Accessed July 10, 2010).

58. U.S. Department of Justice, Office of Community Oriented Policing Services, "Community Policing Dispatch: Preparing for Crime in a Bad Economy," http://www.cops.usdoj.gov/html/dispatch/January_2009/crime_economy.htm (Accessed July 9, 2010).

59. Michael S. Scott and Herman Goldstein, *Shifting and Sharing Responsibility for Public Safety Problems*, August 2005, pp. 23–24, http://www.popcenter.org/responses/responsibility/ (Accessed July 11, 2010).

60. Ibid.

61. Ibid., p. 4.

3

COPPS
Problem Oriented Policing

KEY TERMS AND CONCEPTS

Analysis

Assessment

Guardian

Handlers

Incident-driven policing

Manager

Problem analysis triangle

Problem-oriented policing
 (POP)

Problem solving

Response

Scanning

Situational policing

Small wins

LEARNING OBJECTIVES

As a result of reading this chapter, the student will:

- Comprehend the development of problem solving for the police

- Be aware of the basic principles of problem-oriented policing and how it differs from incident-driven policing

- Understand the four major steps in the S.A.R.A. problem-solving process, including their role and methods of accomplishment

- Be able to explain the potential difficulties with problem solving

- Recognize the three identifiable stages of neighborhoods

- Understand the four different types of neighborhoods

- Know the meaning of situational policing

- Be able to explain, after reading an example, the fundamentals of how problem-oriented policing functions

It seemed that the next minute they would discover a solution.
Yet it was clear to them that the end was still far, far off, and that
the hardest and most complicated part was only just beginning.
—ANTON CHEKOV

INTRODUCTION

In this chapter, we analyze problem oriented policing: its origin and operation, and the four-stage problem-solving process that rests at its core. Included in this discussion is an overview of some possible difficulties that are involved with problem solving and how different types of neighborhoods require different approaches by the police in terms of overall strategies.

As we noted in Chapter 2, although the concepts of community policing and problem-oriented policing are commonly treated as separate and distinct entities, we maintain here and throughout the remainder of the book that they are complementary core components. Therefore, here as in other chapters we use the term "community oriented policing and problem solving," or COPPS. We believe this term best captures the nature of this approach to policing.

Note that there are several important adjuncts to COPPS, including situational crime prevention, crime prevention through environmental design (CPTED), technologies, crime analysis, and mapping. Those topics are addressed in Chapters 4 and 5.

PROBLEM SOLVING

Early Beginnings

Problem solving is not new; police officers have always tried to solve problems (we define the word "problem" below). The difference is that, in past eras of policing, officers who were dealing with problems did not have an in-depth understanding of the nature and underlying causes of those crime problems, nor receive much guidance, support, or sophisticated methods (e.g., crime analysis or mapping tools) to support their efforts. The routine application of problem-solving techniques is new. It is based on two facts: that problem solving can be applied by officers throughout the agency as part of their daily work and that routine problem-solving efforts can be effective in reducing or resolving problems.

Problem oriented policing (POP) was grounded in principles different from community oriented policing (COP), but, again, they are complementary. POP is a strategy that puts the COP philosophy into practice. It advocates that police examine the underlying causes of recurring incidents of crime and disorder. The problem-solving process, discussed in later chapters, helps officers identify problems, analyze them completely, develop response strategies, and assess the results.

Herman Goldstein is considered by many to be the principal architect of POP. His book, *Policing a Free Society* (1977),[1] is among the most frequently cited works in police literature. A later work, *Problem Oriented Policing* (1990),[2] provided a rich and complete exploration of POP. Goldstein first coined the term "problem oriented policing" in 1979 out of frustration with the dominant model for improving police operations: "More attention [was] being focused on how quickly officers responded to a call than on what they did when they got to their destination."[3] He also bemoaned the linkage between the police and the telephone: "The telephone, more than any public or internal policy, dictates what a police agency does. And that problem has been greatly aggravated with the installation of 911."[4]

As a result, Goldstein argued for a radical change in the direction of efforts to improve policing—a new framework that should help move the police from their past preoccupation with form and process to a much more direct, thoughtful concern with substantive problems. To focus attention on the nature of police business and to improve the quality of police response in the course of their business, Goldstein argued that several steps must be taken:[5]

1. Police must be equipped to define more clearly and to understand more fully the problems they are expected to handle. They must recognize the relationships between and among

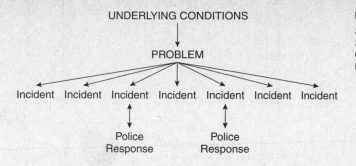

UNDERLYING CONDITIONS

PROBLEM

Incident Incident Incident Incident Incident Incident Incident

Police
Response

Police
Response

FIGURE 3-1 **Incident-Driven Policing**
Source: John E. Eck and William Spelman, *Problem-Solving: Problem-Oriented Policing in Newport News* (Washington, D.C.: U.S. Department of Justice, National Institute of Justice, 1987), p. 4.

incidents—for example, incidents involving the same behavior, the same address, or the same people.

2. The police must develop a commitment to analyzing problems. It requires gathering information from police files, from the minds of experienced officers, from other agencies of government, and from private sources as well. It requires conducting house-to-house surveys and talking with victims, complainants, and offenders.

3. Police must be encouraged to conduct an uninhibited search for the most effective response to each problem, looking beyond just the criminal justice system to a wide range of alternatives; they must try to design a customized response that holds the greatest potential for dealing effectively with a specific problem in a specific place under specific conditions.

Basic Principles

In earlier chapters, we mentioned several limitations of traditional policing methods in trying to deal with incidents. The first step in POP, therefore, is to move beyond just handling each incident separately (see **incident-driven policing**, Figure 3-1) and recognizing that incidents are often merely overt symptoms of problems and require that officers take a more in-depth interest in incidents by acquainting themselves with some of the conditions and factors that cause them. Everyone in the department contributes to this mission, not just a few innovative officers or a special unit or function.[6]

Figure 3-1 shows incident-driven policing as it attempts to deal with each incident. Like band-aid application, this symptomatic relief is valuable but limited. Because police leave unresolved the underlying condition that created the incidents, the incident is very likely to re-occur.

A problem-oriented police agency would respond as described in Figure 3-2. Officers use the information in their responses to incidents, along with information obtained from other sources, to get a clearer picture of the problem. Then they address the underlying conditions. As James Fyfe asked, "Can anyone imagine the surgeon general urging doctors to attack [a disease] without giving any thought to its causes?"[7] If successful, fewer incidents may occur; those that do occur may be less serious. The incidents may even cease.[8]

The problem-oriented approach also addresses a major dilemma for the police: the lack of meaningful measures of their effectiveness in the area of crime and disorder. Crime rate statistics are virtually useless because they collapse all the different kinds of crime into one global category and are an imperfect measure of the actual incidence of criminal behavior (evaluating COPPS initiatives is discussed in Chapter 8).[9] Goldstein also maintained that the police should "disaggregate" the different problems they face and then attempt to develop strategies to address

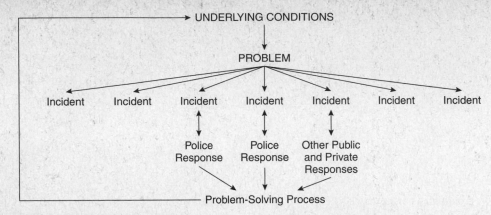

FIGURE 3-2 **Problem Oriented Policing**
Source: John E. Eck and William Spelman, *Problem-Solving: Problem-Oriented Policing in Newport News* (Washington, D.C.: U.S. Department of Justice, National Institute of Justice, 1987), p. 4.

each one.[10] Domestic disturbances, for instance, should be separated from public intoxication; murder should be separated from sexual assault. In this respect, POP is primarily a *planning process.*

Broader Role for the Street Officer

A major departure of POP from the conventional style lies with its view of the line officer, who is given much more discretion and decision-making ability and is trusted with a much broader array of responsibilities. POP values thinking officers, urging that they take the initiative in trying to deal more effectively with problems in the areas they serve. This concept more effectively uses the potential of college-educated officers who have been smothered in the atmosphere of traditional policing.[11] It also gives officers a new sense of identity and self-respect; they are more challenged and have opportunities to follow through on individual cases, to analyze and solve problems, which will give them greater job satisfaction. We ought to be recruiting as police officers people who can "serve as mediators, as dispensers of information, and as community organizers."[12]

Under POP, officers continue to handle calls, but they also do much more. They use the information gathered in their responses to incidents together with information obtained from other sources to get a clearer picture of the problem. They then address the underlying conditions.

S.A.R.A.: THE PROBLEM-SOLVING PROCESS

A four-stage problem-solving process has been developed and is known as "S.A.R.A.," for *scanning, analysis, response,* and *assessment.*[13] This process is depicted in Figure 3-3.

Scanning: Problem Identification

Scanning means problem identification. As a first step, officers should identify problems on their beats and then look for a pattern or persistent repeat incidents. At this juncture, the question might well be asked, "What is a 'problem'?" A problem has been defined this way: A group of two or more incidents that are similar in one or more respects, causing harm and therefore being of concern to the police and the public.

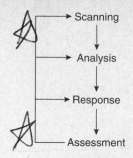

Scanning

Analysis

Response

Assessment

FIGURE 3-3 A Problem-Solving Process

Source: John E. Eck and William Spelman, *Problem-Solving: Problem-Oriented Policing in Newport News* (Washington, D.C.: U.S. Department of Justice, National Institute of Justice, 1987), p. 43.

Incidents may be similar in various ways:

- *Behaviors.* A pattern of behavior is the most frequent type of indicator and includes such activities as drug sales, robberies, thefts, and graffiti.
- *Locations.* Problems occur in hot spots, such as downtown cruising areas, housing complexes plagued by burglaries, and parks where gangs commit crimes.
- *Persons.* They can be repeat offenders or victims; both account for a high proportion of crime.
- *Times.* There may be a time pattern (e.g., seasonal, day of week, hour of day) due to traffic congestion, closing times for bars, or tourist activity.
- *Events.* Crimes may peak during such events as university spring breaks, rallies, and rock concerts.

There does not appear to be any limit to the types of problems patrol officers can work on; there are several types of problems that are appropriate for problem solving. The following list demonstrates the diversity of problems identified and addressed in several jurisdictions:[14]

- Series of burglaries from trailers at a construction site
- Drug activity, drinking, and disorderly conduct at a community park
- Prescription drug thefts from pharmacies
- Thefts from autos at a shopping mall
- Juvenile loitering at a shopping center and near a bar
- Vagrants panhandling downtown
- Problems with false and faulty alarms at commercial addresses
- Parking and traffic problems
- Street prostitution and related robberies in a downtown neighborhood
- Identity Theft
- Repeat domestic assault calls to certain addresses

If the incidents police are responding to do not fall within the definition of a problem, then the problem-solving model is not applicable. The police should handle the incident according to normal procedures.

There are numerous resources available to the police to identify problems, including calls for service (CFS) data, especially repeat calls from the same location or a series of similar incidents. Other ways are through citizen complaints, census data, data from other government agencies, and media coverage of community issues, officer observations, and community surveys (discussed in Chapter 8).

The primary purpose of scanning is to conduct a preliminary inquiry to determine whether a problem really exists and whether further analysis is needed. During this stage, priorities should be established if multiple problems exist and a specific officer or team of officers be assigned to handle the problem. Scanning initiates the problem-solving process.

Analysis: Heart of Problem Solving

The second stage(**analysis,** is the heart of the problem-solving process, so we will dwell on it at greater length. Comprehensively analyzing a problem is critical to the success of a problem-solving effort.)Effective tailor-made responses cannot be developed unless people know what is causing the problem. Thus, the purpose of analysis is to learn as much as possible about problems in order to identify their causes; officers must gather information from sources inside and outside their agency about the scope, nature, and causes of problems.

RESEARCHING A PROBLEM.   One will greatly reduce the time spent searching for information about a problem if the problem is tightly defined. The best way to begin is by examining related sources and Web sites, such as the following:

- The U.S. Department of Justice, Office of Community Oriented Policing Services, has published a Problem-Oriented Policing Guide entitled *Researching a Problem* (2005); it is available at: http://www.cops.usdoj.gov/files/RIC/Publications/e02052729.pdf
- Center for Problem-Oriented Policing (www.popcenter.org). The center is the first place to look for information concerning how to address problems of crime and disorder; it has myriad resources to draw from, including more than 80 of the problem-oriented guides mentioned above, covering all types of problems of crime and disorder and possible solutions to them (see http://www.popcenter.org/guides). Launched in 2003, the POP Center Web site has provided innovative learning experiences, curriculum guides, teaching aids, problem analysis tools, and countless examples of POP projects in the United States and abroad in multiple languages.
- National Criminal Justice Reference Service (NCJRS) (http://abstractsdb .ncjrs.org). This is an information clearinghouse created by the U.S. Department of Justice for people involved in research, policy, and practice; the Web site includes an online tutorial on how to search its abstracts.
- Office of Community Oriented Policing Services (COPS Office) (www.cops .usdoj.gov). This office funds the aforementioned Center for Problem-Oriented Policing; its Web site allows you to download or order COPS publications, and it has links to regional community policing institutes (RCPIs).
- Police Executive Research Forum (PERF) (www.policeforum.org). PERF is a national membership organization of police executives from large law enforcement agencies. Its Web site may be entered by a guest or a member. It contains POPNet, a searchable database of COPPS projects.

Other sources to be sought out for information on problem solving would include the Police Foundation (www.policefoundation.org), the International Association of Chiefs of Police (IACP) (www.theiacp.org), the RAND Public Safety and Justice Center (www.rand.org/psi), and the *FBI Law Enforcement Bulletin* (www.fbi.gov/publications/leb/htm).

PRINCIPLES OF ANALYSIS.   A complete analysis includes identifying the seriousness of the problem, all the persons/groups involved and affected, and all the causes of the problem and then assessing current responses and their effectiveness. One might be tempted to circumvent or give only passing attention to the analysis phase of S.A.R.A., believing that the nature of the problem

An abandoned residence vandalized with gang graffiti shows how quickly a neighborhood may decline.
Courtesy Sgt. Dominic Licavoli, LAPD.

is obvious, succumbing to pressure to quickly solve the problem, or feeling that the pressure of CFS precludes their having time for detailed inquiries into the nature of the problem. Problem solvers must resist these temptations, or they risk addressing a problem that does not exist and/or implementing solutions that are ineffective in the long run.

There are several considerations to remember when planning and conducting problem analysis:

- *Analysis is based on common sense:* Although good analysis will include some statistical analysis and research methodology that are not typical law enforcement activities, the process also relies on the officer's experience and ability to determine what is known about the offender, offenses, locations, and victims.
- *There is no one way to do analysis:* Done appropriately, analysis will generate valuable knowledge about the problem and suggest potential responses. There are often many ways to produce such information, using multiple analytical approaches.
- *Individual problems require individual analysis:* Because an analysis plan was successful in one location does not guarantee it will succeed elsewhere. Much can be learned from the experiences of other jurisdictions, so it is wise to consult agencies that have encountered similar problems.
- *Analysis requires creativity and innovation:* Many problem solvers limit their analysis to reported incidents. Other sources should be considered, however. Incident reports typically include only information about the offense, not about the general conditions surrounding the incident. Additional sources of information that can clarify the problem include changes in usage of target areas, property values, business profits, medical data, and building occupancy rates.
- *Analysis does not need to be complex:* In most cases, simple frequencies of events, percentages of various categories, and tables showing how characteristics relate to each other (e.g., type of burglary by time of day) are sufficient for adequate analysis[15]

ANALYSIS TOOLS FOR PROBLEM SOLVING.   Many tools or data sources can facilitate analysis and the problem-solving process. Conducting an overall review of source availability and accuracy early in the analysis process helps clearly define a problem, generates useful analysis questions, determines the order of analysis activities, and facilitates discussion for the analysis team.

Table 3-1 lists the most frequently used data sources as determined by a national survey by the Office of Community Oriented Policing Services.

SEEKING "SMALL WINS." Karl Weick explained that people often look at social problems on a massive scale. [16] The public, media, elected officials, and government agencies often become fixated on problems and define them by using the simplest term (gangs, homelessness, poverty, mental illness, violent crime, and so on). Viewing problems in this manner leads to defining problems on a scale so massive that they are unable to be addressed and people become overwhelmed in their attempts. For this reason, Weick introduced the **"small wins"** concept. One must understand that some problems are too deeply ingrained or too rooted in other complex social problems to be eliminated. Conversely, however, adopting the small wins philosophy helps people understand the nature of an analysis and a response to problems.

TABLE 3-1 Data Sources Used by Police for Analysis (in Order of Greatest Frequency)	
Incident reports	88.9
Calls-for-service records	85.5
Officer perceptions, observations, surveys, interviews	77.9
Arrest reports	77.5
Partner or stakeholder information	69.8
Community surveys	62.6
Victim interviews	54.2
Offender interviews	47.3
Field interviews	46.9
Targeted resident surveys	38.9
Mapping and GIS data	38.2
Court and municipal agencies	24.4
Relevant literature	24.0
Social service agencies	20.6
Environmental surveys	19.8
Other law enforcement agencies	17.2
Other government agencies	13.7
Media	13.0
Other criminal justice agencies	11.8
Other sources	11.1
Local real estate and tax records	8.8
Insurance records	4.2
Medical records	1.9
Transit agencies	0.8

Source: Adapted from Timothy S. Bynum, *Using Analysis for Problem-Solving: A Guide for Law Enforcement,* p. 20 (Washington, D.C.: U.S. Department of Justice, Office of Community Oriented Policing Services, http://www.cops. usdoj.gov/pdf/e08011230.pdf (accessed October 6, 2010).

As indicated above, the more appropriate response to these problems is to break them down into smaller, more controllable problems. Although an individual small win may not seem important, a series of small wins may have a substantial impact on the overall problem. Eliminating the harms (graffiti, drug sales, and so on) is a sensible and realistic strategy for reducing the impact of gang behaviors. Therefore, it makes sense to address a large problem at a level where there can be a reasonable expectation of success.

The idea of small wins is also helpful when prioritizing problems and working together in a group. We have discussed the benefits of collaborating with the community and other outside agencies to address problems. Small wins can help the group understand the problem better, select realistic objectives, and formulate more effective strategies. It also helps to build confidence and trust among group members.

USING THE PROBLEM ANALYSIS TRIANGLE.   Generally, three elements are needed for a problem to occur: an offender, a victim, and a location. The **problem analysis triangle** helps officers visualize the problem and understand the relationship between these three elements. In addition, it helps officers analyze problems, suggests where more information is needed, and assists with crime control and prevention.

The relationship between these three elements can be explained as follows. If there is a victim and he or she is in a place where crimes occur but there is no offender, no crime occurs. If there is an offender and he or she is in a place where crimes occur but there is nothing or no one to be victimized, then no crime will occur. If an offender and a victim are not in the same place, there will be no crime. Part of the analysis phase involves finding out as much as possible about the victims, offenders, and locations where problems exist in order to understand what is prompting the problem and what can be done about it.

The three elements must be present before a crime or harmful behaviors—problems—can occur: an *offender* (someone who is motivated to commit harmful behavior), a *victim* (a desirable and vulnerable target must be present), and a *place* (the victim and offender must both be in the same place at the same time) (see Figure 3-4). (We discuss locations more below.) If these three elements show up over and over again in patterns and recurring problems, removing one of these elements can stop the pattern and prevent future harms.[17]

As an example, let us apply the problem analysis triangle to the issue of graffiti, using Figure 3-5. The place is marked buildings and areas immediately around them. The victims are the owners and users of the buildings; the offenders are the writers of the graffiti (see the inside triangle of Figure 3-5; the outside triangle is discussed below). Removing one or more of these elements will remove the problem. Strategies for removing one of these elements are limited only by an officer's creativity, availability of resources, and ability to formulate collaborative responses.

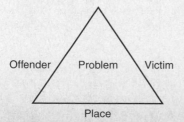

FIGURE 3-4   **Problem Analysis Triangle**

Source: U.S. Department of Justice, Bureau of Justice Assistance, *Comprehensive Gang Initiative: Operations Manual for Implementing Local Gang Prevention and Control Programs* (Draft, October 1993), p. 3.

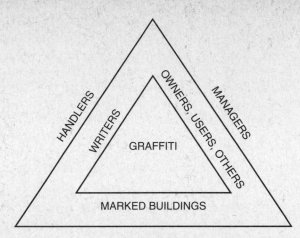

FIGURE 3-5 Graffiti Problem Triangle: The Role of Third Parties
Source: Adapted from John E. Eck, "Police Problems and Research: A Short, Furious, Concise Tour of a Complex Field." Unpublished draft 1.2, January 20, 2002, p. 4; and U.S. Department of Justice, Bureau of Justice Assistance, *Comprehensive Gang Initiative: Operations Manual for Implementing Local Gang Prevention and Control Programs* (Draft, October 2003), pp. 3–11. Used with permission.

Some jurisdictions, for example, are using nonadhesive paint on buildings and property (protecting locations) to discourage taggers ("offenders"). Other jurisdictions have contemplated outlawing the sale of spray paint or limiting the sale of broad-tip markers to juveniles, while still others have enacted graffiti ordinances to help business owners ("victims") to keep their locations graffiti-free.

Police engaged in problem solving need to also be aware of three types of third parties that can either help or hinder the problem-solving effort by attempting to act on behalf of one or more of the three elements discussed above in the problem analysis triangle, at Figure 3-4. We will again use examples and Figure 3-5 to explain the role of third parties:

1. *Handlers.* There are people who, acting in the best interests of the potential offenders, try to prevent them from committing crimes. **Handlers** of gang members might be parents, adult neighbors, peers, teachers, and employers. However, these youths may live in a poor one-parent home or not be attending school or working. Controllers can often restrict the tools used by gang members, such as putting spray cans in locked bins, restricting the wearing of colors, and passing laws obstructing the sale of semiautomatic and automatic weapons.[18]

2. *Guardians.* There are people or things that can exercise control over each side of the triangle so that crime is less likely and are called **guardians**. For instance, if the crime problem is drug dealing in a house and the offender side of the triangle includes dealers and buyers, then a list of guardians would include police, parents of dealers/buyers, probation and parole officers, landlords, city codes, health and tax departments, and neighbors. Tools used by guardians can include crime prevention techniques (discussed more later).[19]

3. *Managers.* People who oversee locations are called **managers.** For example, apartment managers can help prevent or solve problems by installing security equipment in their buildings, screening tenants carefully, and evicting troublemakers or criminals. Conversely, where managers are absent or lax, risks will be higher.[20]

Police should constantly look for ways to improve the effectiveness of third parties, as these groups of individuals have the authority to deal with the problem. There will always be the temptation on the part of society to use the police as handlers, guardians, or managers. Although this may be effective for a short time, there are rarely enough officers to control a recurring problem in the long run.

We conclude our discussion of the critical analysis stage of the S.A.R.A. process by noting that in Chapter 5 we examine additional tools—such as mapping, GPS, CompStat, and computer-aided dispatch systems—that can also be brought to bear on the analysis of crime problems.

Response: Formulation of Tailor-Made Strategies

After a problem has been clearly defined and analyzed, the officer confronts the ultimate challenge in problem-oriented policing: the search for the most effective way of dealing with it. This stage of the S.A.R.A. process focuses on developing and implementing a **response** to the problem. Before entering this stage, an agency must overcome the temptation to implement a response prematurely and need to be certain that it has thoroughly analyzed the problem; attempts to fix problems quickly are rarely effective in the long term.

To develop tailored responses, problem solvers should review their findings about the three sides of the crime triangle—victim, offender, and location—and develop creative solutions that will address at least two sides of the triangle.[21] It is also important to remember that the key to developing tailored responses is making sure that the responses are very focused and *directly linked* to the findings from the analysis phase of the project.

Responses may be wide-ranging and often require arrests (but apprehension may not be the most effective solution), referral to social service agencies, or changes in ordinances. Potential solutions to problems can be organized into five groups:[22]

1. ***Totally eliminating the problem.*** Effectiveness is measured by the absence of the types of incidents that this problem creates. It is unlikely that most problems can be totally eliminated, but a few can.
2. ***Reducing the number of incidents the problem creates.*** A reduction of incidents stemming from a problem is a major measure of effectiveness.

Seeking information from a variety of resources (e.g., business owners) will assist officers in understanding the underlying conditions and factors related to problems.
Courtesy Community Policing Consortium.

3. *Reducing the seriousness of the harms.* Effectiveness for this type of solution is demonstrated by showing that the incidents are less harmful.
4. *Dealing with a problem better.* Treating participants more humanely, reducing costs, and increasing the effectiveness of handling incidents are all possible choices. Improved victim satisfaction, reduced costs, and other measures can show that this type of solution is effective.
5. *Removing the problem from police consideration.* The effectiveness of this type of solution can be measured by looking at why the police were handling the problem originally and the rationale for shifting the handling to others.

Box 3-1 provides an explanation of the possible range of responses to problems. Furthermore, because problem-solving officers must often seek the assistance of the community, other city departments, businesses, private and social service organizations. Box 3-2 is a guide to collaboration—developing networks with people and other agencies in developing appropriate responses.

Assessment: Evaluation of Overall Effectiveness

Finally, in the **assessment,** officers evaluate the effectiveness of their responses. A number of measures have traditionally been used by police agencies and community members to assess effectiveness. These include numbers of arrests, levels of reported crime, response times, clearance rates, citizen complaints, and various workload indicators, such as CFS and the number of field interviews conducted.[23]

Several of these measures may be helpful in assessing the impact of a problem-solving effort; however, a number of nontraditional measures will shed light on whether a problem has been reduced or eliminated:[24]

- Reduced instances of repeat victimization
- Decreases in related crimes or incidents
- Neighborhood indicators (including increased profits for businesses in the target area, increased usage of the area, increased property values, less loitering and truancy, and fewer abandoned cars)
- Increased citizen satisfaction regarding the handling of the problem, determined through surveys, interviews, focus groups, electronic bulletin boards, and so on
- Reduced citizen fear related to the problem

Assessment is obviously the key in the S.A.R.A. process; knowing that we must assess the effectiveness of our efforts emphasizes the importance of documentation and baseline measurement. Supervisors can help officers assess the effectiveness of their efforts.

If the responses implemented are not effective, the information gathered during analysis should be reviewed. New information may need to be collected before new solutions can be developed and tested.[25]

It is also important to distinguish between evaluation and assessment. Evaluation is an overarching scientific process for determining whether a problem declines and whether the solution caused the decline; it begins at the moment the problem-solving process begins and continues throughout the effort. Although assessment is the final stage of both evaluation and problem solving, critical decisions about the evaluation are made throughout the process.

Figure 3-6 shows the relationship between the problem-solving process and critical evaluation questions that should be asked at each stage. The left side of the figure shows the S.A.R.A. process, while the right side lists critical questions to address to conduct an evaluation. We discuss assessment (evaluation) in greater depth in Chapter 4.

BOX 3-1

Range of Possible Response Options

1. *Concentrate attention on the individuals accounting for a disproportionate share of the problem.* A relatively small number of individuals usually account for a disproportionate share of practically any problem, by causing it (offenders), facilitating it (controllers, managers, guardians), or suffering from it (victims).

2. *Connect with other government and private services.* A thorough analysis of a problem often leads to an appreciation of the need for (a) more effective referrals to existing governmental and private services, (b) improved coordination with agencies that exert control over some of the problems or individuals involved in the incidents, and (c) initiative for pressing for correction of inadequacies in municipal services and for development of new services.

3. *Use mediation and negotiation skills.* Often the use of mediation and negotiation teams can be effective responses to conflicts.

4. *Convey information.* Relating sound and accurate information is one of the least used responses. It has the potential, however, to be one of the most effective for responding to a wide range of problems. Conveying information can help (a) reduce anxiety and fear, (b) enable citizens to solve their own problems, (c) elicit conformity with laws and regulations that are not known or understood, (d) warn potential victims about their vulnerability and advise them of ways to protect themselves, (e) demonstrate to people how they unwittingly contribute to problems, (f) develop support for addressing a problem, and (g) acquaint the community with the limitations on government agencies and define realistically what can be expected of those agencies.

5. *Mobilize the community.* Mobilizing a specific segment of the community helps implement a specific response to a specific problem for as long as it takes to deal with the problem.

6. *Make use of existing forms of social control.* Solve problems by mobilizing specific forms of social control inherent in existing relationships—for example, the influence of a parent, teacher, employer, or church.

7. *Alter the physical environment to reduce opportunities for problems to recur.* Adapt the principles of crime prevention through environmental design and situational crime prevention to the complete range of problems.

8. *Increase regulation, through statutes or ordinances, of conditions that contribute to problems.* An analysis of a specific problem may draw attention to factors contributing to the problem that can be controlled by regulation through statutes or ordinances.

9. *Develop new forms of limited authority to intervene and detain.* Examination of specific problems can lead to the conclusion that a satisfactory solution requires some limited authority (e.g., to order a person to leave) but does not require labeling the conduct criminal so that it can be dealt with through a citation or a physical arrest followed by a criminal prosecution.

10. *Make more discriminate use of the criminal justice system.* Use of the criminal justice system should be much more discreet than in the past, reserved for those problems for which the system seems especially appropriate, and used with much greater precision. This could include (a) straightforward investigation, arrest, and prosecution; (b) selective enforcement with articulated criteria; (c) enforcement of criminal laws that, by tradition, are enforced by another agency; (d) more specific definitions of behavior that should be subject to criminal justice prosecution or control through local ordinances; (e) intervention without making the arrest; (f) use of arrest without the intention to prosecute; and (g) new conditions attached to probation or parole.

11. *Use civil law to control public nuisances, offensive behavior, and conditions contributing to crime.* Because most of what the police do in the use of the law involves arrest and prosecution, people tend to forget that the police and local government can initiate a number of other legal proceedings, including those related to (a) licensing, (b) zoning, (c) property confiscation, (d) nuisance abatement, and (e) injunctive relief.

Source: Adapted from Herman Goldstein, *Problem-Oriented Policing* (New York: McGraw-Hill, 1990), pp. 140–141. Used with permission of McGraw-Hill.

BOX 3-2
Problem Solving: Guide to Collaboration

General Background

1. Develop personal networks with members of other agencies who can give you information and help you with problems on which you may be working.
2. Become familiar with the workings of your local government, private businesses, citizen organizations, and other groups and institutions that you may need to call on for help in the future.
3. Develop skills as a negotiator.

Getting Other Agencies to Help

1. Identify agencies that have a role (or could have a role) in addressing the problem early in the problemsolving process.
2. Determine whether these other agencies perceive that there is a problem.
   a. Which agency members perceive the problem and which do not?
   b. Why is it (or isn't it) a problem for them?
   c. How are police perceptions of the problem similar to and different from the perceptions of members of other agencies?
3. Determine whether there is a legal or political mandate for collaboration.
   a. To which agencies does this legal mandate apply?
   b. What are the requirements needed to demonstrate collaboration?
   c. Who is checking to determine whether collaboration is taking place?
4. Look for difficulties that these other agencies face that can be addressed through collaboration on this problem.
   a. Are there internal difficulties that provide an incentive to collaborate?
   b. Are there external crises affecting agencies that collaboration may help address?
5. Determine how much these other agencies use police services.
6. Assess the resource capabilities of these agencies to help.
   a. Do they have the money?
   b. Do they have the staff expertise?
   c. Do they have the enthusiasm?
7. Assess the legal authority of these other agencies.
   a. Do they have special enforcement powers?
   b. Do they control critical resources?
8. Determine the administrative capacity of these agencies to collaborate.
   a. Do they have the legal authority to intervene in the problem?
   b. What are the internal procedures and policies of the stakeholders that help or hinder collaboration?

Working with Other Agencies

1. Include representatives from all affected agencies, if possible, in the problem-solving process.
2. Look for responses to the problem that maximize the gains to all agencies and distribute costs equitably.
3. Reinforce awareness of the interdependence of all agencies.
4. Be prepared to mediate among agencies that have a history of conflict.
5. Develop problem information sharing mechanisms, and promote discussion about the meaning and interpretation of this information.
6. Share problem-solving decisions among stakeholders, and do not surprise others with already-made decisions.
7. Develop a clear explanation as to why collaboration is needed.
8. Foster external support for collaborative efforts, but do not rely on mandates to further collaboration.
9. Be prepared to negotiate with all involved agencies as to their roles, responsibilities, and resource commitments.
10. When collaborating with agencies located far away, plan to spend time developing a working relationship.
11. Try to create support in the larger community for collaborative problem solving.

When Collaboration Does Not Work

1. Always be prepared for collaboration to fail.
2. Have alternative plans.
3. Assess the costs and benefits of unilateral action.
4. Be very patient.

Source: Adapted from John E. Eck, "Implementing a Problem-Oriented Approach: A Management Guide," mimeo, draft copy (Washington, D.C.: Police Executive Research Forum, 1990), pp. 69–70.

Working partnerships with residents to create safer and more secure neighborhoods are vital in community policing.
Courtesy Keith Richards, City of Charlotte, North Carolina.

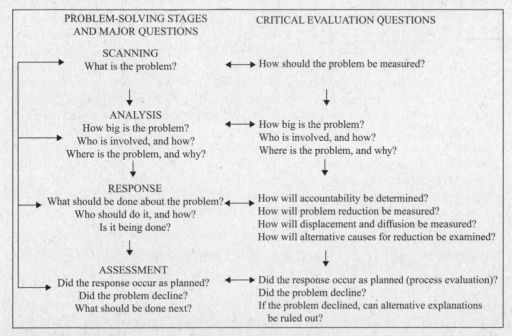

PROBLEM-SOLVING STAGES
AND MAJOR QUESTIONS

CRITICAL EVALUATION QUESTIONS

SCANNING
What is the problem?

How should the problem be measured?

ANALYSIS
How big is the problem?
Who is involved, and how?
Where is the problem, and why?

How big is the problem?
Who is involved, and how?
Where is the problem, and why?

RESPONSE
What should be done about the problem?
Who should do it, and how?
Is it being done?

How will accountability be determined?
How will problem reduction be measured?
How will displacement and diffusion be measured?
How will alternative causes for reduction be examined?

ASSESSMENT
Did the response occur as planned?
Did the problem decline?
What should be done next?

Did the response occur as planned (process evaluation)?
Did the problem decline?
If the problem declined, can alternative explanations
be ruled out?

FIGURE 3-6   The Problem-Solving Process and Evaluation

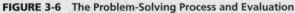

Source: John Eck, *Assessing Responses to Problems: An Introductory Guide for Police Problem Solvers* (Washington, D.C.: U.S. Department of Justice, Office of Community Oriented Policing Services, 2004), p. 6.

DIFFICULTIES WITH PROBLEM SOLVING

Notable community policing and problem-solving researcher and author John Eck has bluntly offered a number of caveats with respect to problem solving. Given his pioneering involvement with and stellar reputation in the field, his musings are certainly worthy of mention.

First, Eck argues that POP suffers from appearing to be simple—beginning with the term "problem solving" itself. It is one of those ubiquitous terms that are used in countless business, mathematics, computer, psychology, and many other books. Another problem is that the term suggests that for every difficulty there is a solution that is easy, cheap, permanent, and 100 percent effective.[26]

Eck also bluntly maintains that several explanations have been offered for why problem-solving efforts are not always successful. Most of these explanations (but not all, he argues) are inadequate.[27]

- *Police officers do not have the analytical skills required to analyze problems.* Eck believes that while more problem-solving training certainly could be given to officers, it should not be assumed that we even know *how* to train police in problem solving, especially in its nuances. (See, however, Chapter 9 on training for COPPS, which includes discussion of the new Police Training Officer [PTO] program.)
- *Police managers and supervisors do not know how to foster problem solving.* Eck believes this is probably true. Can supervisors discriminate between quality problem solving and superficial problem solving? The answer is "no."
- *Police agencies resist change.* Eck argues that despite a large body of literature on policing and COPPS, there is little practical advice that research can provide police executives. Resistance to change is to be expected if research cannot provide practical guidance on how to behave with a new approach.
- *Police workloads prevent anything but superficial analysis.* One thing is clear: Problem solving—which requires days, weeks, even months—has a different time frame than responding to calls, which is measured in minutes and hours. Eck is of the opinion that difficulty with time is not how much is available but how much time the police are willing to devote.
- *There is too little involvement of communities.* There is also merit to this argument. Neighborhoods usually cover much larger areas than most problems, even the most engaged communities are aware of problems, and citizens are often in the dark about how to systematically analyze and fix problems, Eck states.
- *Little is known about what works under what circumstances.* Eck believes this statement is also true. He says that the police and community can therefore experiment with solutions or systematically record and organize their problem-solving experiences; then, they can share them with each other. Neither approach is adequate, however. Experimentation is a slow process, while few problem-solving efforts result in a formal evaluation.

COMMUNITY ORIENTED POLICING AND PROBLEM SOLVING

Basic Principles

As we mentioned in Chapter 2, our view is that the two concepts of community policing and problem-oriented policing are separate but complementary strategies that work together hand-in-glove. And as we emphasized in Chapter 2, the police are severely hampered when attempting to solve neighborhood and community problems without the full cooperation—a partnership and collaboration—with the community and other resources.

The two concepts of community-oriented policing and problem-oriented policing share some important characteristics: (1) decentralization (to encourage officer initiative and the effective use of local knowledge), (2) geographically defined rather than functionally defined subordinate units (to encourage the development of local knowledge), and (3) close interactions with local communities (to facilitate responsiveness to and cooperation with the community).[28]

Herman Goldstein did not see POP as an alternative to community policing or in competition with it. However, he asserted that much of what is occurring in community policing projects begs for application of all that has been described under the label of problem-oriented policing.

Definition

What exactly is COPPS? How does it function? How would we know it if we saw it? Following is our definition—which we believe accurately captures the essence of this concept:

> Community oriented policing and problem solving (COPPS) is a proactive philosophy that promotes solving problems that are criminal, affect our quality of life, or increase our fear of crime, as well as other community issues. COPPS involves identifying, analyzing, and addressing community problems at their source.

One of the strongest advocates of this kind of approach to policing is the California Department of Justice, which has published several monographs on the subject and has taken the following position:

> Community Oriented Policing and Problem Solving is a concept whose time has come. This movement holds tremendous promise for creating effective police-community partnerships to reclaim our communities and keep our streets safe. COPPS is not "soft" on crime; in fact, it is tougher on crime because it is smarter and more creative. Community input focuses police activities; and, with better information, officers are able to respond more effectively with arrests or other appropriate actions. COPPS can unite our communities and promote pride in our police forces.[29]

In order for COPPS to succeed, however, we believe the following measures are minimally required:

- Conducting accurate community needs assessments
- Mobilizing all appropriate individuals for collecting data and brainstorming strategies
- Determining appropriate resource allocations and creating new resources where necessary
- Developing and implementing innovative, collaborative, comprehensive programs to address underlying causes of neighborhood crime and disorder
- Evaluating programs and modifying approaches as needed

CHOICE OF APPROACH: TAILORING STRATEGIES TO NEIGHBORHOODS

Which Strategy Where?

Some interesting research has been done on whether or not COPPS can work in different types of neighborhoods; one study suggests that COPPS should have similar benefits in different types of neighborhoods.[30] Furthermore, a theoretical framework has been developed by Nolan et al. to help police decide which type of COPPS strategy to employ in specific neighborhoods.[31] First, it is important to remember—as noted in Chapter 3 discussions of communitarianism, social capital, mobilization, and alliances—that the level of responsibility for neighborhood safety and problem solving is important and relates to a community's level of crime. Some authors have termed this "collective efficacy": the cohesion among residents combined with shared expectations for the social control of public space that predicts both crime and disorder.[32] Some researchers argue that neighborhood-level collective efficacy is the most significant predictor of crime.

In a related vein, research has indicated that a neighborhood can exist in one of three identifiable stages:[33]

1. *Dependence.* Community members depend on the police to solve problems related to public order, and officers are willing to do so. Most residents view officers as competent and respect them, and officers view the neighborhood as unable or unwilling to care for itself.
2. *Conflict.* Here, officers cannot address community problems or provide safety because residents have become dissatisfied with the police and with each other; they see the police as having primary responsibility for order maintenance in the neighborhoods but consider the police to be ineffective. In defending themselves, officers may initiate high-visibility foot or bicycle patrols or other methods in order to appease residents. To move out of this stage, officers must give up the notion that they alone can address crime and disorder in neighborhoods.
3. *Interdependence.* Once the police and the community have come to recognize their mutual responsibilities for restoring order and safety, development of social networks begins to occur. Officers play a less prominent role in order maintenance and develop a more trusting relationship with the community.

Differing Types of Neighborhoods

Obviously, neighborhoods will differ in their ability to move along these stages of development. Some are stronger than others and have more resources to help them evolve. There are four basic types of neighborhoods:[34]

1. *Strong.* Strong communities experience low levels of crime and have residents who interact or organize themselves on issues of community disorder.
2. *Vulnerable.* Vulnerable neighborhoods also have low rates of crime and disorder, but they have minimal levels of development as well. Residents depend on the police to deal with disorder.
3. *Anomic.* Anomic communities have high rates of crime and disorder and low levels of neighborhood development. Residents are dependent on officers to take care of safety problems and are dissatisfied because of the officers' lack of success.
4. *Responsive.* Responsive neighborhoods have high levels of crime and disorder, but residents work with the police to resolve problems.

Effective policing involves not only reducing crime and disorder but also facilitating neighborhood development. The police must strive to move the community along two dimensions: low levels of crime and disorder and high levels of integration and collective efficacy (interdependence). Therefore, matching the policing style to the neighborhood type represents only the first step in the process.

Figure 3-7 shows **situational policing** in motion. The right side of the figure lists policing strategies that will help to move a community toward the responsive and then to the strong quadrants. If crime is high and the citizens are independent (stage one), police should use a

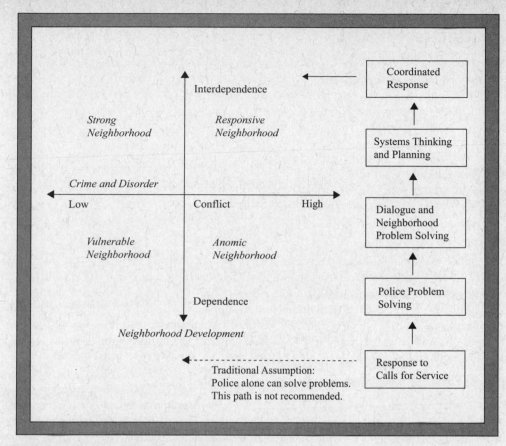

FIGURE 3-7   Situational Policing in Motion
Source: James J. Nolan, Norman Conti, and Jack McDevitt, "Situational Policing," FBI Law Enforcement Bulletin 74 (11) (November 2005), p. 8.

professional service-oriented approach as the logical and preferred first step. The dotted line at the bottom of the figure indicates the direction the police usually want to follow based on the utopian idea that given increased resources or more efficient responses to CFS, they could reduce crime without collective effort. This assumption has proved fictional over the years because the police do not have the resources needed to eliminate crime and disorder through more or better services.

After an initial stage of stepped-up law enforcement, a second wave of activity might include problem solving. At first, the police might do problem solving on their own, without the help of residents. But as officers establish dialogue with residents and as relationships and communication build, police and citizens must reach a shared realization that officers alone cannot fix neighborhood problems and keep residents safe. With this understanding, activities may begin to take place that move the neighborhood toward the responsive quadrant, where residents are ready to organize and plan for addressing crime and disorder.[35]

In sum, situational policing may very well bridge the philosophical gap between traditional policing and COPPS by identifying situations where each style is appropriate. It provides a desired end state at which the police can aim and against which competing strategies can be evaluated.

A WINNING EXAMPLE: THE CHULA VISTA MOTEL AND HOTEL PROGRAM

To illustrate COPPS and S.A.R.A. in action, it would be helpful to see how the Chula Vista, California, Police Department addressed a serious motel and hotel problem. This project won the coveted Herman Goldstein Award for Excellence in Problem-Oriented Policing, conferred at the annual International Problem Oriented Policing Conference. Note the kinds of measures that were taken as the department followed the S.A.R.A. problem-solving model:[36]

Example	Reducing Crime and Disorder at Motels and Hotels in Chula Vista, California

Scanning

In the mid-1990s, business organizations asked for the city's help in improving the quality and safety of Chula Vista's motels. In response, police increased enforcement at motels and implemented a new law requiring all motel guests to show photo ID at check-in. Despite these efforts, police continued to respond to a high number of calls for service at motels, which remained platforms for criminal activity and inhibited efforts to bring tourist dollars to the city. With a mandate for improvement, police staff, along with other city staff and business groups, began working on a problem-oriented policing project to improve public safety levels at motels.

Analysis

The problems at motels were analyzed in a variety of ways, including motel user interviews; motel manager interviews; environmental surveys; analysis of CFS, crime, and arrest data; and a comprehensive review of the literature pertaining to crime and disorder at motels. Project staff tested and rejected a number of hypotheses regarding the cause of the problems at Chula Vista motels. Ultimately, the project team concluded that motel managers and owners could effectively control crime and disorder on their properties through good management practices if they chose to do so.

Response

Working together, police, code enforcement, and chamber of commerce staff spent several years reaching out to motel managers and owners, offering information on the nature and level of problems at motels and ways those problems could be reduced. Code enforcement staff began an annual motel inspection program in 2003, to ensure that the properties met state and local housing codes. However, these efforts did not substantially reduce public safety problems at motels. Recently, police worked with staff from the city attorney's office, planning and building, community development, finance, and fire departments to develop an ordinance that enabled the city to hold motels accountable for meeting a CFS-based public safety performance standard.

Assessment

- CFS to Chula Vista motels declined 49 percent
- Violent crimes and crimes against persons at motels declined 49percent; Part I and Part II crimes at motels went down 70 percent
- Drug arrests at motels decreased 66 percent
- The quality and appearance of several motels improved dramatically

- Motel management practices improved
- The number of motel rooms that did not meet basic safety standards declined from at least 378 to 0
- Aggregate transient occupancy tax reported to the City increased

Summary

This chapter and the discussion of community in Chapter 2 constitute the heart and soul of this book and have set out the basic principles and strategies of the COPPS concepts. This combined approach of COPPS is, we believe, the best philosophy and strategy for the future of policing. We also believe that blending these two concepts results in a better, more comprehensive approach to providing quality police service—combining the emphasis on forming a police-community partnership to fight crime with the use of the S.A.R.A. process to solve problems.

As we noted in the summary of Chapter 2, it is essential for the reader to have a firm, fundamental understanding of these two chapters, as they lay the foundation for what follows in the remaining chapters. Subsequent chapter topics elaborate on COPPS and the problem-solving process and include a large number of examples of COPPS in real-life situations. Furthermore, some chapters, particularly those addressing such topics as crime prevention, information technology, and crime analysis, bear heavily on the S.A.R.A. problem-solving process.

Items for Review

1. Explain what is meant by problem-oriented policing, and how it differs from traditional reactive, incident-driven policing.
2. Briefly describe the four steps of the S.A.R.A. problem-solving process.
3. Review in detail what kinds of activities are involved in the analysis stage of the S.A.R.A. process.
4. Delineate the three elements of the problem analysis and graffiti problem triangles.
5. List the three types of roles of third parties in the problem analysis triangle.
6. List the five potential solutions to problems.
7. Describe five potential difficulties with problem solving.
8. Explain what is meant by COPPS, and provide an example of how it might function in a situation involving neighborhood disorder.
9. Review some of the considerations in tailoring problem-solving strategies to neighborhoods.

Notes

1. Herman Goldstein, *Policing a Free Society* (Cambridge, Mass.: Ballinger, 1977).
2. Herman Goldstein, *Problem-Oriented Policing* (New York: McGraw-Hill, 1990).
3. Herman Goldstein, "Problem-Oriented Policing." Paper presented at the National Institute of Justice Conference on Policing: State of the Art III, Phoenix, Arizona, June 12, 1987.
4. *Ibid.*, p. 4.
5. Ibid., pp. 5–6.
6. John Eck and William Spelman, "A Problem-Oriented Approach to Police Service Delivery," in Dennis Jay Kenney (ed.), *Police and Policing: Contemporary Issues* (New York: Praeger, 1989), pp. 95–111.
7. Quoted in Roland Chilton, "Urban Crime Trends and Criminological Theory," in Chris W. Eskridge (ed.), *Criminal Justice: Concepts and Issues* (Los Angeles: Roxbury, 1993), pp. 47–55.
8. Ibid., p. xvii.
9. Samuel Walker, *The Police in America: An Introduction* (2nd ed.) (New York: McGraw-Hill, 1992), p. 177.
10. Goldstein, *Problem-Oriented Policing*, pp. 38–40.
11. Goldstein, "Toward Community-Oriented Policing: Potential, Basic Requirements, and Threshold

Questions," *Crime and Delinquency* 33 (1987): 6–30.

12. Ibid., p. 21.

13. Ibid., pp. 43–52.

14. Goldstein, *Problem-Oriented Policing,* p. 18.

15. Adapted from Timothy S. Bynum, *Using Analysis for Problem-Solving: A Guide for Law Enforcement* (Washington, D.C.: U.S. Department of Justice, Office of Community Oriented Policing Services, 2002), pp. 13–15.

16. Karl E. Weick, "Small Wins: Redefining the Scale of Social Problems," *American Psychologist,* 39 (1) (1984):40–49.

17. John Eck, *A Dissertation Prospectus for the Study of Characteristics of Drug Dealing Places* (Dissertation, College Park, Md.: University of Maryland–College Park, 1992).

18. Marcus Felson, "Linking Criminal Career Choices, Routine Activities, Informal Control, and Criminal Outcomes," in Derek Cornish and Ronald Clarke (eds.), *The Reasoning Criminal: Rational Choice Perspectives on Offending* (New York: Springer-Verlag, 1986).

19. Lawrence E. Cohen and Marcus Felson, "Social Change and Crime Rate Trends: A Routine Activity Approach," *American Sociological Review* 44 (August 1979):588–608.

20. Eck, *A Dissertation Prospectus for the Study of Characteristics of Drug Dealing Places,* p. 5.

21. Rana Sampson, "Problem Solving," in *Neighborhood-Oriented Policing in Rural Communities: A Program Planning Guide* (Washington, D.C.: U.S. Department of Justice, Office of Justice Programs, Bureau of Justice Assistance, 1994), p. 4.

22. William Spelman and John E. Eck, "Problem-Solving," *Research in Brief* (January 1987):6.

23. Darrel Stephens, "Community Problem-Oriented Policing: Measuring Impacts," in Larry T. Hoover (ed.), *Quantifying Quality in Policing* (Washington, D.C.: Police Executive Research Forum, 1995).

24. U.S. Department of Justice, Office of Community Oriented Policing Services, *Problem Solving Tips,* p. 20.

25. Sampson, "Problem Solving," p. 5.

26. John E. Eck, "Why Don't Problems Get Solved," in Wesley G. Skogan (ed.), *Community Policing: Can It Work?* (Belmont, Calif.: Wadsworth, 2004), pp. 185–206.

27. *Ibid.,* pp. 190–193.

28. Mark H. Moore and Robert C. Trojanowicz, *Corporate Strategies for Policing* (Washington, D.C.: U.S. Department of Justice, National Institute of Justice, 1988), p. 11.

29. California Department of Justice, Attorney General's Office, *Community Oriented Policing and Problem Solving: Definitions and Principles* (Sacramento, Calif.: Author, 1993), p. iii.

30. See W. G. Skogan, S. M. Hartnett, J. DuBois, J. T. Comey, M. Kaiser, and J. H. Lovig, *Problem Solving in Practice: Implementing Community Policing in Chicago* (Washington, D.C.: U.S. Department of Justice, National Institute of Justice, 2000).

31. James J. Nolan, Norman Conti, and Jack McDevitt, "Situational Policing," *FBI Law Enforcement Bulletin* (November 2005):1–9.

32. R. J. Sampson and S. W. Raudenbush, "Systematic Social Observation of Public Spaces: A New Look at Disorder in Urban Neighborhoods," *American Journal of Sociology* 105 (3) (1999):603–651.

33. Ibid, pp. 3–4.

34. Ibid., pp. 4–5.

35. Ibid., pp. 7–9.

36. Center for Problem-Oriented Policing, "Goldstein Awards 2009," http://www.popcenter.org/library/awards/goldstein.cfm?browse=abstracts (accessed July 10, 2010).

4

Crime Prevention
Creating Safe Communities

KEY TERMS AND CONCEPTS

Crime displacement
Crime opportunity
Crime prevention through
 environmental design
 (CPTED)

Crime prevention officers'
 roles
Designing out crime
Evaluation
Publicity campaign

Second-generation CPTED
Situational crime prevention
 (SCP)

LEARNING OBJECTIVES

As a result of reading this chapter, the student will:

- Know how crime prevention evolved
- Understand how crime prevention relates to community oriented policing and problem solving (COPPS)
- Be able to describe crime prevention through environmental design (CPTED) as well as some of the obstacles to adopting it
- Comprehend the meaning and value of situational crime prevention
- Be able to list the principles of crime opportunity
- Be able to delineate the roles of the contemporary crime prevention officer
- Know how to evaluate the outcomes of crime prevention initiatives
- Be aware of the nature and potential for crime displacement
- Know which crime prevention strategies work, do not work, and hold promise

I don't see much improvement in man's heart.
The whole thing is in man's heart: his desire,
his greed, his lust, his pride, his ego.
—BILLY GRAHAM, 2006

The test of police efficiency is the absence of crime and disorder,
not the visible evidence of police action dealing with them.
—Sir Robert Peel's Ninth Principle of Policing, 1829

INTRODUCTION

A multimillion dollar hotel/convention center complex is constructed in the middle of a large Midwestern city. Immediately upon its completion, police begin receiving reports of rapes in the parking garage, robberies in dark hallways, and all manner of other crimes. The parking garage, hallways, lighting, and security system—indeed, much of the facility—had to be retrofitted to prevent such an onslaught of crimes, at a major cost to the owners. The police department commander who headed up the agency's crime prevention bureau later lamented that:

> They [the hotel chain building the complex] came to town and talked with the architects, the health department, the street department, the zoning department, the fire department, and everyone else—but they never came to see me.

Until relatively recently, such was often the angst of one whose career revolved around *preventing* crimes—a time when perhaps only a few, if any, officers were engaged in such activities, and they primarily gave out advice and brochures on "lock it or lose it," and so forth. Thankfully, that simplistic, reductionistic era is now long gone, and today's crime prevention professionals are engaged in much more sophisticated and appreciated work. We also know that it is far cheaper to *prevent* a crime from occurring in the first place, rather than trying to reactively investigate it and then try to arrest, prosecute, and incarcerate the offender.[1]

This chapter begins with a brief history of how crime prevention evolved, and then we discuss how crime prevention works hand-in-glove with community oriented policing and problem solving (COPPS), which is examined in Chapter 3. Two very important components of crime prevention and COPPS are then analyzed: crime prevention through environmental design and situational crime prevention. Following that, we briefly review several issues and problems that can accompany crime prevention efforts: the role of the crime prevention officer, conducting a crime prevention publicity campaign, the displacement of crime, and the evaluation of initiatives. Finally, we view which crime prevention strategies have been shown to work, to not work, and to hold promise. The chapter concludes with a summary, review questions, and several scenarios and activities that provide opportunities for you to "learn by doing."

The underlying theme of this chapter, as demonstrated in Chapter 2, is that the police alone cannot prevent crime and disorder; the community *must* be engaged in a collaborative effort if the physical and social problems that plague the community are to be reduced or eliminated.

A BRIEF HISTORY

Crime prevention may be defined as:

> A pattern of attitudes and behaviors directed both at reducing the threat of crime and enhancing the sense of safety and security to positively influence the quality of life in our society and to help develop environments where crime cannot flourish.[2]

Under COPPS, crime prevention is evolving to more comprehensives situational and environmental intervention strategies. This photo depicts a Neighborhood Watch sign vandalized by local gangs.

Crime prevention is not a new idea. Humans have long known that crime is not simply a matter of motivation; it is also a matter of opportunity. Indeed, for as long as people have been victimized, there have been attempts to protect one's self and family. The term "crime prevention," however, has only recently come to signify a set of ideas for combating crime.[3]

Our earliest ancestors maximized lighting from the sun and moon and employed defensive placement of homes on the side of cliffs, with only one entrance and exit.[4] Cave dwellers established ownership of a space by surrounding it with large boulders; later the Romans developed and enforced complex land laws. Walled cities and castles exist throughout the world. It is a natural human impulse to claim and secure an area to prevent problems.[5]

A more contemporary form of early preventive action was the Chicago Area Project (CAP), based on the research of Shaw and McKay in the 1930s and 1940s, which concerned the altering of the social fabric. Crime and delinquency were concentrated in the central areas of Chicago. Identifying a high level of transiency and an apparent lack of social ties in these areas as the root cause of the problems, Shaw and McKay labeled the problem as "social disorganization," meaning that the constant turnover of residents resulted in the inability of the people to exert any informal social control over the individuals in the area. Consequently, offenders could act with some degree of impunity in these neighborhoods.[6] Shaw's proposed solution to the problem was to work with the residents to build a sense of pride and community, thereby prompting people to stay and exert control over the actions of the people in the area. CAP was founded in 1931 and generated community support by using volunteers and existing neighborhood institutions.[7]

The 1970s saw the rise of community-based crime prevention programs, such as the Neighborhood or Block Watch. These programs used the same premise as physical design approaches: Potential offenders will not commit a crime if they perceive citizen activity, awareness, and concern in an area. The focus is on citizen surveillance and action (such as cutting back bushes, installing lighting, removing obstacles to enhance sight lines, organizing security surveys, and distributing crime and crime prevention news). Signs of resident activity and cohesion should work to protect the neighborhood. The police also recognized that they could not stop crime or solve problems on their own; they needed the help of the citizenry.[8]

Crime prevention experienced perhaps its biggest boost, however, with the emergence of physical design as a topic of debate. Led by the work of Oscar Newman in 1972, flaws in the physical environment were identified as causes of, or at least facilitators for, criminal behavior. In 1969 Newman first coined the term "defensible space," which in his mind did not mean ugly fortress-like buildings where occupants were prisoners. (Table 4–1 depicts Newman's suggestions for defensible space.) Rather, buildings that are properly designed promote a sense of safety and power to their occupants, making them less afraid and vulnerable.[9]

Newman, an architect, argued that the physical characteristics of an area have the potential to suggest to residents and potential offenders that either the area is well cared for and protected or it is open to criminal activity. Design features conducive to criminal behavior—allowing offenders to commit a crime and escape with minimal risk of detection—would include common entrances for a large number of people, poorly placed windows inhibiting casual surveillance of grounds and common areas, hidden entrances, easy access for illegitimate users, and isolated buildings.[10]

Then in the 1970s and 1980s, theories of crime were developed that gave added importance to the role of **crime opportunity**. L. E. Cohen and M. Felson's routine activity theory seeks to explain how physical and social environments create crime opportunities by bringing together in

TABLE 4–1	Oscar Newman's Defensible Space Suggestions

1. Reduce the size of a housing estate or block.
2. Reduce the number of dwellings sharing an entrance way.
3. Reduce the number of stories in a building block.
4. Arrange dwellings in groups to encourage social contact.
5. Minimize the degree of shared public space inside and near blocks.
6. Make the boundaries between public and private space very clear.
7. Make public areas clearly visible to nearby housing.
8. Use external rather than internal corridors in blocks of housing so that they are visible.
9. Make entrances flush with the street rather than set back.
10. Do not have entrances facing away from the street because they are not open to surveillance.
11. Avoid landscaping and vegetation that impede surveillance.
12. Reduce escape routes (elevators, staircases, and multiple exits) for criminals.

Source: U.S. Department of Housing and Urban Development, *Crime Prevention Brief,* "Crime Prevention Through Environmental Design" (no date), p. 2.

one place at a particular time a "likely" offender, a "suitable" target, and the absence of a "capable guardian" against crime (e.g., a police officer or security guard).[11] Routine activity theory was used to explain how large increases in burglary rates occurred in the United States in the 1960s and 1970s because (1) home electronic goods became lighter and (2) women increasingly entered the labor force, resulting in more empty homes during the day that could be entered by burglars.

Another opportunity theory is the rational choice perspective, which holds that all crime is purposive behavior designed to benefit the offender.[12] In committing an offense, the offender makes the choice to balance the effort, risks, and rewards with the costs and benefits of alternative legal means of achieving an end.

James Q. Wilson and George Kelling's 1982 "broken windows" theory extended Oscar Newman's focus on housing projects to entire neighborhoods. "Broken windows" refers to physical signs that an area is unattended: There may be abandoned vehicles and buildings in the area, trash and litter may be present, and there may be broken windows and lights and graffiti.[13] In addition to these physical indicators are social manifestations of the same problems, such as loitering youths, public drunkenness, prostitution, and vagrancy. Both the physical and social indicators are typically referred to as signs of "incivility" that attract offenders to the area.[14]

The glass stairwell in this parking garage demonstrates how natural surveillance can be designed into a facility. People using the stairwell are easily seen by passers-by, thus reducing the likelihood of victimization.

The most recent movements in crime prevention focus efforts and interventions on attacking specific problems, places, and times. Ronald V. Clarke proposed "situational prevention" as "measures directed at highly specific forms of crime that involve environmental changes that reduce the opportunities for crime and increase its risk."[15] Examples of situational prevention include the installation of surveillance equipment in a parking lot experiencing vandalism, erecting security screens in banks to stop robberies, altering traffic patterns in a drug market neighborhood, using electronic tags for library materials, and using caller ID for obscene phone calls.[16] The physical environment as it relates to crime prevention is discussed shortly. Next we discuss the contemporary crime prevention-based philosophy.

CRIME PREVENTION AND COPPS: A SYMBIOTIC RELATIONSHIP

COPPS argues that the police and the community must stop treating the symptoms of the problem. COPPS requires a new age of prevention—as well as improvement of prevention efforts.

Altering physical designs of buildings, for example, is not in itself generally sufficient for altering the level of crime; physical design changes cannot stop a truly motivated offender. Furthermore, altering the physical environment does not guarantee that residents will become involved and take action. Direct efforts to enhance active citizen involvement are necessary.[17]

Crime prevention and COPPS are therefore close companions, attempting to define a problem, identify contributing causes, seek out the proper people or agencies to assist in identifying potential solutions, and work as a group to implement the solution. The problem drives the solution.[18]

Comprehensive crime prevention resource guides for municipal and rural agencies are available through the National Crime Prevention Council at http://www.ncpc.org.
Courtesy National Crime Prevention Council.

At its heart, COPPS is about preventing crime. COPPS and crime prevention are linked in several areas. Crime prevention efforts provide information and skills that are essential to community policing. Furthermore, crime prevention and community policing have six major points in common[19]:

1. *Each deals with the health of the community.* They acknowledge the many interrelated issues that contribute to crime.
2. *Each seeks to address underlying causes and problems.* Although short-term and reactive measures (such as personal security and response to calls for service) are necessary, they are insufficient if crime is to be significantly reduced. Looking beyond symptoms to treat the causes of community problems is a strategy that both, at their best, share in full measure.
3. *Each deals with the combination of physical and social issues that are at the heart of many community problems.* An abandoned building may attract drug addicts; bored teens may become area burglars. Both approaches examine the broadest possible range of causes and solutions.
4. *Each requires active involvement by community residents.* Both have the chief task of enabling people to make themselves and their communities safer by helping them gain appropriate knowledge, develop helpful attitudes, and take useful actions.
5. *Each requires partnerships beyond law enforcement to be effective.* Both efforts can and have involved schools, community centers, civic organizations, religious groups, social service agencies, public works agencies, and other elements of the community.
6. *Each is an approach or a philosophy rather than a program.* Neither is a fixed system for delivery of a specific service; instead, each is a way of doing business and involves the development of an institutional mindset.

Crime prevention provides knowledge about ways to involve the entire community in reducing crime, both individually and collectively; community policing practices can spread that knowledge. Community policing officers need to understand and apply techniques to educate and motivate citizens; crime prevention offers these techniques. Because crime prevention addresses both physical and social aspects of neighborhoods, it offers numerous ways for community policing officers to gain entry into community circles. Crime prevention offers resources to help change community attitudes and behaviors.

CRIME PREVENTION THROUGH ENVIRONMENTAL DESIGN

Designing Out Crime

Crime prevention through environmental design (CPTED) is defined as the "proper design and effective use of the environment that can lead to a reduction in the fear and incidence of crime, and an improvement in the quality of life."[20] At its core are three principles that support problem-solving approaches to crime[21]:

1. *Natural access control.* Natural access control uses elements such as doors, shrubs, fences, and gates to deny admission to a crime target and to create a perception among offenders that there is a risk in selecting the target.
2. *Natural surveillance.* Natural surveillance includes the proper placement of windows, lighting, and landscaping to increase the ability of those who care to observe intruders as well as regular users, allowing them to challenge inappropriate behavior or report it to the police or the property owner.

3. ***Territorial reinforcement.*** Using such elements as sidewalks, landscaping, and porches helps distinguish between public and private areas and helps users exhibit signs of "ownership" that send hands-off messages to would-be offenders.

Ironically, in the past the police were not involved in design planning, whereas fire departments have promulgated and enforced national fire codes for about a half-century. Today, in cities such as Tempe, Arizona, if the police are not involved in the preliminary stages of planning a building, they often become very involved afterward, when crimes are committed in or around the structure.[22]

Cities such as Tempe have become leaders in expanding policing's new role in **designing out crime**. In the late 1900s, Tempe enacted an ordinance requiring that no commercial, park, or residential building permit be issued until the police department had approved it, ensuring that the building fully protected its occupants.

Tempe's CPTED officers advocate that walls around the perimeter of a building be at least eight feet high to make them more difficult to scale. River rocks are banned from parking lots, as they can be used as weapons. Natural surveillance, which can be obtained from proper lighting and window placement, helps people oversee nearby activities. Transparent fences are better than walls to monitor activities. Light switches in rest rooms should be keyed or remotely controlled to prevent tampering, thus perhaps facilitating a possible hiding place for an attacker; rest rooms should not be located at the ends of hallways where they are isolated. Defensive architecture includes "target hardening" through quality deadbolts and other mechanical means and includes proper landscaping (e.g., thorny bushes help to keep burglars away).[23]

Five types of information are needed for CPTED planning[24]:

1. ***Crime analysis information.*** This can include crime mapping, police crime data, incident reports, and victim and offender statistics.

This gated storage facility uses an electronic keyed gate for access control.

2. *Demographics.* This should include resident statistics, such as age, race, gender, income, and income sources.
3. *Land use information.* This includes zoning information (such as residential, commercial, industrial, school, and park zones) as well as occupancy data for each zone.
4. *Observations.* These should include details of parking procedures, maintenance, and residents' reactions to crime.
5. *Resident information.* This includes resident crime surveys and interviews with police and security officers.

Second-Generation CPTED

As emphasized in Chapter 2 and stated by Greg Saville and Gerry Cleveland, "what really counts is a sense of community."[25] In that vein, a **second-generation CPTED** has more recently been developed that, again in the words of Saville and Cleveland, "recognizes that the most valuable aspects of a safe community lie not in structures of the brick and mortar type, but rather in structures of family, of thought, and, most importantly, of behavior."[26]

In addition to the basic elements such as access control and natural surveillance, second-generation CPTED looks at several *social* aspects of how neighborhoods work[27]:

- *Size of the district, population density, and differentiation of buildings.* There is an environmental influence on social interaction. We have relied for too long on large systems for survival. It is difficult to get to know one's neighbors when the neighborhood consists of 100 homes, an apartment building has more than 300 units, and a high school has more than 3,000 students. Size can affect the alienation of a place. We need to live in smaller, locally based neighborhoods, near where we work, go to school, and socialize. We must develop ways to encourage more local contacts for social, economic, and political interaction. (This brings us full circle to the Chicago studies of the 1930s, discussed above.)
- *Urban meeting places.* Providing meeting places is an absolute necessity in neighborhoods, and the lack thereof can make urban spaces empty and dangerous—which is why regional shopping malls fail to become places of community gathering.
- *Youth clubs.* Again, the creation of youth clubs has been a crime prevention and community-building strategy since the aforementioned CAP of the 1930s and can provide activities, meeting places, and life skills training.

Second-generation CPTED also involves the idea of an ecological threshold, or what is called the neighborhood "tipping point." The fundamental idea is that a neighborhood, just like a natural ecosystem, has the capacity to contain only so much; too much of something and the system will collapse.

A study of neighborhood bars and taverns serves as an example. For those persons who are harmed by alcohol-related behavior, for the police who respond to alcohol-related calls for service, and other municipal officials who attempt to control these establishments, too many bars in too small an area can create an excessive amount of crime and disorder. The bars can lead to a drain on municipal services, especially the police, and the neighborhood may reach its tipping point. Studies show that the number of bar seats located in a neighborhood has a multiplier effect on the police calls for service, and at some point the police, social services, and city resources become exhausted, and the situation can no longer be tolerated.[28] More research is certainly warranted concerning this tipping point concept.

Exhibit 4–1 breaks down CPTED activities into their most basic components.

Exhibit 4–1	Breaking Down CPTED Functions and Activities

Following are some examples of actual CPTED activities, reported by the federal Office of Community Oriented Policing Services, that demonstrate how it works. Note that for each example, asking *why here?* compels the person(s) examining the situation to consider the motivations behind the activities, as well as the environmental conditions related to the location. Solving a problem thus requires a detailed understanding of both crime and place, and the response should consider one of the three objectives of CPTED: control access, provide opportunities to see and be seen, or define ownership and encourage the maintenance of territory.

Case #1:   Custodial workers routinely find evidence of smoking, drinking, and vandalism in a high school lavatory.

Why here? The lavatory is in an isolated area of the building, adjacent to a ticket booth and concession stand that are active only during athletic events. The school's open lunch policy allows students to eat anywhere on campus, while monitors are assigned only to the cafeteria.

CPTED response: A lock is installed on the lavatory door, and it remains locked unless there is an athletic event. The open lunch policy has been revised: Students are still allowed to leave the cafeteria but must eat in designated areas, and a faculty member is charged with patrolling these areas during lunch periods.

Case #2:   The back wall of a building in an office center is repeatedly tagged with graffiti.

Why here? The taggers have selected an area that is out of the view of passers-by: a rear corner location where two buildings come together at the end of a poorly lit service lane. Visibility is further reduced by hedges at the site's perimeter. Businesses in the office center are open from 9 AM to 5 PM during the week; however, the tagged building is next to a roller skating rink where activity peaks at night and on weekends.

CPTED response: Hedges are trimmed and wall-mounted light fixtures installed along the service lane, with motion detection lighting in the problem area. The skating rink agrees to change to a "no re-admission" policy to keep skaters inside the building and away from the office property.

Case #3:   ATM patrons at a bank are being robbed after dark.

Why here? The bank is situated along a commercial strip in a neighborhood with vacant properties and abandoned businesses. The ATM is in the front corner of the bank building, and the drive-through teller windows are at the side of the building, around the corner from the ATM. Robbers hide in the darkened drive-through teller area and attack unsuspecting ATM users after they complete a transaction.

CPTED response: The bank installs a fence at the corner of the building, creating a barrier between the ATM and the drive-through teller area.

Source: Diane Zahm, *Using Crime Prevention through Environmental Design in Problem Solving* (U.S. Department of Justice, Office of Community Oriented Policing Services, August 2007, pp. 1–3, http://www.popcenter.org/tools/cpted/ (Accessed July 12, 2010).

Advertising obstructions create poor natural surveillance and may contribute to a location's being an attractive target to offenders.

SITUATIONAL CRIME PREVENTION

Situational crime prevention (SCP) draws from the aforementioned rational choice and routine activities theories and departs radically from most criminology in its orientation. It is focused on the settings for crime and the prevention of crime rather than on persons committing criminal acts. It seeks to forestall the occurrence of crime rather than to detect and sanction offenders. It seeks not to eliminate criminal or delinquent tendencies through improvement of society or its institutions but merely to make criminal action less attractive to offenders.[29]

SCP is a targeted means of reducing crime. It provides an analytical framework for strategies to prevent crime in varying settings. It is an "environmental criminology" approach that seeks to reduce crime opportunity by making settings less conducive to unwanted or illegal activities, focusing on the environment rather than the offender.[30] The commission of a crime requires not merely the offender but, as every detective story reader knows, also the opportunity for crime.[31]

Because "opportunity makes the thief," seven principles of crime opportunity have been developed, some of which draw on the above theories[32]:

1. Opportunities play a role in all crime.
2. Crime opportunities are highly specific (e.g., the theft of cars for joyriding has a different pattern of opportunity than theft for car parts).
3. Crime opportunities are concentrated in time and space (dramatic differences are found from one address to another, even in high-crime areas, and shift by time, hour, and day of week).
4. Crime opportunities depend on everyday movements of activity (e.g., burglars visit houses in the daytime when occupants are away).
5. One crime produces opportunities for another (e.g., a successful burglary may encourage the offender to return in the future, or a youth who has his bicycle stolen may feel justified in stealing someone else's).

6. Some products offer more tempting crime opportunities (e.g., easily carried items such as electronic equipment and jewelry are attractive).

7. Social and technological advancements produce new opportunities (products are most sought after in their new "mass-marketing" stages, when demand for them is greatest; most products reach a saturation stage where most people have them and they are unlikely to be stolen).

Although the concept of SCP was British in origin, its development was influenced by two independent, but nonetheless related, strands of policy research in the United States: defensible space and crime prevention through environmental design—both of which preceded SCP and were discussed earlier in the chapter. Because of the trans-Atlantic delay in the dissemination of ideas, however, there was no stimulus for the development of SCP.[33]

SCP is a problem-oriented approach that examines the roots of a problem and identifies a unique solution to the problem. Experience has shown that successful SCP measures must be

Signage at the entrance to this apartment complex and high school parking lot serves to remove offenders' excuses for loitering and trespassing.

directed against specific crimes and must be designed with a clear understanding of the motives of offenders and their methods. SCP relies on the rational choice theory of crime, which asserts that criminals choose to commit crimes based on the costs and benefits involved with the crime. For example, a potential offender will commit a high-risk crime only if the rewards of the crime outweigh the risks.[34]

Ronald V. Clarke divided crime prevention goals into five primary objectives, each of which is designed to dissuade the criminal from committing the offense by making the crime too hard to commit, too risky, or too small in terms of rewards to be worth the criminal's time.[35] We discuss each of these five objectives:

1. ***Increasing the effort needed to commit the crime.*** Crimes typically happen because they are easy to commit. A person might see an easy opportunity to commit a crime and do so. Casual criminals are eliminated by increasing the effort needed to commit a crime. Following are different methods for increasing the effort needed to commit a crime:
   a. ***Hardening targets.*** Install physical barriers (such as locks, bolts, protective screens, and mechanical containment and antifraud devices to impede an offender's ability to penetrate a potential target).
   b. ***Controlling access.*** Install barriers and design walkways, paths, and roads so that unwanted users are prevented from entering vulnerable areas.
   c. ***Deflecting offenders.*** Discourage crime by giving people alternate legal venues for their activities (such as decreasing littering by providing litter bins or separating fans of rival teams after athletic events).
   d. ***Controlling facilitators.*** Facilitators are accessories who aid in the commission of crimes. Controlling them is achieved by universal measures (such as firearms permit regulations) and specific measures (metal detectors in community centers).
2. ***Increasing the risks associated with the crime.*** Increasing the risks associated with a crime reduces the incidence of that crime, because criminals believe that they will not be caught; offenders who believe that they will be caught are less likely to offend. For example, if a video camera monitors all entrances and exits to a convenience store or bank, potential robbers who know of such surveillance will be less likely to rob such establishments.
   a. ***Entry and exit screening.*** Screening methods include guest sign-ins or a required display of identification; they ensure that residents and visitors meet entrance requirements.
   b. ***Formal surveillance.*** Using security personnel and hardware (such as CCTV and burglar alarms) is a deterrent to unwanted activities.
   c. ***Informal surveillance.*** The presence of building attendants, concierges, maintenance workers, and attendants increases site surveillance and crime reporting.
   d. ***Natural surveillance.*** The surveillance can be provided by people as they go about their daily activities, making potential offenders feel exposed and vulnerable.
3. ***Reducing the rewards.*** Reducing the rewards from crime makes offending not worthwhile to offenders. Methods of reducing rewards include making targets of crime less valuable by the following means:
   a. ***Removing targets.*** Eliminate crime purposes from public areas. Examples include having a no-cash policy and keeping valuable property in a secure area overnight.
   b. ***Identifying property.*** Use indelible marks, establishing ownership and preventing individuals from reselling the property.

    c. ***Removing inducements.*** Related to target removal, this involves removing temptations that offenders have not targeted in advance but that are likely to become the targets of a spontaneous crime (such as vacant houses or other living units or broken windows and light fixtures).

4. ***Reducing the provocations.*** The environment or manner in which places are managed (e.g., busy bars and unmonitored drinking) may provoke crime and violence. Studies show that certain lighting improves people's mood and morale in the workplace. Additional seating and soothing music, measures to avoid long waiting lines, and other such options may reduce people's frustrations in crowded public places.

5. ***Removing the excuses.*** Many offenders say, "I didn't know any better" or "I had no choice." This strategy involves informing individuals of the law and rules and offers them alternatives to illegal activity by eliminating their excuses for committing crime. For example, a "no trespassing" sign is enforceable if posted. It also involves rule setting, such as clearly stating the rules of a housing development, which establish the procedures of punishment for violators. Such methods prevent offenders from excusing their crimes by claiming ignorance or misunderstanding.

Table 4–2 presents an SCP matrix for CPTED, specifically for the five CPTED objectives discussed. Included are organized (procedural measures), mechanical (provision or removal of certain physical objects), and natural (use of native aspects of the environment) means of facilitating each.

OTHER CRIME PREVENTION CHALLENGES

Next we look at four challenges that come into play with crime prevention operations that must be taken into account if the strategy is to function properly: the role of the crime prevention officers, crime displacement, properly publicizing crime prevention campaigns, and the evaluation of results.

Officers' Roles

What do crime prevention officers do? In broad terms, the mission of the crime prevention officer is to solve problems. By using all resources—city agencies, social services, the fire department, power companies, and landlords—the crime prevention effort builds a sense of partnership with other city and community agencies. It is proactive work, investigating suspicious people and activities. It is the police work that recognizes the importance of community input and involves officers trying to solve community problems even if they are not criminal in nature.

Today's crime prevention officers are also specifically engaged in the following activities:

- Obtaining useful information concerning hot spots, crime patterns, and individuals of interest.
- Using resources to put an end to ongoing problems and reduce the number of calls for service that require officer intervention, so as to free up patrol time and afford officers more time to be proactive.
- Acting as liaisons for Neighborhood Watch participants along with conducting public relations events, thus giving the department a human face and improving relationships between the police and the citizens.
- Obtaining and using grant money and other donations to fund programs allow the department to use budgeted funds for other needed activities.[36]

TABLE 4–2	Situational Crime Preventiion Matrix			
Increase the Effort	**Increase the Risks**	**Reduce the Rewards**	**Reduce the Provocations**	**Remove the Excuses**
1. Harden targets immobilizers in cars antirobbery screens	**6. Extend guardianship** cocooning Neighborhood Watch	**11. Conceal targets** gender-neutral phone directories off-street parking	**16. Reduce frustration and stress** efficient queueing soothing lighting	**21. Set rules** rental agreements hotel registration
2. Control access to facilities alley gating entry phones	**7. Assist natural surveillance** improved street lighting Neighborhood Watch hotlines	**12. Remove targets** removable car radios; prepaid public phone cards	**17. Avoid disputes** fixed cab fares; reduce crowding in pubs	**22. Post instructions** "No parking" "Private property"
3. Screen exits tickets needed electronic tags for libraries	**8. Reduce anonymity** taxi driver IDs "How's my driving?" signs	**13. Identify property** property marking; vehicle licensing	**18. Reduce emotional arousal** controls on violent porn; prohibit pedophiles working with children	**23. Alert conscience** roadside speed display signs "Shoplifting is stealing"
4. Deflect offenders street closures in red light district separate toilets for women	**9. Utilize place managers** train employees to prevent crime support whistleblowers	**14. Disrupt markets** checks on pawn brokers licensed street vendors	**19. Neutralize peer pressure** "Idiots drink and drive" "It's OK to say no"	**24. Assist compliance** litter bins public lavatories
5. Control tools/weapons toughened beer glasses; photos on credit cards	**10. Strengthen formal surveillance** speed cameras CCTV in town centers	**15. Deny benefits** ink merchandise tags; graffiti cleaning	**20. Discourage imitation** rapid vandalism repair; V-chips in TVs	**25. Control drugs/alcohol** Breathalyzers in pubs; alcohol-free events

Source: Ronald V. Clarke and Derek Cornish, "Opportunities, Precipitators, and Criminal Decisions: A Reply to Wortley's Critique of Situational Crime Prevention." In M. Smith and D. B. Cornish (eds.), Theory for Situational Crime Prevention. *Crime Prevention Studies*, Vol. 16 (Monsey, N.Y.: Criminal Justice Press, 2003).

It has also been said that every police officer needs to know at least as much as the bad guy knows. Certainly, the knowledge to commit criminal acts is not limited to a few; such information now is widely available on the Internet. For example, the Open Organization of Lockpickers, or TOOOL (www.toool.nl), is an organization dedicated to the so-called sport of lock picking. Although most TOOOL enthusiasts are generally law-abiding people who are interested in the intricacies of locks and keys, that information is available to those with criminal designs as well. Another site where such information proliferates is YouTube, where videos now explicitly show how to open padlocks with a tool made from a soft drink can, and how to get drinks and food from vending machines without paying. Obviously the police must monitor such sites and be aware of what the "bad guys" know, are doing, and are using as tools.[37]

Conducting a Publicity Campaign

Crime prevention **publicity campaigns** target two main audiences: potential victims and offenders. Police agencies should decide which audience to target based on the nature of the problem. For example, if a police department notices there are numerous preventable property crimes in an area, perhaps a short campaign to remind residents about the importance of securing their belongings could be beneficial. On the other hand, if local youths routinely vandalize cars in a parking lot, a campaign threatening police apprehension would be more effective. A dual approach can also be used, whereby two campaigns run simultaneously, one to reduce the number of potential victims and the other to deter offenders.

Victim-Oriented Campaigns

Efforts to reach victims can take one of two forms: Police can try to provide general information to residents concerning crime and its prevention, or they can advertise a specific community program they are undertaking. These campaigns often involve cooperation between the police department and the community in conducting home-security surveys, obtaining steering-wheel locks, or providing classes on various security-enhancing measures. Fliers and newsletters demonstrating techniques to make cars and houses "burglar-proof" are common in these "target-hardening" campaigns.

Offender-Oriented Campaigns

Offender-oriented crime prevention strategies rely on the notion that offenders are rational individuals who seek to maximize their rewards while minimizing their potential costs. With that premise, giving offenders information about the risks of crime becomes an important component of crime reduction efforts. Publicity campaigns that threaten an increased risk of arrest can be more effective in reducing offending.

Offender campaigns are successful not when they threaten later punishment, but when they threaten detection and arrest. Offender campaigns are more efficient when they target specific crime types and focus on a clearly defined geographic area. For offenders to take the message seriously, they need to feel as though the campaign targets them directly. For example, a police initiative to reduce car vandalism after school hours can include posting signs around town stating that "Vandalism is a Misdemeanor," but a more focused approach might include posters in the problem area with messages such as "Smile: Undercover Officers are Watching You," or "Our Officers Have Arrested 12 Students for Vandalism This Month—Will You Be Next?"[38]

Table 4–3 provides the primary considerations when developing both victim- and offender-oriented campaigns.

Displacement of Crime

An issue that emerges in any serious discussion of crime prevention is **crime displacement**, which refers to the idea that rather than eliminate crime, interventions simply result in the movement of crime to another area, shift offenders to new targets in the same area, alter the methods used to accomplish a crime, or prompt offenders to change the type of crime they commit.[39] Displacement has, therefore, been the Achilles' heel of crime prevention in general. Efforts to

TABLE 4–3	Managing Victim- and Offender-Oriented Publicity Campaigns

Publicity directed at VICTIMS can advertise:

- Self-protection techniques
- New ways to report crime
- Locations of police facilities or resources
- Dangerous areas
- Offenders living in the area (e.g., sex offenders)
- Neighborhood crime problems.

Publicity directed at OFFENDERS can advertise:

- Police techniques or future police crackdowns
- Penalties or the risk of apprehension for certain crimes
- Results of past crackdowns or police operations
- Knowledge of an illicit market or drug trade
- Legislative changes

Source: U.S. Department of Justice, Office of Community Oriented Policing Services, Center for Problem Oriented Policing, "Police Publicity Campaigns and Target Audiences," http://www.popcenter.org/responses/crime_prevention/2 (Accessed September 22, 2010).

control drug dealing and crime in neighborhoods and places are often criticized for having displaced the offending behavior instead of reducing it. If crime or drug dealing has only been moved around without any net reduction in harmful behavior, then that would be a valid criticism.

Research indicates, however, that displacement is not inevitable but is contingent on the offender's judgments about alternative crimes. If these alternatives are not viable, the offender may well settle for smaller criminal rewards or for a lower rate of crime. Few offenders are so driven by need or desire that they have to maintain a certain level of offending, whatever the cost. For many, the elimination of easy opportunities for crime may actually encourage them to explore noncriminal alternatives.[40] There are six commonly recognized types of displacement[41]:

1. *Time.* Offenders change the time when they commit crimes (e.g., switching from dealing drugs during the day to dealing at night).
2. *Location.* Offenders switch from targets in one location to targets in other locations (e.g., a dealer stops selling drugs in one community and begins selling them in another community).
3. *Target.* Offenders switch from one type of target to another type (e.g., a burglar switches from apartment units to detached single-family homes).
4. *Method.* Offenders change the way they attack targets (e.g., a street robber stops using a knife and uses a gun).
5. *Type.* Offenders switch from one form of crime to another (e.g., from burglary to check fraud).
6. *Perpetrator.* New offenders replace old offenders who have been removed by police enforcement (e.g., a dealer is arrested and a new dealer begins business with the same customers).

A review of the evidence for displacement shows that when attempts to detect displacement have been made, it is often not found, and if found, it is far less than 100 percent.[42] John Eck found that of 33 studies that looked for displacement effects, only 3 found evidence of much displacement.[43] Eck concluded, "There is more reason to expect no displacement than a great deal.

A reasonable conclusion is that displacement can be a threat, but that it is unlikely to completely negate gains due to an enforcement crackdown or a crime prevention effort."[44]

Research has shown that offenders generally begin offending at places they are familiar with and explore outward into increasingly unfamiliar areas.[45] If opportunities are blocked (by increased enforcement, target hardening, or some other means) close to a familiar location, then displacement to other targets close to familiar areas is most likely. Displacement usually occurs in the direction of familiar places, times, targets, and behaviors. Offenders may desist for varying periods of time, or they may even stop offending, depending on how important crime is to their lives.[46]

Although studies have indicated that displacement may not pose a major threat to crime prevention efforts, it is still a phenomenon that police officials must take into account. Ignoring this problem can lead to inequitable solutions to problems; this is particularly true of problem-solving tactics designed to displace offenders from specific locations. Efforts must be made to track those individuals to ensure that they do not create a problem somewhere else.[47]

Evaluating Crime Prevention Initiatives

The field of crime prevention generally suffers from the same shortcoming and criticisms that many other interventions suffer from: poor or nonexistent **evaluation**. The evaluation component of many initiatives is often poorly conceived, marginally funded, and short-lived. A useful form of evaluation is an outcome or impact evaluation to determine whether the intervention accomplished the expected result. Assessments of this nature require more planning and effort, and consideration must be given to the selection of comparison groups, time frames, outcome variables, potential confounding factors, and analytic techniques.[48] We will discuss such higher levels of evaluation in Chapter 8.)

For now, we will briefly note that evaluations not only provide the police with valuable information, but also give community leaders and residents an indication of the success or failure of crime prevention efforts.[49] That point hopefully will be made as we look at the following discussion of what works and does not work in crime prevention.

CRIME PREVENTION: WHAT WORKS AND WHAT DOESN'T

Many crime prevention programs work; others do not. Most programs have not yet been evaluated with enough scientific evidence to draw conclusions. Enough evidence is available, however, to create tentative lists of what works, what does not work, and what is promising.

Following are the major conclusions of a report to Congress, based on a systematic review of more than 500 scientific evaluations of crime prevention practices by the University of Maryland's Department of Criminology and Criminal Justice.[50] This is the first major evaluation of crime prevention programs, resulting in much attention and debate in the field. There are some surprising findings, particularly in the list of programs that do not hold promise—several of which have become pet projects of police agencies and political leaders.

What Prevents or Reduces Crime

The following are programs that researchers believed with reasonable certainty would prevent crime or reduce risk factors for crime. These programs are thus likely to be effective in preventing some form of crime:

- Providing extra police patrols in high-crime hot spots
- Monitoring known high-risk repeat offenders to reduce their time on the streets and returning them to prison quickly

- Arresting employed domestic abusers to reduce repeated abuse by these suspects
- Offering rehabilitation programs for juvenile and adult offenders that are appropriate to their risk factors to reduce their rates of repeat offending
- Offering drug treatment programs to prison inmates to reduce repeat offending after their release

What Does Not Appear to Be Successful

Sufficient evidence indicated to the University of Maryland researchers that the following programs failed to reduce crime or reduce risk factors:

- Gun buyback programs failed to reduce gun violence in cities (as evaluated in St. Louis and Seattle).
- Neighborhood Watch programs organized with police failed to reduce burglary or other target crimes, especially in higher-crime areas where voluntary participation often fails.
- Arrests of unemployed suspects for domestic assault caused higher rates of repeat offending over the long term than nonarrest alternatives.
- Increased arrests or raids on drug markets failed to reduce violent crime or disorder for more than a few days, if at all.
- Storefront police offices failed to prevent crime in the surrounding areas.
- Police newsletters with local crime information failed to reduce victimization rates (as evaluated in Newark, New Jersey, and Houston, Texas).
- Correctional boot camps using traditional military training failed to reduce repeat offending after release compared to similar offenders serving time on probation and parole, for both juveniles and adults.
- "Scared Straight" programs that bring minor juvenile offenders to visit maximum-security prisons to see the severity of prison conditions failed to reduce the participants' reoffending rates and may increase crime.
- Shock probation, shock parole, and split sentences, in which offenders are incarcerated for a short period of time at the beginning of the sentence and then supervised in the community, did not reduce repeat offending compared to the placement of similar offenders only under community supervision, and they increased crime rates for some groups.
- Home detention with electronic monitoring for low-risk offenders failed to reduce offending compared to the placement of similar offenders under standard community supervision without electronic monitoring.
- Intensive supervision on parole or probation did not reduce repeat offending compared to normal levels of community supervision.

What Holds Promise

Researchers determined that the level of certainty for the following programs is too low for there to be positive generalizable conclusions, but some empirical basis exists for predicting that further research could show positive results:

- Problem-solving analysis is effective when addressed to the specific crime situation.
- Proactive arrests for carrying concealed weapons in gun crime hot spots, using traffic enforcement and field interrogations, can be helpful.

Although both adult and juvenile military-style boot camps increased in number in the 1990s, they had poor results in reducing repeat offending.
Courtesy Washoe County, Nevada, Sheriff's Office.

- Community policing with meetings to set priorities reduced community perceptions of the severity of crime problems in Chicago.
- Field interrogations of suspicious persons reduced crime in a San Diego experiment.
- Gang offender monitoring by community workers and probation and police officers can reduce gang violence.
- Community-based mentoring by Big Brothers/Big Sisters of America substantially reduced drug abuse in one experiment, although evaluations of other similar programs showed that it did not.
- Battered women's shelters were found to reduce at least the short-term (six-week) rate of repeat victimization for women who take other steps to seek help.

Many more impact evaluations using stronger scientific methods are needed before even minimally valid conclusions can be reached about the impact of programs on crime. Again, as previously noted, there is much debate in the field about the research findings. The Maryland report to Congress, however, has raised the consciousness of the crime prevention discipline and will, it is hoped, bring about much more needed research and inquiry.

Summary

It is clear that the field of crime prevention has matured from its earlier forms, originally involving strategic placement of rocks by early cave dwellers and until recently having to do primarily with target hardening one's home with better locks. This chapter has shown its various elements as well as the results of research efforts concerning what good can occur when measures are taken to prevent crimes. The police realize that they alone cannot prevent or address crime and disorder and that a partnership with the community is essential if the physical and social problems that plague communities are to be reduced or eliminated.

Items for Review

1. Describe briefly the history of crime prevention.
2. Explain the relationship between crime prevention and COPPS.
3. Define what is meant by CPTED, what its second generation includes, and what some potential obstacles to implementing it are.
4. Explain the crime prevention officer's roles.
5. Describe what is meant by situational crime prevention, and list its five goals.
6. Review some of the primary considerations for conducting a crime- and victim-oriented publicity campaign.
7. Explain what is meant by crime displacement, and how it relates to crime prevention.
8. Discuss some crime reduction or prevention activities that have been shown by researchers to work, to not work, and to hold promise.

Learn by Doing

1. As part of a class group project, you and a fellow criminal justice student have been assigned to determine what "works, doesn't work, and has promise" in your local area with regard to police practices. You decide to begin by contacting the research, planning, and analysis unit of your local police agency and ask for their input. Based on what you have read and heard about local police initiatives, what do you believe they would say "works" in local policing, and what initiatives have been shown to not work?
2. Your criminal justice professor has the following essay question as part of a take-home exam in a community policing course: "Your police agency is launching a massive crime prevention initiative and desperately needs to get the word out to the general public. How will it do so?" You contact your local agency's Public Information Officer (PIO) for assistance. What will he or she say are some good approaches for publicizing the campaign?
3. Your criminal justice professor asks you to prepare an essay spelling out the definitions of crime prevention, CPTED, and situational crime prevention. What will be your responses?

Notes

1. Ronald V. Clarke, *Situational Crime Prevention: Successful Case Studies* (2nd ed.) (Monsey, N.Y.: Criminal Justice Press, 1997), p. 2.
2. Crime Prevention Coalition of America, *Crime Prevention in America: Foundations for Action* (Washington, D.C.: National Crime Prevention Council, 1990), p. 64.
3. Steven P. Lab, "Crime Prevention: Where Have We Been and Which Way Should We Go?" in Steven P. Lab (ed.), *Community Policing at a Crossroads* (Cincinnati, Ohio: Anderson, 1997), pp. 1–13.
4. Cynthia Scanlon, "Crime Prevention Through Environmental Design," *Law and Order* (May 1996):50.
5. U.S. Department of Housing and Urban Development, "Crime Prevention Through Environmental Design," in *Crime Prevention Brief* (Washington, D.C.: Author, no date), p. 2.
6. Lab, "Crime Prevention," p. 5.
7. Ibid.
8. Ibid., p. 7.
9. Scanlon, "Crime Prevention Through Environmental Design," p. 50.
10. Lab, "Crime Prevention," p. 6.
11. L. E. Cohen and M. Felson, "Social Change and Crime Rate Trends: A Routine Activity Approach," *American Sociological Review* 44 (1997):588–608.
12. D. B. Cornish and R. V. Clarke, *The Reasoning Criminal: Rational Choice Perspectives on Offending* (New York: Springer-Verlag, 1986).
13. James Q. Wilson and George Kelling, "Broken Windows," *The Atlantic Monthly* 211 (1982):29–38.
14. Lab, "Crime Prevention," p. 6.
15. Ronald V. Clarke, "Situational Crime Prevention: Its Theoretical Basis and Practical Scope," in Michael Tonry and Norval Morris (eds.), *Crime and Justice: An Annual Review of Research* (Vol. 4) (Chicago: University of Chicago Press, 1983), pp. 225–256.

16. Lab, "Crime Prevention," pp. 8–9.

17. Lab, "Crime Prevention," p. 6.

18. Ibid., p. 8.

19. U.S. Department of Justice, Bureau of Justice Assistance, *Crime Prevention and Community Policing,* p. 3.

20. C. R. Jeffrey, *Crime Prevention Through Environmental Design* (Beverly Hills, Calif.: Sage, 1971), p. 117.

21. National Crime Prevention Council, *Designing Safer Communities: A Crime Prevention Through Environmental Design Handbook* (Washington, D.C.: Author, 1997), pp. 7–8.

22. "Building a More Crime-Free Environment: Tempe Cops Have the Last Word on Construction Projects," *Law Enforcement News* (November 15, 1998):7.

23. Scanlon, "Crime Prevention Through Environmental Design," pp. 51–52.

24. Ibid., p. 3.

25. Greg Saville and Gerry Cleveland, "2nd Generation CPTED: An Antidote to the Social Y2K Virus of Urban Design." Paper presented at the Third Annual International CPTED Conference, Washington, D.C., December 14–16, 1998.

26. Ibid., p. 1.

27. Ibid.

28. Gregory Saville, "New Tools to Eradicate Crime Places and Crime Niches." Paper presented at the Conference of Safer Communities, Melbourne, Australia, September 10–11, 1998, pp. 9–10.

29. Clarke, "Situational Crime Prevention," p. 230.

30. U.S. Department of Housing and Urban Development, "Situational Prevention," *Crime Prevention Brief* (Washington, D.C.: Author, no date), p. 1.

31. Clarke, "Situational Crime Prevention," p. 231.

32. U.S. Department of Justice, Center for Problem-Oriented Policing, "The 10 Principles of Crime Opportunity," http://www.popcenter.org/about-situational.htm (Accessed March 7, 2006).

33. Clarke, "Situational Crime Prevention," p. 236.

34. Ibid.

35. Ibid.

36. Adapted from Ron Francis and Jeff Wamboldt, "Making Crime Prevention a Priority, *The Police Chief,* January 2010, p. 40, http://www. policechiefmagazine.org/magazine/index.cfm?fuse-action=display_arch&article_id=1989&issue_id=12 010 (Accessed July 12, 2010).

37. Jeffrey Dingle, "Thinking Like a Thief is the Key to Crime Prevention," *The Police Chief,* January 2010, p. 30, http://www.policechiefmagazine.org/magazine/index.cfm?fuseaction=display_arch&article_id=198 6&issue_id=12010 (Accessed July 12, 2010).

38. Ibid., pp. 5–11

39. Lab, "Crime Prevention," p. 12.

40. Clarke, "Situational Crime Prevention," p. 237.

41. Robert Barr and Ken Pease, "Crime Placement, Displacement, and Deflection," in Michael Tonry and Norval Morris (eds.), *Crime and Justice: A Review of Research* (Vol. 12) (Chicago: University of Chicago Press, 1990), pp. 146–175.

42. John E. Eck, "The Threat of Crime Displacement," *Criminal Justice Abstracts* 25 (3) (1993):529.

43. Pat Mayhew, Ronald V. Clarke, A. Sturman, and J. M. Hough, *Crime as Opportunity* (Home Office Research Study No. 34) (London: Her Majesty's Stationery Office, 1976); J. Lowman, "Prostitution in Vancouver: Some Notes on the Genesis of a Social Problem," *Canadian Journal of Criminology* 28 (1) (1997):1–16; Barry Poyner and Barry Webb, "Reducing Theft from Shopping Bags in City Center Markets," in Ronald V. Clarke (ed.), *Situational Crime Prevention: Successful Case Studies* (Albany, N.Y.: Harrow and Heston, 1992).

44. Eck, "The Threat of Crime Displacement," pp. 534–536.

45. Ibid., p. 537.

46. Ibid.

47. Ibid., pp. 541–542.

48. Ibid.

49. William Spelman and John E. Eck, "Problem-Solving: Problem Oriented Policing in Newport News," *Research in Brief* (January 1987):8.

50. Lawrence W. Sherman, Denise C. Gottfredson, Doris L. MacKenzie, John Eck, Peter Reuter, and Shawn D. Bushway, "Preventing Crime: What Works, What Doesn't, What's Promising." *Research in Brief* (Washington, D.C.: National Institute of Justice, 1998), pp. 1–27.

5

Technologies and Tools for the Tasks:
Collecting and Analyzing Information

KEY TERMS AND CONCEPTS

ARJIS
CompStat
Computer-aided dispatch
  (CAD)
Computer statistics
Counterterrorism
Crime analysis

Crime mapping
Decision making structure
  (for IT)
Geographic profiling
Information technology
Intelligence-led policing
Mobile computing

Predictive Policing
Records management system
  (RMS)
Social networking sites
Street-level criminology

LEARNING OBJECTIVES

As a result of reading this chapter, the student will:

- Know the necessary steps and components for establishing an IT framework

- Understand the functions of the three basic crime-analysis tools: computer-aided dispatch, mobile computing, and records management systems

- Comprehend the basics of crime mapping functions, and how crime patterns can be geomapped

- Be able to explain how IT applies to crime analysis

- Know the basic purposes of three new management and analysis tools: CompStat, intelligence-led policing, and predictive policing

- Know about geographic profiling and counterterrorism analysis

- Know how the Internet and an intranet apply to policing and crime analysis

*God hath made man upright; but they have sought
out many inventions.*

—ECCLESIASTES 7:29

INTRODUCTION

According to the Wickersham Commission, 1931, the newly deployed radio-equipped patrol car was "fast, efficient, stealthy . . . [and police were] just as liable to be within 60 feet as 3 miles of the crook plying his trade - and may bring them down about him like a swarm of bees—this lightning swift angel of death."[1] Thus was the age of police technologies born, to turn the tide against criminals.

Now, for more than four decades, the police have been employing myriad technologies to gather, store, and share information. In addition, today's police officers are on smart phones, deploying electroshock weapons against criminals, resuscitating heart attack victims with defibrillators kept in the patrol car, sending latent fingerprints to an automated database for matching, using various means to see whether someone is telling the truth, notifying the public about wanted persons, using social networking sites, creating composite drawings and traffic collision diagrams with computer software, and employing many kinds of databases and tools of the trade (many of which are discussed later in this chapter)—all of which would boggle the minds of the members of the Wickersham Commission.

This chapter examines the current use of technologies and other tools as they can be applied to community oriented policing and problem solving (COPPS). We begin by considering how to lay the foundation—establishing a **decision making structure** for an information technology (IT) project. Next we consider what we call the basic systems of analysis: computer-aided dispatch (CAD), mobile computing, and records management, and then we move into the broad area of **crime mapping**, and what it can provide to COPPS. Then we revisit crime analysis, discussed in Chapter 3 in conjunction with the S.A.R.A. problem-solving process (for scanning, analysis, response, analysis, as discussed in previous chapters) to look more deeply at the tools that are available for a thorough look at crime problems and patterns.

Then we examine several relatively new management and analysis tools that can be used to manage crime: **CompStat**, **intelligence-led policing (ILD)**, and **predictive policing**; those discussions are followed by brief considerations of geographic profiling and hot spots, counterterrorism analysis, a review of how the Internet and an intranet can assist the police in crime analysis and engaging the community (included here is an overview of the popular social networking sites, which are now being used to partner with the community), and the use of surveys. A number of examples of IT applications are disseminated throughout the chapter, as exhibits. The chapter concludes with a summary, review questions, and several scenarios and activities that provide opportunities for you to "learn by doing."

Note that we will not endeavor to list or describe all of the technologies and tools that are available for, or adaptable to COPPS purposes; the IT that is now available is simply too widespread and varied in role, nature, and application for us to attempt to do so. Therefore, here we will only cover the basics.

FIRST THINGS FIRST: BUILDING AN IT FRAMEWORK

Establishing a Decision Making Structure for an IT Project

As expensive, complex, and important as **information technology** (IT) is for today's COPPS efforts, certainly any degree of success in planning, installing, implementing, and managing an IT project involves a major combined effort on the part of many people. The need for careful attention to this process has been recognized and assisted by the U.S. Department of Justice, Office of Community Oriented Policing Services (COPS), in its *Law Enforcement Tech Guide: A Guide for Executives, Managers and Technologists.*[2] Although this publication is primarily designed for larger agencies, small and rural police agencies may also be assisted by a companion publication, also available at the COPS office.[3]

First, the foundation must be established by creating a decision-making structure. Agency leadership (chief or sheriff, upper management) and users (patrol officers, investigators, dispatchers, records clerks, crime analysis, community policing experts, and technical staff) will all rely on this foundation being established.

Figure 5-1 illustrates how a project decision-making structure might be configured. As shown, the executive sponsor will be the person who has ultimate decision-making authority and provides leadership and accountability. Below the executive sponsor are several more layers of key people who are involved, as follows:

- *The Steering Committee.* It includes captains, lieutenants, high-ranking non-sworn employees (i.e., dispatch supervisor, records supervisor, IT manager), whose role is to adopt a shared vision; commit to and guide the project; dedicate staff resources; keep

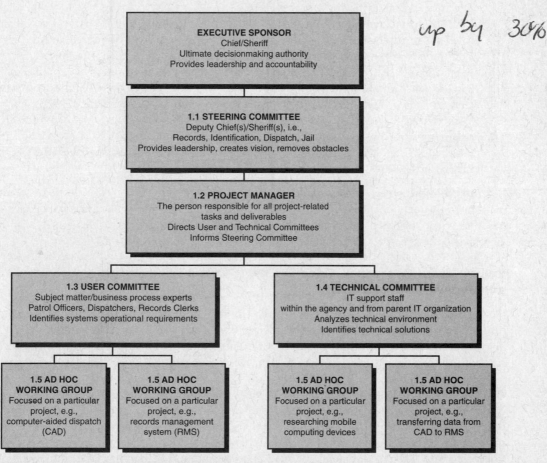

FIGURE 5-1   A Decision Making Structure for an IT Project

Source: Kelly J. Harris and William H. Romesburg, *Law Enforcement Tech Guide: A Guide for Executives, Managers and Technologists* (Washington, D.C.: U.S. Department of Justice, Office of Community Oriented Policing Services, 2002), p. 27; also available at: http://www.cops.usdoj.gov/files/ric/Publications/lawenforcementtechguide.pdf (Accessed July 13, 2010).

abreast of project progress, risks, challenges, successes; provide update reports to the executive sponsor; remove project barriers; deal with policy and personnel obstacles; and render decisions on issues that impact project scope, time, and cost.

- **The Project Manager.** Ideally, this is an individual who has project management skills, experience and/or training, dedicated in a full-time manner to the success of the initiative. His or her role is to provide overall project direction, manage the project's schedule, serve as a single point of contact with vendors, direct/lead team members toward project objectives, review and approve project deliverables, handle low-level problem resolution, and serve as liaison to the Steering Committee.

- **The User Committee.** These are subject matter and business process experts for the functions to be addressed (i.e., patrol officer, detective, dispatcher, records clerk, crime analyst, property manager). His or her role is to assist and support in creating a project charter (Chapter 3 of the Tech Guide) and ultimately the project plan (Part III). To analyze existing workflows, define business processes (Chapter 4), look for efficiencies and establish the requirements of any new system.

- **The Technical Committee.** These people are dedicated technical staff from the agency. Their roles are to understand the vision proposed by the Steering Committee and the User Committee's workflow and business needs, to analyze the agency's existing technical environment, and to research and propose solutions to the agency's business needs and problems.

- **The Ad Hoc Committee.** As shown in Figure 5-1, these are people who, throughout the course of the project, may be convened to focus on particular issues. These groups may be formed to look at specific tasks and business processes that require more in-depth research or analysis, or to carry out research on and development of a variety of project-specific plans, models, policies and directions. Ad hoc working groups are assembled on a temporary basis to address a specific issue or task.[4]

In addition to mentioning available resources concerning police IT for problem solving mentioned throughout this chapter, we also note that the Center for Problem Oriented Policing[5] has a vast array of resources available for research in this area, as well as Hendon Publishing Company's *Public Safety IT* magazine.[6]

Some Basics: Computer-Aided Dispatch, Mobile Computing, and Records Management

Now, we briefly describe several staples of today's system of IT: the CAD system, mobile computing, and records management system. These tools are described in detail because they are the primary technologies for offering *core* data management capabilities for COPPS, such as data capture and entry; search, retrieval, and display; messaging; and linkages between data elements.[7]

COMPUTER-AIDED DISPATCH.   CAD has become an indispensable technology in policing, designed to handle all information related to receiving and dispatching emergency calls for service (CFS). CAD is often the first point of data entry, whether processing an emergency 911 CFS or managing an officer-initiated car stop. CAD fully automates the call-taking and dispatching functions; used with automated vehicle location (AVL) systems that track patrol vehicle status, CAD can help to prioritize CFS and make recommendations for unit and resource dispatching based on beats, zones, closest resources, repeat calls for service, and/or current unit activities. Some CAD systems can also provide the number and type of prior calls that were made at the location, whether there are existing warrants for residents, or if there are specific hazards related to the location.[8]

MOBILE COMPUTING. **Mobile computing** has become the catchall phrase for outfitting an officer's vehicle or person with the technology that, in effect, allows him or her to be a "mobile office." Mobile computing is actually composed of several law enforcement hardware and software technologies working together to allow officers to access, receive, create, and exchange information wirelessly in the field. Officers can proactively query local, state, and national databases; receive and initiate CAD events; view unit status; send e-mail; prepare and file incident reports; issue citations; capture field interview information; access department policies and procedures; research penal codes; and perform many other functions. In sum, they are able to do nearly everything they could do in the station house.[9]

RECORDS MANAGEMENT SYSTEM (RMS). Today a **records management system (RMS)** is a key asset to effective policing, offering robust analytical tools and the ability to seamlessly share information, developing complex linkages between myriad data and information, and assisting in effective management strategies. In its simplest form, an RMS captures, maintains, and analyzes all police agency and incident-related information and is vital for tracking and managing criminal and noncriminal events, investigations, and personnel information. An RMS automates the daily practice of entering, storing, retrieving, retaining, archiving, viewing, and exchanging records, documents, data, information, or files related to persons, vehicles, incidents, arrests, warrants, traffic accidents, citations, pawn tickets, civil process papers, gun registration investigations, property, and evidence.[10]

Together, CAD and RMS can produce most of the data in CompStat (discussed below) with a touch of a button. Otherwise, a data entry clerk or crime analyst must enter the details of *every* incident reported, arrest effected, summons issued, case cleared, and other such information into a spreadsheet or database to produce the reports.[11]

Exhibit 5-1 **How Technology Changed the Chicago Police Department**

In the early 2000s, the Chicago Police Department (CPD) had three goals: to make Chicago the safest U.S. city, to partner with the community to solve problems of crime and disorder, and to share information with hundreds of criminal justice agencies in the greater Chicago area. The CPD had mountains of data stored in an inaccessible, antiquated computer and sitting around in file cabinets, but could do little with it. Efforts to perform a technology upgrade had resulted in CPD becoming mired down with getting information into the database without looking at what it needed to do to accomplish its goals; nor was there an understanding of who needed the information, why and when they needed it, and how best to present it. Sworn personnel were spending all their time putting data into the system without getting anything out that helped them in their job.

Finally the CPD formed a unique partnership with a private corporation, which provided IT and technical assistance; together they developed a new analysis and reporting tool that helped to accelerate its efforts to meet its core mission. The results are as follows:

▶ *Greater productivity.* By linking available information, officers could do more in less time and solve crimes that were unsolvable before.
▶ *Better management and accountability.* The CPD could now provide millions of files at officers' fingertips, monitor in real time the effectiveness of plans to address crime and disorder problems, and make adjustments as needed to COPPS initiatives and to officer deployment.

▶ **Stronger partnerships.** Information is now shared with every law enforcement agency in Illinois.

Source: Adapted from Chuck Wexler, Mary Ann Wycoff, and Craig Fischer, *Good to Great: Application of Business Management Principles in the Public Sector* (Washington, D.C.: Office of Community Oriented Policing Services and the Police Executive Research Forum, 2007), pp. 41–42.

CRIME MAPPING

Conclusive evidence from clay tablets found in Iraq proves that maps have been around for several thousand years—perhaps tens of millennia.[12] A relatively recent development in policing is computerized crime mapping, which has become increasingly popular among law enforcement agencies.[13] In fact, a federal study found that departments with one hundred or more officers used computer crime mapping 35 percent of the time.[14] Computerized crime mapping combines geographic information from global positioning satellites with crime statistics gathered by the department's CAD system and demographic data provided by private companies or the U.S. Census Bureau. (Some agencies acquire information from the Census Bureau's Internet site.) The result is a picture that combines disparate sets of data for a whole new perspective on crime. For example, maps of crimes can be overlaid with maps or layers of causative data: unemployment rates in the areas of high crime, locations of abandoned houses, population density, reports of drug activity, or geographic features (such as alleys, canals, or open fields) that might be contributing factors.[15] Furthermore, the hardware and software are now available to nearly all police agencies for a few thousand dollars.

Exhibit 5-2 describes an innovative yet very practical use for crime mapping: discovering where traffic crashes and crime hot spots are combined to cause many problems.

Exhibit 5-2	Baltimore "Intersects" Traffic Crash and Crime Hot Spots

The connection between traffic law enforcement and the detection of criminal activity has long been known; aggressive officers look beyond the license plate at traffic stops, often leading to major arrests, case clearances, and an effective way to interdict drugs, guns, and wanted criminals. With 800,000 citizens to protect, recently the Baltimore County, Maryland, Police Department (BCOPD) and its 1,900 sworn officers began designing its own study of data relevant to this correlation, looking to tie together crash problems and crime issues in areas that were experiencing both. The Crime Analysis Section identified roadways having significant levels of both traffic crashes and criminal incidents. Software was used to generate maps that identified overlapping crime (robberies and burglaries in particular) and crash areas. Six corridors were selected, with the objective of reducing crashes, robberies, and burglaries by 5 percent over a 10-month period. The level of enforcement was significant, with more than 65,000 enforcement contacts being made—traffic stops in the target area increasing 83 percent above normal—which resulted in 1,169 arrests ranging from impaired driving and other traffic violations to robbery, weapons, drugs, and outstanding warrants. Meanwhile, personal-injury crashes decreased by 15 percent, robberies declined by 14 percent, and burglaries increased by 2 percent. The BCOPD believes that this approach provides a means to deploy limited resources into areas that have shown long-term traffic- and crime-related problems.

Source: Howard B. Hall, "Targeting Crash and Crime Hot Spots in Baltimore County," *The Police Chief* (July 2009): 24–7.

Exhibit 5-3	ARJIS: Power of the Web

The Automated Regional Justice Information System (**ARJIS**) was the first multiagency, interactive, publicly accessible crime-mapping Web site in the nation, serving only San Diego County. ARJIS has now evolved into a complex criminal justice enterprise network used by 71 local, state, and federal agencies in the 2 California counties that border Mexico; it integrates more than 6,000 workstations, and there are more than 11,000 authorized users generating more than 35,000 transactions daily.

ARJIS is used for much more than crime mapping: tactical analysis, investigations, statistical information, and crime analysis. ARJIS is responsible for major public safety initiatives, including wireless access to photos, warrants, and other critical data in the field, crime and sex offender mapping, crime analysis tools evaluation, and an enterprise system of applications that help users solve crimes and identify offenders. ARJIS also serves as the region's information hub for officer notification, information sharing, and the exchange, validation, and real-time uploading of many types of public safety data.

Source: Automated Regional Criminal Justice Information System, "What is ARJIS ?" http://www.arjis.org/WhatisARJIS/tabid/54/Default.aspx (Accessed October 29, 2009).

The importance of crime mapping is evidenced by the fact that in 1997 the NIJ established the Crime Mapping Research Center (CMRC) to promote research, evaluation, development, and dissemination of **geographic information systems** technology for criminal justice research and practice. The CMRC holds annual conferences on crime mapping to give researchers and practitioners an opportunity to gain both practical and state-of-the-art information on the use and utility of computerized crime mapping.[16]

Exhibit 5-3 describes what has become a powerful Web-based crime-fighting tool that provides mountains of information to the police and the public: the Automated Regional Justice Information System, or ARJIS, based in San Diego County, California; the system affords tactical, investigative, statistical, and crime analysis information to police, and offers a wealth of information to the public, including crime mapping.

Another excellent example of mapping success is the New York Police Department's Compstat program, which provides up-to-the-minute statistics, maps, and patterns and establishes causal relationships among crime categories. Compstat also puts supervisors in constant communication with the department's administration, provides updates to headquarters every week, and makes supervisors responsible for responding to crime in their assigned areas.[17]

CRIME ANALYSIS: REVISITING S.A.R.A.

In Chapter 3, we discussed at some length the analysis stage of the S.A.R.A., the problem-solving model. Here we expand somewhat on that discussion, bringing technologies to the subject.

A critical aspect of the problem-solving process, as we noted in Chapter 3, is **crime analysis**, which may be simply defined as "the collection and analysis of data pertaining to a criminal incident, offender, and target."[18] The greater the extent of collecting, analyzing, and relating all data to the components of the crime triangle (victim, offender, and location, as discussed in Chapter 4), the better equipped the police will be to develop innovative solutions that include the full spectrum of suppression, intervention, and prevention options.[19]

It is very important for officers who are engaged in problem solving to understand how, when, where, and why criminal events occur rather than merely responding to them. In this vein, we do not mean to say that patrol officers should develop expertise in understanding the mental processes and theories that are involved in a person's choosing to commit crimes (although criminology or psychology courses at a college or university would certainly benefit the problem-solving officer); rather, we are referring to what might be termed **street-level criminology**. It requires that police learn more about crime occurrences through analysis and experimentation with the problem-solving process.

The collection and analysis of data spanning a long period of time result in *strategic* crime analysis. This type of analysis is research focused because it includes the use of statistics to make conclusions. This analysis can be useful to departments in terms of forecasting crime trends or estimating future crime based on past trends. (*Note:* Although we will not delve into it at this point, it should be mentioned that the Microsoft Word Excel function is very useful for making forecasts of crime trends; this task can be accomplished fairly easily.)

While strategic crime analysis involves the review of data spanning generally a year or more, tactical crime analysis uses real-time data spanning several days. One of its principal uses involves problem identification, or the pattern detection of multiple offenses over a short period of time that have common characteristics, such as the type of crime, modus operandi, and type of weapon used.[20] One example of tactical crime analysis that is discussed later in this chapter is geographic profiling, which can be used to suggest the likelihood of where an offender resides based on the pattern of where victims and offenses occur. Linkage analysis involves connecting a suspect to a series of incidents based on commonalities in modus operandi and suspect descriptions as well as known offenders who live in close proximity to a given area. For example, many states search their databases of registered sex offenders when a series of sexual offenses is identified.[21]

Not to be overlooked in crime analysis is the use of community surveys—discussed in Chapter 3—to identify or clarify problems.

We recommend an excellent resource for one who is engaged in COPPS initiatives and needs to know more about how to use technologies and tools for analyzing crime: *Crime Analysis for Problem Solvers in 60 Small Steps*, published by the U.S. Department of Justice, Office of Community Oriented Policing Services; it is also available online at: http://www.popcenter.org/learning/60steps/[22]

NEW MANAGEMENT AND ANALYSIS TOOLS: USING IT TO MANAGE CRIME

CompStat, Intelligence-Led Policing, and Predictive Policing

COMPSTAT.   A relatively new crime management process used in the problem-solving process is known as CompStat—for comparative or **computer statistics**—which is designed for the collection and feedback of information on crime and related quality of life issues.

Since being introduced by the New York City Police Department in 1994, CompStat has been widely adopted: A national survey found that 58 percent of large agencies (those with 100 or more sworn officers) had either adopted or were planning to implement a CompStat-like program.[23] The key elements of CompStat are as follows:

- Specific objectives
- Accurate and timely intelligence
- Effective tactics
- Rapid deployment of personnel and resources
- Relentless follow-up and assessment[24]

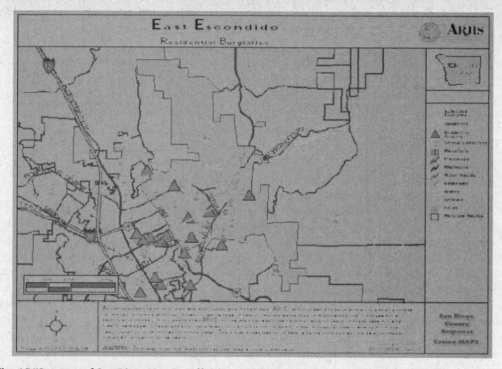

The ARJIS system of San Diego County affords tactical, investigative, statistical, and crime analysis information to police, and a wealth of information to the public. Here, a map shows East Escondido citizens the locations of residential burglaries during a recent one-month time frame
Courtesy ARJIS Crime Mapping Research Center.

CompStat pushes all precincts to generate weekly or monthly crime activity reports. Crime data are readily available, offering up-to-date information that is then compared at citywide, patrol, and precinct levels.

Under CompStat, police begin proactively thinking about ways to deal with crime in terms of suppression, intervention, and prevention. Commanders must proactively respond to crime problems, and explain what tactics they have employed to address crime patterns, what resources they have and need, and with whom they have collaborated. Follow-up by top brass further ensures accountability.

INTELLIGENCE-LED POLICING.   ILP originated in Great Britain, where police believed that a relatively small number of people were responsible for a comparatively large percentage of crimes; they believed that officers would have the best effect on crime by focusing on the most prevalent offenses occurring in their jurisdiction.[25]

The word "intelligence" is often misused; the most common mistake is to consider "intelligence" as synonymous with "information." Information is not intelligence; rather, "information plus analysis equals intelligence," and without analysis, there is no intelligence. Intelligence is what is produced after collected data is evaluated and analyzed by a trained intelligence professional.[26]

Exhibit 5-4 explains the views of the federal Bureau of Justice Assistance concerning the need for and the development and functions of ILP.

To better comprehend what is meant by ILP is to break it down into its core components. For example, many police agencies have both crime analysts and intelligence analysts. Crime analysts keep their fingers on the pulse of crime in the jurisdiction: which crime trends are up, which ones

| Exhibit 5-4 | Intelligence-led Policing: Origins and Functions |

ILP, while a relatively new concept in the United States, was an outcome of British efforts during the late 1990s to manage law enforcement resources efficiently and to respond effectively to serious crime. In 2000, the National Criminal Intelligence Service published the National Intelligence Model (NIM) that established the following priorities for British police service:

► Target prolific offenders through overt and covert means
► Manage crime and disorder hotspots
► Identify and investigate linked series of crime or incidents
► Apply prevention measures that include working with a broad range of other disciplines

NIM priorities were grounded in experience and solid research. Several authoritative longitudinal projects, in America and the United Kingdom, have convincingly demonstrated that a small minority of offenders commit a majority of crimes. It is well known that crime reports and service calls often cluster predominately at specific locations; research has shown that violent crime and neighborhood disorder can be reduced by focused, multiagency efforts in which law enforcement plays an important, if not exclusive role.

ILP does not replace the concepts of problem-solving policing or the community involvement and neighborhood maintenance theories (broken windows), nor the police accountability and information sharing practices (CompStat). It builds on these concepts to keep pace with changes in society, technology, and criminal behavior. ILP encourages greater use of criminal intelligence; attends to offenders more than offenses; and offers a more targeted, forward-thinking, multijurisdictional and prevention point of view to the business of policing.

As such, successful adoption of ILP will generally involve the following practices:

► Information collection is part of the organizational culture—led by the chief executive, supervisors, and managers encourage line officers and investigators to regularly collect and forward intelligence.
► Analysis is indispensable to tactical and strategic planning—record management systems are robust, analysts are well-trained and equipped, actionable intelligence products are regularly produced to inform both tactical and strategic decisions.
► Enforcement tactics are focused, prioritized by community harm assessments and prevention-oriented; operations are mounted against repeat or violent offenders; serious organized (gang, trafficking, etc.) groups are identified and dismantled; and traffic violations are enforced at dangerous intersections or roadways.

Source: Adapted from Office of Justice Programs, Bureau of Justice Assistance, "Intelligence-led Policing," http://www.ojp.usdoj.gov/BJA/topics/ilp.html (Accessed September 20, 2010).

are down, where the hot spots are, what type of property is being stolen, and so on. Intelligence analysts, on the other hand, are likely to be more aware of the specific *people* responsible for crime in the jurisdiction: who they are, where they live, what they do, who they associate with, and so on (see Exhibit 5-4). Integrating these two functions—crime analysis and intelligence analysis—is essential for obtaining a comprehensive grasp of the crime picture. *Crime analysis* allows the police to understand the "what, when, and where," while *intelligence analysis* provides an understanding the "who"—crime networks and individuals.

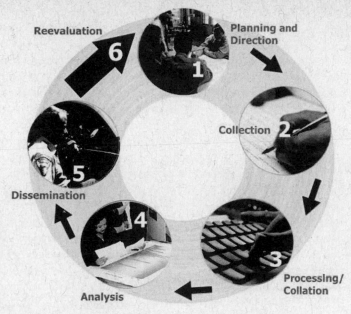

FIGURE 5-2 **The Intelligence Gathering Process**

Source: U.S. Department of Justice, Office of Justice Programs, *National Criminal Intelligence Sharing Plan*, p. 6, http://www.fas.org/irp/agency/doj/ncisp.pdf (Accessed December 7, 2009).

As shown in Figure 5-2, the National Criminal Intelligence Sharing Plan (NCISP)[27] categorizes the intelligence gathering process into six steps: planning and direction, collection, processing/collation, analysis, dissemination, and reevaluation.

PREDICTIVE POLICING.   Have you ever logged onto a Web site to purchase an item and seen something like "other customers who placed similar orders also ordered these items"? Or entered an online auction service and been provided with some items you might also be interested in bidding on? Essentially, in these cases private businesses are harnessing social sciences to predict human behavior. The processes used in predicting your shopping behavior are the same ones used to determine criminal behavior, only they are using different data sets (bearing in mind, however, that private industry may be able to use more personal data than a police agency can).[28]

Welcome to the world of predictive analysis, where the next generation of police problem solving could combine existing technologies like computers, crime analysis, and police reports with a few newer technologies such as artificial intelligence. The future may well bring a system that can predict crimes before they happen—with predictive analytics acting as a force multiplier that are focused on problem solving.[29] Of course, high-tech tools alone cannot solve crimes, but when trained crime analysts and police management combine the tools with their ingenuity, anything is future in this high-tech world.

The term "predictive policing," according to the U.S. Department of Justice (DOJ), is a relatively new law enforcement concept that "integrates approaches such as cutting-edge crime analysis, crime-fighting technology, intelligence-lead policing, and more to inform forward thinking crime prevention strategies and tactics."[30] The DOJ states that, ultimately, predictive policing is intended as a framework to advance strategies like community policing, problem-oriented policing, ILP, and hot spots policing.[31]

The police have always known that robberies surge near check-cashing businesses, that crime spikes on hot days and plummets during the rain, that residential burglaries often occur on Sunday mornings (while people are attending church services), and that Super Bowl Sunday is usually the slowest crime day of the year.[32] But officers' minds can store and remember only so much data. So when the police monitor crime data and query a computer system for historical and real-time patterns, they can predict, more systematically, over a bigger area, and across shifts and time spans, where crimes are likely to occur. More Important, the crime-analysis software does not forget details, get sick, take vacation, or transfer to a different precinct.

Thus, if commercial robberies were high in, say, March 2010, their software would predict another spike in March 2011, and the police could then look at the types of businesses that were hit, their locations, and time of day. The system can even analyze a robber's modus operandi—what was said, type of weapon used, and so on.[33]

How might predictive policing work for the street officer? Well, imagine that you are dispatched to a domestic dispute that involves a man and woman. You arrive at the home, knock on the door, are escorted into the living room, and all is going as it has gone on such calls a thousand times—but now you are engaged in a struggle for your life. Do you believe that you might have approached this call differently if, upon being given the call, your mobile computer had awakened with the following flurry of information? The male subject you are about to confront has been previously arrested for assaulting officers in another jurisdiction and was recently arrested for driving under the influence. Or, if you know there have been copper thefts from construction sites in your city, would it not be better to know the patterns of such thefts so as to predict when and where they are likely to happen, rather than having to rely on parking the patrol car in various areas and hoping for blind luck? These are just a few simple examples of how predictive policing can be applied—simply by looking at patterns of behavior—to the patrol officer in addition to crime analysts.

Other Applications: Geographic Profiling and Hot Spots

GEOGRAPHIC PROFILING. Geographic **profiling**, or the combined use of geography, psychology, and mathematics to identify the location of an offender, is most commonly associated with tracking down serial killers, rapists, and arsonists. However, it is a useful investigative tool in any case in which an individual offender has committed criminal activity across a series of locations. Geographic profiling suggests investigative alternatives based on the "hunting behavior" of the offender. Leading geographic profiler Kim Rossmo argues that criminals are no different in their pattern of carrying out their offenses than ordinary citizens are in going about their day-to-day activities.[34]

Following this principle, geographic profiling uses the nearness principle as a key rule. The nearness principle argues that offenders will remain within a limited range that is comfortable to them when committing their offenses, just as animals will forage within a limited range from their base. This principle has led to the creation of a computerized geographic profiling workstation that includes statistical analyses, geographic features, and database management to aid in calculating investigative suggestions. Crime scenes are broken down by type and entered by location, and addresses of suspects can be evaluated based on their probability of being the actual offender. This can help investigators sort through existing records, such as registered sex offenders, and other information.[35]

Counterterrorism Analysis

In the wake of attacks by terrorists on U.S. soil, the role and function of crime analysts have become even more crucial. Crime analysts' approach to **counterterrorism** involves two major areas—investigation and prevention:[36]

Exhibit 5-5	Neighborhood eWatch Fights Crime in Minnesota

Ramsey County, Minnesota, recently created a virtual neighborhood watch network composed of 30 surveillance cameras targeted at criminal hot spots. Deputies can access live video feeds from their patrol cars and substations.

With Neighborhood eWatch, the public can log onto the site and enter "public" for the username and password. On the Web site (www.ramseycountysheriffwebcop.com), users gain access to 14 of the county's surveillance cameras set up in various public areas. If users spot any suspicious activity, they contact the East Metro Real-Time Information Center (EMRIC), where analysts can pan, tilt, and zoom in on potential incidents and dispatch deputies as needed.

Proponents argue that these digital tools assist agencies to solve problems faster. As an example, the Neighborhood eWatch program helped Ramsey County deputies arrest an auto thief who had been working parking lots for weeks. The Web site also provides information about other criminal activities, a "most wanted" section, and the option for citizens to register to receive e-mail crime reports. A live video from one of the sheriff's cars—which Ramsey County touts as the first in the nation—provides viewers the chance to periodically "ride along" on patrol and see for themselves what is occurring on the county's streets and highways.

Source: Adapted from Russell Nichols, "Neighborhood Watch Goes Digital in Ramsey County, Minn." Government Technology, http://www.govtech.com/public-safety/Ramsey-County-Minn-Neighborhood-eWatch.html (Accessed September 20, 2010).

- *Investigation.* Terrorists operate according to rules and principles that can be identified, analyzed, and predicted. Although they can be fanatical and fiendish, they behave in a logical fashion, picking their targets with precision. This makes them more vulnerable in the sense that analysts can predict their behavior and disrupt their efforts. Analysts must never work alone, however; they must coordinate with the appropriate federal agency, most often the Federal Bureau of Investigation (FBI).
- *Prevention.* Prevention is accomplished by denying the terrorist the opportunity to attack in the first place. The process begins with a threat assessment of the jurisdiction: identifying and evaluating the risk of targets, and constructing countermeasures by using the S.A.R.A. process. Analysts can *scan* for vulnerabilities, *analyze* these methods of attack to determine countermeasures, *respond* by allocating the necessary police resources to try to thwart an attack, and *assess* by performing periodic readiness tests and exercises to determine effectiveness.

Internet/Intranet and COPPS

The Internet has also proven to be an important mechanism for furthering police agencies' COPPS objectives. Important features that are used by many departmental Web sites in reaching their citizens include the following:[37]

- Libraries devoted to crime prevention and safety tips (including information about known scam cases operating within the jurisdiction)
- Virtual tours of the department
- Recent jurisdictional and neighborhood crime statistics (including crime maps)
- Departmental wanted lists and upcoming court cases
- Capability for citizens to anonymously report crime or complaints about officer conduct

Exhibit 5-6	Social Networking and Crime Analysis

Police officers today are more connected and have access to more information than ever before. Social networks are the newcomers to online communities. If a citizen is following the local police department on, say, Twitter, then the citizen will receive all of the police "tweets" on the user's Twitter home page in their e-mail, or on a mobile phone or PDA. If the police are looking for an offender, they can send a message to their community followers. Amber Alerts for missing children, pursuit-in-progress notices, reports of persons apprehended, reminders of neighborhood watch meetings, or other relevant bulletins can also be provided. Citizens can reply to these messages using the same system. Facebook, also free, is also used to advantage, by promoting community events, drawing attention to its podcasts, and adding video clips it has produced. Blogs—sort of an online diary—are an excellent means for police to elevate their community profile as well; it can serve as a daily "police blotter," a log of what officers are doing; they can include photos and YouTube video clips. When a new blog is posted, citizens can be alerted to it on Twitter and Facebook.

Source: Tim Dees, "Social Networks for Better Policing: Facebook Twitter, Blogs, and Google Voice," *Law and Order,* November 2009, pp. 32–34.

Many agencies are also establishing an intranet for their employees. Through the intranet, a department is able to supply a number of important informational needs through access to the following:[38]

- *Problem-solving system.* A searchable database of problems that officers have worked on over the past few years can be accessed.
- *Property evidence system.* A searchable database on property and evidence in the department's custody can be used.
- *Calls for service.* A searchable database on CFS by several categories would be accessible.
- *Records management system.* There would be online access to RMS and a wide range of search capabilities for offense reports.
- *Computer-aided dispatch system.* Online access to CAD system records, including active call information, would be available.
- *Gang database.* There would be online access to the agency's gang information.

The Internet also contains several other means of collecting and analyzing information, as well as communicating with the public: **social networking sites** that are free and whose members now proliferate; some of these networking sites are discussed in Exhibit 5-6.

Summary

This chapter has revisited the S.A.R.A. problem-solving process discussed in Chapter 3, examining how technologies and other tools can assist with what is considered to be the heart of the problem-solving process: the analysis of crime data. This discussion included the kinds of methods and technologies—including various forms of computer hardware and software—that are now in the analyst's quiver and are being applied to COPPS.

It should be abundantly clear now, after reading this chapter, that these are most certainly challenging times for those persons who are charged with trying to determine the who, what, when, where, why, and how of crime.

Items for Review

1. How should a large police department go about establishing a decision making structure for an IT project?
2. Describe the functions of the three basic means for engaging in crime analysis: computer-aided dispatch, mobile computing, and records management systems.
3. Explain how crime mapping can assist in general with COPPS, and how crime patterns can be geomapped.
4. Review the basic functions of three relatively new management tools: CompStat, intelligence-led policing, and predictive policing.
5. Explain how COPPS and IT can assist with counterterrorism analysis.
6. Distinguish between the Internet and an intranet in terms of how they apply to policing and crime analysis.
7. Describe how social networking sites are assisting with community partnership endeavors.

Learn by Doing

1. Today some people indicate concerns with the number of technologies now in use: invasion-of-privacy issues, reducing police interactions with the public, and so on. How would you justify the general use of technologies in policing, and with COPPS initiatives in specific? Do you see any potential problems with police using these technologies?
2. As part of a criminal justice honor society poster project to be presented at a local conference, you opt to illustrate how an IT decision making structure might be configured. Describe how your poster would look when completed.
3. As discussed in the chapter, the Automated Regional Justice Information System (ARJIS) is used for much more than crime mapping. Go online to the ARJIS Web site and locate figures and illustrations that depict at least four functions that ARJIS is capable of providing.

Notes

1. National Commission of Law Observance and Enforcement, *Report on Police* (Washington, D.C.: Government Printing Office, 1931), p. 140.
2. Kelly J. Harris and William H. Romesburg, *Law Enforcement Tech Guide: A Guide for Executives, Managers and Technologists* (Washington, D.C.: U.S. Department of Justice, Office of Community Oriented Policing Services, 2002), p. 23; also available at: http://www.cops.usdoj.gov/files/ric/Publications/lawenforcementtechguide.pdf (accessed July 13, 2010).
3. See William H. Romesburg, *Law Enforcement Tech Guide for Small and Rural Agencies: Guide for Executives, Managers and Technologists* (U.S. Department of Justice, Office of Community Oriented Policing Services, 2005).
4. Harris and Romesburg, *Law Enforcement Tech Guide: A Guide for Executives, Managers and Technologists*, pp. 27–31.
5. At www.popcenter.org.
6. See, for example, http://www.hendonpub.com/publications/publicsafetyit/ (accessed July 15, 2010).
7. Philip Canter, "Using a Geographic Information System for Tactical Crime Analysis," in Victor Goldsmith, Philip G. McGuire, John H. Mollenkopf, and Timothy A. Ross (eds.), *Analyzing Crime Patterns: Frontiers of Practice* (Thousand Oaks, Calif.: Sage, 2000), pp. 3–10.
8. Timothy C. O'Shea and Keith Nicholls, *Crime Analysis in America: Findings and Recommendations* (Washington, D.C.: U.S. Department of Justice, Office of Community Oriented Policing Services, March 2003), p. 7.
9. Heath J. Grant and Karen J. Terry, *Law Enforcement in the 21st Century* (Boston, Mass.: Allyn & Bacon, 2005), pp. 329–330.
10. Ibid., p. 330.
11. U.S. Department of Justice, Office of Community Oriented Policing Services, *Law Enforcement Tech Guide: How to Plan, Purchase, and Manage Technology (Successfully!)* (Washington, D.C.: Author, 2002), p. 247.
12. U.S. Department of Justice, National Institute of Justice, *Crime Mapping and Analysis by Community*

Organizations in Hartford, Connecticut (Washington, DC: Author, March 2001), p. 1.

13. Donna Rogers, "Getting Crime Analysis on the Map," *Law Enforcement Technology* (November 1999): 76–79.

14. U.S. Department of Justice, National Institute of Justice, *Crime Mapping Research Center* (Washington, DC: Author, 2000), pp. 1–3.

15. Lois Pilant, "Computerized Crime Mapping," *Police Chief* (December 1997): 58.

16. U.S. Department of Justice, *Crime Mapping Research Center*, pp. 1–3; the CMRC Web site address is http://www.ojp.usdoj.gov/cmrc.

17. Pilant, "Computerized Crime Mapping," pp. 64–65.

18. Philip Canter, "Using a Geographic Information System for Tactical Crime Analysis," in Victor Goldsmith, Philip G. McGuire, John H. Mollenkopf, and Timothy A. Ross (eds.), *Analyzing Crime Patterns: Frontiers of Practice* (Thousand Oaks, Calif.: Sage, 2000), pp. 3–10.

19. Grant and Terry, *Law Enforcement in the 21st Century*, pp. 329–330.

20. Canter, "Using a Geographic Information System for Tactical Crime Analysis," p. 5.

21. Grant and Terry, *Law Enforcement in the 21st Century*, p. 331.

22. Ronald V. Clarke and John E. Eck, *Crime Analysis for Problem Solvers in 60 Small Steps* (Washington, D.C.: U.S. Department of Justice, Office of Community Oriented Policing Services, 2005).

23. Daniel DeLorenzi, Jon M. Shane, and Karen L. Amendola, "The CompStat Process: Managing Performance on the Pathway to Leadership," *The Police Chief* (September 2006), http://www.Theiacp.org/foundation/Foundation.htm (accessed July 6, 2009).

24. Heath B. Grant, and Karen J. Terry, *Law enforcement in the 21st Century* (Boston: Allyn & Bacon, 2005), pp. 329–330.

25. U.S. Department of Justice, Office of Justice Programs, Bureau of Justice Statistics, *Intelligence-Led /Policing: The New Intelligence Architecture* (Washington, D.C.: Author, 2005), p. 9.

26. Ibid., p. 3.

27. See U.S. Department of Justice, Office of Justice Programs, *National Criminal Intelligence Sharing Plan*, p. 6; http://www.fas.org/irp/agency/doj/ncisp.pdf (accessed December 7, 2009).

28. Eric Mills, "An Ounce of Prevention," *Law Enforcement Technology*, September 2009, pp. 60–64.

29. Ibid., p. 63.

30. Ibid., pp. 12–13.

31. Ibid., pp. 10–11.

32. U.S. Department of Justice, "Predictive Policing: A National Discussion," http://blogs.usdoj.gov/blog/archives/385 (accessed February 11, 2010); also see U.S. Department of Justice, National Institute of Justice, "Predictive Policing Symposium: Agenda," http://www.ojp.usdoj.gov/nij/topics/law-enforcement/predictive-policing/symposium/agenda.htm (accessed February 11, 2010).

33. U.S. Department of Justice, National Institute of Justice, "Predictive Policing Symposium: The Future of Prediction in Criminal Justice," http://www.ojp.usdoj.gov/nij/topics/law-enforcement/predictive-policing/symposium/future.htm (accessed February 17, 2010).

34. A. Onion, "Coordinates of a Killer: A Mathematical Method Can Help Investigators Locate Killers," http://www.abcnews.com (Accessed October 8, 2002).

35. Grant and Terry, *Law Enforcement in the 21st Century*, p. 340.

36. Dan Helms, "Closing the Barn Door: Police Counterterrorism After 9-11 from the Analyst's Perspective," *Crime Mapping News* 4 (Winter 2002):1–5.

37. Grant and Terry, *Law Enforcement in the 21st Century*, pp. 346–347.

38. Darrel W. Stephens, "IT Changes in Law Enforcement," in Ronald W. Glensor and Gerard R. Murphy (eds.), *Issues in IT: A Reader for the Busy Police Chief Executive* (Washington, D.C.: Police Executive Research Forum, 2005), pp. 7–29.

6

From Recruit to Chief
Changing the Agency Culture

KEY TERMS AND CONCEPTS

"Bombshell" technique	"Great" organizations	Recapturing officers' time
Change agent	Level 5 leader	Service orientation
First-line supervisor	Middle manager	Time management
Generational divide	"Moments of truth"	Value-laden leadership

LEARNING OBJECTIVES

As a result of reading this chapter, the student will:

- Have a foundation regarding the key element in COPPS: human resources
- Understand some of the key issues now involving human resources in policing: recruiting quality officers and the generational divide
- Know how a police organization can change from being "good" to "great"
- Understand what is meant by a "moment of truth" and how it relates to COPPS
- Recognize some pitfalls to, and methods of changing policing, and the role of key police leaders as change agents
- Understand how police agencies can capture time for their officers to engage in COPPS activities

Where there is no vision, a people perish.
—RALPH WALDO EMERSON

INTRODUCTION

Police agencies have a life and culture of their own. Powerful forces have a much stronger influence over how a department conducts its business than do managers of the department, courts, legislatures, politicians, and members of the community. At its root, the willingness to change is a fundamental requirement of community oriented policing and problem solving (COPPS); police agencies must modify their culture from top to bottom. This chapter addresses that agency imperative. Change is never easy, however, because there is so much uncertainty and, often, opposition accompanying it.

At its root, of course, a police agency's culture is determined by its *people*; therefore, this chapter gives considerable attention to several human-resources aspects of COPPS. We begin with a discussion of the need for strong values in our leaders, how police leaders can transform their organizations from being "good" to "great." Following those broader discussions of police organizations, we then look at several key issues involving individuals: confronting what are termed "moments of truth," recruiting quality people into police service, and the **generational divide**, the challenges posed by today's new generation of police employees. The chapter concludes with a summary, review questions, and several scenarios and activities that provide opportunities for you to "learn by doing."

Change *per se* in police organizations is then examined, beginning with a look at some lessons learned and how change must occur to accommodate COPPS. The roles of three key leaders in this process—chief executives (and their precarious political position as innovators), middle managers, and first-line supervisors—are then covered, including how sufficient time may be allocated for the latter to engage in problem-solving activities.

OUR MOST VALUABLE ASSET—HUMAN RESOURCES

Needed: Strong (and Value-Laden) Leadership

People are the backbone of every organization, and the importance of properly seeing to their hiring, training, and overall careers cannot be overstated. Countless books, articles, and speeches have been generated concerning personnel administration, and yet we still cannot seem to get it right. Certainly what is needed today is **value-laden leadership**.

According to Christopher Hayes, writing about the failings of American leadership during the past decade:

> Nearly every pillar institution in American society—whether it's General Motors, Congress, Wall Street, Major League Baseball, the Catholic Church or the mainstream media—has revealed itself to be corrupt, incompetent, or both. And at the root of these failures are the people who run these institutions. In exchange for their power, status and remuneration, they are supposed to make sure everything operates smoothly. But after a decade of scandals and catastrophes, that implicit social contract lies in ruins, replaced by mass skepticism, contempt and disillusionment.[1]

The common themes that underlie the failed performance of many of the country's leadership, Hayes believes, are the concentration of power and the erosion of transparency and accountability that extend throughout.[2] And the kinds of problems of which Hayes speaks do not even reach those of a sexual nature that have befallen many of our nation's political, business, and religious leadership.

Although the nation's police chief executives have escaped the "scandals and catastrophes" of which Hayes wrote, he lays bare problems that can easily reach beyond leaders' offices within the institutions of business, baseball, and religion. Certainly there is much to be learned from the crises of faith that have befallen many of our nation's leaders, and everyone who serves in a leadership capacity would do well to heed the lessons of their public—and often criminal—exposure.

Moving from a "Good" to a "Great" Police Organization

Certainly COPPS requires that the police organization be as innovative, efficient, and effective as it can be. In that vein, Jim Collins authored two books[3] that were the result of his organizational studies and looked at how organizations could move from being "good" to becoming "great."

First, regarding their leadership, Collins coined the term **"Level 5 leader"** to describe the highest level of executive capabilities. Level 5 executives' ambitions are directed first and foremost to the organization and its success, not to personal renown. Such leaders, Collins stressed, are "fanatically driven, infected with an incurable need to produce results."[4] They are also self-effacing, quiet, reserved, even shy.

Collins also uses a bus metaphor when talking about transforming from good to great:

> The executives who ignited the transformations . . . did not first figure out where to drive the bus and then get people to take it there. No, they *first* got the right people on the bus (and the wrong people off the bus) and *then* figured out where to drive it (emphasis his).[5]

Collins wrote, "The main point is not about assembling the right team—that's nothing new."[6] Rather, the main point is that great leaders assemble their teams *before* they decide where to go; the right people will be self-motivated. **"Great" organizations**, Collins found, also have a "culture of discipline" in which employees show extreme diligence and intensity in their thoughts and actions, always focusing on implementing the organizations mission, purpose, and goals.[7]

Therefore, people are not an organization's most important asset; rather, the *right* people are. Collins states that picking the right people and getting the wrong people off the bus are critical. "*By whatever means possible, personnel problems have to be confronted in an organization that aspires to greatness.*"[8]

Of course, Collins was not writing about the transition to COPPS and the inherent change in agency culture; however, his viewpoints are certainly apropos in this regard—particularly when considering that there are some people who will not be in the right seat on the COPPS bus, and there are younger officers waiting in the wings who are in need of the challenge and training involved with COPPS—and for the purpose of accepting the mantle of leadership in a COPPS organization when the current baby-boomers retire.

Certainly the kinds of issues and challenges discussed in this textbook—particularly in such areas as crime analysis, CompStat, intelligence-led policing, predictive policing, and technologies where higher levels of cognitive ability are necessary—demand that succession planning (discussed in Chapter 15, concerning the future development of police leadership) be part of the organizational fabric.

"Moments of Truth"

Jan Carlzon, former president of Scandinavian Airlines, wrote a book entitled **Moments of Truth,** in which he defined the moment of truth in business as follows: "Anytime a customer comes into contact with any aspect of a business, however remote, is an opportunity to form an impression."[9]

Moments of truth are anywhere that someone has an opportunity to make a lasting impact on others. Certainly such opportunities present themselves each day in policing, and are unequivocally a part of the fabric of COPPS. Every contact an officer makes with a citizen—from the way the officer looks in his or her uniform, to the tone of voice used—provides an opportunity for them to make a lasting impact for good or for bad.

Although most if not all officers probably understand that they can have such an impact, the Scottsdale, Arizona, Police Department (SPD) has taken the moment-of-truth concept to a higher level, realizing that, as one police executive stated, "Safe communities are developed and maintained through community partnerships. The public's willing cooperation to help prevent crime and disorder is the cornerstone of the agency's system of policing."[10]

Realizing that police leaders play the most critical role in changing an agency's culture and adopting a customer **service orientation**, an article in SPD's monthly employee newsletter explained the theory, history, and advantages of moments of truth. All employees were encouraged to submit for publication examples of employees proving enhanced customer service through moments of truth; meanwhile, command staff discussed and reinforced moments of truth with employees at squad briefings, manager meetings, and employee forums. Almost immediately, supervisors began to submit examples of positive moment of truth encounters through their chains of command to underscore personnel performance. Soon, employees at all levels and across all bureaus began to draw attention to the many examples of moments of truth carried out by their peers and manifested through enhanced customer service. Moments of truth are now part of the department's vernacular and culture. These published moments of truth can be accessed at: http://www.scottsdaleaz.gov/Police/about/Customer/MOT.asp.

Addressing a Front-End COPPS Problem: Recruiting Quality Officers

Certainly the **recruitment** of quality police officers is the key to the values and culture of any police organization and for the successful conduct of the COPPS strategy. Indeed, an inadequate supply of quality personnel would not bode well at all for the future of COPPS. Police recruitment issues are such a concern at present that a national meeting was recently convened to discuss these issues by the U.S. Department of Justice, the National Institute of Justice, and the RAND Corporation.

The current "cop crunch" is exacerbated in many cities by exploding growth, a competitive job market, natural catastrophes (e.g., Hurricane Katrina in New Orleans), and struggles to retain diversity.[11] Furthermore, this crunch comes at a time when today's police need a stronger focus on problem-solving skills, ability to collaborate with the community, and a greater capacity to use technology.[12] Adding to the problems are today's higher incidence of obesity, major debt, drug use, and criminal records that are found among potential recruits.[13]

This national meeting produced several recruiting measures that can be adopted, however, toward generating a satisfactory applicant pool:

- Have one leader in charge of the entire recruiting process, from marketing to testing to background investigation through academy training.
- Consider the academy dropout rate: Are recruiters signing up the most promising candidates for the academy?[14]
- Publicize hiring campaigns on business cards, use department vehicles as billboards, and make the agency Web sites more effective by emphasizing the positive reasons for joining rather than focusing on the challenges faced by police officers.

- Limit recruiting trips to those locations where candidates are likely to be found, such as areas with economic difficulties; out-of-town recruiting trips are generally not effective.[15]
- Look at the academy program to see whether something is hindering diversity and in effect "washing out" candidates, particularly those whose native language is not English.[16]
- Make the department's recruiting efforts focus on the positives of police work, such as job security, the satisfaction of public service, and superior pay and benefits; too often, they emphasize the challenges involved in becoming a police officer.[17]
- Use bonuses for officers who refer candidates to the academy.
- Include an online sample test on the agency Web site to give recruits an idea of the types of questions they will be facing.
- Allow other standardized tests such as the Armed Services Vocational Aptitude Battery to substitute for the police department's own written test; this will speed the acceptance process.[18]

The Oakland, California, Police Department may well represent the best example of a city that rebounded from hard times (see Exhibit 6–1).

Another Looming Challenge: Arrival of the Millennials

Today's new generation of police officers—which, as we will see, is much different from the current generation of veteran officers—when confronted with the need to find the definition of, say, a terroristic threat, is as likely to grab his computer and consult its search engine as he or she is to flip through many pages of state statute books. And if asked what time of day it is, he or she is as likely as not to remove a cell phone from its holster and obtain the time from its display screen. Such is the world of the coming "new generation" of police officers.

Here are some cold, hard facts. Half of the baby boomers will be eligible to retire within the next decade. This will produce the largest workplace shortage in U.S. history. The 70 million-strong

---

| Exhibit 6–1 | Oakland Rebounds: Hiring for Community Needs |

The Oakland, California, Police Department (OPD), like many agencies, experienced hiring freezes, ultimately resulting in an 8 percent reduction in force. Oakland voters passed legislation that provided about $19 million for community policing and other public-safety initiatives over a 10-year period; OPD was to hire more than 60 new officers. To attract new candidates, OPD launched a 1 million dollar advertising campaign featuring billboards and other saturation advertising; it streamlined its hiring process so that a candidate could pass the background check within three weeks—helping the department hire promising candidates who were considering other agencies. OPD sent applicants e-mails concerning the status of their applications, and accepted applications from other academies. To foster retention, OPD established a new shift schedule with seven 12-hour shifts over a two-week period, increased pay 20 percent, added a 4.5 percent increase for those officers meeting standards and training qualifications, and offered another 4.5 percent for officers with a bachelor's degree.

Source: Adapted from Jeremy M. Wilson and Clifford A. Grammich, *Police Recruitment and Retention in the Contemporary Urban Environment: A National Discussion of Personnel Experiences and Promising Practices from the Front Lines* (Santa Monica, CA: RAND Corporation, 2009), pp. 11–12.

Millennial generation, whose members were born between 1977 and 1994, will take the place of the boomers. Millennials will have a profound impact on the workplace.[19]

Being unknown cultural territory, they will of course change the face of policing, and many observers have concerns about what differences will be wrought by the younger generation. As one observer stated:

> Today's young men and women seem more concerned with outside interests than in a career or profession. Overtime is a foreign word, and do not even think of interfering with their days off. They do not know the depth of dedication or the experiences of veteran officers. They understand technology better than we do and constantly ask questions about job performance. Today's officers seek motive in addition to fact.[20]

This same observer struck a more positive tone, however, in noting that there are means by which these traits—that often fly in the face of veteran officers and administrators—can be assuaged. For example, it is recommended that the veterans pass along knowledge and experiences if the young officer is struggling with a work issue, be certain that they understand orders that are given them, and model appropriate behavior with them. Most veteran officers remember times when, as a young employee, a more senior officer mentored them, and served as a confidant and even a hero.[21]

Certainly this is sage advice—particularly at this point in time, with many baby boomers now retiring and so-called Gen Xers (persons born after born between 1976 and 1980) looking to retire within the next decade or so. Law enforcement must understand these new generations, including their work ethic and workplace needs—as well as the fact that the traditional paramilitary, chain-of-command structure may well cause friction with them—many of whom are quicker to challenge the status quo and higher authority than earlier generations. Police agencies looking to recruit younger-generation employees may be well-advised to examine their policies and structure in light of these differences.

Exhibit 6–2 discussed one agency's approach to its personnel concerns as it transitioned to COPPS.

CHANGE IN POLICE ORGANIZATIONS

As shown in Exhibit 6–2, organizational change can and must occur when an organization adopts new ideas or behaviors. Any change in the organization involves an attempt to persuade employees to change their behavior and their relationships with one another. Therefore, it is not surprising that most people find change uncomfortable. Studies on change in organizations have shown that only about 10 percent of the people in most organizations will actively embrace change; approximately 80 percent will wait to be convinced or wait until the change is unavoidable, and the remaining 10 percent will actively resist change. For these people, change is very upsetting; they may even seek to subvert or sabotage the process.[22]

Lessons Learned

Change is difficult for any organization and is particularly so for police departments, which are paramilitary, bureaucratic, and somewhat socially isolated from the community. How did change come about in those many agencies that have adopted COPPS?

A general transition process appears to have emerged: First, the agencies recognized that traditional approaches did not succeed; second was a change in attitude about the functions of

| Exhibit 6–2 | Hayward, California: Hiring, Training, and Evaluation of Personnel |

After making the decision to change its policing philosophy, a systems change was required that would greatly affect personnel. Therefore, the initial focus was on personnel systems such as recruiting, hiring, training, performance appraisals, and promotability guidelines. To transform the recruiting and hiring processes, the Hayward, California, Personnel Department and Police Department began exploring the following three questions:

1. Overall, what type of candidate, possessing what types of skills, should be recruited?
2. What specific knowledge, skills, and abilities reflect the COPPS philosophy—particularly regarding problem-solving abilities and sensitivity to community needs?
3. How can these attributes best be identified in the initial screening process?

The department also analyzed the city's demographics, finding that it had a diverse ethnic composition. To promote cultural diversity and sensitivity to the needs of the community, a psychologist was employed to develop a profile of an effective COPPS officer in Hayward. These considerations became an integral part of the department's hiring process.

Next the training and performance evaluation systems were reappraised. All personnel, both sworn and civilian, had to receive COPPS training to provide a clear and thorough understanding of the history, philosophy, and transition to COPPS. The department's initial training was directed at management and supervisory personnel and was designed to assist these employees in accomplishing the department's goals of reinforcing COPPS values, modifying the existing police culture, strategically transitioning the organization from traditional policing to the new philosophy, and focusing on customer relations. Rank-and-file officers were given 40-hour blocks of instruction.

Performance and reward practices for personnel were modified to reflect the new criteria. Emphasizing quality over quantity (e.g., arrest statistics, number of calls for service, response times), new criteria included an assessment of how well a call for service was handled and what type of problem-solving approach was used to reach a solution for the problem. Other mechanisms were developed to broadcast and communicate successes, including supervisors' logs, a COPPS newsletter, and city-wide recognition of extraordinary customer service efforts.

The department's promotional process was also retooled; a new phase was added to the department's promotional test—the "promotability" phase—to evaluate the candidate's decision-making abilities, analytical skills, communication skills, interpersonal skills, and professional contributions.

Source: Adapted from Joseph E. Brann and Suzanne Whalley, "COPPS: The Transformation of Police Organizations," in California Department of Justice, Attorney General's Office, Crime Prevention Center, *COPPS: Community Oriented Policing and Problem Solving* (Sacramento, Calif.: Author, 1992), p. 72.

administrators, line personnel, and citizens; third, community assessments were performed to identify new police responsibilities; fourth, new organizational and operational approaches were conceived to meet the newly defined police responsibilities; and fifth, the community was enlisted to work cooperatively with the police to achieve the desired results.[23]

Decentralized decision making is key to the success of COPPS.
Fort Lauderdale, Florida, Police Department.

Lessons were also learned about the political environment in which police administrators managed change and included the following eight points:

1. There must be a stimulus for change. A leader must have a vision, be willing to take the first step in challenging the status quo, involve people at all levels, and maintain that commitment (reallocating resources, amending policies and procedures, experimenting with new ideas).
2. Change must be grounded in logical and defensible criteria as opposed to effecting change just to "shake things up" in the organization.
3. There must be sufficient time for experimentation, evaluation, and fine-tuning of new ideas.
4. Major change might require a generation; people tend to be impatient, but resocialization of employees and citizens is a long-term endeavor requiring patience and stamina.
5. Not everyone will buy into new ideas.
6. Flexibility in a view of change is necessary. Many ideas are "losers," so a leader must maintain the freedom to fail, even though in U.S. culture success is often mandated.
7. Change carries risks, and change agents might be placed on the hot seat to explain new endeavors; in short, a leader's political neck may be on the line.
8. Organizational personnel evaluation systems must measure and reward effective involvement in change. Benefits do not have to be monetary, but they can include such things as positive reinforcement, creative freedom, and awards or commendations.

"Bombshell" Technique

Police organizations develop considerable inertia and can develop a resistance to change. Having a strong personal commitment to the values with which they have "grown up" in the organization, patrol officers may find any hint of proposed change in the department extremely threatening.

Therefore, the chief executive who simply announces that COPPS is now the order of the day—the **"bombshell" technique**—without a carefully designed plan for implementing that change is in danger of "losing traction" and of throwing the entire force into confusion. In addition, the chief executive confronts a host of difficult issues: What structural changes, if any, are needed? How do we get the people on the beat to behave differently? What should we tell the public, and when? How fast can we bring about this change? Do we have enough external support?[24]

Change in Organizational Values

A related subject is that of values in police organizations. All organizations have values, the beliefs that guide an organization and the behavior of its employees.[25] Police departments are powerfully influenced by their values, and policing styles reflect a department's values.

COPPS reflects a set of values rather than a technical orientation toward the police function. There is a service orientation, which means that citizens are to be treated with respect at all times. When riding in patrol vehicles, supervisors and managers must listen for the "talk of the department" to determine whether values expressed by officers reflect those of the department.

Also, values are no longer hidden but serve as the basis for citizen understanding of the police function, judgments of police success, and employee understanding of what the police agency seeks to achieve.[26] Values are a guidepost by which the agency will provide service to the community and a means by which the community can evaluate the agency.

TRANSITIONING TO COPPS

Potential for Resistance and Conflict

As Fresno, California, Police Chief Jerry Dyer has observed, managing change in police agencies is not working as it should, for a variety of reasons: Officers and labor unions block change by claiming memorandum of agreement violations, filing grievances, utilizing their political influence with council members, or making calls to local news media outlets. Such obstacles may prevent many police leaders from seeking change in their organizations.[27]

In the many jurisdictions where COPPS has been implemented and is flourishing and succeeding, however, the traditional orthodoxy of policing, rooted in military command and scientific management theory, had to be changed. In short, the traditional orthodoxy became "taboo."[28] This included management style, performance measures (as one author put it, "Bean-counting performance measures have little meaning in such a system"[29]), and disciplinary measures.[30] The new required leadership style meant (1) a shift from telling and controlling employees to helping them develop their skills and abilities; (2) listening to the customers in new and more open ways; (3) solving problems, not just reacting to incidents; (4) trying new things and experimenting, realizing that risk taking and honest mistakes must be tolerated to encourage creativity and achieve innovation; and (5) avoiding, whenever possible, the use of coercive power to effect change.[31]

A Washington State University graduate student determined that there were three significant reactions by Spokane officers to the shift to community policing[32]:

1. *Meaning.* Some officers saw community policing as a way of validating who they were, allowing them to do the kind of policing they believed they should have been doing all along.

2. *Resistance.* Community policing, being a philosophy rather than a program, made it more difficult for management to describe, so some officers who were said to be resistant were merely trying to determine what community policing meant in relation to how they were currently doing their jobs.

3. *Sabotage.* Some employees went beyond resistance, engaging in sabotage and being obstructionist; some supervisors would wait until a ranking officer was out of earshot and then proceed to tell their staff "how it's really going to be."

"We're Too Busy to Change"

It is not uncommon for consultants to go into police agencies to assist in implementing or training COPPS and be told, "We're too busy for community policing and problem solving." As William Geller and Guy Swanger noted, it may be true in some organizations that people are too busy to change. They said:

> [This may be the case] if the senior leadership insists that middle managers continue doing all the old things they shouldn't be doing plus all the new things they should. The classic problem here is being too busy bailing out the boat to fix the hole in the hull.[33]

Indeed, preoccupation with the task at hand prevents people from pausing to reflect critically on whether what they are doing has any value. As Price Pritchett and Ron Pound observed, "Ditch those duties that don't count much, even if you can do them magnificently well."[34] Beliefs that police are too busy to change can be compounded by fears that COPPS will only intensify the workload. But when the community is an organized, active partner in problem solving, the problem-solving process is not as labor-intensive for the police as some have asserted.[35]

ROLES OF KEY LEADERS

Earlier in this chapter, we discussed briefly the roles of chief executives, middle managers, and first-line supervisors in the implementation of COPPS. Here we briefly examine their respective roles in the change process.

Chief Executives

Of course, the police chief executive is ultimately responsible for all of the facets of COPPS, from implementation to training to evaluation. Therefore, what is needed are chief executives who are willing to do things that have not been done before, or as one writer put it, "risk takers and boat rockers within a culture where daily exposure to life-or-death situations makes officers natural conservators of the status quo."[36] These are chief executives who become committed to getting the police and neighborhoods to work together to attack the roots of crime. For them, "Standing still is not only insufficient . . . it is going backwards."[37]

Therefore, a police executive must be a viable **change agent**. In any hierarchy, the person at the top is responsible for setting both the policy and tone of the organization. Within a police agency, the chief or sheriff has the ultimate power to make change, particularly one as substantive as COPPS. The chief executive must be both visible and credible and must create a climate conducive to change. Under COPPS, chief executives must focus on the vision, values, mission, and long-term goals of policing in order to create an organizational environment that enables officers, government officials, and community members to work together. By building consensus, they can establish programs, develop timelines, and set priorities. They should honor the good

COPPS is not soft on crime—and first-line supervisors are key to its success.

Courtesy Washoe County, Nevada, Sheriff's Office.

work done in the past but exhibit a sense of urgency about implementing change while involving people from the community and the department in all stages of the transition. The chief executive's roles and responsibilities during the change to COPPS include the following:

- Articulating a clear vision to the organization
- Understanding and accepting the depth of change and time required to implement COPPS
- Assembling a management team that is committed to translating the new vision into action
- Being committed to removing bureaucratic obstacles whenever possible

Many police organizations boast talented and creative chief executives who, when participating in the change process, will assist in effecting change that is beneficial and lasting. James Q. Wilson put it this way:

> The police profession today is the intellectual leadership of the criminal justice profession in the United States. The police are in the lead. They're showing the world how things might better be done.[38]

Middle Managers

Middle managers—lieutenants and captains—also play a crucial role in the operation of a COPPS philosophy. The COPPS emphasis on problem-solving necessitates that middle managers draw on their familiarity with the bureaucracy to secure, maintain, and use authority to empower subordinates, helping officers to actively and creatively confront and resolve issues, sometimes using unconventional approaches on a trial-and-error basis.

There are many really significant contributions middle managers can make to the changing culture of the agency to embrace and sustain COPPS. First, they must build on the strengths of their subordinates, capitalizing on their training and competence.[39] They do so by treating people as individuals and creating talented teams.[40] They must "cheerlead," encouraging supervisors and patrol officers to actually solve the problems they are confronting.[41] It is also imperative that middle managers *not* believe they are serving the chief executive's best interests by preserving the status quo. The lieutenants are the gatekeepers and must develop the system, resources, and support mechanisms to ensure that the officers, detectives, and supervisors can perform to achieve the best results. The officers and supervisors cannot perform without the necessary equipment, resources, and reinforcement.[42]

Middle managers, like their subordinates, must be allowed the freedom to make mistakes—and good middle managers protect their subordinates from organizational and political recrimination and scapegoating when things go wrong. Put another way, middle managers cannot stand idly by while their people are led to the guillotine, and they must protect their officers from the political effects of legitimate failure.[43] They must not allow their problem-solving officers to revert to traditional methods. They must be diplomats and facilitators, using a lot more persuading and negotiating (toward win-win solutions) than they did under the traditional "my way or the highway" management style.

The roles and responsibilities of middle managers during the change to COPPS include the following:

- Assuming responsibility for strategic planning
- Eliminating red tape and bottlenecks that impede the work of officers and supervisors
- Conducting regular meetings with subordinates to discuss plans, activities, and results
- Assessing COPPS efforts in a continuous manner

The position of middle managers in a COPPS environment was well described by Kelling and Bratton:

> The idea that mid-managers are spoilers, that they thwart project or strategic innovation, has some basis in fact. Mid-managers improperly directed can significantly impede innovation. Yet, ample evidence exists that when a clear vision of the business of the organization is put forward, when mid-managers are included in planning, when their legitimate self-interests are acknowledged, and when they are properly trained, mid-managers can be the leading edge of innovation and creativity.[44]

First-Line Supervisors

It is widely held that the most challenging aspect of changing the culture of a police agency lies in changing the attitudes and beliefs of **first-line supervisors**. The influence of first-line supervisors is so strong that their role warrants special attention.

The primary contact of street officers with their organization is through their sergeant, so the quality of an officer's daily life is often dependent on his or her immediate supervisor. Most officers do not believe their sergeants are sources of guidance and direction but rather are authority figures to be satisfied (by numbers of arrests and citations, manner in which reports are completed, officer's ability to avoid citizen complaints, and so on). There is just cause for the reluctance of first-line supervisors to avoid change. Herman Goldstein stated it this way:

> Changing the operating philosophy of rank-and-file officers is easier than altering a first-line supervisor's perspective of his or her job, because the work of a sergeant is greatly simplified by the traditional form of policing. The more routinized the work, the easier it is for the sergeant to check. The more emphasis placed on rank and the

| Exhibit 6–3 | Characteristics of a Good Problem-Oriented Supervisor |

1. Allowing subordinates freedom to experiment with new approaches.
2. Insisting on good, accurate analyses of problems.
3. Granting flexibility in work schedules when requests are appropriate.
4. Allowing subordinates to make most contacts directly and paving the way when they are having trouble getting cooperation.
5. Protecting subordinates from pressures within the department to revert to traditional methods.
6. Running interference for subordinates to secure resources, protect them from criticism, and so forth.
7. Knowing what problems subordinates are working on and whether the problems are real.
8. Knowing subordinates' beats and important citizens in it, and expecting subordinates to know it even better.
9. Coaching subordinates through the process, giving advice, helping them manage their time.
10. Monitoring subordinates' progress and, as necessary, prodding them along or slowing them down.
11. Supporting subordinates even if their strategies fail, so long as something useful is learned in the process and the process was well thought through.
12. Managing problem-solving efforts over a long period of time; not allowing efforts to die simply because they get sidetracked by competing demands for time and attention.
13. Giving credit to subordinates and letting others know about their good work.
14. Allowing subordinates to talk with visitors or at conferences about their work.
15. Identifying new resources and contacts for subordinates and making them check them out.
16. Stressing cooperation, coordination, and communication within the unit and outside it.
17. Coordinating efforts across shifts, beats, and outside units and agencies.
18. Realizing that this style of policing cannot simply be ordered; officers and detectives must come to believe in it.

Source: Police Executive Research Forum, "Supervising Problem-Solving" (Washington, D.C.: Author, training outline, 1990).

symbols of position, the easier it is for the sergeant to rely on authority—rather than intellect and personal skills—to carry out [his or her] duties. . . . [S]ergeants are usually appalled by descriptions of the freedom and independence suggested in problem oriented policing for rank-and-file officers. The concept can be very threatening to them. This . . . can create an enormous block to implementation.[45]

Supervisors must be convinced that COPPS makes good sense in today's environment, and they should possess the characteristics of a good problem-oriented supervisor; see Exhibit 6–3.

The roles and responsibilities of first-line supervisors during a change to COPPS include the following:

- Understanding and practicing problem solving
- Managing time, staff, and resources

- Encouraging teamwork
- Helping officers to mobilize stakeholders
- Tracking and managing officers' problem solving
- Providing officers with ongoing feedback and support

Another matter implicating police supervisory personnel concerns the amount of time required for patrol officers to engage in problem-solving activities. We examine that issue next.

Ways to "Recapture Officers' Time" for Problem Solving

One of the ongoing controversies with respect to COPPS—as noted in the "We're Too Busy to Change" section earlier—concerns whether police officers can garner the time required to engage in problem-solving activities. On the one hand, officers complain that they are going from call to call and have little time for anything else; on the other hand, administrators say there is plenty of time for problem solving because calls account for only 50 to 60 percent of an officer's time. The following four methods of **time management** can be used to overcome the problem of finding time for problem solving while still handling calls effectively:

1. *Allow units to perform problem-solving assignments as self-initiated activities.* Under this approach, a unit would contact the dispatcher and go out of service for a problem-solving assignment. The unit would be interrupted only for an emergency call in its area of responsibility; otherwise, the dispatcher would hold nonemergency calls until the unit becomes available or send a unit from an adjacent area after holding the call for a predetermined amount of time.
2. *Schedule one or two units to devote a predetermined part of their shift to problem solving.* As an example, a supervisor could designate one or two units each day to devote the first half of their shift or even only one hour to problem solving. Their calls would be handled by other units so that they have an uninterrupted block of time for problems. Of course, this approach means that the other units will be busier. The trade-off is that problem solving gets done and the supervisor can rotate the units designated for these activities.
3. *Take more reports over the telephone.* Many departments take certain nonemergency complaints by telephone rather than dispatch a patrol unit. The information about the incident is recorded on a department report form and entered in the department's information system as an incident or crime. The average telephone report taker can process four times as many report calls per hour compared to a field unit. The department might increase the types of calls handled by telephone, or the staffing for a telephone report unit can be increased to cover more hours of the day.
4. *Review the department policy on assist units.* In some departments, several units show up at the scene of a call even though they are not needed. Some units assist out of boredom or curiosity. The units may initiate themselves out of service to assist, or the dispatcher may send several units to the scene. This problem is particularly acute with alarm calls. Many departments have a policy of dispatching two or more units to alarms, even when the source has a long history of false alarms. A department should undergo a detailed study on the types of calls for which assist units are actually appearing, with the aim of reducing the number of assists and discouraging officers from assisting other units unless it is necessary.

As a more general approach, a department should review its patrol plan to determine whether units are fielded in proportion to workload. Time between calls is a function not only of the number of incoming calls but also of the number of units in the field. More units result in more time between calls.

Indeed, we can calculate the number of units needed to ensure that the time between calls averages, for example, 35 minutes. A department may also want to consider changes in officer schedules to facilitate overlapping during busy times of the day; however, adjustments within a shift may be the more effective approach. Delaying response time to calls for service can also provide more time for officers. For example, by refining the manner in which 911 calls are dispatched in non-life-threatening cases, responses may be significantly reduced annually.[46]

Response time research implied that rapid responses were not needed for most calls. Furthermore, dispatchers can advise citizens of an officer's arrival time. Slower police responses to nonemergency calls has been found satisfactory to citizens if dispatchers tell citizens an officer might not arrive right away. Managers have also garnered more time for officers by having nonsworn employees handle noncrime incidents.[47] Time between calls is an important, but frequently overlooked, element of any problem-solving strategy. The overall aim should be to provide officers with uninterrupted amounts of time for problem-solving assignments. There are many ways to accomplish this aim, but they require a concerted planning effort by the department.

Exhibit 6–4 shows the 15-step exercise developed for police managers needing to engage in **recapturing officers' time** while working in a problem-solving framework. If during the recapturing time exercise a police manager finds potential ways to effectively solve problems and recapture time lost to repetitive incidents, then problem-oriented policing may be a smart approach.

Exhibit 6–4   A 15-Step Exercise for Recapturing Officers' Time

1. Assemble a group of patrol officers and emergency communications center personnel representing each shift.
2. Have each of them write down three to five locations where the police respond regularly to deal with the same general problem and people repeatedly.
3. Determine the average number of responses to those locations per month and approximately how long the problem has existed.
4. Determine the average number of officers who respond each time to those incidents.
5. Determine the average length of time involved in handling the incidents.
6. Using the information from 3, 4, and 5, determine the total number of staff hours devoted to each of these problem locations. Do this for the week, month, and year.
7. Identify all the key players that either participate in or are affected by the problem—all direct and indirect participants and groups such as the complaining parties, victims, witnesses, property owners and managers, and bystanders.
8. Through a roundtable discussion, decide what it is about the particular location that allows or encourages the problem to exist and continue.
9. Develop a list of things that have been done in the past to try to deal with the problem, and a candid assessment of why each has not worked.
10. In a free-flowing brainstorming session, develop as many traditional and nontraditional solutions to the problem as possible. Try to include alternative sources like other government and private agencies that could be involved in the solution. Encourage creative thinking and risk taking.

11. After you have completed the brainstorming session, consider which of those solutions are (a) illegal, (b) immoral, (c) impractical, (d) unrealistic, or (e) not affordable.
12. Eliminate all those that fall in categories a and b.
13. For those that fall in categories, c, d, and e, figure out if those reasons are because you are thinking in conventional terms like "We've never done it this way," "It won't work," "It can't be done." If you are satisfied that those solutions truly are impractical, unrealistic, or not affordable, then eliminate them, too. If there is a glimmer of hope that some may have merit with just a little different thinking or approach, then leave them.
14. For each remaining possible solution, list what would have to be done and who would have to be involved to make it happen. Which of those solutions and actions could be implemented relatively soon and with a minimum of difficulty?
15. If the solution were successful, consider the productive things officers could do with the time that would be recaptured from not having to deal with the problem anymore.

Source: Jerald R. Vaughn, *Community Oriented Policing: You Can Make It Happen* (Clearwater, Fla.: National Law Enforcement Leadership Institute, no date), pp. 6–7. Used with permission.

FEDERAL GUIDANCE. This issue of time for COPPS activities is of such importance that the federal Office of Community Oriented Policing Services recently developed a guidebook to show agencies ways and means of freeing up officer time for COPPS functions; this 100-page guide-book—which discusses such topics as using call intake strategies, managing call responses, and collecting and analyzing call data—should be a part of the COPPS agency's "toolbox" for sustaining these efforts. It discusses in detail all the time-related subjects we have mentioned in this chapter section.[48]

Summary

This chapter has been about police personnel and change. Both of these aspects of policing can pose serious challenges, as we have seen. Certainly the work of policing is made much more difficult today when one considers the challenges involved with developing future leaders, recruiting new officers, and coping with a new generation of employees whose wants and abilities are quite different from those of earlier generations.

Change itself can be quite difficult to accomplish in police organizations, as we have seen—especially those police agencies with the traditional entrenched culture and management styles. The chapter pointed out the major roles played by leaders at all levels in effecting change.

This chapter has underscored the importance and means of changing the culture of the police agency, from recruit to chief, to accommodate the new philosophy and the operation of COPPS. Also called for is a requisite radical change in the way the police organization views itself, hones its values, and conducts its affairs. The chief executive must be a risk taker, and all employees, sworn and civilian, must believe that change is needed within the organization, if COPPS is to succeed. This modified approach to policing is also required in the view and latitude given to the middle managers and first-line supervisors and especially to the very important problem-solving street officer. We also emphasized the need to examine—and probably shift—the organization's means for recruiting people as police problem solvers.

Items for Review

1. Describe some of the key issues now involved in recruiting quality officers.
2. What is the generational divide, and why could it be problematical for policing in the future?
3. How can a police organization change from being "good" to "great," according to Collins?
4. What is meant by a "moment of truth," and how can it relate to COPPS?
5. Describe why change must occur within police organizations in order to accommodate COPPS, and review some of the common forms of potential resistance to such change.
6. How might police agencies recapture time for their officers to engage in COPPS activities?
7. Explain the roles of chief executives, middle managers, and first-line supervisors as change agents.

Learn by Doing

1. Assume that you are part of a classroom group that is studying police administration, and you are to make a five-minute presentation on ways of assisting a "good" police organization in becoming "great." What would be the major points of your presentation, according to Collins?
2. You are instructing your police department's Police Reserves unit on the basic organizational structure of your agency. One of the officers states that he heard a regular officer complain that "We're so busy going call to call, we don't have time to do community policing and problem solving." What is your reply? (Include in your response the roles of key leaders in transitioning and maintaining COPPS, as well as how first-line supervisors can help officers recapture their time and engage in problem solving.)

Notes

1. Christopher Hayes, "The Twilight of the Elites: Why We Have Entered the Post-Trust Era," *Time*, March 22, 2010, p. 56.
2. Ibid.
3. Jim Collins, *Good to Great: Why Some Companies Make the Leap...And Others Don't* (New York: HarperCollins, 2001); Jim Collins, *Good to Great and the Social Sectors: A Monograph to Accompany Good to Great* (New York: HarperCollins, 2005).
4. Quoted in Chuck Wexler, Mary Ann Wycoff, and Craig Fischer, *Good to Great: Application of Business Management Principles in the Public Sector* (Washington, D.C.: Office of Community Oriented Policing Services and the Police Executive Research Forum, 2007), p. 5.
5. Ibid., p. 6.
6. Ibid.
7. Ibid., p. 22.
8. Ibid.
9. *Moments of Truth: New Strategies for Today's Customer-Driven Economy* (New York: Ballinger, 1987), p. 24.
10. Sean Duggan, "Moments of Truth in Policing," June 2010, http://www.policechiefmagazine.org/magazine/ index.cfm?fuseaction=display&article_id=2114&iss ue_id=62010 (Accessed July 14, 2010).
11. Jeremy M. Wilson and Clifford A. Grammich, *Police Recruitment and Retention in the Contemporary Urban Environment: A National Discussion of Personnel Experiences and Promising Practices from the Front Lines* (Santa Monica, CA: RAND Corporation, 2009), p. 5; also available at: http:// www.rand.org/pubs/conf_proceedings/2009/RAND_ CF261.pdf (Accessed July 14, 2010).
12. Ibid., p. 2.
13. Stephanie Slahor, "RAND Study Suggests Strategies to Address Recruiting Shortage," *Law and Order*, December 8, 2008, p. 32.
14. Ibid., p. 18.
15. Ibid., pp. 18–19.
16. Ibid.
17. Slahor, "RAND Study Suggests Strategies to Address Recruiting Shortage," pp. 32–38.
18. Wilson and Grammich, *Police Recruitment and Retention in the Contemporary Urban Environment*, p. 33.
19. James Uhl, "Mentoring: Nourishing the Organizational Culture," *The Police Chief*, June 2010,

pp. 66–72, http://www.policechiefmagazine.org/magazine/index.cfm?fuseaction=display_arch&article_id=2115&issue_id=62010 (Accessed July 20, 2010)

20. Tom Saprony, "Legacy: Leaving Our Best Behind," *The Associate*, FBI National Academy Associates, January/February 2008, p. 27.

21. Ibid., p. 28.

22. Community Policing Consortium, *Curricula: Module Four: Managing Organizational Change* (Washington, D.C.: Author, August 2000), pp. 4–5.

23. David L. Carter, "Community Police and Political Posturing: Playing the Game." Policy paper for the Regional Community Policing Training Institute, Wichita State University, Wichita, Kansas, 2000.

24. Malcolm K. Sparrow, "Implementing Community Policing," *Perspectives on Policing* 9 (November 1988):1–2.

25. Thomas J. Peters and Robert H. Waterman Jr., *In Search of Excellence* (New York: Harper & Row, 1983), p. 15.

26. Robert Wasserman and Mark H. Moore, "Values in Policing" (Washington, D.C.: U.S. Department of Justice, National Institute of Justice, November 1988), pp. 6–7.

27. Jerry Dyer and Keith Foster, "Managing Change: Reorganizing and Building Community Trust," in symposium paper "Risk Management Issues in Law Enforcement," http://www.riskinstitute.org (Accessed May 28, 2003).

28. Mark H. Moore and Darrel W. Stephens, *Beyond Command and Control: The Strategic Management of Police Departments* (Washington, D.C.: Police Executive Research Forum, 1991), pp. 1, 3–4.

29. Gordon Witkin and Dan McGraw, "Beyond 'Just the Facts, Ma'am,'" *U.S. News & World Report* (August 2, 1993):29.

30. Malcolm K. Sparrow, Mark H. Moore, and David M. Kennedy, *Beyond 911: A New Era for Policing* (New York: Basic Books, 1990), p. 149.

31. California Department of Justice, Attorney General's Office, Crime Prevention Center, *COPPS: Community Oriented Policing and Problem Solving* (Sacramento, Calif.: Author, November 1992), pp. 67–68.

32. Lunell Haught, "Meaning, Resistance, and Sabotage—Elements of a Police Culture," *Community Policing Exchange* (May/June 1998):7.

33. William A. Geller and Guy Swanger, *Managing Innovation in Policing: The Untapped Potential of the Middle Manager* (Washington, D.C.: Police Executive Research Forum, 1995), p. 41.

34. Price Pritchett and Ron Pound, *A Survival Guide to the Stress of Organizational Change* (Dallas, Tex.: Pritchett and Associates, 1995), p. 12.

35. Warren Friedman, "The Community Role in Community Policing," in Dennis P. Rosenbaum (ed.), *The Challenge of Community Policing: Testing the Promises* (Thousand Oaks, Calif.: Sage, 1994), p. 268.

36. Mike Tharp and Dorian Friedman, "New Cops on the Block," *U.S. News & World Report* (August 2, 1993):23.

37. Ibid., p. 24.

38. James Q. Wilson, "Six Things Police Leaders Can Do About Juvenile Crime," *Subject to Debate* (September/October 1997):1.

39. Geller and Swanger, *Managing Innovation in Policing*, p. 105.

40. Ibid., p. 131.

41. Ibid., p. 109.

42. Ibid., p. 112.

43. Ibid., pp. 137–138.

44. George L. Kelling and William J. Bratton, "Implementing Community Policing: The Administrative Problem," *Perspectives on Policing* 17 (1993):11.

45. Goldstein, *Problem-Oriented Policing*, p. 29.

46. Lee P. Brown, "Community Policing: Bring the Community into the Battle Against Crime." Speech at the 19th Annual Lehman Lecture Series, Long Island University, Brookville, New York, March 11, 1992.

47. John Eck and William Spelman, "A Problem-Oriented Approach to Police Service Delivery," in Dennis Jay Kenney (ed.), *Police and Policing: Contemporary Issues* (New York: Praeger, 1989), pp. 95–111.

48. U.S. Department of Justice, Office of Community Oriented Policing Services, *Call Management and Community Policing: A Guidebook for Law Enforcement* (Washington, D.C.: Author, February 2003).

7

Planning and Implementation
Translating Ideas into Action

KEY TERMS AND CONCEPTS

Decentralized services
Economic effects
Elected officials (and COPPS)
Environmental scanning
Force field analysis

Implementation
Investigations (in COPPS context)
Needs assessment
Planning cycle

Planning document
Strategic planning
Strategic thinking

LEARNING OBJECTIVES

As a result of reading this chapter, the student will:

- Know the primary elements of strategic thinking and strategic planning, and why they are important for today's police executives.

- Understand what is involved in a planning cycle, an environmental scanning exercise, and a needs assessment.

- Comprehend the roles of chief executives, middle managers, first-line supervisors, detectives, and patrol officers in the planning and implementation of COPPS.

- Be able to review several possible obstacles that can militate against, and undermine, the implementation of COPPS.

- Be able to delineate some of the major considerations that come into play when one is assigned to develop a plan for transitioning your police agency to COPPS.

- Delineate some of the major considerations that would come into play if you were to be assigned to address a major problem solving project.

- Be able to explain Lewin's force field analysis, and how it functions in anticipating and planning for resistance to change.

*Alice: Cheshire Puss, would you tell me, please, which way I
ought to go from here?*

> *Cheshire Cat: That depends a good deal on where you want to get to.*
>
> *Alice: I don't much care where . . .*
>
> *Cheshire Cat: Then it doesn't matter which way you go.*
>
> —LEWIS CARROLL, *ALICE'S ADVENTURES IN WONDERLAND (1865)*, CHAPTER 6

INTRODUCTION

Having identified in the previous chapters the core components of and tools for analysis for community oriented policing and problem solving (COPPS), we now look at how to strategically plan for and implement this concept. Because we are often an instant-gratification, "plan ahead through next Friday" oriented society, this chapter will begin with a look at the general need for strategic thinking and planning, particularly as they concern police executives and their organizations. Then we shift to the implementation of COPPS per se, considering four of that function's principal components: leadership and administration, human resources, field operations, and external relations. We then review several general obstacles to implementation and by delineating 10 ways that COPPS can be undermined. The chapter concludes with what we hope will provide the reader with a hands-on, real-world flavor. The reader is invited to consider some of the major considerations that would ensue if someone were assigned to developing a plan for transitioning their police agency to COPPS; following that, you are to deliberate on some of the considerations that would come into play someone were to be assigned to a major problem-solving project. Then the chapter concludes with a summary, review questions, and several scenarios and activities that provide opportunities for you to "learn by doing."

The bottom line for this chapter is that police personnel of all ranks long ago passed the point where they only needed to "plan ahead through next Friday," engage in major changes haphazardly and with little planning and forethought, and do not have to be concerned with the repercussions of those changes. This chapter provides a rational and formal approach to anticipating and performing change to COPPS, as well as for other innovative initiatives.

STRATEGIC THINKING

In order for a chief executive to engage in strategic planning (strategic management is discussed below), he or she must first become engaged in **strategic thinking** and then assist the organization in thinking strategically. This means seeing both the big picture and its operational implications. As Herocleous observed, the purpose of strategic thinking is to discover novel, imaginative strategies "that can rewrite the rules of the competitive game and to envision potential futures significantly different from the present."[1] Strategic thinking refers to a creative, divergent thought process. It is a mode of strategy making that is associated with reinventing the future.[2]

Strategic thinking is, therefore, compatible with strategic planning (see Figure 7–1). Both are required in any thoughtful strategy-making process and strategy formulation. The creative strategies emerging from strategic thinking still have to be operationalized through convergent and analytical thought, however, which is strategic planning. Thus, both strategic thinking and

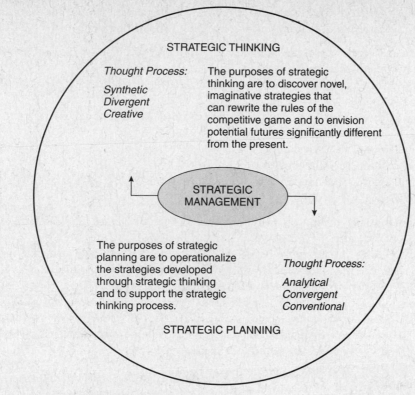

FIGURE 7–1   Strategic Thinking and Strategic Planning

Source: Loizos Heracleous, "Strategic Thinking or Strategic Planning?" *Long Range Planning* 31 (June 1998):485. Used with permission.

strategic planning are necessary, and neither is adequate without the other for effective strategic management.[3] Herocleous stated:

> It all comes down to the ability to go up and down the ladder of abstraction, and being able to see both the big picture and the operational implications, which are signs of outstanding leaders and strategists.[4]

STRATEGIC PLANNING

Basic Elements

Strategic planning is a leadership tool and a process; it is primarily used for one purpose: to help an organization do a better job—to focus its energy, ensure that members of the organization are working toward the same goals, and assess and adjust an organization's direction in response to a changing environment. In short, strategic planning is a disciplined effort to produce fundamental decisions and actions that shape and guide what an organization is, what it does, and why it does it, with a focus on the future.[5]

The history of strategic planning begins in the military, in which strategy is the science of planning and directing large-scale military operations. Although our understanding of strategy as applied to management has been transformed, one element remains: aiming to achieve competitive advantage. Strategic planning also includes the following elements:[6]

- It is oriented toward the future and looks at how the world could be different 5 to 10 years in the future. It is aimed at creating the organization's future.
- It is based on thorough analysis of foreseen or predicted trends and scenarios of possible alternative futures.
- It thoroughly analyzes the organization, both its internal and external environment and its potential.
- It is a qualitative, idea-driven process.
- It is a continuous learning process.
- When it is successful, it influences all areas of operations, becoming a part of the organization's philosophy and culture.

Excellent examples of strategic planning abound; for example, see the strategic plan of the U.S. Department of Justice.[7]

For police leaders, strategic planning holds many benefits. It can help an agency anticipate key trends and issues facing the organization, both currently and in the future. The planning process explores options, sets directions, and helps stakeholders make appropriate decisions. It facilitates communication among key stakeholders who are involved in the process and keeps organizations focused on outcomes while battling daily crises. Planning can be used to develop performance standards to measure an agency's efforts. Most important, it helps leaders facilitate and manage change (which was the subject of Chapter 6).

Planning Cycle

A **planning cycle** is used for strategic planning—the initial steps to be taken in the process—with appropriate involvement by all stakeholders. The process is as follows; however, it must be flexible enough to allow rapid revision of specific strategies as new information develops:

1. Identify the planning team: Include the involvement of several key stakeholders, both internal and external to the organization.
   a. *Department and city leadership.* Police chief executives and other officeholders should be involved.
   b. *Department personnel.* Supervisors, officers, nonsworn staff members, and all members of the department should be included.
   c. *The community.* The plan must be developed in partnership with the community it is designed to serve.
   d. *Interagency partners.* These include both staff and other government agencies and representatives of key social welfare agencies.
2. Develop a **planning document** (also discussed later).
3. Engage in environmental scanning: Conduct a needs assessment (discussed below).

The steps in the planning cycle are presented in Figure 7–2.

Environmental Scanning and Needs Assessment—In a Dire Economy

Certainly there are tremendously dire **economic effects** on the way police organizations plan and are conducting business, and we would be remiss in not mentioning the financial aspect of policing in discussing program planning and **implementation**.

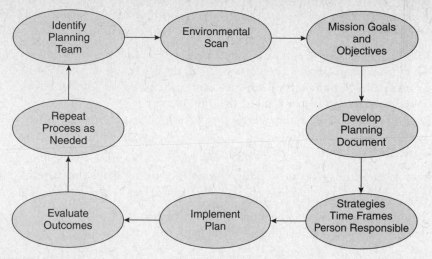

FIGURE 7–2 Planning Cycle

This is, simply put, an unprecedented time in the history of policing. For the first time in a field known for being stable and recession-proof and affording a high degree of job security, the economy has altered policing such that some agencies are closing precincts, merging with other departments, and even shutting down completely. In some jurisdictions, recruits who have been hired are being released while in, or upon graduating from the training academy. And in addition to hiring freezes across the nation, following are other examples of reactions to fiscal challenges in the field:

- In Pennsylvania, more than 20 suburban and rural police agencies closed and 7 others cut patrols. These closures and cuts forced the state police—who face their own budget struggles—to assume full or partial public safety responsibility for about 54,000 more people.
- In Minnesota, nine small police agencies closed, leaving sheriffs' departments to provide police service.
- In Portland, Oregon, police consolidated operations by eliminating two of five patrol precincts. Portland residents fear response times will increase and that experienced officers will be replaced by others who are unfamiliar with local problems.
- Several California cities—including Indio, Palm Springs, Desert Hot Springs, Cathedral City and Beaumont—merged some key functions and also plan to combine dispatch operations to increase efficiency.[8]

All efforts by the police to plan and implement new programs, projects, and policies should be assessed in light of today's economic challenges.

Environmental scanning is a part of the planning cycle that deserves special attention because it refers to the collection and analysis of information required to determine the nature and extent of crime in a community, community residents' perceptions of crime and how they are affected by it, and information about the environment or conditions of a community.

The purpose of the **needs assessment** is to determine and exchange information about specific types of community crime and disorder problems, their causes and effects, and the resources available to combat them. The needs assessment provides the foundation for a community's entire COPPS effort.

Therefore, in order to develop a comprehensive implementation plan for community policing, a needs assessment should be completed at the earliest possible time for several reasons:

- To list in order of priority and clarify the existing crime and drug problems
- To provide a view of resident perceptions about the crime and drug problems, and to provide an excellent means of involving the community in problem identification
- To provide information to the public about problems
- To provide initial direction for developing a work plan, and to assist in setting program goals, strategies, and objectives
- To provide baseline data for evaluation

Needs assessment is ultimately a process conducted for outlining the current issues of the community and the resources needed to resolve those issues. This document will do the following:

- Result in a clearer picture of community needs and resources
- Allow the planning team to develop a strong rationale for decision making

Information sources for needs assessment include:

- City planning reports
- Newspaper articles
- Police reports (including local crime analysis and dispatch calls for service [CFS] data, as well as police officers' knowledge of the community, the Federal Bureau of Investigation's *Uniform Crime Reports*, and other related sources)
- Interviews with community leaders
- Community surveys (see "Community Survey in Fort Collins, Colorado," in Appendix B)
- Employment, housing, education, and health information

PLANNING DOCUMENT: A GUIDE FOR IMPLEMENTATION

Strategic planning is both a document and a process. A written document or plan is the product of a planning team's efforts, is helpful for organizing key objectives, and serves as a guide for those persons involved in the implementation process. The detail and structure of a plan may vary greatly: It may be highly detailed and cover goals, objectives, tasks, and timelines, or it may be less formal, identifying general areas targeted for change.

The structure and formality of a plan will depend largely on the needs and capacity of the organization (based on the environmental scanning and needs assessment). Large organizations with funding and staff support may desire a more comprehensive plan to keep track of the many details and numbers of people involved in implementation. Conversely, smaller police organizations may be capable of implementing change with less detailed plans.

Following are some format and content issues for the planning process and the development of a planning document:

1. Develop statements of vision, mission, and values:
   a. Vision is a scenario or description of how the agency and community will change if the plan is successful.
   b. Mission defines the "business" of COPPS. The statement can be expected to include both traditional aspects of policing (such as public safety, enforcement, "protect and serve") and aspects of COPPS philosophy (community engagement, shared responsibility for public safety).

    c. Values guide decisions and actions. Prioritize and develop a short list of key principles that people who are involved in COPPS implementation should consider.

2. Identify primary objectives that define critical outcomes anticipated from the change to COPPS.

3. Select strategies from among various options outlined during the process that clearly outline the primary avenues and approaches that will be used to attain objectives.

4. Set goals that are general statements of intent. They are the first step in translating a mission statement into what can realistically be attained. Goals should be obtainable and measurable, often beginning with such phrases as "to increase," "to reduce," or "to expand."

5. Set objectives, specific statements of what must be done to achieve a goal or desired outcomes. Usually, several objectives are developed for each goal. A meaningful and well-stated objective should be:

    a. *Specific:* stating precisely what is to be achieved

    b. *Measurable:* answering how much, how many, how well

    c. *Time-bound:* indicating when results will be achieved

6. Set activities, detailed steps necessary to carry out each strategy; they should be time-framed and measurable.

7. Identify a responsible person for every task.

8. Set timelines for the completion of tasks.

Leadership and Administration

MANAGEMENT APPROACHES. COPPS requires changing the philosophy of leadership and management throughout the entire organization. This begins with the development of a new vision/values/mission statement, as noted earlier. Leadership should be promoted at all levels, and a shift in management style from controller to facilitator is necessary. The organization should invest in information systems that will assist officers in identifying patterns of crime and support the problem-solving process. Progressive leaders will need to prepare for the future by engaging in long-term strategic management and by developing continuous evaluation processes, but at the same time these leaders should be flexible and comfortable with change.

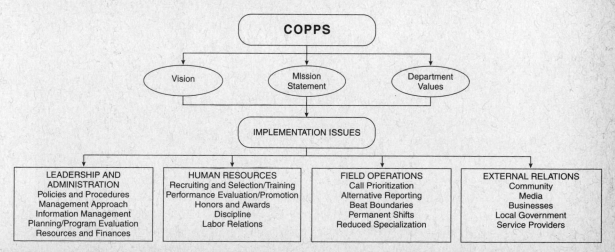

FIGURE 7–3 Principal Components of Implementation

Finances and resources will no longer be firmly established within boxes in the organizational chart; rather, they will be commonly shared across the organization, with other city departments and the public engaged in neighborhood problem solving.

CHIEF EXECUTIVES. It is essential that chief executives communicate the idea that COPPS is department-wide in scope. To get the whole agency involved, the chief executive must adopt four practices as part of the implementation plan:[9]

1. Communicate to all department members the vital role of COPPS in serving the public. Executives must describe why handling problems is more effective than simply handling incidents.
2. Provide incentives to all department members to engage in COPPS. This includes a new and different personnel evaluation and reward system as well as positive encouragement.
3. Reduce the barriers to COPPS that can occur. Procedures, time allocation, and policies all need to be closely examined.
4. Show officers how to address problems. Training is a key element of COPPS implementation. The executive must also set guidelines for innovation. Officers must know they have the latitude to innovate.

The top management of a police agency must consciously address these four concerns. Failure to do so will result in the COPPS approach being conducted by a relatively small number of officers; as a result, relatively few problems will be addressed.

Police chief executives must constantly address their staff, communicating that COPPS is department-wide and that handling problems is preferred to simply handling incidents, along with many other key points concerning this strategy.
Courtesy Shutterstock.

The general task of the chief executive is to challenge the fundamental assumptions of the organization, its aspirations and objectives, the effectiveness of the department's current technologies, and even the chief's own self-perception. This is an awkward stage in the life of the organization. It seems to be a deliberate attempt by the chief to upset the agency. The remedy lies in the personal commitment of the chief and his or her senior managers and supervisors. Ensuing surveys may well find that morale improves once it becomes clear that the change in direction and style was more than a "fleeting fancy," that the chief's policies have some longevity.[10]

MIDDLE MANAGERS.   In the early twentieth century, a powerful midlevel management group emerged that extended the reach of chiefs throughout the department and became the locus of the practice and skill base of the occupation. As such, middle managers—captains and lieutenants—became the leading edge in the establishment of decentralized control over police departments' internal environment and organizational operations.[11] Furthermore, in the past one of the basic functions and practices of middle managers was to forestall creativity and innovation.

Times have changed in this regard, however; today these middle managers play a crucial role in planning and implementing COPPS as well as encouraging their officers to be innovative, to take risks, and to be creative.[12] As George Kelling and William Bratton observed, "Ample evidence exists that when a clear vision of the business of the organization is put forward, when mid-managers are included in planning, when their legitimate self-interests are acknowledged, and when they are properly trained, mid-managers can be the leading edge of innovation and creativity."[13]

FIRST-LINE SUPERVISORS.   Research has provided additional information for leaders to consider when implementing a COPPS philosophy. To begin, first-line supervisors and senior patrol officers seem to generate the greatest resistance to community policing, largely because they have long-standing working styles cultivated from years of traditional police work and because these officers can feel disenfranchised by a management system that takes the best and brightest out of patrol and (they often believe) leaves them behind. The press of 911 calls also makes it difficult to meet the need for community outreach, problem solving, and networking with other agencies. Officers may become concerned about the size of the area for which they are responsible; community policing beats are typically smaller than those of radio patrols.

The role of middle managers and first-line supervisors is covered in greater detail in Chapter 6, on changing the culture of the organization.

EXAMINATION OF THE ORGANIZATION.   An important aspect of COPPS is that its implementation occurs not over a period of days or weeks but more likely over many months or even years. The bigger the organization, the longer it will take to change. Also, throughout the period of change, the office of the chief executive is going to be surrounded by turbulence. An executive may be fortunate enough to inherit an organization that is already susceptible to change; however, the executive who inherits a smoothly running bureaucracy, complacent in the status quo, has a tougher job.

With regard to the organization, one of the first steps the executive and managers must take is an analysis of existing policies and procedures. Although a need remains for some standing orders and some prepared contingency plans and procedures, in the past such manuals have been used more to allocate blame retrospectively after some error has been discovered. It is not surprising that street officers have adopted a mindset of doing things "by the book." Many executives have deemphasized their policy and procedure manuals in implementing community policing. As an extreme example, the manual of an English police force had grown to four volumes, each more than three inches thick, totaling more than 2,000 pages of instructions. Under COPPS, the manual was discarded in favor of a one-page "Policy Statement" that gave 11 brief "commandments." These commandments related more to initiative and "reasonableness of action" than to rules and regulations. Each officer was issued a pocket-size laminate copy of the policy statement.[14]

The organization should conduct an in-depth analysis of the existing departmental rank structure, which itself can be a principal obstacle to the effective communication of new values and philosophy throughout the organization. A large metropolitan police force may have 10 or more layers of rank. The chief executive must talk with the officers; therefore, it is necessary to ensure that the message not be filtered, doctored, or suppressed.[15]

Human Resources

As shown in Chapter 6, human resources constitute the basis of organizational culture. Developing COPPS as a part of daily police modeling behaviors and practices presents a major challenge. To accomplish this requires that the mechanisms that motivate, challenge, reward, and correct employees' behaviors comport with the principles of COPPS. They include recruiting, selection, training, performance evaluations, promotions, honors and awards, and discipline, all of which should be reviewed to ensure that they promote and support the tenets of COPPS.

LABOR RELATIONS.   Another challenge for leadership and administration in the implementation of COPPS centers is labor unions. Since the 1960s, police unions and associations have evolved quickly, making great strides in improving wages, benefits, and working conditions. Yet there is a concern about police administrators' ability to run their agencies and the impact of unions on police-community partnerships. Unions are often viewed by administrators and the public as a negative force, focusing only on financial gain and control over administrative policy making without regard for the department or community.

Does COPPS conflict with the philosophy of police unions? It is understandable that this approach could be construed as antithetical to union interests. For example, COPPS asks officers to assume a proprietary interest in the neighborhoods where they work and to be flexible and creative in their work hours and solutions to problems. This approach often conflicts with collective bargaining contracts in which unions have negotiated for stability of work hours and compensation when working conditions are altered. The idea of civilianization, reductions of rank, and decentralized **investigations** can also be viewed as a threat to officers' lateral mobility, promotional opportunities, and career development. Labor organizations are also concerned with any proposed changes in shifts, beats, criteria for selection, promotion, discipline, and so on.

It is wise to include labor representatives in the planning and implementation process from the beginning. When the unions are excluded from the planning process, officers perceive the implementation of COPPS as a public relations gimmick in management's interests. It is also important that union leaders understand management's concerns and collaborate in planning an agency's future.

Remember, COPPS is important from both the labor and management perspectives. Both sides are interested in creating a quality work environment for employees. This translates to a healthy and productive workforce. COPPS provides officers the opportunity to use their talents, and it removes layers of management and quota-driven evaluations that are often opposed by officers.

Field Operations

DECENTRALIZED SERVICES. The need for available time to engage in problem solving presents a supervisory challenge that begins with managing CFS. This may well require comprehensive workload and crime analyses, including call prioritization, civilianization of some services, and alternative means of handling calls. This information helps an agency when its managers are considering a decentralized approach to field operations that involves assigning officers to a beat and shift for a minimum of one year to learn more about a neighborhood's problems. It is also helpful in reconstructing beat boundaries to correspond more closely with neighborhoods.

Decentralized service is an important part of the general scheme of COPPS. Under the traditional incident-driven style of policing, officers have little permanent territorial responsibility. They know that they may be dispatched to another area at any time and that they are not responsible for anything that occurs on their beat when they are off duty. This responsibility for their area only during a specific period of time reinforces the officer's focus on incidents rather than on long-term area problems. When the chief executive says to the officer, "This area is yours, and nobody else's," however, the territory becomes personalized. The officer's concern for the beat does not end with a tour of duty; concerned officers will want to know what occurred on their beat while they were off duty and will often make unsolicited follow-up visits, struggling to find causes of incidents that would otherwise be regarded as inconsequential.[16]

DETECTIVES. Detectives may view the introduction of COPPS as a matter strictly for the patrol officers—that "Our job is still to solve crime"[17]—and thus have to be incorporated into the COPPS context (see Exhibit 7–1). Valuable intelligence information gained by detectives through investigations can be fed to the patrol division. Also, detectives must believe that crime prevention is their principal obligation and not the exclusive responsibility of the patrol force.

Exhibit 7–1	Investigations in the COPPS Context

One problematic issue for police departments that are implementing COPPS is the appropriate organization of investigative functions. How can agencies structure investigations to best support these approaches? Who in the organization should conduct which types of investigations? Should agencies decentralize investigative functions? Should there be a separate command structure for detectives?

A group of chiefs leading organizations through the change process first identified this whole issue. The National Institute of Justice will fund a research project surveying 900 law enforcement agencies, all those serving populations of at least 50,000 and having at least 100 sworn personnel. The Police Executive Research Forum will ask these agencies about their status with respect to COPPS, as well as detailed questions about the structure of their investigative functions. Researchers will then develop several models of the investigative function in the COPPS context.

Source: Workshop presentation, Mary Ann Wycoff, Police Executive Research Forum, "The 8th Annual International Problem Oriented Policing Conference: Problem Oriented Policing 1997," November 16, 1997, San Diego, California.

Detectives have opportunities to establish and enhance positive working relationships with victim advocacy groups, civic organizations, police district advisory councils, and other stakeholders in the system. Detectives, like patrol officers, attend regular community meetings and impart valuable knowledge relating to criminal activities, trends, and patterns; in addition, quicker, easier investigative responses can be realized. After analyzing the problem—and examining the environment of the offenses, including victims' family situations, economics, and social pressures involved in lack of prosecutions—detectives can work with the patrol division to encourage victims to follow through with prosecutions, engage in follow-up investigations, and even devise a rudimentary witness protection unit, with impressive outcomes.

TOP PRIORITY: PATROL PERSONNEL.   There is one very important positive aspect of considering whether to implement a COPPS philosophy, one that all chief executives should remember: It encourages many of the activities that patrol officers would like to do, that is, to engage in more inquiry of crime and disorder and get more closure from their work. When asked why they originally wanted to enter policing, officers consistently say that they joined in order to help people.[18] By emphasizing work that addresses people's concerns and giving officers the discretion to develop a solution, COPPS helps make police work more rewarding.

Among the most frequent complaints voiced by patrol officers, however, are that they are given little support, they are accorded low esteem by their organization, and they are simply a pool of employees from which to draw for other special assignments. For COPPS to be successful, the agency must ensure that patrol staffing is maintained and that its officers believe that their work is most important to the organization's success.

Allowing officers to identify and resolve neighborhood problems can improve morale by making the job more rewarding.
Courtesy Community Policing Consortium.

External Relations

In Chapter 4 we discussed the various stakeholders and partners that police will find in the community for assistance in the COPPS initiative. Enlisting the assistance of the community is often a more complex undertaking than one might assume.

Collaborative responses to neighborhood crime and disorder are essential to the success of COPPS. This requires new relationships and the sharing of information and resources among the police and community, local government agencies, service providers, and businesses. Also, police agencies must educate and inform their external partners about police resources and neighborhood problems using surveys, newsletters, community meetings, and public service announcements. The media also provide an excellent opportunity for police to educate the community. Press releases about collaborative problem-solving efforts should be sent to the media, and news conferences should be held to discuss major crime reduction efforts.

Exhibit 7–2 shows how Sacramento, California, approaches external relations by providing comprehensive neighborhood services.

Elected officials must also provide direction and support through policy development and resource allocation. They must realize that the police exercise considerable discretion, and can and should do more than merely enforce the laws, such as: mobilizing the community (as witnesses), requesting that citizens exercise greater informal social control over one another (e.g., parents over children, teachers over students, landlord over tenants, and so on), using mediation skills to resolve disputes, altering the physical environment to reduce crime opportunities, intervening short of arrest (e.g. issuing warnings, placing people in temporary custody), enactment of new laws, and concentrating on those repeat offenders who account for a disproportionate share of crime problems.[19]

Elected officials can assist COPPS in other ways, such as those described in Exhibit 7–3.

Exhibit 7–2	City of Sacramento Neighborhood Services Department: "The Bridge"

An excellent example of a community's external relations efforts is that of the City of Sacramento, California's Neighborhood Services Department (NSD), which, as its mission statement reads, "bridges and engages Sacramento's diverse residents with resources to maintain, revitalize, and promote healthy communities." The NSD, established in 1993, has a full-time professional staff of nine, five of whom are responsible for a specific Council District. NSD publishes a semi-annual newsletter, "The Bridge" (see: http://www.cityofsacramento.org/ns/documents/March2010Final-color.pdf). NSD is an excellent clearinghouse of information, providing links at its website to all city services and queries (e.g., how to pay a parking fine); it contracts with a vendor to translate citizens' requests for information in more than one hundred languages. NSD encourages people to be *organized*, be it in Neighborhood Watch or in a wide variety of other neighborhood groups. NDS partners with police and more than 200 groups to sponsor a "National Night Out," held in August each year and including a variety of events to promotes crime awareness and crime prevention.

Source: Adapted from the City of Sacramento Neighborhood Services Department Web site, http://www.cityofsacramento.org/ns/ (Accessed July 16, 2010).

| Exhibit 7–3 | COPPS for Mayors and Elected Officials |

COPPS requires police and citizens to join together as partners in the course of both identifying and effectively addressing problems involving crime and disorder. A publication by the federal Office of Community Oriented Policing Services exists to better inform elected officials of the invaluable role they occupy in this endeavor, and what they can do to foster the implementation and operation of such strategies.

Elected officials, in close coordination with their police chief executives, can help to make COPPS work best and potentially expand beyond law enforcement. Their administration likely has dozens of partnerships with members of the business community, faith-based organizations, community groups, nonprofit groups, victim service providers, health service providers, the media, individuals, and other city agencies. They can also promote a more coordinated approach to these partnerships across municipal agencies, ensuring that they are strategic and structured to identify and deal with specific problems that are relevant to all members. Indeed, it is vital to include those government agencies that have a stake in the outcome, and can bring resources to bear on the development and implementation of jurisdiction-wide solutions.

Elected officials can also:

▶ facilitate and provide leadership to their public service executives to join into partnerships when their participation is warranted
▶ encourage and provide funds for the growth of interconnected technology and information systems across government to facilitate the sharing of COPPS-related information
▶ provide, or advocate for, necessary resources to sustain these partnerships, as well as support the implementation of their proposed solutions
▶ use their influence to encourage participation from important segments of the community through direct contact with key stakeholders, or media access to promote and provide information regarding these partnerships

Source: Adapted from U.S. Department of Justice, Office of Community Oriented Policing Services, *Community Policing for Mayors: A Municipal Service Model for Policing and Beyond*, August 2006, p. 4, http://www.cops.usdoj.gov/files/RIC/Publications/e05060064.pdf (Accessed July 16, 2010)

TEN WAYS TO UNDERMINE COPPS

In closing this chapter section on COPPS, Exhibit 7–4 offers, to the tradition-bound police chief, John Eck's "ten things you can do to undermine COPPS"—a prescription for preventing COPPS from gaining a foothold for many years to come.[20] Many of these tactics are being practiced today, sometimes out of ignorance and sometimes intentionally. With apologies to the U.S. Surgeon General, we issue a prefatory warning: "Practicing these techniques in a police department may be hazardous to the health of community policing and problem solving."

YOU BE THE CHANGE AGENT: SOME HANDS-ON ACTIVITIES

To "put some meat on the bones" of strategic thinking and planning, next we add a real-world flavor to the matter using two case study activities that will engage you in the process. A number of questions are posed, and new concepts are discussed for each.

| Exhibit 7–4 | Ten Ways to Undermine COPPS |

1. *Oversell it:* COPPS should be sold as the panacea for every ill that plagues the city, the nation, and civilization. Some of the evils you may want to claim COPPS will eliminate are crime, fear of crime, racism, police misuse of force, homelessness, drug abuse, gangs, and other social problems. COPPS can address some of these concerns in specific situations, but by building up the hopes and expectations of the public, the press, and politicians, you can set the stage for later attacks on COPPS when it does not deliver.

2. *Don't be specific:* This suggestion is a corollary of the first principle. Never define what you mean by the following terms: community, service, effectiveness, empowerment, neighborhood, communication, problem solving. Use these and other terms indiscriminately, interchangeably, and whenever possible. At first, people will think the department is going to do something meaningful and won't ask for details. Once people catch on, you can blame the amorphous nature of COPPS and go back to what you were doing before.

3. *Create a special unit or group:* Less than 10 percent of the department should be engaged in this effort, lest COPPS really catch on. Since the "grand design" is possibly the return to conventional policing anyway (once everyone has attacked COPPS), there is no sense in involving more than a few officers. Also, special units are popular with the press and politicians.

4. *Create a soft image:* The best image for COPPS will be a uniformed female officer hugging a small child. This caring and maternal image will warm the hearts of community members suspicious of police, play to traditional stereotypes of sexism within policing, and turn off most cops.

5. *Leave the impression that COPPS is only for minority neighborhoods:* This is a corollary of items 3 and 4. Since a small group of officers will be involved, only a few neighborhoods can receive their services. Place the token COPPS officers in areas like public housing. With any luck, racial antagonism will undercut the approach. It will appear that minority, poor neighborhoods are not getting the "tough on crime" approach they need.

6. *Divorce COPPS officers from "regular" police work:* This is an expansion of the soft image concept. If the COPPS officers do not handle calls or make arrests, but instead throw block parties, speak to community groups, walk around talking to kids, visit schools, and so on, they will not be perceived as "real" police officers to their colleagues. This will further undermine their credibility and ability to accomplish anything of significance.

7. *Obfuscate means and ends:* Whenever describing COPPS, never make the methods for accomplishing the objective subordinate to the objective. Instead, make the means more important than the ends, or at least put them on equal footing. For example, to reduce drug dealing in a neighborhood, make certain that the tactics necessary (arrests, community meetings, etc.) are as important as, or more important than, the objective. These tactics can occupy everyone's time but still leave the drug problem unresolved. Always remember: The means are ends, in and of themselves.

8. *Present community members with problems and plans:* Whenever meeting with community members, officers should listen carefully and politely and then elaborate on how the department will enforce the law. If the community members like the plan, go ahead. If they do not, continue to be polite and ask them to go on a ride-along or witness a drug raid. This avoids having to change the department's operations while demonstrating how difficult police work is, and why nothing can be accomplished. In the end, they will not get their problems solved, but will see how nice the police are.

9. *Never try to understand why problems occur:* Do not let officers gain knowledge about the underlying causes of the problems; COPPS should not include any analysis of the problem and as little information as possible should be sought from the community. Keep officers away from computer terminals; mandate that officers get permission to talk to members of any other agency; do not allow COPPS officers to go off their assigned areas to collect information; prevent access to research conducted on similar problems; suppress listening skills.

10. *Never publicize a success:* Some rogue officers will not get the message and will go out anyway and gather enough information to solve problems. Try to ignore these examples of effective policing and make sure that no one else hears about them. When you cannot ignore them, describe them in the least meaningful way (item 2). Talk about the wonders of empowerment and community meetings. Describe the hours of foot patrol, the new mountain bikes, or shoulder patches. In every problem solved, there is usually some tactic or piece of equipment that can be highlighted at the expense of the accomplishment itself. When all else fails, reprimand the COPPS officer for not wearing a hat.

Source: John E. Eck, "Helpful Hints for the Tradition-Bound Chief," *Fresh Perspectives* (Washington, D.C.: Police Executive Research Forum, June 1992), pp. 1–7.

First is an exercise on transforming the police agency from one that is primarily traditional and reactive, to one that practices the COPPS philosophy; second is "Opening a POP Project," in which COPPS is already established and practiced in your agency, and you must use the philosophy to address a problem of crime and disorder.

I. You Lead the Transition to COPPS

Assume that you are a middle manager in your local police department and have been tasked with laying the foundation for launching the COPPS philosophy throughout your agency. You must develop an action plan, taking into account all kinds of preliminary requirements and activities for the transition.

- What kinds of training—for both sworn and non-sworn personnel—will be necessary (first, peruse Chapter 9)?
- What kinds of technologies (Chapter 5) must be obtained for performing the necessary crime analyses?
- How much regular and overtime staffing will be required, particularly during the initial phase of the initiative? What forms, Web sites, brochures, and other informational and communications resources will be required?
- If there are not enough funds available locally, how will the additional funding needed be obtained? What resource providers exist (e.g., social services, other organizations that can provide funding assistance or in-kind services)?

Other possible funding sources include:

1. *Local, state, or federal government agencies.* Federal agencies are most likely to have specific grant announcements; local (city or county) agencies are most likely to fund specific programs that address their mission.
2. *Governmental funds designated for special purposes.* Find out if city, state, or federal agencies have designated specific funds for certain programming areas (e.g., crime prevention, drug awareness education, and violence prevention).

3. *User fees.* In some cases, nominal fees may be charged to the clients, although these fees are usually far less than actual program costs. In many criminal justice programs, such "user fees" are not popular, but we have seen more creative user fees in recent years (e.g., an intensive supervision probation program charges a daily fee to all participants, which helps to offset program costs).

4. *Private and nonprofit agencies* (e.g., nonprofit agencies such as the MacArthur Foundation, the United Way, and the Pugh Foundation provide funding for programs which address their mission statements).

5. *Donations from businesses.* Many large corporations and even many small community businesses have become increasingly involved in providing resources for programs that address community needs. In addition to "giving something back to the community," many businesses may qualify for tax breaks by making donations of equipment, goods, services, or money.

6. *Volunteers.* Many programs make extensive use of volunteers to provide some of the program's services (e.g., tutoring and mentoring in after-school delinquency prevention programs).

7. *Fund-raising projects.* Special projects may occasionally be undertaken to raise money for the program's services.

- How will you inform and train your elected officials, including those in other government agencies, and all members of your police agency about the transition to COPPS?
- By which dates will the above and other implementation tasks be accomplished, and responsibilities assigned to staff members for carrying out the tasks? This is a very important task at this stage—developing a timeline, and your Gantt chart (see Figure 7–4) should specify the following:
  1. All the specific implementation activities that need to be accomplished.
  2. Assignment of responsibility for each specific task to one or more individuals, and
  3. A specific date by which each task is to be completed.

  Without a specific plan that incorporates all three elements listed above, the program is likely to experience difficulty (or even mortality) before it gets off the ground.
- What mechanisms will you develop to ensure that progress is being made, to monitor staff performance and enhance communication, including procedures for orienting participants, coordinating activities, and managing resistance and conflict?
- What sources of resistance to change should you anticipate, and how will you address them (see the **force field analysis**, below)?

Resistance to Change: Using Force Field Analysis

One particularly popular and useful technique for analyzing sources of support and resistance is called *force field analysis*, developed in 1943 by Kurt Lewin, a German social psychologist.[21]

Lewin believed that participation and communication are keys to change, and collaborative strategies are preferred to conflict strategies. The force-field analysis technique is based on an analogy to physics: A body will remain at rest when the sum of forces operating on it is zero. When forces pushing or pulling in one direction exceed forces pushing or pulling in the opposite one, the body will move in the direction of the greater forces. In planned change, we are dealing with social forces rather than physical ones. Generally, we want to try to reduce resistance to change.

Such a change as transitioning to COPPS and thus transforming the culture of the police agency will involve one of three options: (1) increasing forces in support of change, (2) decreasing

	TASK	Start	End	Duration	Jan	Feb	Mar	Apr	May	Jun	Jul	Aug	Sep	Oct	Nov	Dec
1	Assemble implementation team; develop mission & goals statements; meet with key union, first-line, mid-management and outside agency personnel	1/1/2012	3/3/2012	60		▌										
2	Determine technologies and related funding required for analysis	1/1/2012	2/7/2012	30	▌											
3	Develop new recruiting literature, employee testing/ selection/evaluation processes	1/1/2012	5/7/2012	120				▌								
4	Develop training programs for sworn & non-sworn personnel	4/1/2012	6/27/2012	90					▌	▌						
5	Conduct COPPS training for all personnel	7/1/2012	9/28/2012	90							▌	▌				
6	Train key external agency personnel and elected officials	10/1/2012	11/27/2012	45										▌		▌
7	Evaluate outcomes of the above; adjust as necessary	11/17/2012	1/1/2012	45												▌

FIGURE 7–4 Example of a Gantt Chart for COPPS

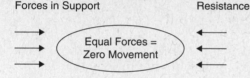

FIGURE 7–5   Force Field Analysis

forces against change (usually creates less tension and leads to fewer unanticipated consequences), or (3) doing both in some combination. There is always resistance to change. At best,
there is inertia that the change agent must anticipate and overcome. Force field analysis is a valuable tool for doing this. Generally, we focus on reducing resistance.

Three steps are involved in conducting a force field analysis:

1. *Identifying driving forces* (those supporting change) and restraining forces (those resisting
   change)
2. *Analyzing the forces* identified in step 1. Assess (for each):
   • *Amenability to change* (how likely is it that this force can be changed?)
   • *Potency* (how much impact would reducing this source of resistance have on moving the
     intervention forward?)
   • *Consistency* (does this force remain stable or change over time?)
3. *Identifying alternative strategies* for changing each force identified in step 1. Focus on
   reducing sources of resistance

To engage in a force-field analysis for a COPPS initiative, you might begin by drawing the diagram as shown in Figure 7–5, and then drawing a line down the middle of the page; you then put
the idea or situation to be considered above the top of the line. Write "for" and "against" on either
side of the line. Next, determine the existing forces for and against the change, writing these on
the appropriate side of the line. Show the significance of these forces with an arrow, where the
length indicates the size of the force.

Now, study the diagram, considering the forces identified, and ask questions such as:

• What is the overall force, for and against?
• How can you tip the balance?
• How can you neutralize forces against?
• How can you increase the "for" forces?

Finally, draw your conclusions. You now have a good idea of those forces that will be in support
and resistant to the proposed change to COPPS, an analysis of those forces, and possible alternative strategies for reducing sources of resistance.

PROGRAM/POLICY IMPLEMENTATION.   At some point, you should attempt to find out if the
transition is being implemented properly. *Monitoring* refers to the collection of information to determine to what degree the program/policy design or blueprint is being carried out as planned. The
purpose is to identify gaps between the program/policy on paper (design) and the program/policy in
action. Adjustments are made either to revise the design of the intervention (e.g., program components) or to make what is being done conform to the intended design. Major activities include:

• Design monitoring instruments to collect data
• Designate responsibility for data collection, storage, and analysis

- Develop information system capacities
- Provide feedback to staff, clients, and stakeholders

II. Opening a POP Project

In addition to many of the same activities described in the above section, transitioning to COPPS, there are some unique tasks that might well be undertaken when becoming involved in an actual problem oriented policing (POP) initiative, as will be seen in this chapter section.

Assume that you are a member of a police agency that adopted the COPPS philosophy many years ago. Upon being informed of a potentially serious neighborhood problem of crime and disorder in your sector, further assume that you have performed the scanning and analysis stages of the S.A.R.A. problem-solving process, and that you have established that there is indeed a problem You now realize that tailor-made responses (per stage three of S.A.R.A.) must be developed, to include obtaining citizen input and feedback from other governmental/social services agencies, and thus you must open a problem-solving project.

Following are some additional measures that are to be carried out: (1) setting goals and objectives and (2) planning and carrying out some intervention.

SETTING GOALS AND OBJECTIVES.   Every criminal justice intervention attempts to achieve some kind of outcome (i.e., some change in the problem). Many expensive and otherwise well-designed interventions fail due to their inadequately defining the desired outcomes of the intervention.

Major activities at this stage include:

- Seeking participation from different individuals and agencies in goal setting.
- Writing goal statements specifying the general outcome to be obtained. Goals should be broad in nature, perhaps no more than a sentence or two in length. An example might be "To significantly reduce criminal victimization involving bank properties."
- Writing specific outcome objectives for each goal. Goals should be quantifiable (and attainable), such as, "Reduce the incidents of weekend ATM robberies in Beat X by 50 percent during the next year." These should include a time frame for measuring impact, and a specific measure of impact.
- Specifying an impact model: How the intervention will act upon a specific cause so as to bring about a change in the problem.
- Identifying compatible and incompatible goals in the larger system: Where do values of different stakeholders overlap or conflict?
- Identifying needs and opportunities for interagency collaboration. For example, police and property managers need to collaborate to make landlord-tenant laws work.

OTHER ACTIVITIES CONCERNING THE PROGRAM OR POLICY DESIGN.   Next it would be helpful to specify, in as much detail as possible, who does what to whom, in what order, and how much? It is the guts of the initiative, including its staff, its services, and its clients. While the planning steps for programs and policies are generally similar, at the design stage we find it best to distinguish activities for programs and policies separately.

Major activities for *program design* include:

- Defining the target population: Who is to be served, or changed? Would it be best to perform a community or neighborhood survey? Other than providing order maintenance in the area, what other needs exist that must be addressed (e.g., level of fear of crime among residents) and what are the characteristics of intended clients (e.g., age, gender, geographic residence).

- Defining program components: The precise nature, amount, and sequence of services provided must be specified. Who does what to whom, in what order, and how much?
- Determining what we need to know: Are there POP Guides (see Chapters 3 and 4) covering this particular problem that will provide insight concerning causes and possible solutions for this problem? Are other activities required, for example, a series of neighborhood meetings, steering a neighborhood or graffiti cleanup?
- Determining whether new legislation is going to be required, such as new laws concerning curfew, cruising, or loitering laws; problem-solving training, education concerning laws pertaining to juveniles; and so on.
- Determining who will write job descriptions for the officers who will have their "boots on the ground," and which kinds of knowledge, skills, and abilities they must possess for the particular problem(s) to be addressed.
- Establishing how many and what kind of staff are required to operate the problem-solving intervention: What specific duties will they carry out? What kinds of qualifications do they need? How much money is needed for regular as well as overtime deployment?[22]

MEASURING AGENCY IMPLEMENTATION: CP-SAT

In Chapter 8, which concerns program and policy evaluation, we will be discussing the Community Policing Self-Assessment Tool, known as CP-SAT, which was developed by the federal Office of Community Oriented Policing Services, the Police Executive Research Forum, and ICF International (a management, technology, and policy consulting firm). It allows agencies to assess, among many other things, their implementation of COPPS. CP-SAT operationalizes the philosophy of COPPS across different ranks and provides resources that assist agencies' efforts to determine their strengths and gaps in several areas discussed in this chapter, including problem solving, partnerships, and organizational transformation.

Last, we should mention an excellent resource that is available for persons who are interested in police planning and research: the Law Enforcement Organization for Planning and Research Directors; see http://www.leoprd.org.

Summary

This chapter has shown how police executives must think and plan strategically, and provided examples of how to implement COPPS using a structured approach and developing a planning document. Four keys to successful implementation—leadership and administration, human resources, field operations, and external relations—were examined, and we considered several obstacles that can undermine COPPS. We also examined how one must expect and be prepared to address and formally analyze resistance to change.

The reader was also given an opportunity to "be" the person in the trenches, looking at the kinds of planning and implementation questions and issues might arise for both transitioning an agency to COPPS as well as launching a problem solving project. This exercise demonstrates that there are many preliminary steps to be taken prior to entering into any form of change.

It should be quite evident—particularly when looking at the chapter *en toto* as well as the 10 ways to undermine COPPS—that there is no substitute for having a well-thought-out, well-laid-out plan of implementation for the COPPS philosophy. As with any new venture, there must be a "road map" to show the executive and the agency how to travel the "highway" in order to reach the ultimate destination.

Items for Review

1. Explain what is meant by strategic thinking and strategic planning, including the primary elements of the latter.
2. Define what is involved in a planning cycle, an environmental scanning effort, and a needs assessment.
3. Explain the roles of chief executives, middle managers, and first-line supervisors in the planning and implementation of COPPS.
4. Review the roles of detectives and patrol personnel in COPPS planning and implementation.
5. Describe Lewin's force field analysis, and how it functions in anticipating and planning for resistance to change.
6. Delineate some of the major considerations that would come into play if you were to be assigned with developing a plan for transitioning your police agency to COPPS.
7. Delineate some of the major considerations that would come into play if you were to be assigned to address a major problem-solving project.

Learn by Doing

1. Assume that you are sitting as an assessor for another police agency's promotional board, which is interviewing candidates for the director's position with its Research and Analysis division. Some of the questions to be posed of all candidates concerns (1) what they know about strategic planning, (2) how they would go about engaging in a planning cycle (including environmental scanning), and (3) how the economy has affected planning in general. What key answers would you look for the candidates to provide for each of these three items?
2. Your agency is well-known nationally for its COPPS efforts and has won a Herman Goldstein Award for innovative problem solving. You are consulting with an agency in another state that is only half-heartedly engaged in problem-solving activities; it now wishes to transform the entire agency so as to fully embrace that philosophy. What will you attempt to "teach" them regarding the many requirements for a successful transition?
3. Looking at item #2 above, how would you explain CP-SAT as a tool for assisting the agency in implementing COPPS? What advice would you provide that they follow so as not to undermine COPPS?

Notes

1. Loizos Heracleous, "Strategic Thinking or Strategic Planning?" *Long Range Planning* 31 (1998):481–487.
2. Eton Lawrence, "Strategic Thinking: A Discussion Paper," Research Directorate, Policy, Research, and Communications Branch, Public Service Commission of Canada, Ottawa, Ontario, Canada, April 27, 1999, pp. 6–7.
3. Ibid.
4. Heracleous, "Strategic Thinking or Strategic Planning?" p. 482.
5. Internet Nonprofit Center, "What Is Strategic Planning?" (San Francisco, Calif.: Author, 2000), p. 1.
6. "Brief History of Strategic Planning," http://www.des.calstate.edu/glossary.html (Accessed September 24, 2000), p. 2.
7. U.S. Department of Justice, "Information Technology Strategic Plan," http://www.usdoj.gov/jmd/irm/imss/2002itplan/strategic_plan.htm (Accessed September 12, 2006).
8. Kevin Johnson, "Economy limiting services of local police," *USA Today*, May 18, 2009, http://www.usatoday.com/news/nation/2009-05-17-police-closure_N.htm (Accessed September 20, 2010).
9. John E. Eck and William Spelman, *Problem-Solving: Problem-Oriented Policing in Newport News* (Washington, D.C.: Police Executive Research Forum, 1987), pp. 100–101.
10. Malcolm K. Sparrow, "Implementing Community Policing," *Perspectives on Policing* 9 (November 1988):2–3.
11. George L. Kelling and William J. Bratton, "Implementing Community Policing: The Administrative Problem," *Perspectives on Policing* 17 (July 1993):4.
12. Ibid., p. 9.
13. Ibid., p. 11.
14. Sparrow, *Implementing Community Policing*, pp. 4–5.
15. Ibid., p. 5.

16. Ibid., p. 6.

17. Ibid., p. 7.

18. Jesse Rubin, "Police Identity and the Police Role," in Thomas J. Sweeney and William Ellingsworth (eds.), *Issues in Police Patrol: A Book of Readings,* (Kansas City, Mo.: Kansas City Police Department, 1973); John Van Maanen, "Police Socialization: A Longitudinal Examination of Job Attitudes in an Urban Police Department," *Administrative Science Quarterly* 20 (1975): 207–228.

19. Adapted from Joel B. Plant and Michael S. Scott, *Effective Policing and Crime Prevention: A Problem-Oriented Guide for Mayors, City Managers, and County Executives* (Washington, D.C.: U.S. Department of Justice, Office of Community Oriented Policing Services, 2009), pp. 13–14.

20. John E. Eck, "Helpful Hints for the Tradition-Bound Chief," in *Fresh Perspectives* (Washington, D.C.: Police Executive Research Forum, June 1992), pp. 1–7.

21. Kurt Lewin, "Defining the Field at a Given Time," *Psychological Review* 50 (1943): 292–310.

22. Some of the materials for this chapter section were adapted from Wayne N. Welsh and Phillip W. Harris, *Criminal Justice Policy and Planning* (3d ed.) (Cincinnati, Ohio: Anderson, 2008), Chapters 2–4.

8

Assessing and Evaluating COPPS Initiatives

KEY TERMS AND CONCEPTS

Assessment
CP-SAT
Data analysis
Empirical study

Evaluation
Impact evaluation
Outcome (process)
  evaluation

Research methodology
Statistical technique
Surveys
"What works"

LEARNING OBJECTIVES

As a result of reading this chapter, the student will:

- Know the rationale for determining "what works" in criminal justice in general, as well as with COPPS initiatives in specific
- Understand the major differences between conducting an assessment and an empirical impact evaluation of a COPPS strategy
- Be able to explain why conducting an impact evaluation of COPPS is extremely challenging for police agencies and a means for securing assistance for doing so
- Understand the kinds of knowledge, skills, and abilities that a police officer engaged in COPPS must possess, as well as the criteria for assessing an officer's problem-solving performance
- Know the benefits of using surveys to obtain input for evaluative purposes
- Know why it is desirable for a police agency to employ the CP-SAT system

All things have two handles: beware of the wrong one.
—RALPH WALDO EMERSON

*Not everything that counts can be counted; and not everything
that can be counted counts.*
—ALBERT EINSTEIN

INTRODUCTION

During the past several decades, America's criminal justice system has invested billions of dollars in policies and initiatives that were not needed and/or did not work. In times of fiscal exigency such as these, there is a greater need than ever for accountability and *evidence-based* initiatives that will bring bang for the buck.

Unfortunately, despite the widespread use and popularity of the community oriented policing and problem solving (COPPS) strategy, almost no empirical research exists concerning whether or not those initiatives are cost-efficient and successfully reduce public fear and incidence of crime and disorder. And, to be sure, a long-standing criticism COPPS of initiatives has concerned this lack of rigorous examination and **evaluation**. As Mears observed, "Comparison is the gold standard—the hallmark—of any evaluation."[1]

We want to know whether or not one approach is better than another. This is not unlike when you are considering two types of automobiles for purchase, and contrast their prices, resale value, safety record, comfort, style, handling, and so forth.

Similarly, in criminal justice we need to know if a particular practice "works" and is better than not having the practice at all. Indeed, policy makers and politicians may well require that the implementation and continuation of a COPPS initiative involve an impact evaluation of the outcome. However, as will be seen below, truly evaluating COPPS is a challenging undertaking because of the required specialized knowledge, skills, and abilities involved.

We begin by discussing the general rationale for looking at "what works," and then consider some of the challenges involved with empirically evaluating COPPS initiatives. Then we examine the two complementary but different means of measuring the results of those initiatives: *assessment* (as it is defined in the S.A.R.A. problem-solving model in Chapter 3) and impact evaluations. Included is a review of the use of community surveys. Next is a review of the kinds of knowledge, skills, and abilities that are required by COPPS police officers, as well as several criteria for a performance evaluation of an officer's problem-solving skills. Then we discuss a new tool developed by the federal government for measuring COPPS implementation and operation, Community Policing Self-Assessment Tool (**CP-SAT**), and then consider two examples of empirical studies of COPPS initiatives. The chapter concludes with a summary, review questions, and several scenarios and activities that provide opportunities for you to "learn by doing." Several excellent resources for developing the ability to perform impact evaluations and assessments are provided throughout the chapter as well as in the endnotes.

PERFORMING ASSESSMENTS AND IMPACT EVALUATIONS: WHY AND HOW

Looking at "What Works," Generally

Of the hundreds of new programs and strategies in our communities, businesses, and criminal justice organizations, which of them succeed? We need to know **"what works."** In policing, that need-to-know exists both for strategies dealing with existing crime and neighborhood disorder as well as with crime prevention. Indeed, Congress mandates evaluations of state and local crime prevention programs that are funded by the U.S. Department of Justice.

At its root, addressing a research question involves the proper means of obtaining data and then examining it. Examples of such research questions would number in the thousands, but following are a few—all of which have been subjected to rigorous empirical analysis and have in some way changed the way police conduct business:

- Does the arrest of the primary aggressor at scenes of domestic violence significantly reduce or prevent such violence in the future?
- Do gun buyback programs reduce street crimes committed with weapons?
- Are programs such as "Scared Straight," D.A.R.E., Neighborhood Watch, and jail or prison boot camps successful in reducing crime?
- Do after-school recreation programs reduce vandalism in public housing?
- Will such strategies as increasing the numbers of officers in a jurisdiction, the use of two-person patrol cars, or random patrolling reduce crime?
- Are therapeutic programs for drug-using offenders in prisons effective in reducing drug offenses?[2]

In these examples, the dependent variable—that which is being acted on—is crime (or, more specifically, its reduction or elimination).

Today, as seen in Chapter 5, technologies and other management tools provide real-time and trend data access for reported crime, arrests, repeat calls for service, and other information. However, many researchers are concerned that more attention is given to evaluating the planning and implementation of a strategy than what effects the program actually had on crime. While process evaluations can produce much valuable data on the implementation of programs and the logic of their strategies, they cannot offer evidence as to whether the programs "work" to prevent crime.

An officer's efforts to improve overall safety in a shopping mall may decrease crime and increase safety and profits for merchants.
Courtesy Community Policing Consortium.

Challenges Involved—and "Tech Support" Needed

As indicated above, very few sworn agents or officers in federal, state, or local law enforcement agencies possess the kinds of knowledge, skills, and abilities required to perform sophisticated impact evaluations of their efforts. This is not a criticism; indeed, even if one has attained a college degree, there is no guarantee that he or she possesses such requisite knowledge and ability. Another legitimate consideration is time: quantitative research efforts such as these are very labor-intensive, and it is highly doubtful that sworn personnel would be able to forego their other duties in favor of engaging in such analyses.

This situation is analogous to the world of computer science: Most of us know the basics of what makes our computer function; however, when we have serious problems with our computer, we must turn to a technician who has the capability to make it work properly again. And so it is with empirical studies of COPPS, with the police agency either necessarily hiring or—if fortunate—being able to obtain the *pro bono* assistance of a trained social scientist in a nearby college or university to set up and perform the impact evaluation. In the *social sciences* (i.e., disciplines such as criminal justice, sociology, political science, anthropology), quantitative research involves the use of empirical investigations, concepts, and variables to test hypotheses in the search for relationships.

This is an opportune point for us to mention the need for greater expansion and use of the "town-gown" relationship: the police calling on civilian academics to assist in their evaluation and assessment efforts. Indeed, typically a person cannot be awarded a doctoral degree and thus become eligible to work in academia without having first demonstrated (in the form of a written dissertation) that he or she possesses requisite skills in both **research methodology** and statistics. The same can also be said of some persons who, as part of their master's studies, were required to write and defend a thesis. In sum, colleges and universities are certainly prime resources for locating individuals who have the ability to assist the police in accomplishing evaluations.

Complementary but Different Approaches: Assessments Vis-à-vis Impact Evaluations

It is important to remember that evaluation and assessment are different from, but complementary to one another. Next we discuss and compare both.

Assessments, which can also be termed outcome evaluations, occur at the final stage of the S.A.R.A. problem-solving process. Outcome evaluations ask the following kinds of descriptive questions: Did the response occur as planned, and did all the response components work? Did the response result in fewer calls for service to the area? More arrests? Fewer reported gang activities?

An example would be as follows: After performing a careful analysis, COPPS officers determine that in order to curb a street prostitution problem, they will heighten patrols in the area, change several streets to one-way and thus create several dead-end streets to thwart cruising "johns," and work with courts and social services to get convicted prostitutes probation and help them to gain the necessary skills for legitimate employment. An **outcome (process) evaluation** will determine whether the crackdown occurred, and if so, how many arrests police made; whether the street patterns were altered as planned; and how many prostitutes received job skills assistance.

Note, however, that an outcome evaluation does *not* answer the question, "What happened to the problem?" Assessments (outcome evaluations) establish whether the COPPS initiative resulted in some sort of outcome: fewer calls for service, more arrests, and so forth. However, assessment or outcome evaluations do not allow us to know if the COPPS initiative actually *caused* the outcome. That is where impact evaluations come into play. Exhibit 8–1 describes how one community has quantitatively assessed its COPPS efforts.

Exhibit 8–1	COPPS Assessment in Lawrence, Massachusetts

Lawrence, a community of 70,000 near Boston, experienced a wide gap between its police and the public, and the department's budget was cut as well. The department began exploring new means of delivering police services.

The police chief and a nine-member management team developed a bilingual community questionnaire (to identify crime and disorder issues) as well as a vision for the department; from this process, new mission and values statements were written. The department began to explore how to strategically address problems. The team chose a 45-square-block neighborhood; a team of six COPPS officers was assigned to seek citizen input, analyze problems, and develop intervention strategies. To evaluate whether the strategy was worth the effort, a pre-post citizen survey approach was adopted with a random sample of households, using a 60-item questionnaire distributed to 3,676 households (with a 30.3 percent response rate). Responses to each question were given a numerical weight, and an average score was computed. The following formula was developed and helped obtain a fear index for the neighborhood:

$$\frac{(\# \text{ increased} \times 5) + (\# \text{ same} \times 3) + (\# \text{ decreased} \times 0)}{\text{Total responses}}$$

A disorder index was also developed from the survey, based on the following formula:

$$\frac{(\# \text{ big problem} \times 5) + (\# \text{ problem} \times 3) + (\# \text{ no problem} \times 0)}{\text{Total responses}}$$

Using this procedure, a summary measure of disorder for each neighborhood was obtained.

The findings indicated that the residents in the target area experienced substantial reductions in actual crimes as well as in their fear and perceptions of crime and disorder. This carefully planned community intervention strategy makes Lawrence an important case study in the systematic implementation of COPPS in a medium-size city.

Source: Adapted from Allen W. Cole and Gordon Bazemore, "Police and the 'Laboratory' of the Neighborhood: Evaluating Problem-Oriented Strategies in a Medium Sized City," *American Journal of Police* 18 (1994):131.

Impact evaluations thus go a step farther by establishing not only whether a COPPS initiative is associated with the outcomes, but also whether it actually produced or caused them. Impact evaluation is an empirical process for determining if a problem declined and if the solution caused the decline. Evaluation begins at the moment the S.A.R.A. problem-solving process begins and continues through the completion of the effort.[3] To determine what did in fact happen to the problem, an **impact evaluation** is needed. An impact evaluation asks the following questions: Did the problem decline? If so, did the *response* cause the decline? We encourage much more frequent use of the former (impact evaluations); as one academic stated, "There needs to be an evaluation process/system that makes reality out of conjecture."[4]

In our prostitution example, assume that during the analysis stage vice detectives conducted a census of prostitutes operating in the target area. They also asked the traffic engineering department to install traffic counters on the major thoroughfare and critical side streets to measure traffic flow and to determine how customers move through the area. The vice squad made covert video recordings of the target area to document how prostitutes interact with potential customers.

Many agencies use neighborhood meetings as a method to evaluate their performance and to identify residents' needs and priorities.
Courtesy Arlington County, Virginia, Police Department.

Then, after the response was implemented, the team decided to repeat these measures to see if the problem has declined. They discover that instead of the 23 prostitutes counted in the first census, only 8 can be found. They also find that there has been a slight decline in traffic on the major thoroughfare on the weekends, but not at other times; however, there has been a substantial decline in side street traffic on Saturday nights. New covert video recordings show that prostitutes in the area have changed how they approach vehicles. In short, the team has evidence that the problem has declined after response implementation.[5] Thus, an impact evaluation has two parts: measuring the problem and systematically comparing changes in measures by using an evaluation design to determine whether or not the response was the primary cause of the change in the measure.

Figure 8–1 depicts and compares critical questions to be asked in the S.A.R.A. problem-solving stages (the left side of the figure) as well as in an impact evaluation. The figure also draws attention to the fact that the assessment may produce information requiring the problem solver to go back to earlier stages to make modifications. Also, note that in the following discussion concerning **surveys**, we discuss some of the kinds of data analyses that can be performed with impact evaluations.

Use of Surveys

Surveys are a vital part of a COPPS strategy. About one-fourth of local police departments, employing 50 percent of all officers, survey citizens in their jurisdiction.[6] Furthermore, citizen survey information is used for a variety of purposes—primarily to provide information to patrol officers, evaluate program effectiveness, and prioritize crime and disorder problems. Police agencies should attempt to "feel the pulse" of their communities, so the importance of surveying community needs cannot be overstated. The mood of the public should be a vital consideration when the police make public policy decisions.[7]

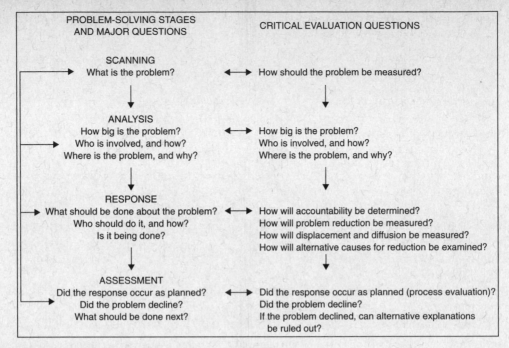

FIGURE 8–1 The Problem-Solving Process and Evaluation

Source: John E. Eck, *Assessing Responses to Problems: An Introductory Guide for Police Problem-Solvers* (Washington, D.C.: U.S. Department of Justice, Office of Community Oriented Policing Services, 2002), p. 6.

METHODS AND ISSUES.   Done properly, surveys are quite labor-intensive and expensive; therefore, consideration should be given to the use of volunteers for the former, and budgetary limitations with the latter. Persons who are about to conduct community surveys will find a very valuable resource in a joint publication by the federal Bureau of Justice Statistics and the Office of Community Oriented Policing Services: *Conducting Community Surveys: A Practical Guide for Law Enforcement Agencies.*[8] It explains the use of surveys by police agencies and includes survey development, administration, and interpretation of results. Many other books have been written that are devoted exclusively to the subject of evaluation.[9] Following are several key issues to resolve before developing a questionnaire:[10]

- *What are the specific purposes of the survey, and what kinds of questions will be consistent with those purposes?* Without clear goals, the number of questions tends to mushroom. This increases the amount of time required to administer each survey, which is a burden on both interviewer and interviewee.
- *How will the survey be administered—by mail, by telephone, or in person?* A questionnaire can be mailed to everyone in the sample to complete and return; the sampled respondents can be interviewed by telephone; or they can be interviewed in person (at home, in the office, on the bus, or wherever they are). Mail surveys can be quite expensive if there is a large population to be sampled.[11] There are advantages and disadvantages to each type of survey that should be explored prior to determining which type is to be used.
- *How much time will it take to complete the survey, and is this a reasonable amount of time to impose on respondents?* Remember that completion of a survey is an intrusion on the time of others. About 10 to 15 minutes to complete a questionnaire is reasonable, but if

examining, say, problems involving drugs and violence, 30 to 40 minutes might be reasonable. The key is to be considerate about demands on others.

Surveys allow a broad range of individuals and groups to provide input on the problem-solving activities. Victim surveys can determine such information as:

- Did victims of auto theft lock their cars or park in lighted areas?
- What actions have residents reporting loitering taken to address the problem?
- How many times have residents experiencing prowlers in a neighborhood contacted the police?
- Who else is affected by the problem, and what do they view as its causes?

Furthermore, surveys can explore residents' participation in community organization, perceptions of the police, victimization experiences, and fear of crime.[12]

OBSERVATIONS.   Certainly not to be overlooked is the use of common observations for understanding problems and response development. Residents can organize themselves to record specific activities at specific locations in their community; activities can be videotaped, and surveys of police can be conducted to determine what was observed at specific times.

As with other analysis tools, observations must be systematic to avoid collecting biased and unreliable data. Observations must be conducted at specific times to document how the nature of the problem changes. They must also be conducted at differing times of day and day of week so that location activity is completely represented.[13]

Neighborhood surveys are often employed by police officers in problem solving; they can provide large amounts of information that are not available in crime statistics. Surveys can help measure the characteristics of neighborhood residents, the background of crime victims, or the background of offenders. Surveys also seek information on the "mental state" of the community, and they frequently address issues such as these:

- Attitudes toward police performance
- Fear of crime
- Future plans and intentions
- Concerns about specific problems
- Suggestions for police actions

There are alternative sources of information as well. For example, census data provides a great deal of information about neighborhoods. Characteristics of victims can be obtained from offense reports, and offender background information can be obtained from arrest reports.

ANALYSIS OF DATA.   To handle large sets of survey data, a computer will probably be needed. Today computers are inexpensive, and user-friendly software programs are available for analyses. Also, police agencies can partner with local colleges and universities for assistance with **data analysis**. Someone will have to read each questionnaire, note how each question was answered, determine the code for each answer, and enter the codes into a data file. This must be done with care to minimize data entry errors.[14] Once the data has been entered, there are four types of analyses to be performed:[15]

1. ***The central tendency of the sample.*** Here, the frequency, central tendency (the average or typical response to a question, which includes the mean, median, and mode), and dispersion of responses (i.e., standard deviation or variance) to each question are calculated.

2. *A determination of how representative of the population being studied the sample really is.* The principal method for checking representativeness is by comparing answers to a few of the questions with information known about the population. If there are no substantial differences, the sample is likely representative of the entire population under study. It may not always be possible to make such a comparison, however.

3. *Make inferences from the sample to the population it represents.* There are two types of inferences that can be made about the population based on sample data. First, characteristics of the population can be determined from what is learned from the sample. Second, one can determine whether there are relationships among the characteristics of members of the population (e.g., whether the age and sex of a person have an influence on fear of crime).

4. *Determine whether or not there are relationships among the attitudes, behaviors, and characteristics identified in the sample population.* When analyzing relationships, social scientists usually talk about variables. Two variables can be noncausally or causally related. A noncausal relationship means that neither variable causes the other; they merely happen to be associated, perhaps because a third variable is causing both of them. An example of a noncausal relationship might be that it is found that be a city's taxi robberies are highest when tourism rates are also at their lowest. To allege that low tourism rates cause high taxi robberies, or vice-versa, would be to imply a spurious relationship between the two. In reality, the economy may have caused both. The economy is an example of a hidden or unseen variable. In a causal relationship, one variable is causing the other. In statistical analysis, the causes are called *independent* variables, and the effects are the *dependent* variables.[16]

COPPS OFFICER PERFORMANCE: ESTABLISHING STANDARDS, EVALUATING WORK

Knowledge, Skills, and Abilities

Evaluating police officer knowledge and performance with COPPS initiatives is also a major need of police agencies; agencies need to know if their officers possess and are applying COPPS skills to crime and disorder issues. Police supervisors in particular should assess how well officers perform problem-solving functions during the course of their tour of duty, and should work with them to correct any deficiencies regarding the following performance criteria[17]:

1. *Time management.* Use uncommitted time to scan neighborhoods and identify problems; balance problem-solving efforts with other responsibilities.

2. *Awareness.* Have knowledge of problems in assigned areas; take steps to stay informed via citizen contact; be familiar with current events; review departmental information; share information with colleagues.

3. *Communication.* Elicit information from colleagues, supervisors, and citizens to facilitate problem solving; convey information in a clear, concise manner.

4. *Analysis.* Be able to relate symptoms to underlying circumstances; identify factors that cause incidents to occur and know what questions to ask.

5. *Judgment.* Identify legitimate alternatives that can be used as responses in addressing problems; select the best alternative based on resource availability, ease of implementation, and perceived effectiveness of response.

A guide for evaluating COPPS officers' performance was developed by the Community Policing Consortium in Washington, D.C.
Courtesy Police Executive Research Forum.

6. *Goal seeking.* Distinguish between short- and long-term goals of response; identify goals that are measurable; relate the goals to the problem.
7. *Planning.* Prepare a legitimate action plan to implement a response; identify responsibilities of participants, appropriate procedures, and a timetable.
8. *Coordination.* Demonstrate competency in organizing efforts of participants involved in implementing responses.
9. *Initiative.* Be self-motivated and engaged in the problem-solving process, identifying and addressing problems; help others when appropriate.
10. *Assessment.* Identify the proper variables to assess; know the types of information to collect to assess results; describe the implications of results attained.

A NEW TOOL FOR MEASURING COPPS: CP-SAT

As mentioned in previous chapters, particularly Chapters 3 and 7, the most challenging aspects of implementing COPPS is fully defining and measuring the concept, as well as how various ranks and functions of an agency practice it over time. Now, however, the federal COPS Office, along with ICF International and the Police Executive Research Forum, has developed a new resource that fills this void: CP-SAT.

CP-SAT is a measurement system that is limited to authorized users for tracking their COPPS efforts over time. It is an online survey platform that assesses the agency's COPPS practices, both within and outside their agency. The CP-SAT meets scientific rigors, is easy to use, and allows departments to implement the tool cost-effectively.

CP-SAT is organized into three modules that correspond to the three primary community policing elements:

1. *Community Partnerships.* This module measures the extent to which agency staff support and develop collaborative relationships among individuals and organizations in the community. Three aspects of partnerships are measured: multisciplinary partnerships, the resources/commitment of an agency's community partners, and the level of interaction with an agency's community partners.
2. *Problem Solving.* This module measures the agency's commitment to crime and disorder. General questions are posed concerning agency problem-solving processes, and problem-solving skill levels are examined.
3. *Organizational Transformation.* Here, the extent to which the agency environment, personnel, practices, and policies are supportive of COPPS philosophy and activities is measured. Specifically, it measures (1) agency management, (2) organizational structure, (3) personnel practices, and (4) technology and information systems.

To ensure a comprehensive assessment, surveys are tailored for each individual role and level of responsibility to COPPS, including officers, supervisors, command staff, civilian personnel, and community partners.

Once the agency and its employees complete the assessment, the agency receives an automated summary report that shows the status of their COPPS initiative across the primary elements and sub-elements. This information is provided to the chief executive, and allows him or her to establish a baseline of COPPS practice, monitor its implementation across ranks over time, and identify COPPS' relative strengths and areas for improvement.[18]

Figure 8–2 depicts a framework for police agencies engaging in a self-assessment of their COPPS efforts.

TWO EMPIRICAL STUDIES OF COPPS INITIATIVES

As indicated in the introduction to this chapter, performing an **empirical study** of a COPPS initiative is always desirable, but it also is highly esoteric, requiring specialized knowledge and abilities. Following are two examples of such studies that will demonstrate the kinds of abilities that are required. Bear in mind that, for the purpose of space and brevity, much has been omitted in terms of the **statistical techniques** employed for data analysis and discussion of findings.

EXAMPLE #1   "Can a Community Policing Initiative Reduce Serious Crime? A Local Evaluation"

Connell et al.,[19] premised their study on the notion that it could help reduce crime and disorder. They observed, however, that this strategy has not been implemented uniformly across the nation, nor were the tactics employed standardized:

> Unfortunately, when crime rates are the dependent variable, varied implementations and strategies cloud the evaluation waters. Although there is evidence that this

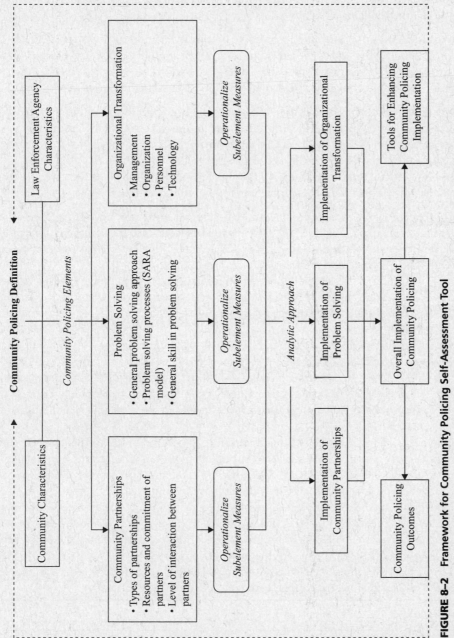

FIGURE 8–2 Framework for Community Policing Self-Assessment Tool

Source: U.S. Department of Justice, Office of Community Oriented Policing Services, "Examining and Assessing Your Community Policing: A Self-Assessment Tool," p. 11, http://www.cops.usdoj.gov/files/ric/Publications/diamond-27.pdf (Accessed September 22, 2010).

strategy reduces disorder and increases positive community–police relations, its effect on crime rates is mixed. This is troubling because the lion's shares of police departments in the United States rely on the community policing model in some manner. If . . . ineffective, researchers, policy makers, and practitioners alike might well seek other policing alternatives.

This study sought to address those shortcomings by evaluating whether or not a well implemented, defined, and comprehensive community policing initiative would have an impact on local crime rates. Officers and first-line supervisors who were selected for the initiative "bought into" community policing and were involved in its implementation. Furthermore,

- every officer was responsible for crime in a particular geographic region within the police beat.
- officers were expected to meet with business owners; make contacts with area schools and other service agencies; and work with apartment managers to identify problem tenants, as well as parole and probation officers concerning repeat offenders.
- patrol officers and sergeants were given the authority to determine how to prevent crime in the targeted area and to use their discretion to find solutions to problems.

Each of three crime rate categories studied—violent, property, and drug crimes—was measured as the crimes known to the police. Crime reports were the dependent measures instead of calls for service or arrests, because it is possible that both of the latter measures may be confounded with the intervention.

To test the impact of the intervention in the treatment police beat, they used three separate dependent variables or dependent series: a violent crimes series, a property crimes series, and a drug series. An intervention series was fit to the data, and served as the independent variable for this analysis.

Using sophisticated statistical techniques, Connell et al. found that for each of the three categories, there was a significant difference between the pre-intervention and the post-intervention means in the intervention site. In other words, the findings suggested that community policing does have the capacity to affect serious crime rates: The intervention resulted in an abrupt and permanent decline in the level of violent and property crimes in the treatment site, though not in the comparison sites.

Connell et al., felt the success of this program may have been due to the comprehensive approach of the program and the fact that it reflected the tenets of community policing. Furthermore, as noted above, the "hearts and minds" of the patrol officers involved were dedicated to problem solving, and those officers who did not buy into the new approach were able to leave the police beat and take other positions within the agency. Finally, the model was not implemented in the entire department; rather, it was limited to a single unit. Connell et al., believed that it is probably easier to implement a comprehensive strategy and maintain standards within a unit rather than an entire department. The hierarchy of command was relatively short; all officers answered to one of two sergeants assigned to the beat. Therefore, more oversight was probably exerted on the officers than would happen within a department-wide initiative.[20]

EXAMPLE #2   "COPS Grants and Crime Revisited"

Worrall et al.,[21] sought to determine whether or not COPS funding had reduced crime; they examined a six-year time frame during which the COPS Office awarded 30,000 grants to more than 12,000 agencies and funded the hiring of more than 105,000 new police officers. From auditing, policy making, and legislative standpoints, it is important to ensure that COPS grants were spent according to plan and, as the enabling legislation emphasized community policing, it was deemed important to consider whether COPS grants had encouraged, altered, or thwarted community policing initiatives.

The source for these data was the FBI's Uniform Crime Reporting program. The dependent variables in these analyses were the rates per 100,000 people of seven index crimes (excluding arson). They merged the COPS data used previously in other studies, with 11 years of panel data from a sample of 189 large cities. They also controlled for pre-existing effects on crime of police spending, and included several conventional control variables: the percentage of people between 18 and 24; the percentage of people between 25 and 44; the percentage of people living beneath the poverty line; the percentage of black residents; the percentage of Hispanic residents; the percentage of female-headed households; and the percentage of the population living alone, per capita income, and state prisoners per 100,000 people. They estimated a series of two-way fixed-effects regressions.

Expecting to find an inverse relationship between COPS grants and crime, and that the spending of $8 billion in taxpayer dollars would be found to have significantly reduced crime, their findings suggested otherwise: COPS spending had little to no effect on crime and thus, in their words, tended to "fly in the face" of other similar studies. They believed the reason for this finding was clear: The average grants for hiring—the largest type of COPS grant—averaged only $407,515.70, a mere one half of 1 percent of the typical police budget.

Worrall and Kovandzic concluded that:

> It may well be the case that federal funding for local law enforcement is not the best way to go, even after controlling for other important variables such as annual fiscal expenditures. A strategy of throwing money at the crime problem, of simply *hiring* more police officers, does not seem to help reduce crime to a significant extent.[22]

The authors would add to these conclusions by Worrall and Kovandzic that history has shown that having more police officers does not necessarily equate with safer communities or better policing. Nor is the number of officers hired as important as what they are doing. Are they trained adequately in problem solving? Is an infrastructure in place to support those officers? Are the supervisors managing officers' time to ensure that they are working on neighborhood problems? These are all essential considerations as well.

Summary

This chapter began with the general proposition that the criminal justice field, today more than ever, needs to know "what works" in terms of its policies and practices. We also emphasized the fact that assessing and evaluating the impact of COPPS is critical and, if done properly, highly challenging. Although there is no one measurement process that will work for COPPs initiatives in all communities, this chapter offered a comprehensive view of the rationales, general guidelines, methods, and criteria for measuring social interventions. Several examples of successful empirical evaluations of COPPS initiatives were also provided.

Items for Review

1. Discuss the general rationale for learning "what works" in criminal justice in general, and for measuring (assessing and evaluating) COPPS initiatives in specific.

2. Describe the major differences between assessments (as defined in the S.A.R.A. problem solving process) and an empirical impact evaluation of a COPPS strategy.

3. Explain why the accomplishment of an actual impact evaluation is uniquely challenging for the police agency in terms of one's knowledge, skills and abilities—and some means for acquiring the services of one who can perform such an evaluation.

4. Describe the kinds of knowledge, skills, and abilities that a police officer engaged in COPPS must possess, as well as the criteria for assessing an officer's problem-solving performance.

5. Explain the benefits of using surveys for evaluative purposes.

6. Describe the benefits of an agency's employing the CP-SAT system for its COPPS initiatives.

Learn by Doing

1. Knowing you excelled in your research methods and statistics courses at university, a local police lieutenant—now supervising its crime research and analysis unit—contacts you for assistance. It seems that the department will soon initiate a POP project involving crime and disorder at motels in a rundown part of town. The lieutenant asks you to explain how they might go about examining outcomes of their S.A.R.A. efforts as well as performing a full-blown impact evaluation. What general recommendations will you make? How would you describe what a truly empirical study contains?

2. You are contacted for advice by a police supervisor. It seems that her community policing team—composed of four deputies who are supposed to be dedicated to COPPS efforts in a particular area of the county—are not getting the job done. Citizens are complaining about crime and disorder and that nothing is accomplished at advisory board meetings. The deputies seem to lack overall knowledge of the area as well as any sort of plan, direction, or motivation to engage in problem solving efforts. The supervisor is in desperate need of advice concerning criteria for evaluating the deputies' performance so as to determine whether they should be retrained or reassigned. How will you proceed, and what criteria will you recommend?

3. You are consulting with a small agency in another state that is engaged in problem-solving activities. It now wishes to survey the community concerning their fears and concerns, views toward the police, observations of crime and disorder, and so on. What information and caveats will you provide concerning the types of surveys that might be developed?

Notes

1. Daniel P. Mears, *American Criminal Justice Policy: An Approach to Increasing Accountability and Effectiveness* (Cambridge University Press, 2010), p. 195.

2. For an overview of methodologies for determining what works, what does not work, and what has promise with respect to criminal justice programs, see Lawrence W. Sherman, Denise C. Gottfredson, Doris L. MacKenzie, John Eck, Peter Reuter, and Shawn D. Bushway, *Preventing Crime: What Works, What Doesn't, What's Promising* (U.S. Department of Justice, July 1988), http://www.ncjrs.gov/pdffiles/171676.PDF (Accessed June 11, 2010).

3. John E. Eck, *Assessing Responses to Problems: An Introductory Guide for Police Problem-Solvers* (Washington, D.C.: U.S. Department of Justice, Office of Community Oriented Policing Services, 2002), p. 5.

4. See, for example, Donald S. Quire, "Models for Community Policing Evaluation: The St. Petersburg Experience," http://www.fdle.state.fl.us/Content/Florida-Criminal-Justice-Executive-Institute/Docs/Quire.aspx (Accessed July 18, 2010).

5. Ibid., pp. 7–9.

6. U.S. Department of Justice, *Law Enforcement Management and Administrative Statistics* (Washington, D.C.: Author, 2003), p. 17.

7. Mervin F. White and Ben A. Menke, "A Critical Analysis on Public Opinions Toward Police Agencies," *Journal of Police Science and Administration* 6 (1978):204–218.

8. Deborah Weisel, *Conducting Community Surveys: A Practical Guide for Law Enforcement Agencies* (Washington, D.C.: U.S. Department of Justice, Bureau of Justice Statistics, Office of Community Oriented Policing Services, 1999).

9. See, for example, Carl A. Bennett and Arthur A. Lumsdaine, *Evaluation and Experiment* (New York: Academic Press, 1975); Ronald Roesch and Raymond R. Corrado (eds.), *Evaluation and*

Criminal Justice Policy (Beverly Hills, Calif.: Sage, 1981); Malcolm W. Klein and Katherine Teilmann Van Dusen, *Handbook of Criminal Justice Evaluation* (Beverly Hills, Calif.: Sage, 1980); Richard H. Price and Peter E. Politser, *Evaluation and Action in the Social Science Environment* (New York: Academic Press, 1980).

10. See, for example, Ken Peak, "On Successful Criminal Justice Survey Research: A 'Personal Touch' Model for Enhancing Rates of Return," *Criminal Justice Policy Review* 4 (3) (Spring 1992):268–277; Don A. Dillman, *Mail and Telephone Surveys: The Total Design Method* (New York: John Wiley & Sons, 1978); Arlene Fink and Jacqueline Kosecoff, *How to Conduct Surveys: A Step-by-Step Guide* (Beverly Hills, Calif.: Sage, 1985); Floyd J. Fowler, *Survey Research Methods* (Newbury Park, Calif.: Sage, 1988); Abraham Nastali Oppenheim, *Questionnaire Design, Interviewing, and Attitude Measurement* (New York: St. Martin's Press, 1992); Charles H. Backstrom and Gerald Hursh-Cesar, *Survey Research* (2nd ed.) (New York: Macmillan, 1981).

11. Police Executive Research Forum, *A Police Practitioner's Guide*, p. 22.

12. Adapted from Timothy S. Bynum, *Using Analysis for Problem-Solving: A Guide for Law Enforcement*, 2002, pp. 25–26, U.S. Department of Justice, Office of Community Oriented Policing Services, http://www.cops.usdoj.gov/pdf/e08011230.pdf (Accessed July 19, 2010).

13. Ibid., pp. 40–41.

14. For a more detailed introduction to analyzing data in policing, see John Eck, *Using Research: A Primer for Law Enforcement* (Washington, D.C.: Police Executive Research Forum, 1984).

15. Adapted from Police Executive Research Forum, *A Police Practitioner's Guide*, pp. 31–34.

16. See, generally, Deborah Weisel, *Conducting Community Surveys: A Practical Guide for Law Enforcement Agencies*, October 1999, http://www.popcenter.org/library/reading/PDFs/Conducting_Surveys.pdf (Accessed July 19, 2010); *A Police Guide to Surveying Citizens and Their Environment*, October 1993, http://www.ncjrs.gov/pdffiles/polc.pdf (Accessed July 19, 2010).

17. Adapted from Columbia, South Carolina, Police Department, *Columbia Patrol Officer Performance Evaluation Workbook* (Columbia, S.C.: Author, March 1997), pp. 6–7; also see Timothy N. Oettmeier and Mary Ann Wycoff, *Personnel Performance Evaluations in the Community Policing Context* (Washington, D.C.: Community Policing Consortium, 1997).

18. "CP-SAT: A New Measure for Community," *Community Policing Dispatch* 3 (May 2010), http://www.cops.usdoj.gov/html/dispatch/May_2010/cp_sat.htm (Accessed July 18, 2010).

19. Adapted from Nadine M. Connell, Kristen Miggans, and Jean Marie McGloin, "Can a Community Policing Initiative Reduce Serious Crime? A Local Evaluation," *Police Quarterly* 11 (2) (June 2008): 127–150.

20. Ibid.

21. Adapted from John L. Worrall and Tomislav V. Kovandzic, "COPS Grants and Crime Revisited," *Criminology* 45 (1) (2007): 159–190.

22. Ibid.

9

Training for COPPS
Approaches and Challenges

KEY TERMS AND CONCEPTS

Adult learning	Higher education	Police training officer (PTO)
Andragogy	In-service training	Problem-based learning
Curriculum (for COPPS)	Learning organization	(PBL)
Distance learning	Mentoring	Recruit academy
E-learning	Needs assessment	Roll call training
Field training officer (FTO)	Online training	Training technology

LEARNING OBJECTIVES

As a result of reading this chapter, the student will:

- Understand the foundations of adult- and problem-based learning, as espoused by Knowles and Bloom, and how they apply to training for COPPS

- Understand why it is important for police agencies to become learning organizations

- Be familiar with the unique challenges that are involved with training police officers

- Understand how knowledge is imparted at the basic recruit academy as well as with post-academy, in-service, and roll call methods

- Have a grasp of why higher education can be beneficial for officers engaged in COPPS

- Know the kinds of technologies that exist in police training

- Have a fundamental understanding of how to determine officers' training needs

A man can seldom—very, very seldom—fight a winning fight
against his training: the odds are too heavy.

—MARK TWAIN

INTRODUCTION

As we have noted in previous chapters, the movement toward community oriented policing and problem solving (COPPS) involves a change in the philosophy, culture, and the organizational structure of the police agency. New knowledge, skills, and abilities must be developed, as well as a reorientation of perceptions and a refining of skill sets. This is a difficult challenge for those involved in the training and education of police officers.

This training is of utmost importance, and the challenge greatly enhanced, because the successful implementation of COPPS requires the training of *every* employee inside the agency as well as an orientation for a number of people and organizations outside the police department. Indeed, police administrators, federal and state criminal justice planning officials, and criminal justice policy advisory groups have rated training as the primary need in order for COPPS to reach its fullest potential. Furthermore, it is important that the police educate the public and other public and private agencies and organizations in the concept because they will be required, at times, to help carry out the COPPS effort. This chapter analyzes training from these disparate yet related perspectives.

We begin this chapter with a look at the concepts of adult- and problem-based learning, and the important contributions they make to COPPS training, as well as the need to create a learning organization. Next we consider why having police officers in the classroom constitutes another sort of challenge, and the various means by which training is provided to these individuals (including the recruit academy and via field training, in-service, roll call, and specialized means); included in this section is a brief description of the use of training technologies.

Then we focus on a combined program for accomplishing COPPS training; this comprehensive section includes the extent to which such training is occurring nationally, the methods for determining officers' training needs, and some ideas for curricular content. Exhibits containing examples and new developments in police training initiatives are provided throughout the chapter. The chapter concludes with a summary, review questions, and several scenarios and activities that provide opportunities for you to "learn by doing."

Also note that, due to space limitations precluding its being in this chapter, Appendix I at the book's end shows a *Model Academic Curriculum for Problem-Oriented Policing,* as espoused by the U.S. Department of Justice, Center for Problem-Oriented Policing.[1]

ADULT AND PROBLEM-BASED LEARNING, GENERALLY

As anyone can attest, there are certain challenges and obstacles to learning that must be overcome before we can expand our knowledge. Therefore, prior to specifically examining the training of police officers in the context of COPPS, it is important to consider how adults learn best; we will briefly discuss adult learning, problem-based learning, and the learning organization.

Knowles' Andragogy

In order for adult training to succeed, the certain conditions for **adult learning** to occur should be borne in mind:

- Adults must be partners in their own educational plans and evaluations.
- The material must be relevant.
- Adult learning should be problem centered rather than content oriented.

Based on these ends, the writings of Malcolm Knowles and Benjamin Bloom are important. Knowles's theory of **andragogy** was developed specifically for adult learners. Andragogy emphasizes that adults are self-directed and need to be free to direct themselves; teachers must actively involve class participants in the learning process and serve as facilitators for them through such means as allowing presentations and group leadership. Knowles wrote that adults are characterized by the following:[2]

- Adults have life experiences and knowledge that may include work-related activities, family responsibilities, and previous education. They need to connect learning to this base, so try to draw out their experience and knowledge that are relevant to the topic.
- Adults are goal oriented and appreciate an educational program that is organized and has clearly defined elements. Instructors should explain how their course assists participants in obtaining their goals.
- Adults are relevancy oriented and must see a reason for learning something; learning must be applicable to their work or other purposes to be of value to them. Therefore, when possible, allow participants to choose projects that reflect their own interests.
- Adults need to be shown respect, and teachers should treat them as equals in experience and knowledge and allow them to voice their opinions freely in class.

Adult Learning—Millennial-Style

In Chapter 6 we discussed today's new generation of police officers, known as the Millennials, and the differences they bring to the workplace in terms of knowledge and expectations. As adult learners, Millennials are felt to be almost unresponsive to didactic or lecture-type instruction; they appreciate team work and desire experiential and engaging activities that they can immediately put to use, and of course are technological and expect their learning to come from a variety of sources. Therefore, it is recommended that today's policing training incorporate the following techniques:

- Use of active and engaging learning activities
- Integrating everyday technology into the classroom
- Minimizing lecture
- Encouraging nonlinear thinking
- Using mentorship as a way to bridge generation gaps
- Using group discussions and collaborative groups
- Showing students the immediate application of skills
- Using a variety of sources for building knowledge[3]

Bloom's Taxonomy

Benjamin Bloom's taxonomy is also helpful. Bloom's cognitive domain for learning emphasizes intellectual outcomes. Bloom's taxonomy of six learning activities, in ascending order, is as follows:[4]

1. *Knowledge*—remembering or recalling previously learned material
2. *Comprehension*—understanding meaning, and explaining and restating ideas
3. *Application*—applying learned material in new and different situations
4. *Analysis*—categorizing material into segments and demonstrating their relationships
5. *Synthesis*—grouping or combining the separate ideas to form a new whole and establishing new relationships
6. *Evaluation*—evaluating the material for appropriate outcomes based on established criteria

Problem-based learning (PBL) is a learning process that also has application to COPPS training, as it stimulates problem solving, critical thinking, utilization of nontraditional

Officers receive in-service computer training to expand their capabilities.
FBI Law Enforcement Bulletin.

resources, and team participation. Like the adult learning theory discussed above, the purpose of PBL is to make learning relevant to real-world situations. In PBL, the trainee engages in self-teaching; trainees begin with a problem rather than follow the traditional approach whereby a class is given a problem to solve at the end of the class.[5]

The aim of PBL is not solely to solve the problem but rather to help the students fill gaps in their knowledge and to involve them in self-directed learning techniques. The students are guided by instructors and facilitators so that they can ultimately learn what they are supposed to learn. PBL departs from traditional learning models by beginning with the presentation of a real-world problem that the trainee must attempt to solve. The trainee follows a path of inquiry and discovery whereby he or she expresses initial ideas about how to solve the problem, lists known facts, decides what information is needed, and develops a course of action to solve the problem. This approach to learning teaches the trainees to look at problems from a broader perspective. It encourages trainees to explore, analyze, and think systemically, while they also collaborate with peers, open lines of communication, and develop resources for solving future problems.

PBL is therefore both a **curriculum** and a process. The curriculum consists of carefully selected problems that demand from the learner acquisition of critical knowledge, problem-solving proficiency, and team participation skills. The process involves resolving problems or challenges that are encountered in life and careers. With PBL, students assume increased responsibility for their learning, giving them more motivation and feelings of accomplishment. Adult learning and PBL are essential for creating a learning organization, which is discussed next.

THE LEARNING ORGANIZATION

Peter Senge's concept of **learning organizations** certainly applies to COPPS training and is very important for training adult learners. Senge feels that the organization must allow its employees to continually expand their capacity to nurture new and expansive patterns of thinking, allow their collective aspiration to be set free, and continually learn to see the whole picture.

To help effect change in their organizations, police administrators are increasingly turning to Senge's writings, which evolved into a book that popularized the concept, *The Fifth Discipline.*[6] Senge states:

> Learning organizations are those where people continually expand their capacity to create the results they truly desire, where new and expansive patterns of thinking are nurtured, where collective aspiration is set free, and where people are continually learning to see the whole together.[7]

Three indicators will determine whether an organization can be identified as a learning organization:

1. How do individuals view their current assignment? If they attend staff meetings and are only concerned about how decisions affect their area of responsibility, it is not; if, however, they view the organization as a system where decisions affect all of its parts, it is open to learning new methods.
2. How do individuals in the organization view their co-workers? There must be a balance between competition and cooperation; without those aspects of work, there will be no dialogue, and without dialogue, new ideas will not be raised, and only the views the command staff will prevail.
3. How does the individual view the change process in the organization? The "we've always done it this way" or "if it ain't broke, don't fix it" mentality has no place in a learning organization, and consideration must be given to external forces of change as well as internal.[8]

In sum, the learning organization requires a new view of leadership; leaders are responsible for building organizations where people continually expand their capabilities to understand complexity, clarify vision, and improve shared mental models. Leaders do not teach but foster learning.

How does COPPS relate to learning organizations? As police organizations implement COPPS and assess its efficacy, the learning organization capitalizes on its own and others' experiences—successes as well as failures—to continually hone strategies, tactics, operations.

TRAINING OF POLICE OFFICERS: CHALLENGES AHEAD

Anyone who undertakes to train police officers must be mindful of the challenges at hand. Michael E. Buerger provided food for thought concerning police training:

> Training is usually discussed in terms of a benefit provided to the rank-and-file. From the perspective of those receiving it, however, training is easily divided into two main categories: the kind officers like, and the kind they despise. What they like fits into their world view; what they despise is "training" that attempts to change that view.[9]

There are challenges in training officers in the COPPS strategy. First, because policing often attracts action-oriented individuals, officers tend to be more receptive to hands-on skills training, such as arrest methods, weaponless defense, pursuit driving, firearms proficiency, and baton usage. Certainly these measures are needed from time to time, and for that reason (and because of the specter of liability) police personnel must receive training in those areas. As many studies have demonstrated, however, only a small fraction of the typical officer's work routine involves the use of weapons, defensive tactics, high-speed chases, and so forth. If training is to help officers do their jobs better, it must focus on what they need to know in order to do their job well. It should also be driven by the mission of the agency.

It must also be remembered that police training is best conducted—and is better received by the officers—when it reflects skills with immediately recognizable application to the job and when that message is constantly reinforced throughout training. Thus, it is not surprising that officers prefer to be instructed by persons who both possess expertise in the activity and have "walked the walk" of police patrol, that is, other police officers.[10] It is also worthwhile to remember that an environment that is conducive to learning, with a clearly stated outcome that inspires learners' physical and mental engagement, and activities that precipitate critical thinking and problem solving are important training processes as well.

NEW KNOWLEDGE AND RETENTION OF LEARNED SKILLS

Police training may be obtained through four primary means—recruit academy, postacademy field training/police training officer, in-service training, and roll call training—in addition to the many excellent conferences and workshops that also now exist to provide COPPS training. Each is extremely important for imparting values and information concerning the COPPS philosophy.

Recruit Academy

Academy training (the recruit or cadet phase) sets the tone for newly hired officers. It is at the **recruit academy** that new officers begin to develop a strong mindset about their role as police. Ideally, academy training will provide comprehensive instruction in the two primary elements of COPPS—community engagement and problem solving—if the proper philosophical mindset for recruits is to be formed. In many cases, this will require that traditional courses, such as those in history, patrol procedures, police-community relations, and crime prevention, be revamped to include the topics and information recommended in this chapter; this information will teach officers to be more analytical and creative in their efforts to address community crime and disorder. A primary emphasis on the nature of crime and disorder and problem-solving methods should be the foundation for this training.

In 1996, Maryland became the first state in the nation to initiate a community policing academy, with the goal of providing training in COPPS to officers in every local police agency. The academy serves as a central resource for providing agencies with continuing education as well as training in resource development and community involvement.

Exhibit 9–1 shows what a training academy in New Jersey is doing to instruct recruits on the basics of community policing in the classroom, and applying their problem solving knowledge in their neighborhoods.

Exhibit 9–1	Community Policing in the Academy and Beyond

Recently the Somerset County, New Jersey, Police Academy developed a recruit program in which community policing was the underlying foundation. That's not usual. Today, however, this academy stands apart in its promotion of partnerships and problem solving, both inside and outside the classroom. In the classroom, police recruits learn the fundamentals of community policing. But the centerpiece of the six-month program is a Capstone Project, which requires the recruits to work with members of the community to identify a problem or community concern. Senior citizens, educators, community members, business leaders, and representatives of the faith community are invited to the academy to participate in the project. Community members, referred to as "community facilitators," are recommended by their local police chiefs and agency heads and then paired with recruits based on either common interests or jurisdictions. These community facilitators work with recruits as they implement the S.A.R.A process to identify and develop responses to actual community problems.

Part of the project involves recruits writing a detailed analysis of the identified issue that often results in a 25–40 page paper. Many Capstone Projects lead to the development of handbooks, curriculum, and/or strategic plans that recruits can take with them when they embark on their new careers. At the end of the academy, each Capstone team gives an oral presentation, sharing how they addressed their community problem. Since the program was established, approximately 800 recruits have successfully completed a Capstone Project and received their community policing certification.

Source: Adapted from "Report from the Field: Community Policing in the Academy and Beyond," _Community Policing Dispatch 2_ (11) (November 2009), http://www.cops.usdoj.gov/html/dispatch/November_2009/police_academy.htm (Accessed July 20, 2010).

Field Training Officer (FTO) Program

The next phase of training for newly hired officers is the **field training officer (FTO)** program, which is provided immediately on leaving the academy. The field training program was begun in the San Jose, California, Police Department in 1972, and assists recruits in their transition from the academy to the streets while still under the protective arm of a veteran officer.[11] Most FTO programs consist of an introductory phase (where the recruit learns agency policies and local laws), training and evaluation phases (the recruit is introduced to more complicated tasks confronted by patrol officers), and a final phase (the FTO may act strictly as an observer and evaluator while the recruit performs all the functions of a patrol officer). This last phase of the recruit's training can obviously have a profound effect on his or her later career based on whether or not the neophyte officer is allowed to learn and put this strategy into practice.

Police Training Officer (PTO) Program

Many police executives have come to believe, however, that the traditional FTO approach that was implemented in 1972 is not relevant to the challenges of contemporary policing, especially those agencies that have adopted COPPS. Therefore, many police agencies are retooling their FTO programs to emphasize community policing and to better meet the needs of their officers with what is termed the **police training officer (PTO)** program.

The Reno, Nevada, Police Department—with assistance and about a half million dollars in funding from the Police Executive Research Forum and the federal Office of Community Oriented Policing Services—recently developed a model PTO program that recognizes the importance of problem-solving skills and critical thinking. PTO uses a number of tools that embrace the aforementioned adult- and problem-based learning concepts as well as a learning matrix that shows core competencies, which are specific knowledge, skills, and abilities that are essential for community policing and problem solving.

Exhibit 9–2 shows the learning matrix that is used with the Reno model. Each cell (A1 through D15) has a corresponding list of skills required to achieve competency in the areas listed. The learning matrix serves as a guide for trainees and trainers during the training period, and it demonstrates the interrelationships between the core competencies and daily policing activities.

Problem solving is woven throughout the training process, and the matrix assists trainees to determine what they have learned, what they need to learn to improve their performance, and which performance outcomes will be utilized to evaluate their performance. PTO covers two primary training areas: substantive topics (the most common activities in policing) and core competencies

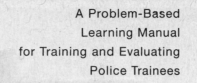

A Problem-Based
Learning Manual
for Training and Evaluating
Police Trainees

pto
manual

The federal Office of Community Oriented Policing Services publishes a manual on the PTO approach for training new police officers.
U.S. Department of Justice, Office of Community Oriented Policing Services, 2005.

(the required common skills that officers use and that are required to utilize in the daily performance of their duties). As shown in the matrix, the four substantive topics that define the key phases of training are nonemergency incident response, emergency incident response, patrol activities, and criminal investigation. In addition, the 15 core competencies that are listed must be met under PTO; these are specific knowledge, skills, and abilities that have been identified as essential for good policing.

Exhibit 9–2	Reno PTO Learning Matrix

	Phase A Nonemergency Incident Response	Phase B Emergency Incident Response	Phase C Patrol Activities	Phase D Criminal Investigation
Core Competencies				
Police Vehicle Operations	A1	B1	C1	D1
Conflict Resolution	A2	B2	C2	D2
Use of Force	A3	B3	C3	D3
Local Procedures, Policies, Laws, Philosophies	A4	B4	C4	D4
Report Writing	A5	B5	C5	D5
Leadership	A6	B6	C6	D6
Problem-Solving Skills	A7	B7	C7	D7
Community-Specific Problems	A8	B8	C8	D8
Cultural Diversity & Special Needs Groups	A9	B9	C9	D9
Legal Authority	A10	B10	C10	D10
Individual Rights	A11	B11	C11	D11
Officer Safety	A12	B12	C12	D12
Communication Skills	A13	B13	C13	D13
Ethics	A14	B14	C14	D14
Lifestyle Stressors/ Self-Awareness/ Self-Regulation	A15	B15	C15	D15
Learning Activities	Introduction of Neighborhood Portfolio Exercise	Continuation of Neighborhood Portfolio Exercise	Continuation of Neighborhood Portfolio Exercise	Final Neighborhood Portfolio Presentation
	Problem-Based Learning Exercise	Problem-Based Learning Exercise	Problem-Based Learning Exercise	Problem-Based Learning Exercise
Evaluation Activities	Weekly Coaching and Training Reports	Weekly Coaching and Training Reports	Weekly Coaching and Training Reports	Weekly Coaching and Training Reports

Source: Reno, Nevada, Police Department, *PTO Program: The Reno Model, 2004.*

In-Service Training

In-service training provides an opportunity to impart information and to reinforce new skills learned in the academy and FTO program. In-service classes are useful for sharing officers' experiences in applying COPPS to a variety of problems as well as for their collaboration with other city agencies, social service organizations, or the community. In-service training is also one of the primary means of changing the culture and attitudes of personnel.[12]

Obviously, a tremendous challenge for large police departments is providing COPPS training for all of the many hundreds or even thousands of officers and civilians. Some large agencies have used videotaped or computer-assisted training. Many departments, using drug forfeiture funds, have also purchased high-technology equipment for use with training. In addition to COPPS courses and orientations, departmental newsletters can disseminate information to personnel on a regular basis.

Roll Call Training

Roll call training is that period of time—from 15 to 30 minutes prior to the beginning of a tour of duty—in which supervisors prepare officers for patrol. Roll call sessions usually begin with a supervisor assigning the officers to their respective beats. Information about wanted and dangerous persons and major incidents on previous shifts is usually disseminated. Other matters may also be addressed, such as issuing officers court subpoenas, explaining new departmental policies and procedures, and discussing shift- and beat-related matters.

Roll call meetings afford an excellent opportunity for supervisors to update officers' knowledge and to present new ideas and techniques. This is particularly advantageous for small police agencies that have limited training staff and resources. For example, videotapes or problem-solving case studies can be used at briefing sessions to provide relevant information.

HIGHER EDUCATION

Certainly a feature of the COPPS strategy concerns **higher education** for officers. To begin with, from 1967 to 1986 every national commission that studied crime, violence, and policing in America was of the opinion that a college education could help the police to do their jobs better.[13] Advocates of higher education for the police maintain that it improves the quality of policing by making officers more tolerant of people who are different from themselves; in this view, educated officers are more professional, communicate better with citizens, are better decision makers, and have better written and verbal skills.

A ringing endorsement for higher education for the police came in 1985, when a lawsuit challenged the Dallas, Texas, Police Department's requirement that all applicants for police officer positions possess 45 credit hours and at least a C average at an accredited college or university. The Fifth Circuit Court of Appeals and eventually the U.S. Supreme Court upheld the educational requirement. The circuit court—in language that could be speaking of COPPS—said:

> A significant part of a police officer's function involves his ability to function effectively as a crisis intervenor, in family fights, teen-age rumbles, bar brawls, street corner altercations, racial disturbances, riots and similar situations. Few professionals are so peculiarly charged with individual responsibilities as police officers. Mistakes of judgment could cause irreparable harm to citizens or even to the community. The educational requirement bears a manifest relationship to the position of police officer. We conclude that the district court's findings . . . are not erroneous.[14]

Exhibit 9–3	Maine's Online Training Initiative

Since 2004, the Maine Chiefs of Police Association (MCOPA) has led an effort to implement an online component within Maine's overall public safety training delivery system. Using funds supplied by a host of state and federal agencies, coupled with subscription fees for expanded services, the online training program is a comprehensive and technically advanced online training system serving the state's law enforcement community. Guided by adult-learning instructional design principles, the online classes are specifically engineered to engage the interest of participants using graphics, animations, photography, audio components, hyperlinks, and interactive exercises. More than 90 classes currently available and 160 law enforcement agencies employ the online training system. User agencies range from the largest law enforcement organization in the state (the Maine State Police) to the smaller agencies. There are some small departments in Maine that employ only part-time officers, and they have access to the same quality training as the larger agencies. All Maine law enforcement agencies have an account in the system, and active system users currently represent nearly 90 percent of Maine's sworn officers.

Source: Adapted from Robert M. Schwartz, John Rogers, and Paul Plaisted, "Partnering for Progress: Maine Law Enforcement Online Training Initiative," *The Police Chief* (November 2009): 32, http://www.policechiefmagazine .org/magazine/index.cfm?fuseaction=display_arch&article_id=1944&issue_id=112009 (Accessed July 20, 2010).

There is abundant empirical evidence indicating that college-educated police officers are better officers, including the fact that these officers have more favorable attitudes toward community policing.[15] Certainly the kinds of abilities that are required for officers to work through the S.A.R.A. process (described in Chapter 3), as well as the skills needed by officers to communicate with citizens and to deal with them with respect and cooperation, would seem to result from having officers who have received higher education. Exhibit 9–3 underscores this benefit as it applies to COPPS.

MENTORING

A training concept that is certainly related to both leadership development/succession planning (discussed in Chapter 15) and training the Millennials, discussed above, is **mentoring**. Mentor was the name of the man charged with providing wisdom, advice, and guidance to King Odysseus's son in the ancient Greek epic *The Odyssey.* Later, in a non-fictional sense, during the Middle Ages boys served as apprentices to masters in a craft or trade while gaining skills to qualify as a master.[16]

In today's context, the very fabric of organizational culture is affected and transmitted by mentoring. De Pree[17] termed it "tribal storytelling." Every police agency has its very own historical context, value system, and stories that give employees a unique sense of organizational pride. "Tribal elders," or agency employees with the most seniority, must routinely share these stories and their significance with others so that the culture remains vibrant and purposeful. Effective mentors can and should be these tribal storytellers. Mentoring is even more important when one considers that an entire generation of seasoned officers, supervisors, and command staff is retiring at an accelerated rate. This is creating a void of experienced leadership, which also means that younger officers stepping in to fill these vacancies will most likely occupy formal leadership positions for many years.[18]

It is therefore very important that younger officers have a sense of the organization's artifacts (e.g., history, organizational structure, dress code, acceptable language, and standards of ethical behavior) and espoused beliefs (e.g., ideologies or organizational values).[19]

Mentors have the following responsibilities, all of which are key to both the individual being mentored and the organization:

- Encouraging and modeling value-focused behavior
- Sharing critical knowledge and experience
- Listening to personal and professional challenges
- Setting expectations for success
- Offering wise counsel
- Helping to build self-confidence
- Offering friendship and encouragement
- Providing information and resources
- Offering guidance, giving feedback, and cheering accomplishments
- Discussing and facilitating opportunities for new experiences and skill building
- Assisting in mapping a career plan[20]

TRAINING TECHNOLOGIES

As technology progresses, new and better methods of instruction and delivery of material continue to evolve. **Training technologies** include distance learning, interactive computer disks, satellite television, and even correspondence courses. On-demand learning allows students to receive their training without placing too great a burden on their personal or professional lives.[21] **Online training** can be self-paced, around-the-clock, and interactive and can contain one-on-one coaching and mentoring. Individuals as well as corporations, colleges, and universities now offer COPPS courses online.[22]

Distance learning is a method of training that does not require people to be physically present with the instructor. People may use written materials such as books and workbooks; videos, audiotapes, and CD-ROMs; or courses on the Internet to learn. Grading of papers and tests can be done by mail, fax, e-mail, the Internet, or videoconferencing over broadband network connections.

There is also a growing trend within distance learning called **e-learning** (see Exhibit 9–3). The continuing explosion of Internet-based services—distance education now reaches 12 million college students alone—provides new opportunities for police training. The advantages of e-learning are obvious: a wide variety of course offerings at significant cost savings; the ability to train greater numbers of officers; and students can learn at their own pace and on their schedules, without having to leave home. However, there are potential pitfalls as well that must be sorted out by training officials: Determining what training offerings best suit their needs as well as which training modalities will best serve their officers (live broadcasts, multi-media programs on CD or downloaded, interactive scenario-based training, or a combination) is important given the above discussion of how to train Millennials. Of course, an ongoing concern exists about the quality of the training; descriptors such as "certified" or "approved" do not guarantee quality, unless the course is attached to an accredited college or university.[23]

Exhibit 9–3 shows how one state is providing its officers and other first responders quality online instruction: the Maine Law Enforcement Online Training Initiative; following that, Exhibit 9–4 provides a listing of some helpful resources for developing and conducting police training of all kinds.

| Exhibit 9–4 | Use of the Internet for COPPS |

The Internet provides police officers and trainers with a lower-cost means of communicating with their colleagues across the nation or abroad about policies and programs. Following are some Internet addresses where trainers can conduct research and gain information concerning virtually anything about law enforcement:

▶ *www.usdoj.gov*—U.S. Department of Justice (DOJ) site provides a link to all DOJ agencies and includes information about a wide range of research, training, and grants.

▶ *www.officer.com*—This directory is related to law enforcement issues.

▶ *www.census.gov*—U.S. Census Bureau site provides demographic information by jurisdiction.

▶ *www.cops.usdoj.gov*—The COPS Office site promotes policing strategies and offers a variety of grants, training, and education to state agencies and local communities nationwide.

▶ *www.ncjrs.org*—The National Criminal Justice Reference Service site functions as a clearinghouse of publications and is an online reference service for a broad range of criminal justice issues.

▶ *www.justnet.org/Pages/home.aspx*—The Justice Technology Information Network provides information about new equipment and technologies.

▶ *www.ojp.usdoj.gov/bjs*—The Bureau of Justice Statistics site includes a variety of information about criminal justice statistics and provides links to other research Web sites.

▶ *www.copnet.org/directory.html*—COPNET site provides information about police training, job opportunities, links to other agencies, and chat rooms.

▶ *http://www.popcenter.org/*—The Center for Problem Oriented Policing makes readily accessible information about ways in which police can more effectively address specific crime and disorder problems.

▶ *http://www.theiacp.org/*—The International Association of Chiefs of Police has always been a primary source of information concerning policing, but in recent years it is also leading the way in developing and commissioning research and reports on COPPS.

▶ *www.ncpc.org/*—The National Crime Prevention Council, discussed in Chapter 4, seeks to help people keep themselves, their families, and their communities safe from crime, and provides tools they can use to further that goal.

Determination of Training Needs

Of primary importance is a **needs assessment** to provide the trainer with vital information about the new or veteran officers, including how they view their daily work and what obstacles exist that may prevent them from using COPPS training. It can also provide important information for changing officer performance evaluation systems, extending beyond such traditional assessments as traffic citations or numbers of arrests. The assessment is a tool to establish department-wide training needs and can be used for various purposes—academy training, in-service training, supervisory and nonsupervisory training, and so forth—to survey trainees prior to their receiving instruction.

Exhibit 9–5 provides a preliminary COPPS training needs assessment questionnaire. The exhibit shows the kinds of questions that could be used by a police agency to do a preliminary survey of its training needs. Obviously, Question 3 of the survey is critical and will require considerable deliberation.

| Exhibit 9–5 | Needs Assessment Survey |

1. Does our department currently have a community policing strategy or plan?
2. Which of the following best describes our department's community policing practice?
   a. All uniformed officers are/will be actively involved in community policing.
   b. All sworn officers are/will be actively involved in community policing.
   c. Only specifically assigned officers are/will be involved in community policing.
   d. The department does not use community policing.
3. What are our primary training needs related to community policing? (Responses might be wide-ranging, from community engagement issues to knowledge about crime prevention, the S.A.R.A. process generally, management of patrol time, resources and referrals, organizational change, responsibilities of administrators and supervisors, and so on.)
4. Have any of our officers received community policing training?
   a. Who presented/provided the training?
   b. What percentage of our officers received the training?
5. Does our department have at least one computer with a modem? Access to the Internet?
6. Does our department currently have a Web page?
7. Does our agency currently have e-mail external to the department?
8. Have our officers had any Internet training?
9. Which programs does our department currently have? (Responses might include Drug Abuse Resistance Education [DARE], Neighborhood or Business Watch, ride-alongs, Gang Resistance Education and Training [GREAT], and so forth.)

Source: Adapted from Andra J. Katz, *The Community Policing Needs Assessment in Kansas and Nebraska: Final Report* (Wichita, Kans.: Regional Community Policing Training Institute, December 1997).

It is also important for COPPS curriculum development that (1) trainees be determined, (2) a task analysis be conducted, (3) performance measures be constructed by which trainees can be evaluated (to determine successful or unsuccessful course completion), (4) existing courses be identified that might address needs, and (5) the appropriate environment for the training be selected.

Ideas for Curricular Content

As we noted above, Appendix I contains a complete recommended COPPS training program as developed by the federal Center for Problem-Oriented Policing. Here, however, we broadly explain the nuts-and-bolts of the training modules contained in such a program, and their rationales and objectives, which include the followiing:

EVOLUTION OF POLICING. Here, we recommend emphasizing that in order to understand policing today, one must first understand its antecedents. Chapter 1 traces this evolution, through its three broad eras and including the three eras of COPPS itself. It is important to include in this history a discussion of how our society is changing and what the police must do to confront these challenges (Chapter 2) as well as the history of the local agency where the training is being conducted. This section of training should end by providing participants with clear definitions of the separate but complementary notions of community- and problem-oriented policing.

COMMUNITY ENGAGEMENT.   Here, participants are introduced to the concept of community policing and its primary components. The desired outcomes for this part of the training are that they be able to:

- Define what is meant by the word "community" and the concept of "community policing" and its components
- Identify why police must collaborate with the community to solve problems.
- Know how to develop a community profile that analyzes its problems and identifies its leaders and available resources
- Know how to communicate and collaborate with the community (including other city or county departments, local businesses, social services agencies, and so forth) through public meetings, newsletters, and contact with leaders, groups, and organizations
- Understand a community's cultural, ethnic, and racial diversity
- Discuss community-oriented government, including the concepts of "total quality" and "customer service" in policing

DIVERSITY TRAINING.   COPPS training should include a training strategy for policing in a multicultural society. As Chapter 2 described, we live in an increasingly diverse society with many new cultural mores and languages that pose new challenges for police. Policing these new communities requires understanding and new skills. (Chapter 10 addresses diversity, the history of police-minority problems, bias-based and racial policing, and ways COPPS can build bridges in these areas.) Especially given our "global village" and its current state of affairs, it is important that police personnel be exposed to different cultures in order to generally make them better and more effective officers and assist in their problem-solving efforts.

In attempting to determine both the role of training in promoting policing in a manner that is culturally sensitive and responsive and an approach to training that will yield the greatest success, police agencies must consult with the ethnocultural communities served.[24]

PROBLEM SOLVING: BASICS AND EXERCISES.   The PBL concept was introduced earlier in this chapter. Here we discuss this approach more specifically as it relates to COPPS. The problem-solving session of training entails teaching officers the basics of conflict resolution, which is the focus of COPPS; it puts the COPPS philosophy into practice, or "walks the talk" of COPPS. The analysis of problems is the most important component of problem solving. In-depth analysis provides the information necessary for officers to develop effective responses. The S.A.R.A. (scanning, analysis, response, and assessment) problem-solving model (which was discussed in detail in Chapter 3) is presented through an interactive lecture and use of case studies. The desired outcomes for this segment include the following:

- Identifying each component and principal element of the S.A.R.A. process
- Learning the importance of in-depth analysis in the complete identification of a problem
- Learning to identify and apply a variety of responses to a problem
- Discussing the application of situational crime prevention and crime prevention through environmental design (CPTED) concepts on the environmental influences on crime and disorder
- Discussing the importance of both quantitative and qualitative evaluation measures of problem-solving efforts
- Discussing how accountability, empowerment, service orientation, and partnership fit into problem solving

Facilitators should divide the classes into small workgroups and ask them to examine each problem, developing strategies for analyzing, responding to, and assessing the effectiveness of their problem-solving efforts. Figures and tables throughout Chapter 3 can be used to lead officers through the process. Brainstorming should be discussed and used as an appropriate tool to foster innovative and creative thinking in the workgroups.[25] The desired outcomes for this segment include the participants' ability to do the following:

- Identify problems on the officer's beat
- Demonstrate an understanding of the problem analysis triangle
- Identify the diversity of resources available, the variety of strategies to address the problem, and some crime prevention techniques
- Evaluate the results using methods similar to those used in the analysis of the problem
- Discuss the advantages and disadvantages of the methods used

Once the problem-solving exercises are completed, each group will have the opportunity to present its problem to the entire class and explain each step of the S.A.R.A. model. Through these presentations, the participants will be exposed to the problem-solving efforts of the other groups. This method of instruction not only provides officers with a practical exercise but also gives them the opportunity to work through an actual problem on their beat.

CASE STUDIES.   Trainers can use case studies involving the use of the S.A.R.A. model of problem solving for neighborhood crime and disorder. Case studies allow the instructor to put the theory into practice, and demonstrate the flexibility of the model as well as emphasize important steps, such as analysis. As mentioned above, it is best to localize the case studies in order to provide a real-world flavor and to help trainees gain a better understanding of the material. For this purpose, the Problem Oriented Guides, utilized or cited in many of this book's chapters, can be invaluable. These guides—now with more than 40 different titles—summarize knowledge about how the police can address a variety of problems.

LEADERSHIP AND MIDDLE MANAGERS.   Executive leadership and middle managers' support are critical to implementing and maintaining the organizational changes required by COPPS (Chapters 6 and 7 discussed the roles of leadership and management as they relate to the implementation and cultural change of an organization). In many instances, the ultimate challenge to a police organization is to change its hierarchical, paramilitary structure. Supervisors, managers, and executives working within a flattened COPPS-oriented organization would require new skills to ensure the successful adaptation and functioning of the police organization.[26]

FIRST-LINE SUPERVISOR AS COACH AND MANAGER.   As we pointed out in previous chapters (and thus do not need to cover in-depth here), COPPS requires the support of the first-line supervisor in particular. Supervising in a COPPS environment means a change from being a "controller," primarily concerned with rules, to being a "facilitator" and "coach" for officers involved in problem solving. Supervisors must learn to encourage innovation and risk taking among their officers and be skilled in problem solving. Finding the time for officers to engage in problem solving and tracking their efforts are also challenges for first-line supervisors. Chapter 6 includes a section on "recapturing officers' time."

SUPPORT PERSONNEL.   Support personnel provide officers with information that is vital to the success of COPPS. For example, it would be difficult for officers to engage in problem solving if

Guide books provided by the federal Office of Community Oriented Policing Services on a variety of topics use research and problem solving case studies to provide a useful tool for training officers.
Courtesy Office of Community Oriented Policing Services.

2010 POP/IACA Conference

September 27–30, 2010

Arlington Convention Center
Arlington, Texas

Analysis
is the most critical step in
the problem-oriented
policing process...

Crime analysis is essential to effective problem-oriented policing. To strengthen this connection, the Center for Problem-Oriented Policing and the International Association of Crime Analysts are co-sponsoring the **2010 International Problem-Oriented Policing and Crime Analysis Training Conference**, with support from the U.S. Department of Justice Office of Community Oriented Policing Services (COPS).

Featuring:

- Eighty-plus training sessions, ranging from fundamentals and foundations to advanced tools and tactics
- 2010 Herman Goldstein Award for Excellence in Problem-Oriented Policing

- Forums and networking functions
- Exhibitors
- Hands-on computer lab training

The conference is an opportunity for analysts and police officers at all levels to improve their abilities to analyze crime and disorder problems and develop and implement more effective responses to them.

Conference Information: Registration and hotel information can be found at the conference web site at **www.popcenter.org**. Conference questions can be directed to the Center for Problem-Oriented Policing at **events@popcenter.org** or **704-788-8302**.

Center for
Problem-Oriented Policing

Center for Problem Oriented Policing.

the dispatcher, unaware of the COPPS philosophy, was concerned only with eliminating pending calls and continued to dispatch officers to low-priority calls.

COMMUNITY AND BUSINESS LEADERS. Because the community plays a vital role in COPPS, there the department and officers must educate citizens about COPPS; these include newsletters, public service announcements, neighborhood meetings, and citizens' police academies. It is also important that business leaders be oriented in the operation of COPPS. Business and industrial leaders can be valuable allies, maybe even providing financial support in causes they believe will help the community.

OTHER GOVERNMENT AGENCIES. Previous chapters have also discussed how problem solving necessarily involves agencies other than the police or sheriff's departments. A large percentage of calls for service (CFS) handled by the police involve noncriminal matters that can be better addressed by other city or county agencies. Furthermore, there is considerable overlap between agencies; for example, a deteriorating neighborhood might involve the health, fire, zoning, prosecutor's, street, social services, or other departments. Thus, it is imperative that key persons in those organizations be trained in the philosophy and workings of COPPS and CPTED.

ELECTED OFFICIALS. Politicians must be involved and educated early in the planning of COPPS (see Chapter 7 and other chapters). They often have the final word on whether new ideas or programs will be funded and implemented. The education of politicians regarding COPPS is important for understanding that this philosophy is unique.

It is important to educate the public about community policing.
Courtesy Kris Solow, City of Charlotte, North Carolina.

Summary

This chapter has presented some of the obstacles to learning, an overview of those persons and groups needing to receive COPPS training, and types and component parts of a COPPS training program.

COPPS must become a philosophy before it can become a practice. This change in thinking is the major challenge facing those involved in the training and education of police officers and the public. This challenge is enhanced because large numbers of police officers and citizens require orientation and training in COPPS.

Police executives who have implemented the COPPS strategy must give due consideration to the training issue—a major aspect of COPPS that is a sine qua non of this strategy. Without training, there is nothing.

Items for Review

1. Explain the basic schools of thought as per Knowles and Bloom concerning the concepts of adult- and problem-based learning, and apply them to training for COPPS.
2. Describe the characteristics of a learning organization, and why it is important for police agencies to become as such.
3. Delineate the unique challenges that are involved with training police officers.
4. Review how knowledge is imparted at the basic recruit academy as well as with the postacademy, in-service, and roll call methods.
5. List some kinds of technologies that exist in police training.
6. Detail the means for determining officers' training needs.

Learn by Doing

1. You are enrolled in a criminal justice internship with the regional police academy. Knowing of your prior coursework, your academy advisor assigns you to prepare a position paper that sets forth the different approaches to teaching adults. You are to emphasize Knowles' andragogy—to include how Bloom's emphasis on problem-based learning can be applied to police academy students. What will you report?
2. Assume the same facts as in the previous scenario. The academy staff sees a need to implement a more solid, core COPPS curriculum at the academy. You are assigned the task of drafting a model COPPS curriculum for comprehensively training the recruits. What courses will your curriculum include?
3. Having successfully completed your internship at the regional police academy, your criminal justice professor asks you to prepare an essay on the potential use of online, distance, and e-learning courses for COPPS. What will you write and emphasize?

Notes

1. U.S. Department of Justice, Office of Community Oriented Policing Services, Center for Problem-Oriented Policing, *Model Academic Curriculum for Problem-Oriented Policing*, http://www.popcenter.org/learning/model_curriculum/files/Model_Academic_Curriculum_Syllabus.pdf (Accessed July 20, 2010).
2. Malcolm Knowles, *Andragogy in Action* (San Francisco: Jossey-Bass, 1981).
3. Eric P. Werth, "Adult Learning: Similarities in Training Methods and Recruits Learning Characteristics," *The Police Chief*, November 2009, p. 43, http://www.policechiefmagazine.org/magazine/index.cfm?fuseaction=display_arch&article_id=1947&issue_id=112009 (Accessed July 20, 2010), pp. 42-43.
4. Benjamin S. Bloom, *Taxonomy of Educational Objectives, Handbook I: The Cognitive Domain* (New York: David McKay, 1956).

5. Howard Barrows and R. M. Tamblyn, *Problem Based Learning* (New York: Springer, 1980).

6. Peter M. Senge, *The Fifth Discipline: The Art and Practice of the Learning Organization* (London: Random House, 1990).

7. *Ibid.,* p. 3.

8. Adapted from George Cartwright, "A Learning Organization, *Law and Order,* September 2008, pp. 71–73.

9. Michael E. Buerger, "Police Training as a Pentecost: Using Tools Singularly Ill-Suited to the Purpose of Reform," *Police Quarterly* 1 (1998):32.

10. *Ibid.,* p. 39.

11. Roger G. Dunham and Geoffrey P. Alpert, *Critical Issues in Policing* (Prospect Heights, Ill.: Waveland Press, 1989), p. 112.

12. *Ibid.*

13. Gerald W. Lynch, "Why Officers Need a College Education," *Higher Education and National Affairs* (September 20, 1986):11.

14. *Davis v. City of Dallas,* 777 F.2d 205 (5th Cir. 1985).

15. For a comprehensive listing of studies of higher education for police officers, see Michael G. Aamodt, *Law Enforcement Selection: Research Summaries* (Washington, D.C.: Police Executive Research Forum, 2004), pp. 1–426.

16. Harvey Sprafka and April H. Kranda, "Institutionalizing Mentoring in Police Departments," *The Police Chief,* January 2008, pp. 46–49, http://www.policechief magazine.org/magazine/index.cfm?fuseaction=display _arch&article_id=1375&issue_id=12008 (Accessed July 20, 2010).

17. Quoted in James Uhl, "Mentoring: Nourishing the Organizational Culture," *The Police Chief,* June 2010, pp. 66–72, http://www.policechiefmagazine.org/ magazine/index.cfm?fuseaction=display_arch& article_id=2115&issue_id=62010 (Accessed July 20, 2010).

18. *Ibid.,* p. 68.

19. *Ibid.*

20. *Ibid.,* p. 47.

21. Thomas Dempsey, "Cyberschool: Online Law Enforcement Classes," *FBI Law Enforcement Bulletin* (February 1998):10.

22. See, for example, the John Jay College of Criminal Justice School Safety and Security Professional Development course outline, "Community Policing in Schools," at http://www.jjay.cuny.edu/conference/ teleconf/.

23. Adapted from Russ Schanlaub, "Online Training," *Law and Order,* April 2009, pp. 36-43.

24. Frum Himelfarb, "A Training Strategy for Policing in a Multicultural Society," *The Police Chief* (November 1991):53–55.

25. Nancy McPherson, "Problem Oriented Policing" (San Diego, Calif.: San Diego Police Department Training Outline, 1992), p. 2.

26. Province of British Columbia, Ministry of Attorney General, Police Services Branch, *Community Policing Advisory Committee Report,* p. 56.

Police in a Diverse Society

KEY TERMS AND CONCEPTS

Bias-based policing
Contagious shootings
Cultural cues

Diversity
Hate crime
Police-community relations

Police-minority relations
Racial profiling
Toolkit (for police recruitment)

LEARNING OBJECTIVES

As a result of reading this chapter, the student will:

- Understand the sordid history of race relations in the United States
- Know what studies and perceptions exist concerning whether or not the criminal justice system discriminates against minorities
- Comprehend what is meant by bias-based policing (racial profiling) and measures being taken to mitigate or eliminate it
- Be aware of the legal definition of a hate crime, and what the police can do to address them
- Have an understanding of a number of federal, state, and local initiatives to improve police-minority relations as well as minority recruitment practices
- Know why it is important for the police to be aware of different cultural customs

> *No man will treat with indifference the principle of race.*
> *It is the key of history.*
>
> —Disraeli

INTRODUCTION

In any contemporary discussion of community oriented policing and problem solving (COPPS) and diversity, it must first be recognized that the meaning of **diversity** is changing along with demographics and social values. Diversity now means more than embracing variations in race, ethnicity, and gender; it also encompasses variations in age, language skills, culture, religion or belief system, and sexual orientation. Indeed, diversity is increasingly being used to stress the importance of individual differences rather than merely stressing group differences.

As a publicly funded service profession, policing is ethically bound to serve the entire community. A commitment to diversity in an agency that reflects the community it serves sends a message of inclusiveness and equality and is consistent with fundamental notions of democracy.[1]

At its root, however, the subject of diversity and its related problems involve race and ethnicity; unfortunately, with this nation's population becoming more and more diverse, as well as its wave of immigration from Mexico, general economic turmoil, war, natural disasters, and a bevy of other social problems that now beset it, there comes greater divisiveness among its citizens. Indeed, in Chapter 2 we discussed some examples of the current legal malaise involving immigration and the legal malaise now found in a number of states as well as the U.S. government.

We begin this chapter with a brief history of police-minority conflict. Our focus is on the major, not-to-be-overlooked history of racial problems in the U.S. involving African Americans. Then we examine whether criminal justice in the United States systematically discriminates against minorities; included is a discussion of bias-based policing (racial profiling). We then consider the companion problem of hate crimes, including its definition and legal aspects. Then we turn to a review of a number of initiatives at the federal, state, and levels to enhance police-minority relations; included is a discussion of the need for police to understand cultural customs, differences, and problems.

After looking at a **toolkit** that can assist the police in recruiting and achieving diversity in their ranks, we conclude the chapter with "Learn by Doing" scenarios, where you are invited to "be the officer" in some delicate situations that police officers might confront. Included throughout are exhibits that demonstrate some programs and activities that exist to enhance and improve diversity in policing.

POLICE AND MINORITIES: A HISTORY OF CONFLICT

A minority group is a group or category of people who can be distinguished by special physical or cultural traits that can be used to single them out for differential and unequal treatment. As indicated above, conflicts between majority and minority groups have a long history.

Modern-day attempts to "protect" America against people who came from other shores—including the Ku Klux Klan in the South who victimize blacks, the vigilantes who patrol the southwestern U.S. borders looking for illegal Mexican aliens, and people who engage in hate crimes against Muslims since 9–11—have their roots in the early twentieth century. Indeed, in 1900 the African American scholar and activist W. E. B. DuBois said the problem of the twentieth century is the problem of the color line. More than 100 years later, we are still proving him right. In the past four decades, many changes in society have influenced the nature of **police-minority relations**:

- The 1954 *Brown v. Topeka Board of Education*[2] decision of the U.S. Supreme Court declared that separate educational facilities were inherently unequal.
- The use of civil disobedience and nonviolent resistance increased in the 1950s and 1960s, and the Civil Rights Act was passed in 1964. Almost all of the riots in the 1960s were sparked by incidents involving the police.[3]

A scene from the Walker Report of the 1968 Democratic National Convention in Chicago.
Courtesy of the Walker Report, from the Department of Justice.

- The Equal Employment Opportunity Commission was established, and the 1972 Amendment to the Civil Rights Act became law.[4]

Collectively, these actions prohibited discrimination in education, hiring and promotion, voting, and use of public accommodations, among other things.

Of particular importance in the history of U.S. race relations are the events that occurred between 1960 and 1970, when police-minority encounters frequently precipitated racial outbursts. Specifically, Harlem, Watts, Newark, and Detroit all were scenes of major race riots during the 1960s. There were 75 civil disorders involving African Americans and the police in 1967 alone, with at least 83 people killed, mostly African Americans. In addition, many police officers and firefighters were killed or injured. Property damage in these riots totaled hundreds of

A scene from the Walker Report of the 1968 Democratic National Convention in Chicago.
Courtesy of the Walker Report, from the Department of Justice.

millions of dollars.[5] The 1970s busing programs that were introduced to integrate schools resulted in white backlash and more interracial conflict.

In the late 1980s, **police-community relations** appeared to worsen, with a major riot in Miami, Florida, in 1989. Also in the 1980s, affirmative action programs led to charges of reverse discrimination and more dominant-group backlash.[6] More recently, of course, there have been incidents of burning and looting in Miami, Los Angeles, Atlanta, Las Vegas, Washington, D.C., and St. Petersburg, Florida as well as other cities. These incidents have demonstrated that the same tensions that found temporary release on the streets of African American communities in the past still remain with us.

The police were involved in all the social changes described. At times the police have been used to prevent minority group members from demonstrating on behalf of civil rights, and on occasion the police have had to use force against protesting groups. At other times the police have been required to protect those same protesting minorities from the wrath of the dominant group and others who opposed peaceful demonstrations. Over time, alienation has developed from these contacts. Thus, members of both groups today have an uneasy coexistence with a good deal of "baggage" based on what they have seen, heard, or been told of their interactions throughout history. The phrase *"police-community relations,"* as Samuel Walker wrote, is really a euphemism for police-race relations:

> The police have not had the same kinds of conflicts with the white majority community as they do with racial minorities. The most serious aspect of the . . . problem involves *black Americans*. Similar problems exist with respect to other racial-minority groups. In areas with large numbers of *Hispanic Americans* . . . there are also serious conflicts with the police. *Native Americans* . . . have also had conflict with the police. Similar problems exist in cities with large *Asian-American* communities (emphases in original).[7]

Police-community problems are part of a larger problem of racism in our society. The highly respected National Academy of Sciences concluded nearly two decades ago that "black crime and the position of blacks within the nation's system of criminal justice administration are related to past and present social opportunities and disadvantages and can be best understood through consideration of blacks' overall social status."[8] Recent mass gatherings in Washington, D.C., engendered by such groups as the Southern Christian Leadership Conference and the Rainbow Coalition, have involved protests against racial profiling (discussed later), police brutality, and other perceived prejudices toward people of color; such assemblies would indicate that the Academy's statement is still valid today. Minority group members remain frustrated because the pace of gains in our society has not kept up with their expectations.

To many minorities the police are an "occupying force," more concerned with restricting their freedom than providing services to their community. From the police's point of view, minority neighborhoods have not always been supportive of their efforts to combat crime. Which perspective is more accurate? Perhaps that question cannot be answered; however, a key element in police-community relations—and one that is often overlooked—is how the police perceive the public.

MINORITIES AND THE CRIMINAL JUSTICE SYSTEM

Systemic Discrimination Against Minorities?

Studies of the criminal justice system vis-à-vis minorities are infrequently conducted. In fact, perhaps the best-known such study was conducted in 1983 by the highly reputed RAND Corporation concerning whether the justice system discriminates against minorities. It found no consistent, statistically significant racial differences in the probability of arrest or in case processing, even though minority suspects were more likely than whites to be given longer sentences and to be put in prison instead of jail. RAND determined that the criminal justice system did not discriminate against minorities, who were not overrepresented in the arrest population *"relative to the number of crimes they actually commit"* (emphasis in original), nor were they more likely than whites to be arrested for those crimes.[9]

Today, however, a perception persists—and as the saying goes, "Perception is reality"—including among some high-profile organizations that there is indeed unequal and discriminatory treatment toward minorities. As examples:

- According to the Web site of the Leadership Conference on Civil and Human Rights, a coalition of more than 200 national organizations, "The injustices of the criminal justice system . . . characterize every stage of the process. Black and Hispanic Americans, and other minority groups as well, are victimized by disproportionate targeting and unfair treatment by police and other front-line law enforcement officials; by racially skewed charging and plea bargaining decisions of prosecutors; by discriminatory sentencing practices; and by the failure of judges, elected officials and other criminal justice policy makers to redress the inequities that become more glaring every day."[10]
- According to the Drug Policy Alliance Web site, "Street sweeps, buy and bust operations and other police activities have targeted people in street level retail drug transactions in low-income communities of color. Blacks and Latinos are victimized by unfair treatment by police; by racially skewed charging and plea bargaining decisions by prosecutors; by discriminatory sentencing practices and by the failure of judges, elected officials and other criminal justice policy makers to redress the inequities that have come to permeate the system. The rate of drug admissions to state prison for black men are thirteen times greater than the rate for white men."[11]

Exacerbating the perception of police mistreatment of minorities are police shootings, which can clearly inflame a community and raise tensions like nothing else. Unfortunately, there has been no dearth of high-profile police shooting incidents during the early part of this millennium:

- In April 2007, three NYPD officers were indicted for manslaughter and reckless endangerment for a shooting incident where they fired 50 rounds at a car of unarmed men leaving a bachelor party at a strip club; the groom died on his wedding day.[12]
- In July 2005, more than 30 Los Angeles officers, including its SWAT team, responded to a hostage situation; the 19-month-old daughter of the suspect was killed. The probe involved microscopic analysis of about 130 bullets and more than 100 casings involving 13 firearms.[13]

These are what are known as **contagious shootings**—gunfire that spreads among officers who believe that they or their colleagues are facing a threat.

A reading of the above case studies demonstrate how important it is that police agencies continue to provide diversity-related education and training to their officers, and that internal systems monitor officers' treatment of citizens and address any individual behavioral or systemic issues that are discovered.

Racial Profiling and Bias-Based Policing

Biased treatment of minorities has thus been and continues to be one of the most sensitive charges against the criminal justice system. **Racial profiling** has become a despised police practice in the new millennium. (Actually, a more inclusive term is "bias-based profiling," which includes

Minority community members often believe they are unnecessarily detained and interviewed by police.
Courtesy Washoe County, Nevada, Sheriff's Office.

unequal treatment of any persons on the basis of race, ethnicity, religion, gender, sexual orientation, or socioeconomic status.) Although the exact number is unknown, many states have adopted legislation related to racial profiling; most of these laws include data collection requirements (discussed below).[14]

Bias-based policing on the basis of race—also known as "driving while black or brown" (DWBB)—where a police officer, acting on a personal bias, stops a vehicle simply because the driver is of a certain race, is given no public support. Such incidents can take various forms, as demonstrated in the following accounts[15]:

- A young black woman trades her new sports car for an older model because police repeatedly stop her on suspicion of possession of a stolen vehicle.
- An elderly African American couple in formal dress are stopped and questioned at length, allegedly because their car resembles one identified in a robbery.
- A prominent black lawyer driving a luxury car is frequently stopped on various pretexts.
- A Hispanic deputy police chief is stopped various times in neighboring jurisdictions on "suspicion."
- A black judge far from her hometown is stopped, handcuffed, and laid face down on the pavement while police search her car (no citations were issued).

The best defense for the police may be summarized in two words: collect data. Collecting traffic stop data helps chiefs and commanders determine whether officers are stopping or searching a disproportionate number of minorities and enables them to act on this information in a timely fashion. Technology—including mobile data computers and wireless handheld devices—is available to the police for this purpose.

The International Association of Chiefs of Police (IACP) has issued a comprehensive policy statement on bias-based policing and data collection. The association "believes that any form of police action that is based solely on the race, gender, ethnicity, age, or socioeconomic level of an individual is both unethical and illegal" but that data collection programs "must ensure that data is being collected and analyzed in an impartial and methodologically sound fashion."[16] To demonstrate the problem has not gone away, one of the IACP's stated goals for 2009 was to promote police training programs that are designed to address problems of disparate treatment of individuals, including biased-based policing, and to increase the skills that individual officers use during officer/violator contacts.

A COLLABORATIVE INITIATIVE.   A major initiative to examine and address the problem of racial bias was implemented in a collaborative effort at Stanford University. The "Policing Racial Bias Project" was launched at a 2004 conference attended by more than 160 researchers and agency representatives, from 34 agencies and 13 states. The Project, which is a partnership between the Psychology Department at Stanford, the Los Angeles County Sheriff's Office, the San Francisco Police Department, and the San Mateo County Sheriff's Office, provides free updates about policing-related research in psychology and particularly effective approaches to combating racial bias in policing. The primary methods of addressing racial issues in policing thus far have been to collect race data on traffic stops and searches and to require sensitivity training for patrol staff. The Project believes these approaches leave many unanswered questions, such as the following: Under what situations might race unintentionally influence patrol officers' decision-making? How can we examine and isolate unintentional racial bias in the policing context? What types of police training would be most effective in reducing racial bias? The Project also examines how the public reads encounters with police, and considers such related questions as: What causes people in the community to believe that the actions of police officers are motivated by race? What steps can be taken to change negative perceptions of the police? The initiative is also grounded on the premise that understanding the conditions under which unintentional racial bias operates could have important implications and may lead to significant interventions in policy, supervision, and training to reduce its influence.

Benefits to be derived by agencies participating in the Policing Racial Bias project is that many of them will be involved in cutting-edge social psychological research designed to answer many of the above questions—while also being in a position to proactively address racial issues in their own communities by participating in ongoing research.

RESPONSES TO HATE CRIMES

Definition and Legislation

Hate crimes and hate incidents, defined in Exhibit 10–1, are major issues for the police because of these crimes' unique impact on victims and the community. Such crimes can have a special emotional and psychological impact. Hate violence can exacerbate racial, religious, or ethnic tensions in a community and lead to a cycle of escalating reprisals. Police executives must demonstrate a commitment to be both tough on hate crime perpetrators and sensitive to the impact of hate violence on the community.[17]

At present, 45 states and the District of Columbia have crime statutes that enhance the penalties for hate crimes and address hate violence. The 1990 Hate Crime Statistics Act, as amended in 1994, requires the Department of Justice to collect and publish data on bias-motivated crimes across the United States. Furthermore, at the federal level hate crimes are investigated by

Exhibit 10–1 Legal Aspects of Hate Crimes

A hate crime, also known as a bias crime, is a criminal offense committed against a person, property, or society that is motivated, in whole or in part, by the offender's bias against a race, religion, disability, sexual orientation, or ethnicity/national origin. In response to mounting national concern over crimes motivated by bias, Congress enacted the Hate Crime Statistics Act of 1990. The law directed the attorney general to collect data "about crimes that manifest evidence of prejudice based on race, religion, sexual orientation, or ethnicity." The attorney general delegated the responsibility for developing and implementing a hate crime data collection program to the director of the FBI, who assigned the task to the Uniform Crime Reporting (UCR) Program. In September 1994, Congress passed the Violent Crime Control and Law Enforcement Act, which amended the Hate Crime Statistics Act to include both physical and mental disabilities. The UCR Program began collecting statistics on offenses motivated by bias against physical and mental disabilities in January 1997. The Church Arson Act of 1996 mandated that hate crime data collection become a permanent part of the UCR Program.

Source: U.S. Department of Justice, Federal Bureau of Investigation, "Hate Crime," http://www.fbi.gov/ucr/cius_04/offenses_reported/hate_crime/index.html (Accessed July 21, 2010).

the Federal Bureau of Investigation (FBI) Bias Crimes Unit and the Bureau of Alcohol, Tobacco, Firearms, and Explosives church arson and explosives experts.[18]

Each year, approximately 8,000 hate crimes are reported in the United States. Racial bias accounted for about half of the incidents, about 1 in 5 are based on religious intolerance, about 1 in 6 is triggered by sexual orientation, and bias regarding ethnicity/national origin is responsible for about 1 in 10.[19]

There is much a law enforcement organization can do with respect to hate crimes to take a leadership role in the community: provide victims with a point of contact in the department to whom they can report hate crimes and express concerns, inform victims on case progress, participate in hate crime training as well as educate the public about these crimes, establish a zero tolerance of prejudice within the department, track the criminal activities of hate groups, and sponsor and participate in community events that promote tolerance and diversity.[20] A good example of a police agency's effort to fight hate crimes is that of Madison, Connecticut. Every officer has a laminated hate crimes response card, providing officers with information for responding to hate crimes, working with victims, and pursuing perpetrators. The card includes the definition of a hate crime, questions responding officers should ask, and tips for recognizing signs of organized hate groups.[21]

An Attempt to Strengthen the Federal Hate Crimes Law

In April 2009, a bill entitled "Local Law Enforcement Hate Crimes Prevention Act of 2009" was passed in the House; as of mid-2011 it was still awaiting action by the U.S. Senate. If enacted into law, it would authorize the attorney general to provide technical, forensic, prosecutorial, or other assistance in the criminal investigation or prosecution of a violent crime, a hate crime, or any felony crime. Significantly, the law would authorize the attorney general to award grants to state, local, and tribal law enforcement agencies for extraordinary expenses associated with the investigation and prosecution of hate crimes.[22]

SELECTED FEDERAL, STATE, AND LOCAL INITIATIVES

Federal Infusion of Funds and Programs

As indicated earlier in this chapter, issues relating to police and community diversity have long been at the forefront of governmental initiatives, and there has been no abatement of such activities in this millennium. For example, since 1996, the federal Office of Community Oriented Policing Services (COPS) Office has invested approximately $70 million to promote and advance ethics and integrity through its *COPS Police Integrity Initiative*. The overall goal of that initiative is to assist agencies in creating or strengthening local programs that build trust between police and their communities, and helping agencies address issues such as racial profiling.

Another federal initiative is the Community Relations Service, an arm of the U.S. Department of Justice, described in Exhibit 10–2.

Following are other initiatives that are in progress.

Training Programs

The key to managing diversity and accommodating cultural differences is training and education. But training in both COPPS and diversity, if not conducted correctly and supported by changes in the organization, is better left undone. Gayle Fisher-Stewart notes:

> [Too often both COPPS and the management of diversity are introduced] with a "shot in the arm." A curriculum is developed, and the entire staff of the department is marched through for their inoculation. After the first dose, there are no boosters. The curriculum is not modified on the basis of rank . . . officers are often viewed as the only ones who need training, because they are viewed as the ones causing problems in the community.[23]

Exhibit 10–3 describes a new program that is being funded by a federal agency and is based on new research concerning why people have biases.

Exhibit 10–2   DOJ's Community Relations Service

The Community Relations Service (CRS) is termed the Department of Justice "peacemaker" for community conflicts and tensions arising from differences of race, color, and national origin. Created by the Civil Rights Act of 1964, CRS is the only federal agency dedicated to assist state and local units of government, private and public organizations, and community groups with preventing and resolving racial and ethnic tensions, incidents, and civil disorders, and in restoring racial stability and harmony. CRS facilitates the development of viable, mutual understandings and agreements as alternatives to coercion, violence, or litigation. It also assists communities in developing local mechanisms, conducting training, and other proactive measures to prevent or reduce racial/ethnic tension. CRS does not take sides among disputing parties and, in promoting the principles and ideals of non-discrimination, applies skills that allow parties to come to their own agreement. In performing this mission, CRS deploys highly skilled professional conciliators, who are able to assist people of diverse racial and cultural backgrounds.

Source: U.S. Department of Justice, "Community Relations Service," http://www.justice.gov/crs/ (Accessed July 21, 2010).

Exhibit 10–3   COPS Funds New Model Training Curricula to Address Police Biases

Realizing that biased policing and the perceptions of it threaten police and community relationships, the COPS office is funding the development of two model curricula, one for academy recruits and one for first-line supervisors. These curricula are based on social psychological research on human biases, which indicates that even the best law enforcement officers may manifest bias because they are *human*. While some bias is intentional in nature, social psychologists have shown that "implicit" or "unconscious" bias can affect what people perceive and do - even people who consciously hold non-prejudiced attitudes.

Implicit bias might lead the patrol officer to automatically perceive a crime in the making, as when observing two young Hispanic males driving in an all-Caucasian neighborhood; or, it might lead an officer to be "under-vigilant" with a female subject because he associates crime and violence with males. The "implicit system" of our brain is designed to be "reactive rather than reasoned" and produces mental shortcuts which at times can produce detrimental outcomes and include automatic associations between social groups and concepts. One example is the automatic or implicit association between minorities, particularly blacks, and crime.

While training cannot easily undo the implicit associations that took a lifetime to develop, with information and motivation, people can implement controlled (unbiased) behavioral responses that override automatic (bias-promoting) associations. The implication

Lasting improvements between the police and minorities require that both groups make necessary changes.
Courtesy of City of Charlotte.

is that law enforcement departments need to provide training that makes personnel aware of their unconscious biases so that they are able and motivated to activate controlled responses to counteract them.

Source: Adapted from Community Policing Dispatch, "Reducing Biased Policing Through Training," February 2009, http://www.cops.usdoj.gov/html/dispatch/February_2009/biased_policing.htm (Accessed July 21, 2010).

Following are other suggested resources published by the COPS office and available at: http://www.cops.usdoj.gov/default.asp?Item=2274:

- *A Suggested Approach to Analyzing Racial Profiling: Sample Templates for Analyzing Car-Stop Data*
- *COPS Evaluation Brief No. 3: Creating A Culture of Integrity*
- *How to Correctly Collect and Analyze Racial Profiling Data: Your Reputation Depends On It!*
- *Protecting Civil Rights: A Leadership Guide for State, Local, and Tribal Law Enforcement*
- *Mediating Citizen Complaints Against Police Officers: A Guide For Police And Community Leaders*
- *Racially Biased Policing: A Principled Response*
- *Understanding Race Data from Vehicle Stops: A Stakeholder's Guide*

Community Programs

Following are some examples of various activities some jurisdictions have undertaken to help address problems and bring about unity among their diverse populations.

LOS ANGELES: ESTABLISHMENT OF FORUMS. Ethnic diversity defines the city of Los Angeles. To take advantage of that wealth of varied knowledge, the Los Angeles Police Department (LAPD) turned to the community for ideas, establishing six Community Forums to promote community policing with reliance on trust, respect, cooperation, and partnership. Each forum has about 25 members as well as direct access to the police chief. Following are brief descriptions of each[24]:

1. *Black Forum.* As a response to the forum's recent concerns about racial profiling, the LAPD publishes a pamphlet to improve relations between motorists and officers, explains procedures of traffic stops, and provides a means to commend officers and to lodge complaints.
2. *Hispanic Forum.* This forum's main concerns include immigration rights and LAPD's policy concerning undocumented aliens, and it attempts to ensure that police comply with a policy against initiating action for the sole purpose of determining a person's immigration status.
3. *Asian/Pacific Islander Forum.* This forum has developed a video on ethnic diversity.
4. *Gay/Lesbian Forum.* Concerns regarding arrests based on lewd conduct and the perceived use of police "baiting" to arrest gays are addressed, and the forum helps police to reduce hate crimes and to hire recruits who respect varied lifestyles.
5. *Religious Forum.* This forum promotes collaboration among the many religious groups in Los Angeles.
6. *Youth Forum.* This forum exposes young people to the scope of law enforcement so that they may better appreciate the importance of laws and justice in their lives.

HARVARD UNIVERSITY POLICE DEPARTMENT DIVERSITY AND COMMUNITY LIAISON.   To support its commitment to maintain open and accessible relationships with all members of the community, the Harvard University Police Department assigns one of its officers to the Chief's Office to serve as the department's Diversity and Community Liaison. The Liaison, with the HUPD community policing teams, fosters a working relationship between the department and the university's many and varied communities, which may be defined by ethnicity, culture, language, sexual orientation, or other types of diverse interests.[25]

SANTA ANA, CALIFORNIA: HANDS-ON CITIZEN ACADEMY.   The Santa Ana, California, Police Department has launched a unique 12-week citizen police academy that enhances its efforts in community policing by emphasizing problem solving and hands-on activities that expose students to what it is like to be a police officer.

Students are given a simulated burglary case, and they interview the victim and witnesses, investigate the case, and solve it. They dust for fingerprints, process evidence, and write reports of their activities. Graduates become "ambassadors" for the department; Cesar Dias and Alicia Ramos said the program is a vital source of information about COPPS, and they "go out and spread the word about law enforcement."[26]

LINCOLN, NEBRASKA: SERVICES FOR NON-ENGLISH-SPEAKING POPULATIONS.   The Lincoln, Nebraska, Police Department (LPD) provides a host of services for residents who do

Citizens' academies expose people to what it is like to be a police officer, and they help officers understand public concerns.

not speak English as their primary language. The most common foreign languages spoken in Lincoln are Spanish and Vietnamese, so the LPD makes interpreters available to officers on the street when needed in those and virtually all languages. The LPD Web site contains information in Spanish and Vietnamese and has produced several bilingual videos on various topics for broadcast on cable television. Officers conduct training sessions for new immigrants on a number of topics as well, and LPD provides telecommunications device for the deaf (TDD) service to the deaf and hearing impaired; closed captioning is available for the city's public television programs.[27]

Discussing the Issues

One of the problems with addressing police-minority relations issues is that police and people in general do not like to discuss the topic because "you step on somebody's toes or it's embarrassing."[28] The COPPS philosophy helps address this complex issue. In addition to getting the two groups talking with each other and, therefore, thwarting conflict, it enables police to pinpoint racial tension in their city.

What can COPPS do to improve relations between the police and minorities? To begin with, COPPS, by its very nature, encourages officers to find out exactly what is occurring in neighborhoods, including who is involved and what their motives are. At its most fundamental level, COPPS emphasizes the interrelationship between the police and the community and dictates that officers understand their unique problem-solving relationship with the community as they execute the law. There is no denying that this is at times a huge task, given the history of problems between the two groups.

In a related vein, Exhibit 10–4 contains 15 appropriately pointed questions compiled by the Minneapolis, Minnesota, police department, for "balancing crime strategies and democratic principles."

Exhibit 10–4 **Self-Evaluation: Balancing Crime Strategies and Democratic Principles**

1. Is your department really doing community-oriented policing: a continual discussion of implementation of crime control strategies involving the direct input of the citizens affected by police action?
2. Does your department routinely give detailed cultural awareness/diversity training to recruits, with followup in-services yearly to the rest of the police department?
3. Does your police department have a reputation in the minority community for taking swift internal discipline when serious police misconduct occurs?
4. Have you developed true school liaison and additional police interaction—other than enforcement—with young people?
5. Are there incentives or requirements for the chief and upper staff and/or other members of the department to reside in the city in which they are responsible for policing?
6. Has your department established strong community ties, particularly with the leadership of all relevant organizations representing people of color, so that when crisis happens—and it will—the department will have immediate access and assistance in dealing with it?

7. Has the department and its political leadership made clear to all its employees that racial intolerance will not be permitted, crushed at the slightest hint of its appearance, and that the public, particularly people of color, feel confident that their city will address those issues?

8. Who polices the police or chief in your community? Is there an alternative to internal affairs? Is the police chief held accountable by the appropriate elected body for [e]nsuring a corruption-free police department?

9. Is the chief executive clearly supported by mayor and council in their community policing and other activities designed to include, rather than exclude, all their constituents?

10. Does your department have a hiring process that will not only [e]nsure diversity within the ranks, but is fair and does not exclude people, and is designed to bring in candidates who wish to join for the spirit of service and not the spirit of adventure? Has your department created an internal atmosphere where people of color would want to become a member and have a rewarding 20-year career?

11. Does each department offer internal promotional and assignment opportunities equally to all? Do the promoted ranks clearly reflect the diversity of the whole organization and the community that it serves?

12. Is the community routinely involved in the discussion of all issues that affect policing within their neighborhoods?

13. Is your police organization structured to ensure there is accountability at every level for the performance and actions of each and every officer who encounters citizens in their daily work?

14. Does your department have consistent institutionalized citizen communication instruments that allow the department to not only keep the citizens informed of police activity, but to receive citizen input on a regular basis on a wide variety of issues?

15. Does your police department have a reasonable standard of behavior and protocol for the stopping of citizens, particularly in high crime areas? Are persons being stopped and clearly being advised of the reason for the stop? Are they being told exactly what the police are doing? Most particularly, does your police training include disengagement techniques—how to get out of a situation where, in fact, the officer may well have been wrong in their assumption, and must appropriately explain and apologize to the citizen for their inconvenience?

Source: List compiled by Chief Robert K. Olson of Minneapolis, Minnesota. Police Executive Research Forum, *Subject to Debate* 13(6) (June 1999):5. Used with permission.

UNDERSTANDING CULTURAL CUSTOMS, DIFFERENCES, AND PROBLEMS

There are negative consequences if the police lack an understanding the cultural differences or discerning the **cultural cues** of the people they confront. Indeed, actions that are common in mainstream American culture can result in miscommunication and have dire consequences if the police do not recognize cultural nuances. As a fundamental example, it is not uncommon for an officer to get someone's attention by beckoning with a crooked index finger, repeatedly moving it back and forth; although this is an innocuous gesture to Americans, it is an insult to an Ethiopian man, who uses it to call a person a dog.[29]

Hmong
Circles of
Peace

A program of the
Upper Midwest
Community Policing
Institute

**Integrity, Compassion, Respect,
Honesty, Consensus and Fairness.**

**Office: (651) 917.2811
Fax: (651) 917.2253**

Criminal justice agencies in the St. Paul, Minnesota, area developed a program to enhance citizens' understanding of the Hmong culture and to train Hmong people in the justice process.
Upper Midwest Community Policing Institute, Woodbury, Minnesota.

A more serious example would be the custom of certain Asian cultures to exchange gifts at initial meetings. On meeting with members of such a culture, the COPPS officer can be placed in an uncomfortable position at having to offend those persons whom he or she is there to serve either by not offering a gift or by refusing to accept a gift. These are true ethical (if not legal) dilemmas that today's police officer—and his or her administrators and supervisors—must address. It has been stated that "law enforcement professionals need to develop cultural empathy."[30]

There are other cultural cues about which the police should be cognizant. For example, during an argument it would not be uncommon for a Mexican American to shout to his friend, "I'm going to kill you if you do that again." In the Anglo culture, this statement would clearly signal one's intent to do harm; however, in the context of the Latino/Hispanic culture, this simply conveys anger. Therefore, the Spanish word *matar* (to kill) is often used to show feelings, not intent. Another example is that Anglo Americans tend to assume that there is a short distance between an emotional verbal expression of disagreement and a full-blown conflict. For African Americans, though, stating a position with feeling shows sincerity. For most African Americans, threatening movements, not angry words, indicate the start of a fight. In fact, some would argue that fights do not begin when people are talking or arguing but rather when they stop talking.

Many possible breakdowns in verbal communication can cause difficulties for police officers and those of different cultures.[31] For example, for many Tongans, being handcuffed when arrested for minor crimes is a cultural taboo; that treatment is reserved for only the very worst offenders in their culture. To many Southeast Asians, being asked by an officer to assume a kneeling position with fingers interlocked behind the head is cause for rebellion; to them, this posture is a prelude to being assassinated. For the Chinese, causing someone to lose face through disrespect—such as not being able to use both hands to convey an object—is one of the worst things one person can do to another.[32]

For Latinos/Hispanics, the concept of masculine superiority is important, as are the dominance of the father in the family, the division of labor according to sex, and the belief that the family is more important than the individual. Arguing politics on street corners is an old tradition that, in its frenzy, might appear to be assaultive behavior. It is culturally taboo for a stranger to touch a small Hispanic girl. The use of surnames and last names may be confusing to some police officers. Latin custom dictates the use of the father's and the mother's last name (e.g., Jose Jesus Leon Flores). The legal name is the surname (Leon); the maternal name is the last name in the series (Flores).[33]

Native Americans, unfortunately, suffer severe social problems. Alcohol has been found to be a factor in 80 percent of all Native American suicides and in 90 percent of all homicides. Alcohol has also been found to play a part in the social, physical, psychological, economic, and cultural disruption experienced by Native Americans.[34]

In addition to the traits discussed above, other cultural differences that might be observed by the police include the following:

- *Body position.* A police sergeant relaxing at a desk with feet up, baring the soles of the feet, would likely offend a Saudi Arabian or Thai because the foot is considered the dirtiest part of the body.
- *Facial expression and expressiveness.* A smile is a source of confusion for police officers when encountering Asian cultures. A smile or giggle can cover up pain, humiliation, or embarrassment; on hearing something sad, an Asian may smile, appearing to be a "smart aleck." Whereas Latin Americans, Mediterranean Americans, Arab Americans, Israeli Americans, and African Americans tend to show emotions facially, other groups tend to be less facially expressive; officers may assume that these persons are not being cooperative.

Preservice and in-service police training should cover these cultural differences. At the very least, police officers should know what terms are the least offensive when referring to ethnic or racial groups. For example, most Asians prefer not to be called Orientals; they prefer their nationality of origin, such as Korean American. Many American Indians resent the term "Native American" because that term was invented by the U.S. government. They prefer to be called American Indian or to be known by their tribal ancestry (e.g., Crow, Winnebago). The terms "black American" and "African American" can usually be used interchangeably; however, the latter is more commonly used among younger people. Mexican Americans usually refer to themselves as Chicanos, whereas the term "Latino" is preferred by those from Central America.[35]

RECRUITING FOR DIVERSITY: A TOOLKIT

The importance of recruiting for diversity in today's COPPS world cannot be overstated. As former Gaithersburg, Maryland, police chief Mary Ann Viverette stated:

> Every day, our officers come into contact with individuals from different cultural backgrounds, socioeconomic classes, religions, sexual orientations, and physical and mental abilities. Each of these groups brings a different perspective to police-community relations and, as a result, our officers must be prepared to respond to each group in the appropriate fashion. Failure to recognize and adjust to community diversity can foster confusion and resentment among citizens and quickly lead to a breakdown in the critical bond of trust between a law enforcement agency and its community.[36]

As we noted above, policing is a publicly funded service profession, and is thus ethically bound to serve and represent the entire community. That is easier said than done, however, and the recruitment and retention of a large pool of qualified applicants to help in changing the culture of the agency—as discussed in general in Chapter 6—can be a daunting task. The task of recruiting and retaining women and minorities as police officer is doubly daunting.

There are some means of doing so, however, and that is the subject of a major publication by the federal COPS office in its 2009 *Law Enforcement Recruitment Toolkit*; those recommendations include the following methods and approaches:

a. ***Take stock of the department's diversity.*** Determine which groups are underrepresented in the agency (a simple tally, using a data grid such as that shown in Figure 10–1, can be used). Does the department reflect the community's diversity? What community does the agency want to reflect?

b. ***Tap into internal knowledge.*** Assess the experiences of current minority and female members of the department, including the recruitment and selection process. These forms of engagement can be informal or formal, such as a candid discussion among trusted colleagues or in the context of supervisory meetings.

RACIAL AND ETHNIC COMPOSITION OF _____ POLICE DEPARTMENT ON __/__/__						
	MALE		FEMALE		TOTAL	
	#	%	#	%	#	%
White						
Black or African-American						
American Indian or Alaska Native						
Asian						
Native Hawaiian or Other Pacific Islander						
Hispanic or Latino						

FIGURE 10–1   **Department Quantitative Diversity Assessment**

Source: U.S. Department of Justice, Office of Community Oriented Policing Services, *Law Enforcement Recruitment Toolkit,* June 2009, p. 35, http://www.cops.usdoj.gov/files/RIC/Publications/e080921223-RecruitmentToolkit.pdf (Accessed July 21, 2010).

RACIAL AND ETHNIC COMPOSITION OF ANY TOWN PD ON ___/___/___ COMPARED WITH COMPOSITION OF ANY TOWN							
	Department						Town
	Male		Female		Total		All Genders
	#	%	#	%	#	%	%
White	130	61.9	16	40.0	146	58.4	40.0
Black or African-American	39	18.6	19	47.5	58	23.2	35.5
American Indian or Alaska Native	2	1.0	0	0.0	2	0.8	1.0
Asian	6	2.9	1	2.5	7	2.8	6.0
Hispanic or Latino	33	15.7	4	10.0	37	14.8	17.5
Total	210	100.0	40	100.0	250	100.0	100.0
			% Female	16.00			

FIGURE 10–2 **Example of Statistical Standing of Departmental Diversity**

Source: U.S. Department of Justice, Office of Community Oriented Policing Services, *Law Enforcement Recruitment Toolkit,* June 2009, p. 37, http://www.cops.usdoj.gov/files/RIC/Publications/e080921223-RecruitmentToolkit.pdf (Accessed July 21, 2010).

c. *Assess the potential recruiting pool.* This assessment includes a basic understanding of the community's racial and ethnic composition to indicate appropriate marketing strategies and to provide a quantitative picture of where agency is falling short of ideal representation. Figure 10–2 is a relatively simple example.

d. *Engage the community.* As an example, Sacramento, California, uses a community recruiter program wherein community members are involved in the process of screening acceptable candidates. These recruiters also serve on entry-level and promotional oral panels, enhancing the recruitment process and providing a valuable opportunity for the department to understand cultural differences, particularly as they relate to interviewing and testing.

e. *Use officers as recruiters.* Police leaders have discovered that the most successful recruitment programs involve every member of the police department in the recruitment of new officers. Studies have shown that officers' demeanor and professionalism during contact with someone powerfully shapes that person's impressions of the police department and policing as a career.

f. *Reach out to where prospects live, work, worship, and pray.* Recruiters can get their information into the hands of potential recruits by engaging them on their terms and in their neighborhoods. Women- and minority-owned businesses, grocery stores, health clubs, neighborhood council meetings, YWCAs, schools, and universities—especially criminal justice programs, career fairs, and sporting events—are all excellent venues in which to engage potential recruits.[37]

Women and minorities are underrepresented in policing. The organizational culture of policing has been noticeably slow to change in this regard, recruitment pools are shrinking, and the recruitment of minority officers remains a difficult task. Probably the single most difficult barrier has to do with the image that police officers have among these groups. Unfortunately, for many African Americans and Latinos/Hispanics, police officers are symbols of oppression;

Agencies seek to employ a force that is as diverse as the population they serve.
Courtesy Fort Lauderdale, Florida, Police Department.

meanwhile, recruiters must overcome the perception by many women that policing is a male-dominated occupation.

Some very successful methods are being used by some law enforcement agencies to recruit women and minorities and to generally diversify their workforce. For example, the Philadelphia Police Department (PPD) has a very informative and easily navigable Web site, and officers visit all the minority communities and such organizations as the Latino Organization; minorities are offered a tour of the police academy to view the training. The Omaha, Nebraska, Police Department (OPD) works closely with local television and radio stations and newspapers to develop videos and publicity spots that highlight various aspects of police work and the department's recruiting efforts. Recruiting information is disseminated nationally to colleges, universities, community agencies, churches, health clubs, libraries, female- and minority-owned businesses, special-interest groups, and community leaders. The Chicago Police Department's Web site offers minorities the opportunity to utilize the latest law enforcement methodologies and technological tools and describing some of the different career and promotional opportunities, benefits, and minimum qualifications as well as the hiring process. Recruiters visit community and college job fairs, military installations, community meetings, religious organizations, and neighborhood organizations, both in and out of state.

LEARN BY DOING: FIVE SCENARIOS

Following are five scenarios based on actual events that demonstrate some of the situations that COPPS officers might confront. For each scenario, we have provided some of the cultural beliefs and practices that might come into play. You should try to determine how, as the police officer involved in each case, you would address each situation. Also consider the possible repercussions if you fail to recognize the underlying nonverbal communication, beliefs, and practices that are present in each scenario

> *Scenario 1.* You, the officer, witness a traffic violation. When you stop the driver of the vehicle, you notice a couple of things. First, the driver speaks with a heavy Spanish accent; second, he appears very nervous. You ask for his driver's license and registration. When he hands them over, you observe that he has also enclosed a $100 bill. The traffic offense carries a fine of $25, but now the offense of bribery has been committed. How would you handle this situation?[38]

Here, you might consider the fact that in some Latin American countries, the way to do business with any public official—especially the police—is to offer money. It is expected, and there are severe penalties for noncompliance. The offense of bribery has been committed, so you would be well within the law to arrest the driver. After further questioning the driver regarding his country of origin, you could explain that the exchange of money is a punishable offense in the United States and charge him only for the traffic offense.

> *Scenario 2.* You are summoned to a local school by the principal, who has been informed of a case of child abuse by a sixth-grade teacher. On arriving at the principal's office, you are shown a Vietnamese girl who had been absent from school for several days with a high fever. The girl has heavy bruising on the left side of her neck. You go to the child's home and question her father, who admits in broken English that he caused the bruising on the girl's neck. What is your response?

In parts of Asia, a medical practice called "coining" involves rubbing the skin with a heated coin, leaving highly visible marks on the neck or back. This practice, intended to heal the child, may easily be misinterpreted as child abuse by police, school, or social service agencies. This is a good example of why police officers must avoid being ethnocentric or interpreting what they see through their own cultural "filters."

> *Scenario 3.* You are summoned to a murder scene involving a family picnic in a neighborhood park. On arriving, you learn that a Mexican woman, who was recently involved in an extramarital affair, had been bragging about her activities in front of her husband and many extended-family members; she also made inappropriate comments about her new lover's sexual prowess and her husband's inabilities in that regard. Her husband then left the park. Returning shortly thereafter with a shotgun, he shot and killed his wife. He gives himself up. For what criminal charge(s) do you believe the defendant should be arrested and convicted?

In probably all states, a case such as this would result in a minimum charge of second-degree murder against the defendant. However, in this actual case (in California), because the jury took into consideration the cultural background of this couple, the husband was convicted of a lesser charge of manslaughter. It was argued that the wife's boasting about her lover and the emasculation of her husband created a passion and emotion that completely undermined his "machismo," pride, and honor—what it means to be humiliated in the context of the Latin culture in front of one's family.[39]

> *Scenario 4.* While on foot patrol, you, a COPPS officer, respond to a neighborhood complaint concerning loud noise and a party. Upon arrival, you observe a brawl at a

barbecue party in the backyard of a home where Samoans reside and many Samoans are now present. How should you proceed?

You could immediately summon backup assistance, and then you and the other officers could make a show of force, breaking up the fighting but also acquiring the undying disrespect and possible wrath of the Samoan community and widening the gap between the two groups. Alternatively, the police could locate the "chief" of this group and let that person deal with the problem in a manner in which he would handle it in Samoa. The chief has a prominent role to play and can serve as a bridge between the police and the community (and keep the matter out of court).[40]

> *Scenario 5.* You perform a traffic stop involving a Nigerian cab driver, who moves uncomfortably close to you and ignores your command to "please step back." He also averts his eyes from you, and begins defiantly "babbling to the ground" in a high-pitched tone of voice while making gestures. You are convinced the cab driver is out of control, unstable, and possibly dangerous. How should you deal with this individual?

In Nigeria, the social distance for conversation is much closer than in the United States; it may be less than 15 inches. Furthermore, Nigerian people often show respect and humility by averting their eyes. What you perceive as "babbling" is actually the cab driver's way of sending a message of respect and humility. Most likely, the cab driver is not even aware that he is perceived as out of control, unstable, and possibly dangerous.

Discussion

These case studies—taken together, which certainly point up the need for cultural diversity to be incorporated into basic police academy training curricula—are not presented to question the rightness or wrongness of any group's values, beliefs, or practices. Nor should they be interpreted to mean that serious crimes should be excused on cultural grounds. The point is to illustrate for police officers the importance of understanding cultural differences and individual backgrounds.

Obviously the police must take differences in nonverbal communication into account when dealing with people of different cultures. These case studies also reveal that discretion at the police level is much more important than that practiced at the court's level.

It would be unrealistic to expect all police officers to be aware of every possibility for mis-communication or cultural insult. Policing in a multicultural society, however, requires a human-istic approach through which differences are understood and accommodated rather than viewed as cause for conflict. Opponents of COPPS may believe that adding a multicultural focus will soften an allegedly already soft approach to crime prevention; however, not understanding cul-tural differences can and does result in officer or citizen injury as well as disorder and death.

Summary

This chapter focused on the often-fractured rela-tions that have historically come between the police and the minority communities they serve. Ours is not a perfect world. The Constitution notwith-standing, people are *not* created equal, at least with respect to legal, social, political, and economic opportunities. This disparity creates confronta-tions, mistrust, and enmity between many citizens and the police.

As more studies point to systematic racism within our criminal justice system, the police must work even harder to heal the wounds of the past and to eliminate any vestiges of bias-based policing and vigorously pursue those who would commit hate crimes.

Policing also needs more women and minorities who are willing to assist as citizens or as police officers to join the cause as well as more culturally informed police training.

For these reasons, COPPS offers hope for improvement because this strategy fosters a partnership that is based on trust, communication, and understanding.

Items for Review

1. Explain what is meant in contemporary terms by "diversity."
2. Delineate the historical background of police-minority relations.
3. Review whether or not the criminal justice system discriminates against minorities; include the finding by RAND as well as the perceptions of other notable organizations.
4. Define what is meant by bias-based policing (racial profiling), and explain why it is a destructive practice.

5. Define the elements of a hate crime, and discuss what measures are being taken by the police to address such acts.
6. Describe some of the cultural customs of people of different nationalities, and discuss why it is important for the police to be aware of those difference customs.
7. Explain why it is important for a police agency to be diverse, and provide examples of what some police agencies are doing to enhance their ability to recruit women and minorities.

Learn by Doing

1. In the past six months, there has been a spike in residential burglaries in an older, predominantly Hispanic neighborhood within your city. Residents are becoming quite vocal at council meetings, wanting something done and delays in investigations stopped. Budgets are extremely tight, and your agency has experienced reductions in burglary detectives; as a result, they will only actively investigate cases with known suspects or where an arrest was made. As your agency's community liaison officer, you are tasked to present ideas to the council outlining what measures will be taken to address the problem and to communicate the police department's concern to the residents. What measures will you present?
2. Your county sheriff assigns you the task of using innovative methods for recruiting women and minor-

ity deputies for your agency. Because the county manager has made agency diversity a top priority, a substantial budget has been appropriated for this purpose. Using the "toolkit" ideas presented in this chapter, what will you recommend is done in order to reach these individuals in markets that are not normally recruited?
3. You are a captain in your law enforcement agency and have been invited to speak at a local meeting of the League of Women Voters. During the discussion, you are asked what the organization is doing to work with diverse populations, and particularly whether or not you believe the police should possess knowledge of different cultures' customs and differences. What is your response, including some examples of such customs?

Notes

1. U.S. Department of Justice, Office of Community Oriented Policing Services, *Law Enforcement Recruitment Toolkit*, June 2009, pp. 30, 32, http://www.cops.usdoj.gov/files/RIC/Publications/e080921223-RecruitmentToolkit.pdf (Accessed July 21, 2010).
2. 347 U.S. 483 (1954).
3. Anthony M. Platt (ed.), *The Politics of Riot Commissions* (New York: Collier Books, 1971).

4. *Ibid.*, p. 272.
5. See, for example, Allen D. Grimshaw, *Racial Violence in the United States* (Chicago: Aldine, 1969), pp. 269–298; *Report of the National Advisory Commission on Civil Disorders* (New York: Bantam Books, 1968).
6. Steven M. Cox and Jack D. Fitzgerald, *Police in Community Relations: Critical Issues* (2nd ed.) (Dubuque, Iowa: William C. Brown, 1992), p. 129.

7. Samuel Walker, *The Police in America: An Introduction* (2nd ed.) (New York: McGraw-Hill, 1993), p. 224.

8. National Academy of Sciences, *A Common Destiny: Blacks and American Society* (Washington, D.C.: National Academy Press, 1989), p. 453.

9. Joan Petersilia, "Racial Disparities in the Criminal Justice System: Executive Summary of RAND Institute Study, 1983," in Daniel Georges-Abeyle (ed.), *The Criminal Justice System and Blacks* (New York: Clark Boardman, 1984), pp. 225–258.

10. The Leadership Conference on Civil and Human Rights, "Justice on Trial," http://www.civilrights.org/publications/justice-on-trial/ (Accessed July 21, 2010).

11. Drug Policy Alliance, "Race and the Criminal Justice System," http://www.drugpolicy.org/communities/race/criminaljust/ (Accessed July 21, 2010).

12. Pat Milton, "Grand Jury Indicts 3 in NYPD Shooting," http://abcnews.go.com/US/wireStory?id=2957956 (Accessed April 19, 2007).

13. LAPD Shooting Blamed on Poor Supervision," http://www.latimes.com/news/local/los_angeles_metro/la-me-pena6dec06,0,5058221,print.story?coll=la-commun-los_angeles_metro (Accessed January 12, 2007).

14. Lorie A. Fridell, *Racially Biased Policing: Guidance for Analyzing Race Data from Vehicle Stops—Executive Summary* (Washington, D.C.: Police Executive Research Forum and Office of Community Oriented Policing Services, 2005), p. 1.

15. Lorie Fridell, Robert Lunney, Drew Diamond, and Bruce Kubu, *Racially Based Policing: A Principled Response* (Washington, D.C.: Police Executive Research Forum, 2001), pp. 6–9.

16. G. Voegtlin, "Bias-Based Policing and Data Collection," *The Police Chief* (October 2001):8.

17. Adapted from Stanford University, "Policing Racial Bias Project," http://waldron.stanford.edu/~policingproject/ (Accessed March 7, 2011).

18. Anti-Defamation League, "ADL Welcomes Release of FBI 2004 Hate Crimes Statistics," http://www.adl.org/PresRele/HatCr_51/4811_52.htm (Accessed April 11, 2006).

19. Federal Bureau of Investigation, "Hate Crimes Statistics 2008," http://www.fbi.gov/ucr/hc2008/incidents.html (Accessed July 21, 2010).

20. International Association of Chiefs of Police, "Responding to Hate Crimes: A Police Officer's Guide to Investigation and Prevention," http://www.theiacp.org/documents (Accessed April 28, 2003).

21. Madison, Wisconsin, Police Department, "Special Programs: ADL and Police Launch Statewide Effort to Fight Hate Crimes," http://www.madisonct.org/pdspcprog.htm (Accessed April 28, 2003).

22. See govtrack.us,, "H.R. 1913," http://www.govtrack.us/congress/bill.xpd?bill=h111-1913&tab=summary (Accessed July 21, 2010).

23. Gayle Fisher-Stewart, "Multicultural Training for Police," *MIS Report* 26 (9) (1994):7.

24. Sharon K. Papa, "L.A. Brass Listens to the Forums," *Community Links* (March 2002):14.

25. Harvard University Police Department, "HUPD Diversity and Community Liaison," http://www.hupd.harvard.edu/diversity_and_community_liaison.php (Accessed July 21, 2010).

26. Alan Caddell, "Citizen Academy: Hands-On Classes Stress Challenges, Responsibilities of Real Thing," *Community Links* (August 2002):1–2.

27. "Lincoln Police Department Community Policing Projects," http://www.ci.lincoln.ne.us/city/police/pdf/cbpprog.html (Accessed April 28, 2003).

28. Quoted in Patricia A. Parker, "Tackling Unfinished Business," *Police* (December 1991):19, 84.

29. Gary Weaver, "Law Enforcement in a Culturally Diverse Society," *FBI Law Enforcement Bulletin* 61 (September 1992):1–7.

30. Ibid.

31. Pamela D. Mayhall, *Police-Community Relations and the Administration of Justice* (3rd ed.) (Englewood Cliffs, N.J.: Prentice Hall, 1985), pp. 308–309.

32. Ibid., pp. 312–313.

33. Ken Peak and Jack Spencer, "Crime in Indian Country: Another 'Trail of Tears,'" *Journal of Criminal Justice* 15 (1987):485–494.

34. Mayhall, *Police-Community Relations*, p. 6.

35. Fisher-Stewart, "Multicultural Training for Police," p. 8.

36. Quoted in U.S. Department of Justice, Office of Community Oriented Policing Services, *Law Enforcement Recruitment Toolkit*, June 2009, p. 32, http://www.cops.usdoj.gov/files/RIC/Publications/e080921223-RecruitmentToolkit.pdf (Accessed July 21, 2010).

37. Ibid., pp. 36-40.

38. Adapted from Robert M. Shusta, Deena R. Levine, Philip R. Harris, and Herbert Z. Wong, *Multicultural Law Enforcement: Strategies for Peacekeeping in a Diverse Society* (Englewood Cliffs, N.J.: Prentice Hall, 1995), pp. 21–22.

39. Ibid., p. 22.

40. Fisher-Stewart, "Multicultural Training for Police," p. 4.

11

COPPS on the Beat
Drugs, Gangs, and Youth Crimes

KEY TERMS AND CONCEPTS

Clandestine drug lab
Cyberbullying
Gang
Graffiti
Hazardous materials
 (HAZMAT)

Intervention
Methamphetamine initiative
Open-air drug market
Pharmaceutical
 counterfeiting

"Pharming parties"
Suppression
Underage drinking
Youth crime

LEARNING OBJECTIVES

As a result of reading this chapter, the student will:

- Be aware of the level of drug problems that now confronts the U.S., and what street-level interventions work and do not work toward meeting the challenges posed by methamphetamine, clandestine drug labs, open-air drug markets, pharmaceutical counterfeiting, and "pharming parties"

- Know the extent of gangs and graffiti in our nation, how they both affect our quality of life and economic well-being; and some successful efforts toward identification, prevention, and suppression of such behaviors

- Understand what can be done toward addressing the problem of youth crime, including gun violence, disorderly conduct in public places, underage drinking, school violence, and cyberbullying

*Destroying the life or safety of other people, through teasing,
bullying, hitting or otherwise, "putting them down," is as
destructive to themselves as to their victims.*
—LEWIS P. LIPSITT

*A team is where a boy can prove his courage on his own. A gang
is where a coward goes to hide.*

—BRANCH RICKEY

*Drug misuse is not a disease, it is a decision, like the decision to
step out in front of a moving car. You would call that not a
disease but an error of judgment.*

—PHILIP K. DICK

INTRODUCTION

How does community oriented policing and problem solving (COPPS) function in practice? While the preceding chapters have traced the origin, preparation, and methods of community policing and problem solving, this chapter (as well as the next chapter) demonstrates its practical application with a variety of problems of crime and disorder. It is quite necessary that we do so, for indeed the litmus test for COPPS is the degree to which it succeeds in our communities and neighborhoods. Included are several examples of this strategy's approaches and accomplishments.

This chapter focuses on three broad areas that are particularly troublesome or challenging for today's society. First we examine the problem of drug offenses, and within this broad area we discuss methamphetamine, clandestine drug labs, open-air drug dealing, and problems involving prescription drugs—**pharmaceutical counterfeiting** and **"pharming parties."** Then we look at the entwined problems of gangs and graffiti. Finally, we consider problems involving our youth, which includes violence, use of firearms, disorderly behavior in public places, underage drinking, and school violence and cyberbullying. The chapter concludes with "Learn by Doing" scenarios, where you can experience some difficult challenges that police officers might confront.

Emphasis for each of the areas is placed on describing the nature of the problem, the extent and nature of its effects on society, and several responses that have been used by the police for coping with the problem. A number of examples and exhibits demonstrate how police agencies and other stakeholders are successfully collaborating to take back their neighborhoods.

OUR NATION'S NIGHTMARE: DRUGS

Societal Conundrum

That the United States is in the throes of a grave drug problem is beyond doubt. In fact, according to the Federal Bureau of Investigation, each year about one of every eight arrests in the United States—1.7 million in total—is for a drug violation.[1] This number of arrests probably represents only the tip of the iceberg in comparison to the actual levels of manufacturing, use, and trafficking that are occurring. The social costs of drug abuse are inestimable; however, we know that drug violations have eroded the environment, created undesirable role models for many youth, given rise to a wide variety of related criminal acts, and resulted in innumerable gun-wielding gang members across the United States who are fighting to expand their turf.

The extent of drug use while people commit crimes is also quite high, and seems to be related to where the offender lives: for example, 49 percent of persons arrested tested positive for at least one illicit drug in Washington, D.C., while an astronomical 87 percent of arrestees in Chicago tested positive. In addition, many arrestees tested positive for more than one illegal drug at the time of arrest—from 15 percent in Atlanta to 40 percent in Chicago. The most common substances present at time of arrest, in descending order, are marijuana, cocaine, opiates, and methamphetamine.[2]

Finally, the annual financial cost of combating drug abuse is significant as well. Indeed, for fiscal year 2011, the federal Office of National Drug Control Policy appropriated $15.5 billion to reduce drug use and availability in four major policy areas: (1) substance abuse prevention, (2) substance abuse treatment, (3) domestic law enforcement, and (4) interdiction and international counterdrug support.[3]

Methamphetamine Initiatives

Methamphetamine (meth) is a central nervous system stimulant often referred to as crack, speed, ice, or crystal. Developed in clandestine laboratories often located in remote areas, meth is cheap and addictive. Its negative effects can include physical addiction, psychotic behavioral episodes, and brain damage; chronic use can cause anxiety, confusion, insomnia, paranoia, and delusions. It is a serious health hazard to anyone who comes in contact with the precursor drugs used to produce it; they include police, medical, and fire personnel.

At present, meth presents a triple threat: Its availability is increasing in the United States, its prices are declining, and it purity is increasing. This situation is directly related to the meth production trends in Mexico, which is the primary source of meth consumed in the United States as a result of precursor chemical restrictions here. Mexican meth traffickers have adapted their operating procedures, including the use of new routes, importing nonrestricted chemical derivatives instead of precursor chemicals, and using alternative production methods.[4]

Exhibit 11–1	Meth's Newest Threat: The "Shake and Bake" Production Method

A new and extremely dangerous method for making methamphetamine is circulating that requires less technical knowledge and is designed to circumvent laws restricting the sale of ingredients needed to make meth. Meth users engage in the so-called "shake and bake" approach, which requires only a little room, can be carried in a backpack, and is easy to conceal. All that is required is a two-liter soda bottle, a few cold pills, and a few household chemicals. The mix of chemicals in the soda bottle can and do explode—if there is only a little oxygen inside the bottle, or it is shaken or opened in an incorrect manner—and become a giant fireball. In sum, if the user is unlucky at all, the result can be a devastating reaction, and a number of severe burns and fatalities have already resulted. Police officers across the nation are being trained in how to handle these new mobile labs.

Sources: "New 'Shake and Bake' Meth Method Explodes," *About.com.* May 13, 2010, http://alcoholism.about.com/od/meth/a/shake_and_bake.htm (Accessed August 10, 2010); Join Together, "New Formula Makes Meth Easier to Manufacture," August 26, 2009, http://www.jointogether.org/news/headlines/inthenews/2009/new-formula-makes-meth-easier.html; "New Meth Formula Avoids Anti-Drug Laws," Associated Press. August, 2009.

Since 1998, the federal Office of Community Oriented Policing Services (COPS) has invested more about $500 million nationwide to combat the spread of meth, supporting training, enforcement, and lab cleanup activities[5] Indeed, training police officers in lab identification and removal is an important first step in any **methamphetamine initiative**. Training public works and hotel/motel staff is also successful in helping to identify meth lab operations. Drug courts are a beneficial option for the criminal justice system because they immediately expose meth-addicted individuals to treatment and provide them with a rigid structure with little tolerance for infractions. Another major part of meth initiatives involves establishing the partnerships that are essential for addressing the problem, such as those developed with prosecutors' offices, environmental protection agencies, agencies involved in cleaning up hazardous materials, child welfare and family services agencies, treatment centers, and federal drug enforcement agencies.[6]

Exhibit 11–2 shows some successful initiatives that have been undertaken in several communities to address their growing meth problem; note the commonalities of the approaches: reliance on training and assistance of outside agencies.

Exhibit 11–2 **What Works: Going After Meth**

▶ *Oklahoma City, Oklahoma.* The Oklahoma City Police Department focused on increased enforcement and training as well as a partnership with a drug court to deal with meth problems. Officers used undercover buys, confidential informants, surveillance, and assistance from patrol officers making traffic stops to apprehend meth users and distributors. A 70 percent increase in meth labs seized occurred in the first year of the initiative. City-wide citizen training in meth use and identification was conducted; part of this training was focused on hotel/motel associations and natural gas employees— the latter responding to over 600,000 service calls in the city and having widespread and frequent access to properties and the potential for identifying lab locations.

▶ *Little Rock Arkansas.* The police in Little Rock also focused on increased enforcement and training of all officers regarding meth identification and response. Other approaches included establishing a telephone hotline for citizens to call if they suspected meth activity, an information campaign for retailers of precursor chemicals (including giving the police license plate numbers of purchasers of large quantities), and interviews with jail detainees regarding meth use and manufacturing to better understand the meth market.

▶ *Salt Lake City, Utah.* The Salt Lake City Police Department used enhanced enforcement and prosecution, child endangerment laws, civil remedies to reduce neighborhood impacts, public awareness campaigns, and formation of a meth training team. More than 30 city, county, and federal agencies participated.

▶ *Minneapolis, Minnesota.* The police in Minneapolis first engaged in comprehensive data collection to obtain information about the extent and nature of the meth problem. Interviews with probationers and drug court clients were conducted (and confirmed police suspicions that meth users were more likely to be white and employed). The department also developed general training videos on lab identification and identification at traffic stops, and it trained community groups, police officers, and transit, housing, sanitation, and park employees who might come in contact with clandestine meth labs.

Source: U.S. Department of Justice, Office of Community Oriented Policing Services, *Combating Methamphetamine Laboratories and Abuse: Strategies for Success* (Washington, D.C: Author, August 2003), pp. 7–9.

Clandestine Drug Labs

A problem that is closely related to meth manufacturing and sales is the clandestine drug labs (meth accounts for 80 to 90 percent of the labs' total drug production). Dealing with **clandestine drug labs** requires extraordinarily high levels of technical expertise. Responders must understand illicit drug chemistry—how to neutralize the risk of explosions, fires, fumes, and burns, and how to handle and dispose of **hazardous materials (HAZMAT)**. They must also know the federal, state, and local laws governing chemical manufacturing and distribution, HAZMAT, and occupational safety. They must collaborate with fire officials, HAZMAT experts, chemists, public health officials, and social service providers.[7]

Cleaning up clandestine drug labs is an enormously complex, time-consuming, and costly undertaking. Seizing a lab potentially makes a police agency liable for some of the costs of cleaning up on-site hazardous materials. If the lab is in operation when found, it must first be safely neutralized so that it does not contaminate the environment; then the materials must be cleaned up and safely disposed of.[8]

Police responses to the problem of these drug labs involve much more than merely finding and seizing the small "mom and pop" labs, because they are so easy to set up that it seems impossible to find all or even most of them. Other responses include the following[9]:

- Using federal and state organized crime and racketeering statutes for dismantling more sophisticated "super labs," run by syndicates
- Searching the homes and vehicles of former lab operators who are on probation and parole regularly to determine if they have resumed operating a lab
- Seizing and filing for forfeiture of clandestine drug lab operators' assets (although this strategy is probably not effective with smaller labs)
- Enforcing environmental protection laws because the burden of proof under these laws is typically less than that required for criminal convictions
- Filing civil actions against persons who allow their properties to be used as clandestine drug labs as well as filing nuisance abatement actions and eviction actions
- Monitoring the sale and distribution of essential and precursor chemicals used in such labs, widely considered to be one of the most effective responses (although doing so requires effort at the local, state, national, and international levels)

Open-Air Drug Markets

Open-air drug markets represent the lowest level of the drug distribution network. These low-level markets need to be addressed, however, because of the risks that are posed to market participants and the harms that drug use can inflict on the entire community.

Open-air markets have several advantages for both buyers and sellers. Buyers know where to go in order to obtain the drugs they want and can weigh quality against price, and sellers are able to maximize customer access. Open-air markets also generate or contribute to a wide range of problems and disorder in the community, including traffic congestion, noise, disorderly conduct, loitering, prostitution, robbery, burglary, theft from motor vehicles, fencing of stolen goods, weapons offenses, assaults, and clandestine drug labs (discussed above).[10]

Dealing with open-air drug markets presents a considerable challenge for the police. Simply arresting market participants will have little impact in reducing the size of the market or the amount of drugs consumed. However, the nature of open markets means that market participants are vulnerable both to police enforcement and to dangers of buying from strangers, which may include rip-offs and robberies.

Shown are drugs, money, and guns seized recently in special operations of the Drug Enforcement Administration.

Courtesy DEA.

Whichever approach the police choose, it is unlikely that they will be able to eradicate open-air drug markets completely; furthermore, a police crackdown or sweep will be a deterrent only if appropriate sentencing is used. Following are some activities the police have engaged in[11]:

- *Policing the area in a highly visible fashion.* Visible policing (including foot patrol) may disrupt the drug market and make it inconvenient for sellers and buyers to engage in drug transactions.
- *Enforcing the law intensively.* The effect of such a crackdown is dependent on the drug market that is targeted and the amount of resources available. Methods include street surveillance and intelligence gathering, hotline for area residents, and increases in drug treatment services.
- *Using intelligence-led investigative work.* Information from drug hotlines and local residents can help to identify and analyze a problem. In addition, an arrest may produce information if officers debrief the offender, and drug buyers may lead undercover officers to drug locations.
- *Arresting drug buyers in "reverse stings."* This response serves to impact the demand side of the market and is most successful against new or occasional drug users. Police in Miami, Florida, found that the process of being arrested, charged, and forced to appear in court and having a vehicle impounded acted as a deterrent.

What Works with Street-Level Drug Enforcement?

To determine what is most effective in street-level drug enforcement interventions, a team of researchers, with federal funding, reviewed a number of rigorous academic studies evaluating a wide range of street-level drug law enforcement interventions. Their findings were instructive in terms of "what works" and "what does not."

First, regarding the use of police crackdowns, defined by Davis and Lurigio as "abrupt escalations in law enforcement activities . . . to increase the perceived or actual threat of apprehension for certain offenses"[12] for drug dealing and use, researchers discovered the following:

- Crackdowns were largely ineffective in disrupting drug problems such as use, dealing, and drug offenses.
- Crackdowns appeared to have more success addressing associated crime problems, such as property crime and violent crime, among others. Displacement (both spatial and temporal) of drug and crime problems was a common problem.
- Crackdowns tend to have minimal, short-term effects on drug, crime, and disorder problems.[13]

Next, the researchers also looked at *community-wide approaches*, which include police interventions that typically are unfocused and involve partnerships (i.e., with local councils, community groups, regulators, inspectors, business groups, and other crime-control agencies). Such programs revealed small and generally insignificant decreases in crime, drug calls, and drug consumption, along with greater citizen satisfaction with the police. Foot and bike patrols showed small reductions in drug-related arrests. Shop fronts (also known as "Cop Shops") revealed improvements in quality of life, reductions in fear of crime, and increased police satisfaction with the community.[14]

Finally, the researchers examined initiatives that centered on problem-oriented policing, with extremely positive results: more than 70 percent (24 of 34) of the problem-oriented policing evaluations reported positive effects on drug outcomes. Almost 80 percent (19 of 24) of the problem-oriented policing evaluations reported positive effects on nondrug outcomes (e.g., property, violent, disorder, offenses).[15]

Submarines are being used by drug cartels to smuggle drugs into the U.S.
Courtesy FBI.

The major policy implication that emerged from this research was that the police will be most effective at reducing street-level drug problems when they work with third parties (community partners), whether they are partnerships within a problem-oriented policing context or not. To reduce street-level drug problems, police need to improve police-citizen relations, forge partnerships with nonpolice agencies (i.e., third parties), utilize a range of civil remedies, and leverage additional resources to deal with a community's drug problems.[16]

These findings can be seen "at work" in Exhibit 11–3, which provides an example of COPPS strategies against drug markets in High Point, North Carolina.

"Pharming Parties" and Pharmaceutical Counterfeiting

A once-serious problem that seems to be abating is that of raves—dance parties that feature fast-paced, repetitive electronic music and light shows. Drug use at raves is intended to enhance ravers' sensations and boost their energy so that they can dance for long periods, usually starting late at night and going into the morning hours.

In the place of raves are so-called "pharming parties." These are essentially parties often arranged while parents are out so that the kids can barter for their favorite prescription drugs. Such parties—or just "pharming" (from pharmaceuticals)—"represent a growing trend among teenage drug abusers."[17]

According to Columbia University's National Center on Addiction and Substance Abuse (CASA), the abuse of prescription drugs has increased sharply. Teens can easily become addicted to painkillers like Oxycontin or Vicodin, antianxiety medicines like Valium or Xanax, or attention-deficit-disorder drugs like Ritalin and Adderall. These medicines can send youths to the

| Exhibit 11–3 | Eliminating Overt Drug Markets in High Point, North Carolina |

High Point is a city of approximately 95,000 population in central North Carolina. The city is 60 percent white and 30 percent African American, and some 13 percent of the population live below the poverty line. This project was designed to eliminate "overt" drug markets—street sales, and associated drug houses—in High Point, North Carolina. The goal was to reduce the full range of harm associated with overt public drug markets, and to repair the damage to race relations associated with the usual approaches to drug issues as well as the associated harms created by traditional drug enforcement.

SCANNING

High Point began experiencing serious drug activity and gun violence in the mid-1990s, and recently decided to focus on overt drug markets. There were chronic problems of street-corner dealing, crack houses, prostitution, and drive-through drug buyers; there were also problems associated with drug dealing, including homicide, gun assault, robberies and other serious violence; sexual assault; prostitution; drive-through drug buyers; and broad community quality of life concerns. These markets were located exclusively in poor minority neighborhoods, although drug and sex buyers often came from outside. A goal was developed to eliminate overt drug markets citywide and to address the key problems associated with them.

ANALYSIS

HPPD mapped drug arrests; calls for service; field contacts; and Part I, weapons, sexual, and prostitution offenses. Within hot spots, serious crimes were individually reviewed for a drug connection. Information from patrol officers, vice/narcotics investigators, informants, and crime tip lines was analyzed. Neighborhoods were identified as major overt markets, and largely included rental and public housing. Careful examination of High Point's markets revealed important patterns, and that heavy enforcement within the hot spot itself would be unproductive.

RESPONSE

The operational plan was designed to address the conflict and misunderstanding between law enforcement and communities, focus on and provide help to dealers, disrupt self-sustaining market dynamics, and support those influences with predictable consequences.

A series of discussions was conducted within and between law enforcement and community circles. HPPD believed that it had a strong relationship with the minority community, but this process established that the community was deeply angry at law enforcement, and felt that they were incompetent or doing deliberate harm. For each market, vice/narcotics detectives surveyed patrol officers, probation officers, street narcotics officers, and community members, and reviewed every arrest report, incident report, and field interview associated with possible dealers. All known associates were reviewed. Suspects' current activities were checked. The process uncovered, as noted, a very small number of active dealers.

A key approach was to enlist those persons close to offenders—e.g., parents, grandparents, guardians, ministers—to create and reinforce positive norms and expectations. For each dealer, one or several "influentials" was identified—primarily mothers and grandmothers—by reviewing the dealer's contact history, booking records, probation officer contact logs, and jail visit lists. A group of ministers, service providers, health care workers, nonprofits, educators, and elected officials worked to ensure that needs—most commonly employment, housing, transportation, and help enrolling in GED programs—were convened. Law enforcement officers watched relentlessly for any dealers to emerge in the target area, stopped them, and "reported" this activity to dealers, their families, and the community: Somebody tried to sell drugs; we stopped them; this activity isn't going to work or be tolerated. Patrol officers maintained systematic contact with offenders, their families, and the community.

Teams consisting of a detective, a service provider, and a minister made home visits to the dealers and influentials. They were told that police had made undercover buys from the offender; that probable cause existed for an arrest; that an opportunity to avoid prosecution and an offer of assistance would be discussed at the call-in; and that family members and others were encouraged to attend. Nine of the 12 dealers came to a meeting, accompanied by many "influentials" and others. They heard an uncompromising message from community speakers: "We care deeply about you, we'll help you, but you're hurting people and destroying the community and you need to stop." From the police they heard, "You could be in jail tonight; we don't want to do that, we want to help you succeed, but you are out of the drug business." Blown-up surveillance photos of drug locations lined the walls; pictures were shown of the offenders who were arrested as part of the operation. Law enforcement's willingness *not* to act on existing cases seemed to make a profound impression on the dealers' families and other community members. Most dealers signed up for services.

ASSESSMENT

There are no remaining overt drug markets in High Point. The quality of life in the affected neighborhoods improved dramatically. The power of the strategy shocked even the police. Street corner and drug house activity, drive-through buyers, and prostitutes were simply not in evidence. No displacement has been evident. Of the 18 dealers initially identified, only 3 have been arrested for dealing. No other hot spots emerged, and gunshot calls for service dropped by over 50 percent. Drug crime is similarly down and has shifted from dealing offenses to minor possession, paraphernalia, and so on. Vice/Narcotics officers are free to pursue more serious traffickers and are making far more productive cases and seizures. Most dealers are now working regular jobs.

Source: Adapted from the Center for Problem Oriented Policing, "Application for the 2006 Herman Goldstein Award," http://www.popcenter.org/library/awards/goldstein/2006/06-20(F).pdf (Accessed August 10, 2010).

---

emergency room and lead to difficulty breathing, a drop or rapid increase in heart rate or trouble responding when driving a car (especially when the drugs are combined with alcohol). Pain medications are particularly dangerous and highly sought after by many youths.[18]

Unfortunately, prescription drugs are often easier to obtain than illegal drugs. Furthermore, some youths obtain such medications legitimately, but then trade them for others, like painkillers, that hold more appeal because of their more potent high. Still other youths order their prescriptions from Internet pharmacies—some of which do not require prescriptions. Finally, the problem is exacerbated by the fact that many of these youths abuse multiple drugs at the same time; indeed, according to CASA, about 75 percent of prescription-drug abusers are such users, who also take those drugs in combination with other drugs or with alcohol.[19]

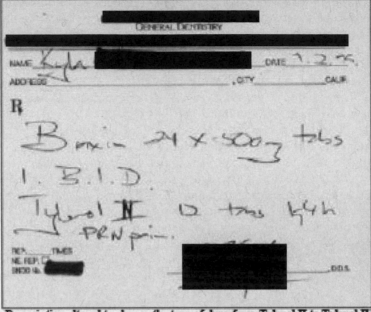

Prescription altered to change the type of drug from Tylenol II to Tylenol IV

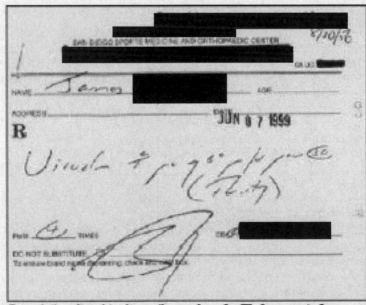

Prescription altered to change the number of refills from one to four

Prescription fraud. As shown above, prescriptions can easily be altered to change the type of drug prescribed or the number of refills allowed.

Courtesy Office of Community Oriented Policing Services.

A related problem and one that is literally killing people is the use of counterfeit pharmaceuticals. The Pharmaceutical Security Institute (PSI) defines counterfeit medicine as those "products deliberately and fraudulently produced and/or mislabeled with respect to their identity and/or source to make them appear to be genuine. This definition applies to branded, generic, and over-the-counter products."[20]

The extent of this international problem is unknown, as government agencies and international organizations have struggled to determine the precise extent and nature of this problem. In 2006, the World Health Organization (WHO) recognized the problem—as hundreds of people are dying each year due to their taking contaminated counterfeit medications—and urged public and private organizations to provide timely exchanges of information concerning this worldwide activity.[21]

Summary

COPPS has wide applications to the problem of drugs. The traditional police approach to a citizen's call about suspected drug activity—showing up, taking a report, and leaving the area or perhaps making a misdemeanor arrest—is neither effective for the long term nor welcomed by COPPS; little analysis or measurement of results would occur under that approach.

Conversely, while a COPPS officer might also use a short-term response (such as an arrest), there would also be an analytical assessment of the situation to determine why the area was the scene of almost constant drug activity: What is the calls for service (CFS) pattern for the location? Are the arrestees youths who are truant from school? When is the activity occurring? Is lighting inadequate? Are grounds littered and vandalized? Are vacant apartments available to foster drug activity? Do abandoned vehicles provide convenient places for drug stashes? The S.A.R.A. process would likely be applied, with follow-up monitoring of the situation. We will examine some COPPS initiatives in jurisdictions that were not content with the traditional approach.

GANGS AND GRAFFITI

Gangs have obviously been known to be a significant problem in this nation for several decades. Following are some disconcerting facts about today's gangs, as determined by the National Gang Intelligence Center:

- Local street gangs, or neighborhood-based street gangs, account for the largest number of gangs nationwide; most engage in violence in conjunction with a variety of crimes, including retail-level drug distribution.
- Nearly 6 in 10 (58 percent) state and local law enforcement agencies report that criminal gangs are active in their jurisdictions.
- Gang members are migrating from urban areas to suburban and rural communities, to expand drug distribution territories, increase illicit revenue, recruit new members, hide from law enforcement, and escape other gangs.
- Criminal gangs commit as much as 80 percent of the crime in many communities, and typical gang-related crimes include alien smuggling, armed robbery, assault, auto theft, drug trafficking, extortion, fraud, home invasions, identity theft, murder, and weapons trafficking.
- Gang members are the primary retail-level distributors of most illicit drugs. They also are increasingly distributing wholesale-level quantities of marijuana and cocaine in most urban and suburban communities.[22]

Furthermore, the line between prison and street gangs is becoming muddled as gang members flow in and out of the correctional system.[23]

Gangs proliferate as well. According to the estimates by the National Criminal Justice Reference Service, there are more than 24,500 gangs and more than 772,000 gang members in more than 3,300 jurisdictions in the United States. Nearly half of all gang members (48 percent) are African American youth, whereas Hispanic youngsters account for 43 percent and Asians total 5 percent.[24]

Street gangs can have a significantly damaging effect on a community. Gangs play a role in firearms transactions and violence, drug sales and use, home invasions, car thefts, homicides, and a number of other crime problems.

For COPPS activities, the police agencies must attempt a problem analysis of the involved street gangs. This is particularly important because no "cookie-cutter" approach will work; gangs are unique phenomena, particular to time and place. Failing to undertake a problem analysis of the crime problems at hand and the general gang landscape will likely result in a futile response strategy.[25]

The options available to the police when attempting to address a street gang problem(s) cover a wide spectrum with regard to both goals and tactics (see Exhibit 11–4). Four programs represent the range of activities that exists for this purpose—prevention, intervention, suppression, and comprehensive strategies:

1. Prevention programs have the broadest audience of interest and are typically aimed at groups that pose some risk or, more broadly, at general populations. For example, a prevention program may focus on preschool children who reside in gang neighborhoods before they show any symptoms of having joined the gang life. Perhaps the best known of these programs is Gang Resistance Education and Training (G.R.E.A.T.). Although evaluation results of G.R.E.A.T. show no long-term impact on gang membership or delinquent behavior, they suggest positive short-term effects on gang-related behavior and attitudes.[26]

2. **Intervention** typically addresses individuals or places that have manifested some problem. In most cases, such intervention programs attempt to persuade gang members or gang-affiliated youth to abandon their current lifestyle or to reduce gang-related crime. At this stage, defining the type of gang of interest, the level of individual involvement in the gang, and the specific problem of focus becomes extremely important and integral to any success. Interventions may include a gang truce or the use of nonmembers to persuade gang members to leave gang life.

3. **Suppression** also has the aim of reducing gang activities, but suppression programs typically rely on the law as a guide and on criminal justice agencies as the primary (and often only) partners. Deterrence principles often include law enforcement task forces or units and sentencing enhancements. Their success hinges on developing a plan based on a problem analysis to understand the gang problem in the jurisdiction. When operating alone, however, suppression tactics are rarely successful in the long term. Even if a program appears successful in the short term, gangs tend to endure because the police can rarely eradicate them completely, nor do they have the resources to sustain such an intensive focus over time and across all gangs and gang members. In addition, crime may simply be displaced. Suppression tactics are important but appear to provide the most benefit when part of a larger comprehensive program.[27] (An example of a collaborative effort is shown in Exhibit 11–4.)

Exhibit 11–4	Sharing Strategies Through a Gang Prevention Network

Early in 2007, 13 cities in California formed a network to identify and share effective strategies for preventing gang violence. The network focuses on cities developing plans that will mobilize the commitment of key stakeholders. To that end, each city has formed a five- to eight-member team with at least one representative from the mayor's office, the chief of police and the community, as well as other municipal leaders, law enforcement officials, school administrators, and faith-based and nonprofit stakeholders.

The four goals of the network are as follows:

1. To create citywide strategies that blend enforcement, prevention, and intervention
2. To create a vibrant network of urban leaders who will work with, and learn from, peers to advance local antigang strategies
3. To identify and document which programs and policies work, and which do not
4. To identify and recommend policies and practices that support effective community-based approaches.

There are also five guiding principles of the program that will hopefully increase the chances of success, all of which mirror the basic tenets of community-oriented policing—that reducing gang violence is not solely a law enforcement problem, but a community problem. These emerging principles are as follows:

1. The mayor and police chief must lead together, to combine the moral ("This will not be tolerated . . ."), the conceptual (a plan), and the bureaucratic (city business will be done in a different way).
2. Law enforcement and social services must partner to reduce gang violence; this requires conveying the certainty of consequences and of help. Police enforce the law, but at the same time many police leaders are ardent proponents of prevention.
3. A comprehensive strategy must be developed. A program here and there will not save a city. All key civic entities must play a role: schools, business, and the faith community, to name a few.
4. An entity must be designated or created. A commission or task force would track the work once a plan is developed.
5. The community must get close to its vulnerable young. The community, police, and social services must know gang members' names in order to stop them, help them, and show them they care.

Source: Adapted from John A. Calhoun, "Thirteen California Cities Share Strategies through Gang Prevention Network," *Community Policing Dispatch*, July 2008, p. 1, http://www.cops.usdoj.gov/html/dispatch/july_2008/13_california.htm (Accessed August 10, 2010).

4. Comprehensive programs typically involve collaboration and include prevention, intervention, and suppression techniques and hinge on the collective work of a variety of agencies, from criminal justice to social service to mental health to faith-based groups. Although they often require intensive resources and time, such programs appear to have the most promise in areas that have an array of problems surrounding a gang problem and fit well

Exhibit 11–5	New Approaches to an Old Problem: Graffiti

All around the world, communities have suffered from the visual blight of graffiti, and police are attempting to deal with it. Making use of community policing partnerships, the police are having some success in abating graffiti, while thus contributing to the economic health of their communities. One such case is that of Indio, California, which recently invested in a state-of-the-art truck and assigned two full-time graffiti abatement technicians to address the problem. These technicians respond to reported graffiti incidents, clean them up, and document them in order to make a prosecutable case. The team also has the capability to match paint colors before removing the graffiti—which it tries to do within 24 to 48 hours, as rapid removal is one of the best deterrents. In addition to removal, the team documents the graffiti with a GPS-enabled camera, so as to track graffiti patterns, locations, and offenders.

Source: Adapted from Amy Schapiro, "Getting a Grip on Graffiti," *Community Policing Dispatch*, February 2010, p. 1.

within an existing COPPS philosophy. In addition, should a particular gang pose numerous problems, such as intense gang recruitment in schools, drug sales, and gang-related homicides, it may require a variety of techniques and partners to address the issues.

A problem that is related to, and arises from gangs involves **graffiti**, which is another social harm that is associated with gangs (harms were discussed in Chapter 3). In addition to its being unsightly and being a general source of irritation, graffiti depreciates property values, adds to the deterioration of neighborhoods, and contributes to economic and urban blight. Exhibit 11–5 describes some new efforts under way to halt or mitigate that blight.

In the United States, the annual cost of graffiti is estimated to be between $10 and $12 billion. In New York City alone, the average cost of removing graffitti has increased from $300,000 to about $10 million. In a 10-year period, Los Angeles removed 162 million square feet of graffiti. A graffiti removal worker painting over a wall was fatally shot in Los Angeles in June 2004 by a man who police believe was angry because his gang's tags were being covered.[28]

Like New York and Los Angeles, most cities fight graffiti with their paintbrushes by quickly dispatching work crews to put on a fresh coat of paint over tagger or gang scribblings. Some experts, however, advocate photographing and filing graffiti markings because they represent actual communication and can be a valuable source of intelligence.

Five types of graffiti communication have been identified by researchers:

1. *Publicity.* Publicity graffiti (47 percent) is the most frequently found form and contains the name or abbreviation of the gang but does not include a threat and does not mark territory.
2. *Roll call.* Roll call graffiti (26 percent) identifies the gang name and a list of gang monikers (member nicknames).
3. *Territorial.* Territorial graffiti (17 percent) is identified by some sort of marking of a gang's territory, often in the form of an arrow pointing down.
4. *Threatening.* Threatening graffiti (9 percent) contains some sort of message aimed at a rival gang or perhaps at the police. It can include one gang crossing out another gang's graffiti.

5. *Sympathetic.* Sympathetic graffiti, the least observed form of graffiti (1 percent), is used to honor a slain gang member, usually in the form of an RIP (rest in peace).[29]

To combat the problem, some cities have enacted ordinances that require property owners to remove graffiti within a specified period of time. For example, in St. Petersburg, Florida, business owners are required to remove graffiti within 48 hours; in other areas, the city will paint over the graffiti for a set fee, usually $50 to $75. Box 11–1 shows an example of an antigraffiti ordinance.

The police must endeavor to eradicate the graffiti problem in order to diminish the gangs' sense of territory, improve the appearance of neighborhoods, and make a community statement that gang-type activities will not be tolerated. Following are some means by which the police and the public can attempt to reduce the rewards for and increase the detection of those who spread graffiti[30]:

- Detect graffiti rapidly and routinely (by monitoring graffiti-prone locations and increasing reporting)
- Remove graffiti rapidly
- Increase natural observation of graffiti-prone locations through use of police, security personnel, and citizens
- Conduct publicity campaigns combined with beautification efforts and cleanup days
- Control access to (and vandal-proof) prone locations, using dark or textured surfaces and special products that are resistant to graffiti and are easy to clean
- Focus on chronic offenders

BOX 11–1
Example of a Municipal Antigraffiti Ordinance

WHEREAS, property defaced by gang members is an act of vandalism and is against the law; and

WHEREAS, gang graffiti constitutes a public nuisance that causes depreciation of the value of the defaced property and the surrounding property and contributes to the deterioration of the neighborhood and the City in general; and

WHEREAS, depreciation of property values and deterioration of neighborhoods lead to economic blight and an increase in criminal activity and are injurious to the public health, safety, morals, and general welfare,

NOW, THEREFORE, BE IT ORDAINED BY THE CITY COUNCIL OF THE CITY OF LAKEWOOD, COLORADO, THAT:

9.85.060 NOTIFICATION OF NUISANCE. (a) The owner of any property defaced by gang graffiti shall be given written notice to abate the public nuisance on his property by removal within five (5) days after service of the notice. Such notice shall be by personal service to the owner or by posting the notice on the defaced property together with written notice mailed to the owner by first-class mail. The notice to the property owner shall contain:

1. The location of and a description of the violation;
2. A demand that the owner remove or eradicate the gang graffiti from the property within five (5) days after service of the notice;
3. A statement that the owner's failure or refusal to remove or eradicate the gang graffiti may result in abatement by the City;
4. A statement that if the costs of abatement plus the $75 fee for inspection and incidental costs are not paid to the City within 30 days after notice, an additional $75 will be assessed for administrative and other incidental costs

Source: Adapted from the Antigraffiti Ordinance of Lakewood, Colorado, 0-91-29, Title 9, Article 85, Chapter 9.85.

Youths remove graffiti from a public wall.
Courtesy Washoe County, Nevada, Sheriff's Office.

YOUTH CRIMES

Extent of the Problem

As any police officer or criminologist knows, crime is a young person's enterprise. In fact, according to the FBI, about 30 percent of all persons arrested in the United States for Part I and Part II offenses are under the age of 21; when raising the age level to 25, the proportion of arrestees jumps to 44 percent.[31] **Youth crime** remains one of the nation's most serious problems, particularly as gang activity continues to spread (discussed above).

Next we briefly consider several significant problems involving criminality and other problems involving youths: gun violence, disorderly youth in public places, underage drinking, and school violence and cyberbullying.

Gun Violence

This is a well-armed nation: It is now estimated that the United States has an estimated 283 million guns in civilian hands, and also that about 4.5 million new and 2 million secondhand firearms are sold each year in this nation.[32] Consequently, gun violence in the United States has become both a criminal justice and a public-health problem; firearms are still the weapons most frequently used for murder and the weapons of choice in nearly two-thirds of all murders. Strategies and programs to reduce gun violence include interrupting sources of illegal guns, deterring illegal possession and carrying of guns, and responding to illegal gun use[33]

At the same time, this nation's youth have become much more violent. There was a time when youths who committed felonies were likely to be engaged in non-violent offenses involving drug possession or trafficking. That is not the case today, however, and the news accounts bear witness to this new breed of youthful offender: the six teenagers who feloniously assaulted from behind an attorney as he jogged in Cleveland (they brandished a metal pole, a set of nunchucks, and a knife),[34] a 15-year old robber who first shot a convenience store clerk and then demanded money from him,[35] the 17-year old who was pulled out of a wrecked stolen car wearing a bullet-proof vest.[36]

All of these cases involved youths who were armed with guns in addition to the other weapons they were carrying. Certainly these youths can be "saved" from a life of felonious behavior, but just as assuredly, there must be special approaches, programs, and people who can bring that outcome to fruition.

Certainly big cities have been hit hard by youth gun violence. The worst hits seem to be in cities with dense populations that are racially segregated and have a high poverty level and lax gun laws.

Some cities and their police departments have begun focusing on these types of gun crimes. For example, in Baltimore, gun offenders are required to keep police informed of where they live. In Boston and in Washington, D.C., police have begun sending officers into high-crime neighborhoods to ask parents for permission to search their kids' rooms for illegal firearms (if any guns are found, they are only removed, and no charges are filed).[37] The cities of Cleveland and Philadelphia have gone even further. In both cities, African American mayors are requiring their police to employ tactics in high-crime, black neighborhoods that few others would dare to use. In Philadelphia, police conduct more "stop-and-frisk" searches, while Cleveland has an aggressive new gun-suppression strategy that hinges on identifying pedestrians who might be carrying guns. In doing so, the Cleveland police are coming face to face with one of the most controversial tactics in policing: use of the "stop and frisk" or pat-down search.[38]

Even though the "stop and frisk" is deeply resented in African American neighborhoods, its current use in such large cities speaks volumes of the levels of frustration cities now have with urban violence. Officers in high-crime areas recognize tell-tale signs of a suspect carrying a concealed weapon, such as frequent belt-tightening (due to one's having a pistol tucked into their pants), or the bulge under one's jacket. Indeed, the federal Bureau of Alcohol, Tobacco and Firearms offers local police a one-day gun-profiling class.[39]

Disorderly Conduct in Public Places

Disorderly conduct by youth in public places constitutes one of the most common problems most police agencies must handle, particularly in suburban and rural communities. Disorderly youth are a common source of complaints from urban residents, merchants, and shoppers. Among the kinds of behaviors (some legal and some not) that are associated with youth disorderly conduct are loud music; cursing; blocking of pedestrians and traffic; alcohol, tobacco, and drug use; fighting; littering; vandalism; and graffiti.[40]

Police responses to this problem might include the following[41]:

- Creating alternative legitimate places and activities for youth (such as youth clubs, drop-in centers, and recreation centers) and employing youth at businesses negatively affected by disorderly behavior
- Encouraging youth to gather where they will not disturb others
- Reducing the comfort level, convenience, or attraction of popular gathering places (such as eliminating places to sit or lean, changing the background music)
- Installing and monitoring closed-circuit television cameras
- Establishing and enforcing rules of conduct
- Denying youths anonymity (getting to know the names and faces of young people without being antagonistic or accusatory)

Underage Drinking

As with the statistics provided above for other problems discussed in this chapter, the numbers concerning **underage drinking** unfortunately are not getting better. The average age when youth first try alcohol is 11 years for boys and 13 years for girls. The average age at which Americans begin drinking regularly is 15.9 years old; adolescents who begin drinking before age 15 are four times more likely to develop alcohol dependence than those who begin drinking at age 21. It has been estimated that over 3 million teenagers are out-and-out alcoholics; several million more have a serious drinking problem that they cannot manage on their own. Finally, of the three leading causes of death for 15- to 24-year-olds—automobile crashes, homicides, and suicides—alcohol is the leading factor in all three.[42]

Although underage drinking (alcohol consumption while under the age of 21) is prohibited throughout the nation, young people use alcohol more than any other drug, including tobacco. Many of the harms associated with underage drinking, such as traffic fatalities, driving under the influence, assaults, cruising, street racing, rave parties, disorderly conduct, acquaintance rape, vandalism, and noise complaints, arise from the overconfidence, recklessness, lack of awareness, aggression, and loss of control that often accompany alcohol abuse.[43] The pressure to drink—to experience as a rite of passage, to become part of a group, to reduce tension, or to forget their worries—also contributes heavily to this problem.[44]

Police have responded to the problem of underage drinking in the following ways[45]:

- *Reducing the community's overall alcohol consumption.* This may sound impossible to do, but some available means for doing so are discouraging price discounts on alcohol, restricting the hours or days retailers can sell alcohol, and limiting the number of alcohol outlets.

Underage drinking is a serious national problem—and is associated with a variety of crimes.
Courtesy Shutterstock

• *Using a comprehensive approach.* Addressing the motivations for drinking and drunken driving, targeting fake IDs, providing counseling or treatment about drinking patterns, enforcing minimum-age purchase laws, and conducting undercover "shoulder tap" operations (having an undercover, underage operative ask adult strangers outside a store to purchase alcohol) could be used in combination. Other options are to check IDs at bars and night-clubs, apply graduated sanctions to retailers that break the law, and require keg registration. The latter is primarily used to identify adults who provide alcohol to minors at large house parties or keg parties on college campuses; several states use keg registration to link information about those who purchase a keg to the keg itself. Developing house party guidelines and walkthrough procedures and imposing fines for each underage person drinking at a party, are other possible methods.

School Violence and Cyberbullying

School violence has been declining: From 1992 to 1999, there were 238 school-associated violent deaths (including the April 1999 massacre of 13 people at Columbine High School in Littleton, Colorado).[46] Yet school safety continues to be a concern and requires broad-based efforts; those efforts must involve students at an early age and must be reinforced throughout their education.[47] Several strategies have been suggested for police and citizens to help prevent school violence[48]:

• Publicizing the philosophy that a gang presence will not be tolerated, and institutionalizing a code of conduct
• Alerting students and parents about school rules and punishments for infractions
• Creating alternative schools for those students who cannot function in a regular classroom
• Training teachers, parents, and school staff to identify children who are most at risk for violent behavior
• Developing community initiatives focused on breaking family cycles of violence, and providing programs on parenting, conflict resolution, anger management, and recovery from substance abuse
• Establishing peer counseling in schools to give troubled youths the opportunity to talk to someone their own age

Many police agencies now use school resource officers (SROs) for safety planning efforts. SROs can assess the school structure to determine where potential problems exist and help to address the social environment by such means as explaining what illegal conduct is, employing surveys to measure safety and security concerns of students and staff, and identifying bullies.[49]

A long-standing problem relating to schools is that of bullying. On a positive note, research indicates that physical bullying appears to be decreasing; the percentage of children who reported being bullied physically declined by 7 percent from 2003 to 2008. However, **cyberbullying** has increased and now eclipses physical bullying: More than 40 percent of teens report being victims of cyberbullying, and 90 percent knew the person who was bullying them.[50]

Cyberbullying, which is sometimes referred to as online social cruelty or electronic bullying, can involve:

• Sending mean, vulgar, or threatening messages or images
• Posting sensitive, private information about another person
• Pretending to be someone else in order to make that person look bad[51]

Of course, given the various means of communications that exist today, cyberbullying can occur through several means, including: e-mails, instant messaging, text or digital imaging messages sent on cell phones, Web pages, blogs, chat rooms or discussion groups, or other information communication technologies.

Cyberbullying can be very difficult to investigate and solve. First, many officers simply are not tech-savvy enough to know how to investigate such an offense, nor do they know how to respond when confronted with an upset parent whose child has been victimized. However, there are measures that can be taken, such as:

- attending training courses in order to learn how to deal with this problem
- attempting to conduct a public information campaign, to inform people about the problem (some organizations offer free cyberbullying toolkits and have CD-ROMs containing both school resource and community-oriented policing resources)[52]
- using the resources of organizations that provide resources for teaching citizens how to protect themselves, including such things as changing their online identity and installing firewalls[53]
- Approaching Internet service providers (ISPs) to assist with online abuse, primarily by removing bullies' Internet access.
- Contacting schools and parents to assist in preventing and ending cyber bullying.

Summary

This chapter has applied COPPS to the street, demonstrating how it works with several specific crimes and problems of disorder: drug violations, including use of methamphetamine, clandestine drug labs, open-air drug dealing, and rave parties; gangs and graffiti; and youth crimes, including gun violence, disorderly behavior in public places, underage drinking, and school violence and bullying. A number of exhibits and examples demonstrated the kinds of methods that the police are adopting to address these problems.

The efficacy of COPPS in dealing with these problems was convincingly demonstrated. The police agencies described in this chapter and their peers across the United States are realizing many successes, breaking with tradition and attacking the contributing or underlying problems while empowering neighborhoods to defend themselves against crime and deterioration.

We also emphasized that for each of the problem areas discussed, the success of COPPS strategies was highly dependent on the police having laid the groundwork—doing the kinds of preparatory work described in earlier chapters and understanding and properly applying the S.A.R.A. process discussed in Chapter 3.

Items for Review

1. Describe the kinds of strategies that may be employed by police to meet the challenges posed by methamphetamine—and the recent "shake and bake" form of drug lab—as well as some of the methods used and the hazards faced by the police to identify, eliminate, and clean up clandestine drug labs.

2. Review what research shows works and does not work with regard to street-level drug enforcement, particularly as it concerns crackdowns, community partnerships, and problem-oriented policing.

3. Explain how open-air drug markets operate, what challenges they pose, and what COPPS efforts have done to meet those challenges.

4. Explain the problem of prescription drugs, particularly pharmaceutical counterfeiting and "pharming parties."

5. Explain how COPPS efforts are being directed toward the identification, prevention, and suppression of gangs.

6. Review the extent and purposes for which graffiti exists, some means by which the problem may be addressed, and how graffiti may be used for intelligence gathering.

7. Explain what some large cities are doing about their crimes of violence in general, and why some of those tactics are controversial.
8. Explain what the police can do about dealing with disorderly conduct by youth in public places.
9. Describe what can be done to address underage drinking.
10. Review some COPPS approaches to school violence and cyberbullying.

Learn by Doing

1. You are a deputy chief of police, and have been invited to appear at a luncheon meeting of a local civic group concerning your agency's priorities and operations. Eventually the topic of discussion involves drug abuse, and someone in the group asks what tactics, in your view, works with street-level drug enforcement. What will be your reply?
2. During the same presentation (in scenario 1 above), you are asked to comment on what approaches seem to be successful with the problem of graffitti. How will you respond?
3. Again, during your luncheon speech, a guest brings up the fact that your community has recently witnessed a spate of violent robberies and attacks involving guns. She wants to know what kinds of initiatives the police can undertake to deal with such crimes involving firearms. How will you answer?

Notes

1. U.S. Department of Justice, Federal Bureau of Investigation, *Crime in the United States 2009: Arrests*, http://www2.fbi.gov/ucr/cius2009/documents/arrestmain.pdf (Accessed June 16, 2011).
2. Office of National Drug Policy, "New Study Reveals Scope of Drug and Crime Connection," http://www.whitehousedrugpolicy.gov/news/press09/052809.html (Accessed August 9, 2010).
3. Office of National Drug Control Policy, National Drug Control Strategy, FY 2011 Budget Summary (n.d.), http://www.whitehousedrugpolicy.gov/publications/policy/11budget/fy11budget.pdf (Accessed June 16, 2011).
4. U.S. Department of Justice, National Drug Intelligence Center, *National Drug Threat Assessment 2010*, February 2010, pp. 32-34, http://www.justice.gov/ndic/pubs38/38661/38661p.pdf (Accessed August 10, 2010).
5. U.S. Department of Justice, Office of Community Oriented Policing Services, "COPS Fact Sheet: Methamphetamine Initiative," p. 1, http://www.cops.usdoj.gov/files/RIC/Publications/e1006527-meth08.pdf (Accessed August 5, 2010).
6. U.S. Department of Justice, Office of Community Oriented Policing Services, *COPS Innovations: A Closer Look*, pp. 3–5.
7. Michael S. Scott, *Clandestine Drug Labs* (Washington, D.C.: U.S. Department of Justice, Office of Community Oriented Policing Services, 2002), p. 1.
8. Ibid., pp. 14–15.
9. Ibid., pp. 24–26.
10. Alex Harocopos and Mike Hough, *Drug Dealing in Open-Air Markets* (Washington, D.C.: U.S. Department of Justice, Office of Community Oriented Policing Services, January 2005), p. 1.
11. Ibid., pp. 24–26.
12. R. Davis and A. Lurigio, *Fighting Back: Neighborhood Antidrug Strategies* (Thousand Oaks, California: Sage, 1996), p. 124.
13. Lorraine Mazerolle, David W. Soole, and Sacha Rombouts. *Crime Prevention Research Reviews No.1: Disrupting Street-Level Drug Markets*. Washington, D.C.: U.S. Department of Justice Office of Community Oriented Policing Services, 2007, p. 13
14. Ibid., pp. 16-17
15. Ibid., p. 19.
16. Ibid., p. 23.
17. Carolyn Banta, "Trading for a high," *Time.com*, July 24, 2005, http://www.time.com/time/magazine/article/0,9171,1086173,00.html (Accessed August 10, 2010).
18. Ibid.
19. Ibid.

20. Quoted in Thomas T. Kubic, "Pharmaceutical Counterfeiting: Understanding the Extent of a New Transnational Crime," *The Police Chief*, August 2008, http://www.policechiefmagazine.org/magazine/index.cfm?fuseaction=display_arch&article_id=1574&issue_id=82008 (Accessed August 10, 2010).

21. Ibid.

22. National Gang Intelligence Center, *National Gang Threat Assessment, 2009*, January 2009, http://www.fbi.gov/publications/ngta2009.pdf (Accessed August 10, 2010).

23. Jean M. McGloin, *Street Gangs and Interventions: Innovative Problem Solving with Network Analysis* (Washington, D.C.: U.S. Department of Justice, Office of Community Oriented Policing Services, September 2005), p. 1.

24. U.S. Department of Justice, National Criminal Justice Reference Service, "In the Spotlight: Gang Resources," http://www.ncjrs.org/gangs/summary.html (Accessed May 27, 2003).

25. McGloin, Street Gangs and Interventions, p. 2.

26. Ibid., p. 4.

27. Ibid., pp. 4–6.

28. Douglas Page, "Taggers Beware: The Writing Is on the Wall," *Law Enforcement Technology* (September 2005):194, 196.

29. Ibid., p. 196.

30. Deborah Lamm Weisel, Graffiti (Washington, D.C.: U.S. Department of Justice, Office of Community Oriented Policing Services, 2002).

31. U.S. Department of Justice, Federal Bureau of Investigation, "Crime in the United States, 2008: Arrests - Persons Under 15, 18, 21, and 25 Years of Age, 2008" (Accessed August 10, 2010).

32. Brady Campaign to Prevent Gun Violence, "Gun Violence: Guns in America," www.bradycampaign.org/facts/gunsinamerica (Accessed August 9, 2010).

33. David Sheppard, "Strategies to Reduce Gun Violence" (Fact Sheet No. 93) (Washington, DC: U.S. Department of Justice, Office of Juvenile Justice and Delinquency Prevention, February 1999), p. 1.

34. John Caniglia, "Last of Teens Charged in the Shaker Beating Case Takes Plea Deal," March 31, 2009, http://blog.cleveland.com/metro/2009/03/last_of_teens_charged_in_the_s.html (Accessed August 10, 2010)

35. John Buntin, "Gundemic: After a Decade of Declining Crime, Urban Gun Violence Is Surging Again. Police Are Being Told to Get Tough," *Governing*, June 2008, p. 24, http://www.governing.com/topics/public-justice-safety/Gundemic.html (accessed August 10, 2010).

36. Donna J. Miller, "17-year-old Charged with Killing Friend in Police Chase," http://blog.cleveland.com/metro/2008/03/17yearold_charged_with_killing.html (accessed August 10, 2010).

37. Buntin, "Gundemic," p. 26.

38. Ibid., pp. 26-27.

39. Ibid., p. 27.

40. Michael S. Scott, *Disorderly Youth in Public Places* (Washington, D.C.: U.S. Department of Justice, Office of Community Oriented Policing Services, June 2002), pp. 2–5.

41. Ibid., pp. 14–21.

42. Focus Adolescent Services, "Teen Drinking," http://www.focusas.com/Alcohol .html (Accessed April 28, 2006).

43. Kelly Dedel Johnson, *Underage Drinking* (Washington, D.C.: U.S. Department of Justice, Office of Community Oriented Policing Services, September 2004), pp. 1, 4.

44. Ibid., p. 5.

45. Ibid., pp. 23–39.

46. Gene Marlin and Barbara Vogt, "Violence in the Schools," *The Police Chief* (April 1999):169.

47. Ira Pollack and Carlos Sundermann, "Creating Safe Schools: A Comprehensive Approach," *Journal of the Office of Juvenile Justice and Delinquency Prevention* 8 (1) (June 2001):13–20.

48. Marlin and Vogt, "Violence in the Schools," p. 169.

49. Center for the Prevention of School Violence, "School Resource Officers and Safe School Planning," http://www.ncsu.edu/cpsv/srossp.htm (Accessed May 27, 2003).

50. U.S. Department of Health and Human Services, Human Resources and Services Administration, "Stop Bullying Now!" http://www.stopbullyingnow.hrsa.gov/adults/cyber-bullying.aspx (Accessed March 20, 2010).

51. Ibid.

52. See, for example, Wired Safety, at http://wiredsafety.org/ (Accessed September 8, 2010).

53. See, for example, CyberAngels, http://cyberangels.org/ (Accessed September 8, 2010).

More COPPS on the Beat
Selected Issues and Problems

KEY TERMS AND CONCEPTS

Domestic violence   Internet crimes   Prostitution
Homelessness   Mental illness   Stalking
Identity theft   Neighborhood disorder

LEARNING OBJECTIVES

As a result of reading this chapter, the student will:

■ Understand how identity theft is accomplished and some ways the police can attempt to prevent and address it

■ Know the definition of mental illness and what kind of training is being developed to deal with it

■ Be aware of homelessness and how the police can attempt to assist people with this problem

■ Know what methods are available for dealing with domestic violence

■ Realize the nature and extent of neighborhood disorder and ways COPPS can help

■ Comprehend the problems surrounding prostitution and some means for addressing it

■ Understand what the police can attempt to do with stalking and Internet crimes

> *But he that filches from me my good name/Robs me of that
> which not enriches him/And makes me poor indeed.*
>
> —SHAKESPEARE, OTHELLO, ACT III, SCENE 3

> *The human story does not always unfold like a mathematical
> calculation on the principle that two and two make four.
> Sometimes in life they make five or minus three; and sometimes
> the blackboard topples down in the middle of the sum and leaves
> the class in disorder.*
>
> —WINSTON CHURCHILL

INTRODUCTION

The three major crime problems that were addressed in Chapter 11 in relation to community oriented policing and problem solving (COPPS)—those involving drugs, gangs, and youth—can and do plague many Americans in their neighborhoods. However, millions of Americans are affected each year by the grave issues and problems that are discussed in this chapter. In that sense, these are in no way lesser problems for those persons who are personally involved with or are being victimized by these situations.

In this chapter, we consider the following crimes and social problems: identity theft, the mentally ill, homelessness, domestic violence, neighborhood disorder, prostitution, stalking, and Internet crimes (the latter including social networking sites). As in Chapter 11, emphasis will be placed on the kinds of problem-solving responses that the police have developed for dealing with these issues and problems. Examples of such responses are provided in five exhibits that are disseminated throughout the chapter. As in the previous chapters, this one concludes with "Learn by Doing" scenarios, where you can experience some difficult challenges that police officers might confront.

IDENTITY THEFT

Identity theft is one of the fastest growing and pernicious crimes in America; one research firm found that there are about 11 million victims of this crime per year, while the total annual fraud amount is about $54 billion.[1] On an individual level, being a victim of identity theft can be devastating, as demonstrated in the following case study:

> The criminal, a convicted felon, not only incurred more than $100,000 of credit card debt, obtained a federal home loan, and bought homes, motorcycles, and handguns in the victim's name, but called his victim to taunt him, saying that he could continue to pose as the victim for as long as he wanted because identity theft was not a federal crime at that time; the offender later filed for bankruptcy, also in the victim's name. The victim and his wife spent more than four years and $15,000 to restore their credit and reputation.[2]

As we will see below, identity theft is indeed now a federal crime.

Basically, identity theft occurs when one steals personal information from a victim, such as a Social Security number, date of birth, or credit card number, and then repeatedly victimizes that individual by opening accounts and/or making purchases in that person's name. Identity theft is facilitated by crimes such as forgery, counterfeiting, check and credit card fraud, computer fraud, impersonation, pickpocketing, and even terrorism.[3]

Identity theft became a federal crime in 1998 with passage of the Identity Theft Assumption and Deterrence Act.[4] Other related crimes might include financial crimes against the elderly, various telemarketing and Internet scams, thefts from autos, burglary, and even trafficking in human beings.[5] Then, in 2004, the Fair and Accurate Transactions Credit Act established requirements for consumer reporting agencies, creditors, and others to help remedy identity theft, while also providing certain rights and privileges to victims to recuperate losses and damages.[6]

Although the notoriety of identity theft arose with publicity on the dangers of buying and selling on the Internet, the ways offenders steal identities are often low-tech and include the following: obtaining a password or checking account by trickery; stealing wallets, purses, or mail;

rummaging through residential trash cans; obtaining people's credit reports or other personal information; hacking into corporate computers and stealing customer databases; buying identities or false documents on the street; counterfeiting checks or credit or debit cards; stealing PINs and user IDs. Then, using the victim's name, the offenders can open new credit card, bank, or phone accounts; file for bankruptcy; take over the victim's insurance policies; take out loans or mortgages; and submit applications for Social Security payments.[7]

This is a complicated issue, and some of the risk factors and solutions will lie beyond the ability of the police to handle them. Also, a number of federal and state laws bear on the subject; therefore, we are only giving minimal coverage to the problem. Following are six recommended police responses to identity theft:[8]

1. *Encouraging businesses' awareness of their responsibility to protect employee and client records.* Having a privacy policy, training employees, and limiting data collection and access to information needed and data disclosure are some approaches.

2. *Educating people about protecting their personal information.* Police can inform people that the Internet has an enormous amount of information about how to avoid becoming an identity theft victim, and they can tell people that the Federal Trade Commission's publications are excellent.

3. *Collaborating with government and other service organizations to protect private information.* It is important that the police work with agencies and businesses to keep Social Security numbers, birth certificates, and other such information out of general circulation; prohibit their sale; restrict access to such information; investigate identity theft cases; and help victims resolve problems.

4. *Working with local banks to encourage credit card issuers to adopt improved security practices.* Although major credit card companies have national reach, the police can work with local banks to establish procedures for local identity theft victims to repair the damage done and to get their accounts operating again. Credit card companies can also be pressured to put policies in place that include better identity verification for credit card usage, photographs on credit cards, identity verification, and passwords on credit accounts.

5. *Tracking delivery.* Much of identity theft involves the delivery of documents and products, and stolen merchandise is often delivered to vacant houses and mailboxes. Maintaining close relationships with local postal inspectors and delivery companies may help to track items back to the thieves.

6. *Preparing a plan to prevent or minimize the harm of identity theft.* When large identity databases have been breached and when such crimes are reported, the police must act quickly to reduce the time the thief has to use the stolen identities. Toll-free phone lines can be set up for victims to call the major credit bureaus to warn of the theft; employee training can be conducted when such breaches occur.

THE MENTALLY ILL

One of the saddest aspects of police work involves trying to help people who are mentally ill or unstable, many of whom suffer from paranoid schizophrenia, hallucinate, are solitary, engage in illegal activities, and/or are addicted to alcohol or drugs. Many such people are also homeless.

It is estimated by the National Institute of Mental Health that **mental illness** or disorders are common in the United States, affecting an estimated 26.2 percent or 57.7 million Americans aged 18 and older, or about one in four adults.[9] And many of those adults wind up in prisons and

| Exhibit 12–1 | Best Practices: Strategies for Addressing Identity Theft |

Following are some strategies that have been adopted by police and prosecutors for dealing with identity theft:

▶ The Charlotte-Mecklenburg Police Department has created a victim alert program to prevent identity theft. Citizen volunteers receive training on identity theft and how personal information is compromised. They are taught to pull crime reports on the types of thefts (e.g., stolen wallets, thefts from autos) that lead to identity theft crimes. Volunteers then contact the theft victims and advise them of the actions they need to take to avoid becoming victims, such as canceling credit cards and activating a fraud alert with the three credit reporting agencies.

▶ The Los Angeles Sheriff's Department's "Victim's Guide" has a brochure that contains detailed information on the steps victims need to take to report and disrupt identity theft. The guide covers nine common types of identity theft, informs victims of their right to have a police report taken in the jurisdiction where they live, and gives the kind of information they need to allow police to assist them in investigating the crime. It offers victims valuable advice on keeping records of conversations with financial institutions and credit card firms, expenses incurred, and so on.

▶ The National Institute of Justice funded a program to enhance the ability of police to cope with identity theft. Project WHO? developed a model framework to manage, analyze, and comprehend identity theft crime data stored in stand-alone police databases across the Internet. This framework addresses the technical and analytical models, methods, tools, and techniques required to effectively share and correlate police identity theft reports with data that are captured in other governmental and private databases. This enhances the understanding of the problem and improves the ability of the police to detect, prevent, and respond to this cross-jurisdictional problem.

Source: U.S. Department of Justice, Office of Community Oriented Policing Services, *A National Strategy to Combat Identity Theft*, May 2006, http://www.cops.usdoj.gov/files/ric/Publications/e03062303.pdf (Accessed September 8, 2010)

jails. Indeed, according to the federal Bureau of Justice Statistics, more than half of all prison and jail inmates have a mental health problem, including 705,600 inmates in state prisons and 479,900 in local jails—representing 56 percent of state prisoners and 64 percent of jail inmates.[10] A related problem involving the police that is of relatively recent origin involves individuals who are mentally unstable and want to die using a technique now termed "suicide by cop"—engaging in a shoot-out with and being killed by the police. Although difficult to measure, one study by a medical organization of deputy-involved shootings in the Los Angeles County, California, Sheriff's Department found that suicide by cop incidents accounted for 11 percent of all deputy-involved shootings and 13 percent of all deputy-involved justifiable homicides.[11]

According to a report by the federal Office of Community Oriented Policing Services (COPS), factors contributing to the problem of mental illness include:

• *Deinstitutionalization.* After 1960, public attitudes, laws, and professional mental health practices changed, leading to the closing of many state hospitals, psychiatric hospitals, and what used to be called insane asylums. There was a shift away from institutionalizing people with mental illness. Unfortunately, this vacuum persists to this day, with many people, and many disturbed people—including families—being left in the streets to fend for themselves.

- *Criminalization.* After deinstitutionalization, many people with serious mental illnesses were returned to the community, and calls to the police about crimes and disorder involving such people increased. Police tried to handle many of these calls informally, but options were limited. Frequently, efforts at civil commitment were unsuccessful, so, inevitably, police often turned to arrest and a trip to jail as the only available solution to the immediate problem. This had the general effect of criminalizing mental illness—but in jail or prison instead of a psychiatric facility.

- *Medicalization.* Medication plays a central role in community-based mental health care; however, getting noninstitutionalized people with mental illness to take their medication as prescribed is difficult, because of the negative side effects associated with some drugs, the high cost of medication, the tendency to self-medicate, and the abuse of illegal drugs and alcohol.

- *Privatization.* Today many community-based mental health facilities are operated by private individuals or companies. Private, for-profit facilities may well have an inherent incentive to cut expenses, which can translate into minimum staffing levels and low-paid staff, resulting in people with mental illness do not get the quality of care that they deserve.[12]

Following are some approaches that the police should bear in mind for addressing persons and problems involving mental disorders:[13]

1. *Working with emergency hospitals.* Police agencies should meet with hospital staff periodically to clarify expectations, develop workable protocols, and address problems and issues.

2. *Appointing police liaison officers.* Issues related to people with mental illness need champions within the police department. Some agencies appoint an officer or commander to serve as liaison to the entire mental health community, including sitting on appropriate boards and committees.

3. *Training generalist police officers.* Training should be provided to all officers for dealing with mental health issues. Some police academies use role-playing, lecture, discussion, and tours of mental health facilities. It is also important to train police to make decisions free of prejudice, preformed attitudes, and stereotypical approaches.

4. *Deploying specialized police officers.* In recent years, a popular approach has been specialization. Departments carefully select and train specialist officers or even special units to handle situations involving the mentally ill, relieving regular patrol officers of that responsibility.

5. *Providing certain types of information to patrol officers.* Information about clinics, shelters, and mental health services available in the community can be invaluable.

6. *Using less-lethal weapons.* Typically, most tense and threatening situations involving people with mental illness can be addressed by maintaining a calm demeanor, using good oral and nonverbal communication, and using proper tactics. However, when those techniques fail, alternative methods short of deadly force can be employed such as pepper spray and electronic control devices. Such methods are especially important when a person with mental illness is wielding a knife or a blunt object, and clear policies and procedures must be in place concerning those use-of-force decisions.

7. *Establishing jail-based diversion.* Some people with mental illness will be arrested for minor crimes and disorder. When these people get to jail, they can be diverted immediately after

Exhibit 12–2	Reaching Out to the Mentally Ill in St. Petersburg, Florida

After mental health advocates began to complain that the police did not understand mental illness and the interventions they should take when encountering such individuals, the police chief instituted a mandatory eight-hour curriculum for all of the agency's 550 officers—the first such training curriculum in the United States. The heart of the course is a four-step approach called CIAF—*calming the subject, investigating* and *assessing* the situation, and *facilitating* a solution. The training, developed by mental health professionals, teaches officers how to look at behavior, intellectual state, attitude, verbal indicators, and environmental factors to optimize the outcome for both the officer and the individual. Instructors emphasize that officers must treat individuals who are mentally ill or unstable with respect, understanding, and compassion, but always have the situation under control. As one observer stated about the program, the police are in effect "untrained mental health counselors. They're problem solvers for people with nowhere else to turn." Officer feedback concerning the training has been positive, and success stories from using the training are beginning to mount, which underscores its effectiveness.

Source: Adapted from Ronald J. Getz, "Reaching Out to the Mentally Ill," *Law and Order* (May 1999):51.

booking (with special conditions), removing those who require services that the jail probably cannot provide, and they benefit the detainee by diverting them from jail to treatment.

8. ***Protecting repeat crime victims, and targeting repeat offenders.*** Previous victimization is generally the best predictor of future victimization, so it is important to identify those who are repeatedly abused. Furthermore, a relatively small proportion of offenders commit a relatively large proportion of offenses. The key is to focus attention on anyone who is responsible for a disproportionate share of a problem.

It is important for the police to recognize that arresting people with mental illness is not an effective response; it may be a short-term solution, but in the long term, arresting and incarcerating people with mental disorders accomplishes little or nothing.

Exhibit 12–2 provides another look at how the police are dealing with the mentally ill under COPPS in a special training program in St. Petersburg, Florida. Similar programs are under way in Albuquerque, New Mexico; Portland, Oregon; and Tampa, Florida.[14]

THE HOMELESS

Although **homelessness** has been a substantive social problem in American society since the early 1980s, it seems that a lot less is written or spoken about this population today than there was then or during the 1990s. However, while the dialogue in the media about homelessness may not be as robust as it once was, this problem is probably never very far from the top of the list of priorities of most governmental entities.

Homelessness is a condition of people who lack regular legal access to adequate housing. Estimates of the homeless population vary widely; according to the National Coalition for the Homeless, there are between 1.6 million and 3.5 million homeless persons in the United States.[15] About one-third of the adult homeless are chronically mentally ill, and about half are alcoholic or

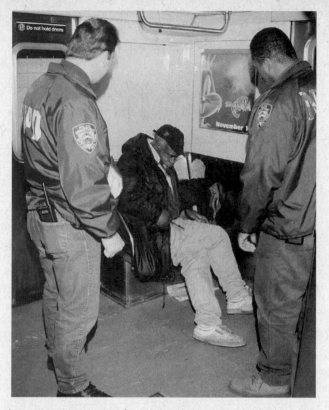

NYPD officers attend to a transient person found sleeping in the city's subway system.
Courtesy NYPD Photo Unit.

abuse drugs.[16] To provide some indication of the extent of the problem, each night there are 80,000 homeless people in Los Angeles County,[17] and Las Vegas, known for its open lifestyle and relatively inexpensive food and beverage industries, has more than 50,000 people experiencing homelessness per year.[18] Therefore, it remains a serious concern for all Americans, especially when so many families are forced to live on the streets and in shelters.

The causes of homelessness are several: Poverty, the declining supply of low-income housing, lack of available public housing, and increases in welfare payments not keeping pace with inflation are a few; other factors implicated in the trend are changes in the treatment of the chronically mentally ill, drug use, the inability of some families to support dependent adult members, and an increasing rate of violence against women.[19] The lack of affordable housing looms large here; it does not require a doctorate in economics to realize that, if a person must earn about $14 per hour just to afford a one-bedroom apartment in a community where the median wage is only $11 per hour, there will be a homelessness problem. Other issues that impact the homeless are the closing of mobile home parks and condominium conversions in cities and rural areas.[20]

Another way of looking at the economic impact of homelessness is by costing out police calls for service with the homeless. If a city spends 1 million dollars per year regarding the homeless on the streets and another 5 million dollars handling calls at low-budget motels where many homeless find temporary refuge from the streets, then spending a few million dollars for shelters and transitional housing does not sound so expensive after all. Cost estimates for daily jail stays must also be taken into account. Figure $80 to $175 per night in jail, $300 per day for substance abuse detoxification, $3,700 per night in an emergency room, $4,500 for a typical three-day hospital stay, and $215 per ambulance ride, and the costs become staggering.[21]

What can be done nationally to stop the cycle of homelessness? Certainly far better and more economical solutions exist than frequent trips to police stations, jails, and emergency rooms: transitional housing and support services. Clearly, the state legislatures and city and county commissions must help to break the cycle of homelessness by appropriating adequate funds to social services. There must be enough money allocated to help the police to not be the initial or sole point of contact for how society addresses the homeless or someone else in crisis. The police argue that, rather than trying to cope with the homeless population, they must instead be allowed to focus their fight against genuine criminals, particularly those who are truly violent.[22]

The police are often caught in the middle here, being pressured by merchants, public officials and private citizens to "do something" about the homeless population. However, police power to arrest the homeless is often limited by court rulings and local ordinances or state statutes. Still, the police can enforce local ordinances if extant in their jurisdiction. As importantly, police can work with mental health agencies and shelters, and make referrals for this population. They can also conduct a census to assess the extent of homelessness in their jurisdiction, have recordkeeping procedures put into place, and generally consider the special needs of this population, particularly during winter months. A well-planned response to homeless populations, with emphasis on the community policing and problem solving approach, would allow police departments to manage significant social problems while making efficient use of police resources.

To raise awareness, recently the police in Reno, Nevada, gave 40 homeless people disposable cameras and asked them to document their life through pictures; 15 homeless people turned in 240 pictures that captured the life of isolation and limited resources. Many of those photos were then put on display in the state's legislative building in Carson City, where 200 homeless advocates slept in cardboard boxes and tents on the legislature's lawn to bring awareness to the problem.[23]

An example of how one agency is addressing it homelessness problem is discussed in Exhibit 12–3.

DOMESTIC VIOLENCE

Clearly the home is not the safest place to be in America; it is the site of many varying acts of violence between intimates. **Domestic violence** (also known as intimate partner violence) involves one person dominating and controlling another by force, threats, or physical violence (including rape).

Each year, according to the Bureau of Justice Statistics, there are about 650,000 nonfatal violent victimizations in the United States; females aged 12 or older experienced about 550,000 such victimizations (rape/sexual assault, robbery, or aggravated or simple assault) by an intimate partner, while men experience about 100,000 of them.[24] Following are some characteristics of these acts:

- Most involved a charge of assault, either aggravated (12 percent) or simple (78 percent)
- Nearly half (46 percent) involved a defendant with a prior history of abuse toward the same victim
- Approximately 1 in 4 cases involved the use of a weapon, such as a gun, a knife, or other blunt object
- Defendants charged with a felony (44 percent) were twice as likely to have used a weapon as defendants charged with a misdemeanor (22 percent)
- A witness to the incident was present in nearly half of intimate partner violence cases; half of those witnesses were children

| Exhibit 12–3 | Homeless-Related Crimes in San Diego |

California's Otay River Valley is a massive tract of undeveloped land covering 8,000 acres. It is bordered by the cities of San Diego, Chula Vista, and Imperial Beach. Businesses surrounding the river valley suffered from burglary, panhandling, theft, and vandalism. People often illegally dumped trash and debris in the valley. Transients, perhaps as many as 300, lived at campsites in the valley in bamboo, metal, plywood, and tarpaulin huts. Many of the transients booby-trapped their campsites to ward off intruders. A large number of them also suffered from infectious diseases, such as AIDS and sexual and skin diseases, and some were mentally ill. Police response was reactive until an increase in crime was noted; transients were becoming more aggressive, and two young boys were found murdered in the area. After political pressure began to mount to remove the transients, a three-phase effort was developed, including the enforcement of trespassing laws, the cleanup of the property, and the restoration of the land that would discourage illegal camping. In addition to the cities that were stakeholders, the state of California, San Diego County, the U.S. Fish and Wildlife Service, and the Army Corps of Engineers joined in the massive project. A prosecutor was assigned as legal counsel as well. Police issued trespassing warnings to transients, provided them with information about area homeless shelters and other services, and photographed the transients in case it became necessary to arrest them. Police also made three sweeps through the area to ensure that all trespassers had been warned, making nearly 100 arrests in the process for outstanding warrants and other offenses. Approximately 200 volunteers collected refuse from the area, a private waste-hauling company removed 31 tons of trash (with the use of donated trash containers), and a private landfill company agreed to waive $1,500 in dumping fees. Burglaries and related crimes dropped 80 percent after the evictions and cleanups. Before the project, San Diego police were spending about 3,000 hours per year on valley-related crimes; since the project's completion, that number has dropped to between 500 and 800 hours.

Source: Rana Sampson and Michael S. Scott, *Tackling Crime and Other Public Safety Problems: Case Studies in Problem Solving* (Washington, D.C.: U.S. Department of Justice, Office of Community Policing Services, 2000), pp. 109–110.

- A history of abuse between the victim and defendant, among other characteristics, was associated with a higher likelihood that the case resulted in a conviction.[25]

Studies in the mid-1980s found that arrests serve as an independent deterrent to future violence, labeled the assailant's actions as criminal, and punished the attacker for his or her actions.[26] Communities with low unemployment rates were instructed to use a mandatory arrest policy; conversely, communities with high unemployment rates were urged to develop some alternative policies and not rely on arrest.[27] Today nearly all states have legislation mandating police officers to effect warrantless arrests where evidence of spousal assault is present. Unfortunately, however, domestic violence remains the most prevalent form of violence confronting our society today.

The advent of COPPS, however, has fundamentally changed the manner in which domestic violence is viewed and addressed by the police; indeed, it is now an article of faith that a collaborative, community-wide approach can enhance existing services to victims of domestic violence. Partnership activities include creating new arrest policies (in keeping with the above mentioned studies of the 1980s), providing follow-up support for victims, prosecuting offenders, monitoring

Domestic violence is not rare; furthermore, it occurs at all social, economic, and cultural levels of society.
Courtesy Fourth Circuit Court, Knoxville, Tennessee.

criminal justice system activity, developing intervention programs, and strengthening civil remedies. In most communities, partnerships are formed to develop a safety net that ensures victims do not go unnoticed or unassisted.[28]

A major study funded by the federal COPS Office involved a survey of 345 police agencies and sought to determine the best practices of the police in the area of domestic violence. The survey resulted in the following key findings:

- Partnership building and problem solving are among the core components of the COPPS philosophy, and a major finding of this study was no different: The police department must be willing to partner with a range of community members (including shelters, victims' advocacy offices, schools, and even animal shelters) as well as criminal justice agencies (such as the court system) to address the problem collaboratively.
- Domestic violence should be treated like any other crime with a solid investigation (involving good evidence collection) and arrests
- The focus should be on, and police should be aware of, victims and their safety, the causes of domestic violence, how relationship violence can be cyclical, and why some partners may not readily leave abusive relationships. This knowledge can underscore both the necessity of arrest and the complexities of why arrest may not always be the most effective response.[29]

NEIGHBORHOOD DISORDER

Neighborhoods deteriorate one home at a time. This deterioration can have many root causes and be accelerated when drug houses, gangs, prostitutes, graffiti, abandoned houses and vehicles, and general neighborhood decay become commonplace. Public housing areas are particularly susceptible to such problems. The police must work in partnership with citizens, tailoring tactics to specific neighborhoods and assisting in their defense against crime and disorder.

As briefly discussed in Chapter 2, certainly the economy—and particularly the recent housing foreclosure crisis—has a deep impact on **neighborhood disorder**. Vacant and/or poorly maintained properties can lead to neighborhood blight, which generates more serious crime and disorder; the police will soon be involved. Overgrown yards, damaged fences and gates, and broken windows make it very inviting for local thieves and drug users, and soon code violations will ensue and some homes will be stripped of everything that is of value, down to the drywall.

Exhibit 12–4 demonstrates how bad the housing foreclosure situation can become, and how one police department tackled the crises and reclaimed its neighborhoods.

As Goldstein mentioned, it is essential that property owners and landlords know their rights with respect to tenants. Because most drug activity occurs on rental property, prevention efforts must involve the property management community. Landlord-tenant training programs are being undertaken by a number of police departments to help owners and managers keep drugs and other criminal activities off their properties.

Such a situation occurred in 1989 in Portland, Oregon, when John Campbell, a resident of a quiet neighborhood, woke up one morning to find a crack house on his block. Campbell's frustration with the drug problem led him to investigate how landlords and neighbors could better detect and stem crime at rental properties. With the Portland police bureau's support— and after researching state and local laws and interviewing more than 40 people—Campbell developed an eight-hour training course for landlords and property managers. Since 1989 Campbell's crusade has resulted in more than 6,000 Portland-area landlords and property managers receiving this training.

Communities in other states have modified Campbell's approach to meet their particular needs.[30] Although such training programs vary, most include the following topics:[31]

- Overview of what landlords and managers can do to keep neighborhoods healthy
- Ways to screen out dishonest applicants while ensuring that honest applicants are encouraged to apply
- Rental agreements and approaches that will strengthen the ability to evict tenants who are drug users or dealers
- Warning signs of drug and other criminal activity, the drugs involved, and the behavior associated with using, growing, and dealing drugs
- Methods to use if a clandestine drug lab is discovered
- Options and process of eviction
- Ways to work with the police
- Rights and responsibilities under Section 8 (subsidized) housing

For many poor urban families, public housing represents the only hope for housing of any kind. Disadvantaged by the lack of education, skills, and health, the urban poor pass on public housing dependency from generation to generation. For young single-parent families who

Exhibit 12–4	Indio, California: From Boom to Bust and Blight— and Lessons Learned

Indio, California, is a city of 84,000 people located 120 miles southeast of Los Angeles in Riverside County. In early 2008, the city was on the front edge of the nation's foreclosure crisis; 4 percent of the city's homes were in foreclosure, compared with just 1 percent nationally. First, the Indio Police Department (IPD) wanted to better understand the nature of the problem. Officers analyzed code enforcement data and citizen complaints of nuisance violations, and conducted visual surveys to determine the locations and conditions of foreclosure properties. They learned that properties that were vacant represented all economic classes and that getting banks to take responsibility for the conditions of vacant properties would be a serious challenge. Next they researched the state's foreclosure laws, learning that lenders were not required to secure or maintain properties during the foreclosure, nor was there a single source of information concerning the property owners, which meant that the IPD would have to devote a tremendous amount of time and resources trying to track down the responsible parties.

The city then developed a multi-pronged solution: First, they enacted a comprehensive foreclosure registration and maintenance ordinance. Lenders had to register all vacant properties with the police department, thus enabling code enforcement personnel to have accurate records of who was responsible for the property's maintenance. The ordinance also held the lenders responsible for securing and monitoring the property against criminal activity and blight. Another new ordinance required lenders to inspect property prior to filing a notice of default and determine if it is vacant. Then they created a resource center that focused on keeping people in their homes.

A media blitz educated lenders, realtors, and community members about the new ordinance and the general program. Partnerships were established with local realtors, property managers, and home owner associations, and trained housing counselors from the provided free, confidential default- and foreclosure-prevention counseling services.

Soon the IPD saw results, with 250 properties being registered in accordance with the new ordinance, and more than 5,000 properties in the city being inspected. More than 500 notices were issued on vacant properties, and more than 200 administrative citations (totaling more than $30,000 in fines) were issued to lenders, realtors, and property managers. The program helped keep 139 families in their homes. The IPD believes that without these efforts the city would have seen an increase in the number of families displaced from their community, the number of unmaintained vacant homes, and the number of crimes associated with those properties.

Source: Adapted from Deborah Spence, "Indio Police Department Tackles the Foreclosure Crisis," *Community Policing Dispatch* 2(3), March 2009, http://www.cops.usdoj.gov/html/dispatch/March_2009/indio.htm (Accessed September 8, 2010).

cannot find decent, safe, and affordable temporary housing, severely distressed public housing becomes the permanent housing of last resort.

In most cases, these young residents have the greatest need for affordable housing; they are also the most vulnerable, the most difficult to manage, and the most difficult to provide security for. Public housing residents ask that the police clear the hallways, stairways, lobbies, and streets of open-air drug sales. The police recognize that distressed housing can be difficult to patrol. Community policing offers the best hope for successful order maintenance in public housing. Sooner or later, a housing authority police force will encounter problems. The conflict usually centers on crime problems, maintenance and repair issues, or turf issues (e.g., who should enforce the "conduct" provisions of the lease).[32]

PROSTITUTION

Prostitution constitutes an offense to the moral standards of the community. It creates a nuisance to passersby, nearby residents, and merchants; parking and traffic problems develop. The behavior may also foment other, more serious crimes as well as the spread of sexually transmitted diseases, including AIDS. Street criminals such as prostitutes may also gather juveniles into their web.

Prostitutes often become brazen, know the law, and develop ways to avoid arrest and conviction. Therefore, police who undertake to address this problem need to perform a systematic inquiry into the extent and nature of the problem: How often are juveniles involved? How much crime (such as robberies of "johns") is related to prostitution? Is organized crime involved? Are prostitutes injuring others or being injured themselves? Answers to these and other related questions will help bring the problem into focus. Officers must also consider alternative strategies to thwarting problems. For example, New York City Police Officers enforced the mandatory seat belt law disproportionately against drivers in areas frequented by street prostitutes. Some jurisdictions now publish the names of johns in local newspapers and send letters to homes of registered owners of vehicles, warning the residents that their vehicles were seen loitering in an area frequented by prostitutes.

At times the officers must also gather information from prostitutes themselves to bring a greater degree of order to the situation. The most severe problems associated with street prostitution can be reduced if prostitutes can be encouraged to bring juvenile prostitutes to police attention, expose those who rob their customers, and respect each other's turf.

Police problem-solving efforts for street prostitution must address both prostitutes' and clients' conduct. These efforts include but are not limited to the following:[33]

- Enforcing laws prohibiting soliciting, patronizing, and loitering for the purposes of prostitution while identifying and targeting the worst offenders
- Establishing a highly visible police presence
- Enhancing fines and penalties for prostitution-related offenses committed within specified high-activity zones
- Banning prostitutes from geographic areas, and serving restraining orders and injunctions against the worst offenders
- Imposing community service sentences in lieu of incarceration or fines (the former have been shown to be more effective)
- Encouraging community members to publicly protest against prostitutes or clients (to intimidate prostitutes and their clients)
- Educating and warning high-risk prostitute and client populations—certain groups are more vulnerable to becoming prostitutes (e.g., juvenile runaways) or being solicited (e.g., conventioneers, soldiers)—through billboards, lectures, signs, or media outlets
- Suspending or revoking government aid to prostitutes (e.g., for housing, unemployment insurance, and/or disability)
- Helping prostitutes to quit (e.g., by providing drug, mental health, housing, job, health care, and/or legal counseling and assistance)

See Exhibit 12–5 for an example of how an Illinois city handled its prostitution problem.

| Exhibit 12–5 | Prostitution in Champaign, Illinois |

Champaign, Illinois, had a chronic prostitution problem in its downtown area. Arrests provided only temporary relief, and the prostitutes were rarely convicted. Collateral crimes (theft, robbery, assaults, and "john rolling") caused a significant drain on police resources. Citizens complained that prostitutes used apartment building foyers, church parking lots, driveways, and private alleys to have sex. Ninety percent of the prostitutes were repeat offenders; 15 of them held the majority of all convictions. The city's antisolicitation ordinance, merely resulting in a fine, offered no long-term solution. Female officers dressed as prostitutes arrested johns for attempted patronizing, but the state attorney's office typically dismissed these cases because entrapment defenses were difficult to refute without evidence of the john's predisposition. The state legislature made a third prostitution conviction a felony, but often many years would pass before an offender would amass a criminal history that made her or him eligible for the enhanced felony sentencing. Finally, court-imposed travel restrictions were investigated. The police crime analysis unit found that 92 percent of 321 prostitution arrests over five years occurred in a 12-block downtown area. Armed with a pin map, police requested that the court impose travel restrictions on one chronic prostitute, thus keeping her away from the downtown area and potential customers. The judge agreed, and within two months Champaign courts imposed such restrictions on 13 chronic prostitutes, taking care of the recidivistic offenders; a state appeals court upheld the restrictions. The following year, the state legislature codified travel restrictions. Over the next year and a half, the city's street prostitution dropped by 90 percent. Limiting access to the area disrupted the market and separated prostitutes from their customers.

Source: Adapted from Rana Sampson and Michael S. Scott, *Tackling Crime and Other Public Safety Problems: Case Studies in Problem Solving* (Washington, D.C.: U.S. Department of Justice, Office of Community Policing Services, 2000), pp. 14–18.

OTHER SELECTED PROBLEMS: STALKING AND INTERNET CRIMES

Next we look at two additional kinds of public safety problems: stalking and Internet crimes—and what the police can do in attempting to respond to them.

Stalking

Stalking, defined as conduct that would cause a reasonable person on at least two separate occasions to feel fear, remains a pervasive problem in our society. In fact, the U.S. Department of Justice reports that stalking is on the rise, and now affecting about 3.4 million Americans per year. Stalking is generally not a random act: Nearly three-fourths of all victims know their stalker in some capacity.[34]

In addition to the increase in such acts, many stalkers are also now "cyberstalking" their victims: About one-fourth of stalking victims report that their stalker had used some form of cyberstalking, such as cell phone "textual harassing" or e-mail. To date, only four states specifically prohibit using cyberstalking methods to instill fear in stalking victims.[35]

There are four types of stalking situations:

1. *Erotomanic.* The stalker has a delusional disorder in which the victim, usually a person of higher status and opposite gender (often a celebrity or a public figure), is believed to be in love with the stalker; the victim does not know the stalker, and the stalking is usually short-lived, lasting one to four months.

2. *Love obsessional.* Similar to the erotomanic stalker, the love obsessional type does not know the victim except through the media and has a psychiatric diagnosis. These stalkers usually write letters and make telephone calls in a campaign to make their existence known to the victim. This behavior lasts much longer, often exceeding 10 years.

3. *Simple obsessional.* Here, the stalker had a prior relationship with the victim (as a former spouse or employer, for example), and the stalking began after the relationship soured. The stalking usually lasts about five months.[36]

4. *False victimization syndrome.* The rarest form, this involves a person who claims that someone is stalking him or her in order to gain attention as a victim. There is no stalker, and this phenomenon is similar to Munchausen syndrome by proxy, in which people intentionally produce physical symptoms of illness in their children in order to gain attention and sympathy.[37]

Evidence collection for crimes of stalking begins with the victims. Victims should record each time they see the stalker or when any contact is made and should document specific details, such as time, place, location, and any witnesses. Messages on answering machines, faxes, letters, and computer e-mails provide useful evidence for building a case against the offender. Police agencies should also consider providing victims with a small tape recorder to facilitate the collection of this information and should encourage victims to report in a journal how the stalking has affected them and their lifestyle, to later help convince a jury of the victims' fear and trauma. Another investigative strategy is doing surveillance on suspects at times when they are likely to stalk their victims. Executing a search warrant for the suspect's personal and work computers, residence, and vehicle can prove useful in many circumstances; officers should look for spying equipment (such as binoculars and cameras), photos, and any property belonging to the victim.[38]

Stalking is a crime that affects victims in all areas of their lives, including the workplace.
Courtesy Shutterstock.

Internet Crimes

The Internet has obviously revolutionized the way people communicate, shop, entertain themselves, learn, and conduct business. However, as we saw above with cyberstalking, and in the discussion in Chapter 11 concerning cyberbullying, "The fleas come with the dog": This high-tech revolution in our homes and offices has opened a whole new world for the criminal element, creating a new type of criminal—the cybercrook.

Pornographers and pedophiles are also on the Web as well as other, newer types of criminals: better educated, upscale, older, and increasingly female. Today's computer crimes include identity theft; cyberterrorism; software piracy; industrial espionage; credit card, consumer, and stock market fraud; baby adoption scams; and embezzlement.

The vast majority of **Internet crimes**—which number about 340,000 complaints per year, according to the national Internet Crime Complaint Center—involve some form of fraud, and average about $560 in losses to the victim per complaint. Of the top five categories of offenses reported to law enforcement, non-delivered merchandise and/or payment composed 19.9 percent of the offenses; identity theft were 14.1 percent; credit card fraud, 10.4 percent; auction fraud, 10.3 percent; and computer fraud (destruction/damage/vandalism of property), 7.9 percent.[39]

The above types of crimes compel the development of new investigative techniques, specialized and ongoing training for police investigators, and the employment of individuals with strong technical backgrounds (and an ability to "follow the money"). The police must become better educated, better equipped, and more adaptable. Social networking sites such as MySpace and Facebook are also becoming one of the most dangerous places on the Internet. According to Reuters, "Scammers break into accounts posing as friends of users, sending spam that directs them to Web sites that steal personal information and spread viruses." Since Facebook alone now has more than 500 million active members (70 percent of whom are outside the United States), the problem is extremely serious.[40]

But such sites are also yielding character evidence to detectives and police who find damaging Internet photos of defendants to use against them. For example, two weeks after a 20-year-old Rhode Island man was charged with driving while intoxicated for seriously injuring a woman, he attended a Halloween Party dressed as a prisoner; pictures from the party showed him in an orange jumpsuit labeled "Jail Bird"; the prosecutor, tipped off to the picture, argued for incarceration, and the young man was sentenced to two years in prison.[41]

Summary

Like Chapter 11, this chapter has applied COPPS to issues and problems that warrant special kinds of attention. Five exhibits were provided, each showing the efficacy of COPPS in addressing a particular problem.

Although we stated it in Chapter 11, it bears repeating that for each of the issues and problems discussed, the success of COPPS strategies is highly dependent on the police having laid the groundwork—doing the kinds of preparatory work described in earlier chapters as well as having a firm grasp of and properly applying the S.A.R.A. process (discussed in Chapter 3).

Items for Review

1. Describe the nature and extent of identity theft and some of the ways that the police can attempt to prevent and address it.
2. Explain what is meant by the term "mental illness," its nature and extent, contributing factors, and what the police can do to cope with it.
3. As with mental illness above, describe the nature and extent of homelessness and some means by which the police can try to cope with it.
4. Review the nature and extent of domestic violence, and how COPPS has affected the approaches to reducing its frequency.
5. Define what is meant by neighborhood disorder, how the economy has contributed to it, and ways COPPS can help to address it.
6. Review the problems surrounding prostitution, and list some means for addressing them.
7. List the four types of stalking situations, and how a COPPS approach would deal with them.
8. Explain how the Internet has contributed to criminality, and how social networking sites have a part in those crimes; review the challenges for, and techniques of the police for investigating them.

Learn by Doing

1. While guest lecturing at your agency's Citizens' Police Academy, one of the attendees inquires about the problem of identity theft; specifically, she wants to know about legal protections that exist for citizens as well as "what works" in terms of police methods for addressing such crimes. What would be your response?
2. As part of a criminal justice honor society poster presentation at a forthcoming conference (which will be focusing on social problems), your group decides to present an overview of the problems of mental illness and homelessness in the United States and focus on "what works." How will you depict each problem, and what will you emphasize for each on your poster(s)?
3. Assume that you are part of a classroom group that is studying domestic violence. You are to make a 10-minute presentation on the nature, extent, and police approaches ("what works") with this serious issue. What would be the major points of your presentation?

Notes

1. Javelin Strategy and Research, "Javelin Study Finds Identity Fraud Reached New High in 2009, but Consumers Are Fighting Back," https://www.javelin-strategy.com/news/831/92/Javelin-Study-Finds-Identity-Fraud-Reached-New-High-in-2009-but-Consumers-are-Fighting-Back/d,pressRoomDetail (Accessed September 8, 2010).
2. U.S. Department of Justice, "Identity Theft," http://www.justice.gov/criminal/fraud/websites/idtheft.html (Accessed September 8, 2010).
3. Graeme R. Newman, *Identity Theft* (Washington, D.C.: U.S. Department of Justice, Office of Community Oriented Policing Services, June 2004), p. 1.
4. P.L. 105-318 (1998).
5. Newman, *Identity Theft,* p. 3.
6. Public Law 108-159, 108th Congress; see Federal Trade Commission, "Provisions of New Fair and Accurate Credit Transactions Act Will Help Reduce Identity Theft and Help Victims Recover," http://www.ftc.gov/opa/2004/06/factaidt.shtm (Accessed September 8, 2010).
7. *Ibid.*, pp. 11–14.
8. *Ibid.*, pp. 32–41.
9. National Institute of Mental Health, "The Numbers Count: Mental Disorders in America," http://www.nimh.nih.gov/health/publications/the-numbers-count-mental-disorders-in-america/index.shtml#Intro (Accessed September 8, 2010).
10. U.S. Department of Justice, Bureau of Justice Statistics, *Mental Health Problems of Prison and Jail Inmates*, September 2006, p. 1, http://bjs.ojp.usdoj.gov/content/pub/pdf/mhppji.pdf (Accessed September 8, 2010).
11. H. Range Huston and Diedre Anglin, "Suicide by Cop," *Annals of Emergency Medicine* 32, no. 6 (December 1998).
12. Adapted from Gary Cordner, *People with Mental Illness* (U.S. Department of Justice, Office of Community Oriented Policing Services, May 2006),

p. 2, http://www.popcenter.org/problems/mental_illness (Accessed September 8, 2010).

13. Ibid., pp. 19-39.

14. Donald G. Turnbaugh, "Curing Police Problems with the Mentally Ill," *The Police Chief* (February 1999): 52.

15. National Coalition for the Homeless, "How Many People Experience Homelessness," http://www.nationalhomeless.org/factsheets/How_Many.html (Accessed April 20, 2010).

16. MSN Encarta, "Homelessness," http://encarta.msn.com/encyclopedia_761579476/Homelessness.html#s3 (Accessed February 22, 2007).

17. Institute for the Study of Homelessness and Poverty, "Homelessness in Los Angeles, http://www.weingart.org/institute/research/facts/pdf/JusttheFactsHomelessnessLA.pdf (Accessed April 3, 2007).

18. Associated Press, "Las Vegas Averages 11,639 Homeless," *Reno Gazette Journal*, April 23, 2007, p. 4A.

19. Ibid.

20. Jaclyn O'Malley, "Assembly tackles homeless problem," Reno Gazette-Journal, February 20, 2007, p. 5A.

21. Ibid.

23. Ibid.

23. Ibid.

24. U.S. Department of Justice, Bureau of Justice Statistics, *Female Victims of Violence*, September 2009, p. 1 (Accessed September 8, 2010).

25. U.S. Department of Justice, Bureau of Justice Statistics, *Profile of Intimate Partner Violence Cases in Large Urban Counties*, October 2009, p. 1, http://bjs.ojp.usdoj.gov/content/pub/pdf/pipvcluc.pdf (Accessed September 8, 2010).

26. Lawrence Sherman and Robert A. Berk, "The Specific Deterrent Effects of Arrest for Domestic Assault," *American Sociological Review* 49 (1984): 261–271.

27. Jacob R. Clark, "Where to Now on Domestic-Violence? Studies Offer Mixed Policy Guidance," *Law Enforcement News* (April 30, 1993):1.

28. Adapted from Melissa Reuland, Melissa Schaefer Morabito, Camille Preston, and Jason Cheney, *Police-Community Partnerships to Address Domestic Violence* (Washington, D.C.: U.S. Department of Justice, Office of Community Oriented Policing Services, March 2006), p. 42, http://www.cops.usdoj.gov/files/RIC/Publications/domestic_violence_web3.pdf (Accessed September 8, 2010).

29. Ibid.

30. Rana Sampson and Michael S. Scott, *Tackling Crime and Other Public Safety Problems: Case Studies in Problem Solving* (Washington, D.C.: U.S. Department of Justice, Office of Community Policing Services, 2000), pp. 13–14.

31. See, for example, Campbell Resources, *The Landlord Training Program: Keeping Illegal Activity Out of Rental Property* (Portland, Ore.: Author, 1992), p. 2.

32. W. H. Matthews, *Policing Distressed Public Housing Developments: Community Policing Could Be the Answer* (Washington, D.C.: U.S. Department of Housing and Urban Development, Crime Prevention and Security Division, no date).

33. Michael S. Scott, *Street Prostitution* (Washington, D.C.: U.S. Department of Justice, Office of Community Oriented Policing Services, August 2001).

34. U.S. Department of Justice, Bureau of Justice Statistics, *Stalking Victimization in the United States* (January 2009), p. 1; http://www.ojp.usdoj.gov/bjs/pub/pdf/svus.pdf (Accessed September 8, 2010); also see National Center for Victims of Crime, *Stalking* (Washington, D.C.: U.S. Department of Justice, Office of Community Policing Services, January 2004), http://www.popcenter.org/problems/pdfs/stalking.pdf (Accessed September 8, 2010).

35. Carolyn Thompson, "Stalkers Turn to Cell Phones to 'Textually Harass,'" ABC News, http://abcnews.go.com/Technology/wireStory?id=6999016 (Accessed July 31, 2009).

36. U.S. Department of Justice, Violence against Women Office, *Stalking and Domestic Violence: Report to Congress* (Washington, DC: Author, May 2001), p. 26.

37. Harvey Wallace, *Victimology: Legal, Psychological, and Social Perspectives* (Boston: Allyn and Bacon, 1998), pp. 333–334.

38. George E. Wattendorf, "Stalking: Investigation Strategies," *FBI Law Enforcement Bulletin* (March 2000): 10–15.

39. Internet Crime Complaint Center, *2009 Internet Crime Report*, p. 1, http://www.ic3.gov/media/annualreport/2009_IC3Report.pdf (Accessed September 8, 2010)

40. Facebook Press Room, "Statistics," http://www.facebook.com/press/info.php?statistics (Accessed May 24, 2011); also see Doug McIntyre, "Cybercrime on Facebook," June 30, 2009, http://blogs.moneycentral.msn.com/topstocks/archive/2009/06/30/cybercrime-on-facebook.aspx (Accessed July 31, 2009); Jim McKay, "Cops on the Tweet to Solve Crimes and Educate the Public," http://www.govtech.com/gt/717300 (Accessed November 24, 2009).

41. Eric Tucker, "Don't Drink and Drive, Then Post on Facebook," Associated Press, July 18, 2008, http://www.msnbc.msn.com/id/25738225/ (Accessed July 31, 2009).

COPPS
Selected American Approaches

KEY TERMS AND CONCEPTS

Chicago Alternative Policing
   Strategy (CAPS)
Drug Abatement Response
   Team (DART)

Geographic Information
   System (GIS)
Neighborhood Watch
Safe Streets NOW!

San Antonio Fear Free
   Environment (SAFFE)

LEARNING OBJECTIVES

As a result of reading this chapter, the student will:

- Understand how COPPS has been adopted and practiced in large, medium, and small communities
- Be aware of COPPS strategies that have been undertaken in federal and state law enforcement agencies and in university settings

Example moves the world more than doctrine.

—HENRY MILLER

INTRODUCTION

Henry Miller is correct: Example is an efficacious means by which to disseminate information and move the world. This chapter provides case studies of community oriented policing and problem solving (COPPS) initiatives. Featured are case studies of COPPS activities in 19 jurisdictions: 5 large (more than 250,000 population), 10 medium-size (between 50,000 and 250,000 population), and 4 small (less than 50,000 population). Also discussed, but in lesser detail, are COPPS initiatives in federal and state agencies (including colleges and universities); described in the chapter as well, in boxed exhibits, are the efforts of three additional agencies.

   The chapter concludes with "Learn by Doing" scenarios, where you can apply some COPPS approaches that have been taken in the domestic venues discussed in the chapter.

LARGE COMMUNITIES

Austin, Texas

Austin, located in central Texas, has about 656,000 residents; the Austin Police Department (APD) consists of approximately 1,536 sworn officers. In the early 1990s, the APD began reviewing the COPPS philosophy and designed a strategy to incorporate the concept throughout the entire organization. A five-year transition was developed and submitted to the city council, and implementation was soon under way. Today, several ancillary programs have been implemented, including a leadership academy for citizens, a landlord training program, a citizen patrol program, and problem-solving projects for cadets at the academy and after graduation. For policing purposes, the city is separated into 7 geographic area commands, each of which is subdivided into 10 to 12 districts staffed by seven shifts of officers.

Strong emphasis is placed on the use of technology. In the mid-1990s a **geographic information system (GIS)** was first employed to see where vehicles were being stolen and recovered. Success in this venture led the APD to incorporate GIS into the crime analysis unit, which soon noticed a pattern of burglaries of churches and residences that were occurring overnight and midweek. A victim told police there was a group of homeless persons who were committing burglaries, and officers went to an area where such persons clustered. Upon arriving, they noticed two transients who were examining some goods; questioning by officers revealed that they had just stolen the articles from a vehicle. The officers learned where they normally fenced their goods: from a woman operating a nearby taco cart. The men agreed to be confidential informants in lieu of arrest, setting into motion a six-week investigation that broke up the largest fencing operation in the history of Austin. In fact, an undercover operation with officers posing as shoplifters determined that three taco carts operated by the woman and three accomplices were receiving stolen property. The four were arrested for engaging in organized crime, three homes were raided, and 395 items were seized along with $62,000 in cash; residential burglaries in the downtown area were reduced by 60 percent.[1]

See Exhibit 13–1 for a discussion of another Texas approach in San Antonio.

Charlotte-Mecklenburg, North Carolina

Charlotte is the largest city in the state North Carolina and the seat of Mecklenburg County, with a combined city/county population 963,000. The Charlotte-Mecklenburg Police Department (CMPD), with 1,650 sworn and 450 nonsworn staff members, is the largest local police agency between Washington, D.C., and Atlanta, Georgia. Its mission: "To build problem-solving partnerships with our citizens to prevent the next crime."

Technology is an important crime reduction tool, and the CMPD takes pride in taking the use of technology to a new level; each officer is assigned a laptop computer in the police cruiser, and each can utilize the GIS, both of which allow officers to have quick and easy access to information for problem solving and to analyze events that have taken place. Their Web site is also a valuable tool.

The CMPD has long been a leader in the COPPS arena, and has served as a shining example of what can be accomplished when an agency is transformed using this strategy in a serious and highly studied and developed manner. But even an award-winning canine has an occasional flea, however, and such was the case recently in Charlotte-Mecklenburg when two particularly serious problems plagued the city. However, CMPD was most fortunate to receive a federal Advancing Community Policing grant to bring Herman Goldstein, the founder of problem-oriented policing,

| Exhibit 13–1 | **COPPS in San Antonio, Texas** |

The San Antonio, Texas, Police Department has embraced COPPS for many decades through its Community Services, School Services, and Crime Prevention programs; storefronts; decentralized patrol substations; and downtown foot and bicycle patrol units. In 1995 the department went a step further, creating a special community policing unit called **San Antonio Fear Free Environment (SAFFE)**, which is linked closely with community involvement programs. First established in 1995 with 60 officers and enlarged to 100 officers in 1996, the SAFFE unit focuses on identifying, evaluating, and resolving community crime problems with the cooperation and participation of community residents. Beginning in 2000 an additional 10 officers were added to the unit each year for five years. SAFFE officers are not tied to radio calls but instead are able to establish and maintain day-to-day interaction with residents and businesses within their assigned beats to prevent crimes before they occur. SAFFE officers also act as liaisons with other city agencies, work closely with schools and youth programs, coordinate graffiti-removal activities, and serve as resources to residents.

Source: San Antonio Police Department Web page: http://www.ci.sat.tx.us/sapd/COPPS.asp (Accessed June 20, 2011).

as well as Ronald Clarke, also renowned in the field and a professor at Rutgers University, to its agency to assist with linking the use of data and computer capacity to address crime and disorder.[2]

One problem involved appliance burglaries from single-family homes under construction. The first step was to investigate why these thefts were occurring. Neighborhoods were surveyed to learn the location of new construction and how many houses would be built during the next few years. Builders were surveyed on their methods and practices while on the construction site. The questioning revealed that:

- Homebuilding in the district was increasing and would continue to do so for the next few years.
- Most homebuilders were installing "plug-in" appliances approximately 21–28 days before houses were sold.
- Before the house was issued a certificate of occupancy, the only appliances required to be installed were those that were hardwired directly into the house.

Next, officers created an appliance profile, noting the types and makes of the appliances stolen, the builders involved, days of the week, incidents per month, and cost per incident. Officers discovered that nearly 75 percent of the appliances stolen were plug-in appliances that did not need to be installed before the sale. The data were presented to the homebuilders, to get them to delay the installation of appliances from the normal 21–28 days in advance to the day of closing.

After a six-month trial period ended and the data were analyzed, officers found a reduction in the number of appliance burglaries (from 76 to 45) and in the rate of burglaries (from 5.3 per 1,000 to 2.5 per 1,000). Using a GIS, officers mapped the areas that had high concentrations of appliances that were installed early. These same areas had most of the appliance burglaries. The results were shared with the builders, most of whom agreed to continue to delay the installation of appliances even after the trial period ended.

The CMPD was also interested in examining pawnshops and their possible connection to burglaries, the recovery of stolen property, and to aid in investigations of robberies and thefts. Of particular interest to CMPD were the activities and behavior of individuals who frequently pawn multiple items.

An examination of data indicated that 10 percent of persons who pawned items did so quite often. Of these frequent pawners, the study also looked at:

- Whether the transaction involved a loan or a sale
- The type of property pawned (e.g., firearms, electronics, tools)
- The addresses and frequency of pawnshops visited for GIS analysis
- The number of items pawned per visit and the average value of these items
- Each customer's criminal record, if any
- The average value of items
- The point at which a pawnshop owner or manager became involved in the transaction, based on the value of the item

The S.A.R.A. problem solving model (discussed in Chapter 3) was applied to this project, with the CMPD Investigative Services Division detectives becoming involved in problem solving. Although the final results of the study are as yet unknown, a major side benefit of this project was that it gave detectives an opportunity to see firsthand the benefits of COPPS.

Chicago, Illinois

We briefly discussed Chicago's COPPS strategy in previous chapters; here we discuss the evolution—and a scientific evaluation—of those COPPS efforts.

Because of soaring crime rates in the early 1990s, the city wanted a smarter approach to policing, one that mobilized residents, police officers, and other city workers around a problem-solving approach. At the time the program began, crime rates were high and the city was—and remains—racially divided into African American, Latino, and white neighborhoods. In fact, race turned out to be an important variable throughout the study.

The important characteristics of the initiative, according to researcher Wesley Skogan, were "turf orientation, community involvement, problem solving, and interagency partnerships."[3] Turf orientation required that the locus of policing not be at headquarters but in a local district. Each district was assigned a beat team of patrol officers under the administration of a sergeant in which the same officers worked the same shifts for at least a year. Community involvement was fostered by the team holding periodic beat meetings at which members of the community could bring problems to the police, be involved with the police in seeking solutions, and hold the police accountable for results.[4]

Problem solving was the centerpiece of the initiative. The police would not only be concerned with criminal behavior of the individual offender, but would also view crime as a "condition" rather than an "event." This process would also involve situational crime prevention, crime mapping, and crime analysis (discussed in Chapters 4 and 5). CPD also recognized that they would have to call on other agencies to do their part. Indeed, the mayor informed the heads of the other agencies that they would cooperate with the police or lose their jobs.[5]

Initiated at the highest levels, the **Chicago Alternative Policing Strategy (CAPS)** was instituted in April 1993 in 5 of the city's 25 police districts. Patrol officers were permanently assigned to fixed beats and trained in problem-solving strategies. Neighborhood meetings between officers and area residents were held, and citizen committees were formed to advice district commanders. Greater participation at beat meetings was in those areas which needed it most. And participants brought their concerns to the police—concerns about social disorder, physical decay, gangs, street drug sales, parking and traffic, and personal and property crimes. The city wanted to avoid the tendency of these beat meetings to become gripe sessions, so the beat teams scheduled the meetings and controlled the agenda.[6]

Has CAPS worked? Studies by Skogan and others resulted in a series of surveys over a period of 10 years that tracked Chicago residents' perceptions in four areas: graffiti, abandoned cars, abandoned buildings, and trash and junk. Whites and Latinos saw little improvement; African Americans, however, saw significant improvement. Roughly the same breakdown occurred regarding loitering, public drinking, and school disruption. There was a significant decrease in crime as well as in fear of crime; Skogan believes that these reductions are attributable to the CAPS program, to general awareness of the CAPS program, and to increasing confidence in the police - one of the major goals of the project.[7]

CAPS is recognized as one of the most ambitious COPPS initiatives in the United States; it has been cited as a model by numerous police experts and the federal government.[8] Mayor Richard M. Daley has described CAPS as a "great program."[9]

Figure 13–1 is a screen of the new Chicago PD "Clearpath" Web site, offering citizens through its many links a variety of means to obtain and share important information.

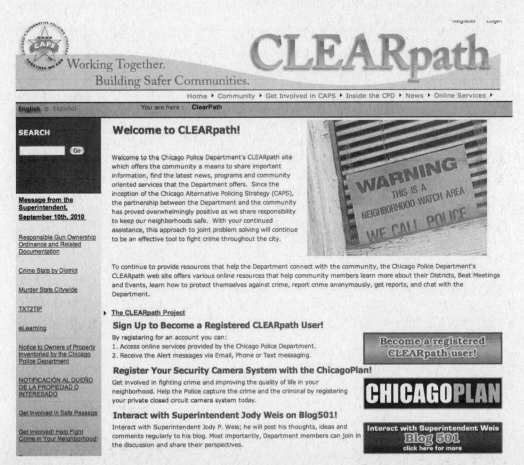

FIGURE 13–1 A screen from the Chicago PD "Clearpath" website; available online at: https://portal.chicagopolice.org/portal/page/portal/ClearPath

Minneapolis, Minnesota

Minneapolis has a population of 385,378; however, as part of the Twin Cities complex (with St. Paul), the area's population exceeds 650,000.[10] Its police department (MPD) has approximately 800 sworn officers and 300 civilian employees, all of whom are, according to the MPD Web site, "fully dedicated to ushering in the twenty-first century with their commitment to community-oriented policing and the people they serve."[11]

Recently the MPD set out to examine several key issues and to determine how citizens viewed the state of policing and the problems of crime and disorder. The department held focus groups with a representative sample of community organizations, interviewed community representatives and MPD personnel, reviewed media files concerning department and community issues, and prepared a preliminary vision for policing the city.

The community perceptions that were brought to light were very informative:

- There was a widely held conviction that there was more violence than ever before
- People perceived that police were reacting to identified problems, but not addressing the root causes
- Illegal drugs seemed to flow freely into the city, but merely arresting street dealers was not solving the problem.
- Gang activity seemed to get much more police attention than did high level drug trafficking
- Judges were perceived as too liberal and contributing to the crime problem

There was also a general sense that many police officers were unnecessarily rude, and treated people differently depending on whom they are and where they live. Many people also complained that police did not live in the neighborhoods they served, nor even remain assigned to their neighborhoods for any length of time; therefore, the officers did not understand local issues or establish effective working relationships with residents. There was also a strong desire for more police visibility at the neighborhood level.[12]

The police officers, at the same time, generally believed that MPD responded well to crises and 911 calls for service (CFS), but that there was not enough time or staffing to address quality of life issues; furthermore, the MPD had no real crime analysis capability; the value of community oriented policing was understood, but implementation had gone awry; overall, staffing shortages had caused a number of problems, with officers being reactive and call-driven, having too little time to spend establishing relationships with the community. Follow-up investigations, they believed, were also weak, and fewer cases were assigned for follow-up. Many officers also perceived that the department had become overly specialized.[13] Both the community and the MPD officers agreed that there was an absence of accountability, a need for stronger collaboration with the community in addressing neighborhood problems, and that arrest was not the best solution to ongoing problems.

Given these findings, a new vision was developed for MPD that sought to correct these problems and change the way was policed. Some of the major aspects of this new vision were the following:

- Neighborhood residents would become deeply involved in developing neighborhood policing strategies
- The police would remain in their assigned neighborhoods for extended periods of time
- Residents would have equal responsibility with police for addressing crime and disorder
- The police would collaborate with citizens on strategy development
- There would be strong outreach to other organizations, and transparency of all efforts

- The MPD would determine, with community input, what service could be provided with current staffing levels
- Working groups would be developed in each area to initiate problem-solving strategies for key neighborhood problems.[14]

San Diego, California

Like Chicago, discussed above, San Diego's police department (SDPD) has a long and storied history of innovation and success with COPPS. Since the early 1970s, community policing has been San Diego's guiding philosophy.[15] The SDPD entered neighborhood policing in a major way. Ten patrol officers formed a team to combine traditional policing with COPPS to target crime; neighborhoods on two beats in midcity were selected as target locations. To professionalize problem solving as an accepted policing strategy, the SDPD and the Police Executive Research Forum founded and was the site of the annual National Problem Oriented Policing Conference, with up to 1,500 attendees from around the world and showcasing the most recent research in the field.[16]

The city, with a population of 1.3 million and about 1,800 sworn officers, was recently forced to reduce its police budget by $16 million through civilian layoffs, a reduced focus on specialized services and shedding some units like harbor patrol and the equestrian unit. The result was the lowest per capita staffing levels in the history of SDPD.[17]

Given this, the SDPD was determined to demonstrate through its Web site that, although the police would still address emergencies, many calls to the SDPD are not police related and can be more effectively handled by other agencies; specifically, its Web site states that as a result:

- Officers are able to spend more time working with citizens to solve crime and disorder problems
- With better police-citizen communication, officers can more effectively use and share crime information with the public

Still, with the budget cuts, recent COPPS accomplishments by SDPD as listed on its Web site include the following:

- The police, community, and city council worked to attack drug and gang problems, leading to an organized community association and a reduction in criminal activity.
- A squad of officers was deployed at a trolley station—the location of gang fights, violent crimes, and narcotic activity—and demonstrated to the transit board that the design of the station contributed to crime (leading to funding to redesign the station).
- Calls of narcotic activity at an 80-unit apartment complex led to a problem-solving approach; working with residents, the on-site manager, the management company, the Housing Commission, and other police units, the officers were able to evict problem residents and stop the drug dealing.[18]
- A redesigned **Neighborhood Watch** and Citizen's Patrol groups throughout the city act as eyes and ears to observe suspicious activity and eliminate problems
- A **Safe Streets NOW!** Program works to eliminate nuisance properties through civil remedies
- The **Drug Abatement Response Team (DART)** involves the City Attorney, Housing Inspection, and the police in identifying properties that have a long history of ongoing narcotic activities. In a six-month period, more than 70 drug houses were targeted for abatement action.[19]

MEDIUM-SIZE COUNTIES AND CITIES

Arlington County, Virginia

Arlington County, Virginia, is an urban community of approximately 26 square miles, located across the Potomac River from Washington, D.C. Being both a residential community and an employment center, its population swells from about 187,000 residents to about 265,000 each workday with the influx of commuters.

Using federal and state community policing grants, five community-based teams were deployed to diverse communities throughout the county. Teams consisting of up to 24 officers and 3 supervisors establish a cooperative relationship with the community and identify broad-based strategies to address crime problems. In addition, community resource officers in each of the county's schools act as a part of the faculty, serving as instructors (teaching antidrug and antigang classes), enhancing the schools' security efforts, and coordinating Neighborhood Watch programs.

Geographic accountability is a management and motivational tool to facilitate agency-wide implementation of COPPS. Officers are responsible and accountable for specific turf rather than a particular shift. Four districts were created, and the department's 10 police beats follow the natural boundaries of their civic organizations. This design enhances department-wide communications and encourages neighborhood focus. Officers are assigned to fixed areas for extended periods of time and are responsible for their specific areas 24 hours per day, 7 days per week. In addition to responding to both emergency and nonemergency CFS, they are responsible for preliminary criminal investigations, special event planning, and school liaison. The middle managers within the department have been identified as the key players in making COPPS work.

The department's COPPS efforts have resulted in a significant reduction in crime and CFS. The department is also working aggressively to develop a technology strategy that will support its new geographic policing strategy. Through another recently funded grant, the department hopes to develop a technology infrastructure to support the requirements of beat officers engaged in problem solving.[20]

Concord, California

In the fall of 1992, the Concord Police Department (CPD) assembled a group of employees into a task force to develop the framework for a unique version of community policing; over the next decade, the CPD refined COPPS so that it reflected the needs of the community and was a "way of being" in public safety service. Thus, COPPS is an evolutionary process that seeks to join the police and the community in reducing crime and enhancing the quality of life.

Officers, first-line supervisors, and middle managers are all held accountable for solving problems and are given annual performance evaluations; their pay is directly tied to their effectiveness. Part of this evaluation concerns the amount of time spent in problem-solving efforts. Of paramount importance are the *results* obtained by the officers in these endeavors. However, the fact that a problem was not eradicated is not viewed as being ineffective per se; rather, it is the analysis of *why* the problem was not solved that offers more satisfying long-term solutions. Automated crime statistics are made available to the public around the clock, and officers go into the community to serve as mentors and trainers concerning COPPS.

The CPD has learned, and counsels others, that it takes time for institutional transformation to occur; the mind-set of employees must change and accept COPPS as a way of being in order to accomplish the agency's mission.[21]

Hawaii County, Hawaii

Hawaii County—on the island of Hawaii, or the Big Island—has a population of about 175,000. The Hawaii County Police Department (HCPD) provides protection on the island with about 300 sworn officers; these officers are distributed throughout two broad Areas (East and West), which are divided into eight policing Districts.[22]

COPPS is taken very seriously by HCPD on the Big Island of Hawaii. Generally, COPPS officers are responsible for developing partnerships within the community in an effort to create a safe and secure environment. This can be accomplished through community mobilization, crime prevention efforts, and problem solving. Specifically, the HCPD operates programs in the schools, a police athletic league, home and business security checks, traffic awareness programs, an identification program for children who go missing, and several other community policing and education programs.[23]

HCPD places heavy emphasis on assisting citizens to initiate a Neighborhood Watch in the county's 6,500 square-mile area, as seen below in a thought-provoking letter posted on the agency's Web site:

> I AM A NEIGHBORHOOD WATCH. My birth certificate is the date a community decides to have me. I am basically conceived to provide citizens an opportunity to address crime and the fear of crime that threatens their community's well being.
>
> I am the opportunity for you and your neighbors to . . . build your community into a safer, friendlier, and nice place to live. I am a strategy that can be used for many things and involve lots of people. I can be found in rural areas, subdivisions, cul-de-sacs, agricultural areas, towns and cities. I am a strong and committed group of citizens wherever I am! I search for a "safe and secure" environment in every program or project I undertake and I am busy at this very moment building a better tomorrow today!!
>
> I am a meeting at a government facility, church, school, business, or in someone's home, built with love and sweat. I am a farmer, a salesman, a retiree, a Christian, a Buddhist, a grandparent, a senior citizen, a teenager, and someone who's trying to be a contributing member of society after having chosen the wrong path in life.
>
> I am a letter to a Council member, government agency, business, or neighbor pleading for assistance to address a problem impacting the community's quality of life. I am growing through all that I undertake. I am never a loser!! I am about roles and responsibilities, communication, planning, training, mobilization, and seeking out resources. I am neighborhood and park cleanups, teen dances, home security checks, finding solutions to traffic problems, collecting toys, clothing and food items for the homeless, organizing after-school activities, helping crime victims, reclaiming playground areas from drug dealers, and task forces that influence policy-makers
>
> I am S.A.R.A., a problem-solving model and CPTED, an environmental approach to crime prevention. I am committed to making Hawaii a nice place to live! Be proud, be great, be still, and know I AM A NEIGHBORHOOD WATCH.[24]

Lansing, Michigan

Lansing has a population of about 119,000, and the Lansing Police Department (LPD) consists of about 250 sworn officers and 94 civilians. LPD began its COPPS efforts in 1990. The city is divided into 18 geographic team areas with assigned officers, investigators, and command staff. As the philosophy evolved, the LPD recognized a critical need to better communicate crime and health data as well as basic social service needs to the community. Accordingly, a seamless network was created between the police problem-solving teams, various service providers, and community members. A digital link provides all Lansing and Tri-County residents access to information related to crime problems, health care, and basic needs such as housing, food, and clothing. A citywide Internet-accessible e-mail system made it searchable by community, police, and government Web sites. An information referral database was also created, allowing anyone with Internet access the ability to connect to nearly all services. Users can search more than 600 agencies that provide basic services.

In order to enhance users' ability to identify neighborhood problems, a GIS was implemented. This system was given reported crime locations, park locations, parcel mapping for identification of registered properties, and county health data. Citizens can also contact their police team to provide information that may lead to the solving of a crime in their neighborhood. The effectiveness of all these efforts is evaluated by measurable questions, analysis measures, and specific evaluator resources to determine whether or not the goals of the LPD were met in a timely and satisfactory manner.[25]

The LPD is not content to rest on its accomplishments, however; it continues to challenge itself to reach more lofty goals. As its web site states:

> As our internal crime information systems change, the availability of data for decision-making allows us to hold ourselves more accountable. We wish to reduce crime and calls for service, while increasing our overall citizen satisfaction levels. As community policing shapes every aspect of our internal decision making process the level of satisfaction within the community also improves. We are committed to providing the best services possible to the residents of Lansing. We continue to look for new and innovative ways to deliver police services and increase our accessibility.[26]

Lincoln, Nebraska

The city of Lincoln has about 225,000 residents, and its police department (LPD) consists of 317 sworn officers and 108 civilian personnel.[27]

According to the LPD Web site, it has been "implementing" community-based policing since 1975, when the police chief announced its first tentative steps:

> into something we called at that time "neighborhood-based team policing." While similar projects came and went, we continued. We are perhaps the only police department in the United States that has been involved so long and so thoroughly in a conscious effort to refine and enhance the community-based approach. Three times (in 1977, 1993, and 2001) we have embarked on comprehensive strategic planning initiatives involving scores of employees and dozens of recommendations for enhancing our efforts.[28]

The LPD Web site is uncommonly candid with citizens concerning what COPPS is and is not:

> When an agency claims to have "implemented" community policing last week, that's a pretty good indication that it has not. You don't start it at the beginning of the fiscal year. It is a process that evolves, develops, takes root and grows, until it is an integral part of the formal and informal value system of both the police and the community as a whole. It is a gradual change from a style of policing which emphasizes crime control and "crook catching," to a style of policing which emphasizes citizen interaction and participation in problem solving. You can't tell whether community policing exists in a city on the basis of the press release, the organizational chart, or the annual report.[29]

The Web site goes on to very poignantly describe for citizens what COPPS *is*, in its view:

> It can best be discerned by observing the daily work of officers. It exists when officers spend a significant amount of their available time out of their patrol cars; when officers are a common sight in businesses, schools, PTA meetings, recreation centers; when most want to work the street by choice; when individual officers are often involved in community affairs-cultural events, school events, meetings of service clubs, etc., often as an expected part of their job duties. It exists when most citizens know a few officers by name; when officers know scores of citizens in their area of assignment, and have an intimate knowledge of their area. You can see it plainly when most officers are relaxed and warmly human-not robotic; when any discussion of a significant community issue involves the police; and when few organizations would not think of tackling a significant issue of community concern without involving the police.[30]

Like the other stellar agencies practicing COPPS that are described in this chapter, the LPD is not content to rest on its laurels, however; its Web site states:

> Community policing in Lincoln will continue to evolve. We will build on some of our most powerful strengths: a highly educated and capable work force, a respect for research and evaluation, and a willingness to change. We will learn from our setbacks, and be constantly open to innovation as we adapt to a changing city, society, and world. We do not have a self-image of the "thin blue line," protecting the helpless public from the ravages of predatory criminals. Rather, we live, work, recreate, raise our children, and enjoy our city as citizens first, even though we are citizens who have a special professional responsibility for protecting others and ensuring the livability of our city. We are wholeheartedly committed to policing Lincoln in concert with our fellow citizens.[31]

Officer with child and Storm Trooper at a kids' function in Lincoln, Nebraska; from the Annual Report 2009, p. 58, at: http://www.lincoln.ne.gov/city/police/annual/2009.pdf
Courtesy of Lincoln, Nebraska Police Department.

Oxnard, California

Oxnard has a population of about 185,000 and is both ethnically and economically diverse. The Oxnard Police Department (OPD), with 238 sworn officers and 151 civilian support personnel, has had COPPS woven into its fabric for several decades, before the term became a popular buzzword.[32]

In the 1970s, officers who were called *Beat Coordinators* acted as a point of contact for resident and business groups within their assigned geographical area. Patrol officers were assigned to work the same beats each shift and were placed into *beat teams* that would work with the respective beat coordinator. In 1999, police commanders were assigned to oversee the efforts in four *districts*, and community policing advisory boards were developed in each district to further formalize the voice of the community.[33]

A Chief's Advisory Board was formed to assure input from various groups, interests, ethnicities and cultures within in the City. A Clergy Council was also developed to partner with people and resources in the faith community. A *crime control* format, roughly based upon a *Compstat* model, was also put into place that would engage managers in anti-crime efforts, as well as hold them accountable to their degree of involvement in their district. An employee performance evaluation system was implemented that rated the quality and degree of participation in community policing efforts; 25 percent of an officer's overall evaluation score was based upon community policing activity.[34]

In 2005, the *Neighborhood Policing Strategy* was developed. As in the 1970s, each beat has a beat coordinator who is responsible for analyzing data, developing partnerships, and coordinating problem solving efforts in his or her area. Teams work from police storefronts. Field teams consisting of a half dozen people are to solve problems. These Neighborhood Teams have developed a strong sense of ownership for their geographical area. Sworn officers, civilian support personnel, employees of other City Departments, and other city agencies join together to address issues such as blight, environmental conditions conducive to crime, residential overcrowding leading to parking and sanitation problems, and graffiti. These teams have expanded their activities into new areas:

- Meeting convicts upon their initial release and monitoring their ongoing term compliance
- Checking sex offender registrants for compliance of accurate address reporting
- Following up with burglary victims and introducing them to Neighborhood Policing, engaging them in the team's efforts, and assuring them that they are important
- Neighborhood canvasses following significant crime or minor crime series to reduce fear
- Periodic surveys of neighborhoods to determine community perceptions
- Proactive public education designed to reduce victimization[35]

COPPS in Oxnard is a long-term success story, with Part I and violent gang crimes reduced, citizen surveys showing confidence in police services, and increases in the number of problems addressed and community meetings attended by officers. The OPD has for several decades been built on a COPPS foundation, and intends to continue working toward achieving new and higher levels of achievement.[36]

Reno, Nevada

Reno is located on the northeastern slopes of the Sierra Nevada mountain range. It is a 24-hour gaming community, consisting of 80 square miles and about 190,000 population (swelling to more than 250,000 persons with the influx of tourists for gaming and during special events).

In April 1987, the Reno Police Department (RPD) reorganized its entire agency to implement a new community policing strategy. The city was divided into three geographic areas, and officers and supervisors were assigned to teams in neighborhoods. Every employee (sworn and nonsworn) attended a 40-hour course in community policing.

A vision statement, "Your Police—Our Community," was adopted to stress the importance of collaborative problem solving. New mission and values statements were also developed by a committee of employees. Hiring, promotional systems, selection for special assignments, personnel evaluation systems, and individual awards and decorations reflected officers' knowledge of COPPS and their related performance.

COPPS training was included in the recruit academy and infused into a new national field training model called the Reno Model Police Training Officer Program. Annual in-service training courses were designed to improve officers' COPPS skills, and all officers were certified in crime analysis and crime prevention through environmental design (CPTED) (discussed in Chapter 4). An advanced COPPS mentoring course was designed to create a cadre of "super" trainers. During this 40-hour course, patrol officers are sent into the field with a trainer and are taught higher problem-solving skills. A computer program was developed to track COPPS projects in neighborhoods.

A new city manager adopted a community-oriented government approach to services. Monthly neighborhood advisory board meetings included representatives of various city agencies and the police department working with residents to resolve problems. Problem-solving and CPTED training has been extended to other city agencies that work closely with officers in neighborhoods. The department supplements its service to neighborhoods with more than 60 senior volunteers who are trained to perform crime analysis functions for field officers, monitor school crossings, and distribute crime prevention materials, among other tasks.

An annual community survey provides vital information by measuring residents' perceptions of police performance, personal safety, and other concerns. The results are presented to the entire department in briefings, and responses to community concerns are developed.

Most recently, the RPD has incorporated COPPS into its training for homeland defense. The RPD feels it is important that officers understand that their knowledge of a beat, its residents,

In the Kids Korner program in Reno, Nevada, beat officers and medical personnel visit low-income rental motels to identify children who are truant and in need of medical and social services.
Courtesy of Ann Munchow Fotografin

and its problems is at the heart of good policing and is the best weapon against the threat of domestic terrorism.

Spokane, Washington

Spokane is unique because of its geographic location and regional orientation. Although the current city population is about 197,000, the city is the urban center of the Spokane–Coeur d'Alene area, which has a combined population of more than 450,000. Many demands for city services are generated daily from a nonresident population base, which includes out-of-state workers, surrounding county residents, and Canadian visitors.

Like most police agencies dealing with increasing violent crimes, more drug-related offenses, and limited staff and resources, the Spokane Police Department (SPD) had fallen into the reactive, incident-driven, call-to-call policing model. Officers became seriously stressed, with as many as 40 officers at one time off work because of fatigue-related illnesses.

In late 1991, the department created a strategic planning team to mold its future and identify and remedy obstacles to change. Members met regularly to tackle separate issues; a monthly department newsletter was created as well. The department then teamed with the Washington State Institute for Community Oriented Policing (WSICOP) to focus on the COPPS philosophy, develop community partnerships, strengthen informal social control, expand police and community empowerment, and increase social and cultural awareness. Written surveys were distributed to police employees and 1,200 citizens.[37]

Also in late 1991, spurred by the grief resulting from the tragic abduction of two local girls, citizens formed a task force to address neighborhood problems. They approached the city council and proposed to open a neighborhood police substation, staffed by community volunteers, as a central distribution point for information on crime and disorder as well as problem solving. The city council and police chief supported the idea, and on May 1, 1992, the facility opened; four years later, there were nine "COPS Shops" in the city, with four more in the planning stages. The volunteers take police reports, deal with nuisances, disseminate resource information, register bicycles, aid victims, and sponsor guest speakers and "get together" nights. Since the original COPS facilities opened, crime rates have declined significantly.[38]

St. Petersburg, Florida

In this community of 244,000, the Community Policing Division was formed following a November 1990 reorganization of the department.[39] Today COPPS in this agency of 540 sworn and 234 civilian staff members involves a department-wide philosophy with citywide deployment. Community policing areas (CPAs) cover every neighborhood, and a community police officer (CPO) is assigned to each CPA.[40] CPOs are responsible for their area 24 hours per day, 7 days per week, and foster a partnership with the community; they identify hot spots and implement strategies to resolve them. CPOs work flexible schedules to meet the needs of the community; they might be in uniform, driving a marked police cruiser or patrolling on a police mountain bike, or be working in plainclothes.

Currently there are 41 CPOs assigned throughout St. Petersburg; in addition, 11 officers are assigned to the downtown area, 2 work at a large shopping mall, and 2 are posted at the city's public housing complexes, for a total of 56 CPOs. There are also zone officers assigned throughout the city whose primary duty is to respond to CFS. Zone officers are encouraged to partner with the CPO in their assigned area, forming a team for each of the shifts. Furthermore, most of the detectives are given geographic responsibilities, thus allowing them to become part of the team to address emerging crime problems.[41]

Tempe, Arizona

Tempe is a growing suburb of Phoenix and the most densely populated city in the state, with about 156,000 residents in a 40-square-mile area. City departments have a reputation for interdepartmental cooperation and problem solving, and citizen surveys have repeatedly indicated the city has an excellent quality of life.

The Tempe Police Department (TPD) employs 256 sworn officers. In response to the changing public safety needs of the city, the TPD initially introduced COPPS on one beat to demonstrate how COPPS strategies could be used to reduce drug demand and overall crime and disorder. This Innovative Neighborhood Oriented Policing (INOP) project was eventually used as a model for citywide implementation of COPPS strategies.[42]

The TPD first ensured that officers had the flexibility to solve problems, using the S.A.R.A. problem-solving model. Patrol officers worked as a self-directed team, sharing information, problem solving, and scheduling with a COPPS philosophy. Officers were in the beat area for extended time periods.

TPD's first task was to perform a comprehensive and detailed profile of the target area using community and business surveys measuring demographic characteristics, fear of crime, perception of quality of life, and so on. Next, the department involved business owners, residents, neighborhood organizations, other city departments, and social services agencies in project coordination. The team of beat officers then used a variety of intelligence and information sources to support drug enforcement and demand reduction efforts. Newsletters, meetings, and a citizen hotline were used to disseminate information.

St. Petersburg, Florida, neighborhood police officers attempt to get to know residents and youths on their beat.

Courtesy St. Petersburg, Florida, Police Department.

An evaluation component was developed by an independent consulting agency to assess INOP's implementation, process, and impact. Although the impact on the community has yet to be determined, the project's impact on the department has been significant. The agency believes that once it made the commitment to INOP, there was no turning back. Changes in organizational structure, management and supervisory roles, policies, goals, recruitment practices, evaluation and award systems, and the COPPS information system are permanent.

A feature of COPPS in Tempe is the department's elaborate system for geographic deployment of patrol officers, allowing officers within a specific area to have varying schedules. Such deployment provides officers with better information about their beats, increases officers' job satisfaction as they take ownership of areas and solve problems, holds officers accountable for their geographic areas, and allows the community to become more involved in solving problems in their neighborhoods.[43] Tempe officers are scheduled individually, rather than by squads, to facilitate greater coverage during peak times. This system has been quantitatively shown to yield higher correlations between CFS and available staffing.

SMALL COMMUNITIES

As seen above, COPPS efforts have been substantial in our nation's large- and medium-sized cities. However, COPPS has also been implemented successfully in smaller cities and rural counties. In fact, a study sponsored by the National Institute of Justice examined COPPS in eight such areas: in California, the cities of Eureka and Redding, as well as in Humboldt and Shasta Counties; in Idaho, the city of Pocatello and Bannock County; in South Dakota, Rapid City and Pennington County.[44]

The study focused on innovative problem-solving initiatives and how these can progress to more advanced stages of community policing. Some insights emerged that are relevant for administrators, planners, and policy makers:

- Community policing was most successful when officers tried innovative approaches directed at specific local problems in tandem with residents and members of the community
- The police chief or sheriff must be fully committed to community policing and drive its implementation, or it will not take hold, let alone advance
- Departments that reached the higher stages of community policing were also supported by local elected officials that were committed to its success.

Furthermore, researchers identified five progressive stages of COPPS that can serve as useful guidelines for evaluating a department's progress in implementation (see Table 13–1).

Next we continue the theme established above, here looking at COPPS efforts in selected small cities.

Arroyo Grande, California

Arroyo Grande provides "an extraordinary quality of life" for its 17,000 residents, with a crime rate that is among the lowest in California.[45] With a complement of 35 full-time and 16 part-time staff members, the Arroyo Grande Police Department (AGPD) also uses the services of more than 50 volunteers. Their COPPS philosophy is based on a "Value-Based Policing" philosophy that involves every member of the organization. Indeed, in the late 1990s the department was a

TABLE 13–1	Progressive Stages of Community Policing

Stage 1 police activities: Establishing a special unit, neighborhood center, or other community policing initiative. Community policing is handled as special assignments, not part of regular patrol. Departmental priority remains rapid response to citizen requests.

Stage 2 police activities: **Getting the community more involved.** Outreach and targeted response to reduce high rates of particular crimes in particular neighborhoods are departmental priorities.

Stage 3 police activities: Solving problems through coordination and cooperation. Officers collaborate with residents on short-term projects to address specific local concerns. Problem-solving initiatives are given priority.

Stage 4 police activities: Broadening collaboration to prevent crime and delinquency. Cross-agency/community-wide coalition plans of action include police. High priority is placed on collaboration through long-term programs.

Stage 5 police activities: Institutionalizing community policing in city and county strategic planning. Community policing activities are practiced throughout the department. Priority is given to sustained, community-based approaches

Source: Adapted from U.S. Department of Justice, National Institute of Justice, *Community Policing Beyond the Big Cities*, November 2004, p. 1, http://www.ncjrs.gov/pdffiles1/nij/205946.pdf (Accessed September 10, 2010).

finalist for the James Q. Wilson Award for Excellence in Community Policing. Furthermore, several police agencies have visited or contacted the department concerning its COPPS initiative and these programs, and the California Peace Officer Standards and Training (POST) has used the department's programs as a resource for developing its training.

In 1989, the AGPD examined its operations and culture—a process that involved every member of the organization and resulted in a new "Mission Statement and Organizational Values," a formal organizational philosophy, long-term departmental goals, and a formal set of principles of leadership. These serve as the foundation of the AGPD operations.[46] Since then, more than 24 community-based programs have been developed—many of which resulting in long-term partnerships being formed within the community. A key factor to the AGPD operations is its flexibility and emphasis on problem solving. The principles involved in problem-oriented policing are integrated into normal operations. The agency is able to quickly and easily adopt short-term strategies and programs to deal with immediate needs and issues in the community.[47]

The agency has developed an organizational culture that seeks to form true partnerships with the community's various stakeholders in order to provide a better quality of life for all residents. The department's operations attempt to anticipate and solve problems before they erupt into major issues.

Elmhurst, Illinois

Elmhurst is a city of about 45,000 in the southern portion of Illinois, with a sworn police complement of 66 officers. The EPD COPPS initiatives, according to its Web site, include procedures that combine partnerships with the community, problem solving and one-stop shopping philosophy to provide service and safety to the residents and visitors.

> Our one-stop shopping philosophy means that all of the employees of the Elmhurst Police Department will try to handle citizen problems without sending citizens from agency to agency.[48]

Given that promise, the EPD has a cadre of officers who can handle the full range of citizens' needs, including noise complaints, broken street lamps, fallen trees, and other problems. When possible, EPD officers handle problems themselves; if need be, the problem is communicated to an appropriate city agency. Steps have been taken to ensure that officers have a stake in the policing process. Each officer has policy- and procedure-making power. They even test and select department equipment and uniforms, and they have developed a new design for police vehicles.

Perhaps a unique aspect of Elmhurst's COPPS strategy lies in its approach to officer evaluation. Instead of relying on traditional quantitative criteria, such as number of arrests, the department uses what it calls "community sensing mechanisms." The chief actively seeks feedback from elected government officials and residents. Random callbacks are conducted to gauge citizen satisfaction with officers and CFS. In addition to letters to the chief, other sources of input that are given weight include newspaper articles, editorials, and comments from the local chamber of commerce.[49]

Orange County, Florida

Tourists are an often-forgotten population in our communities. Orlando, Florida, is the number one tourist destination in the world, with a 78-square-mile tourist corridor. There is also a plethora of criminals seeking to take advantage of unsuspecting victims, many of whom experience armed robbery and theft when items are stolen from their automobiles and hotel rooms. The items most frequently stolen are expensive video cameras, foreign passports, and money.

The Orange County Sheriff's office developed a Tourist Oriented Police Service (TOPS) program, which offers to tourists the same services that are available to locals as well as tourist-oriented services such as crisis intervention, assistance with crime compensation, interaction with foreign consulates, language translation services, and accompaniment throughout the criminal justice system. A tourist advocate is assigned to the patrol unit, and deputies assigned to TOPS make themselves accessible to tourists by leaving their cars, horses, and motorcycles so that they can walk their beats and interact with visitors. The sheriff's office has also developed a training video to teach hotel and business employees how to prevent crimes against tourists.[50]

Pittsburg, Kansas

Pittsburg is located in the southeast corner of the state and is a university town of about 20,000. The region is known as the "Little Balkans" because it was populated in the late nineteenth century by immigrants from European Balkan countries who came to work in the coal mines and smelters. In the latter part of the twentieth century, Pittsburg experienced another wave of immigrants, this one mostly made up of Hispanics who also sought the American Dream in the heartland, in local factories and businesses. But the community was not mentally or structurally prepared for this influx and its subsequent demands on local resources. The police began hearing cries to "get those Mexicans out of Pittsburg"—even by people whose own grandparents or great-grandparents had lived in the community for 50 years without ever learning to speak English.

Sensing the growing tension, the police realized they could either do nothing and face serious problems of crime and disorder, as several other Midwestern communities had, or proactively assist the assimilation of the new residents into the community. The police chief opted for the latter option and with a local female activist (who is bilingual) formed the organization Pittsburg Area Community Outreach (PACO). This body evolved into a 29-person board of directors representing a cross-section of the community who donated their time and professional resources to projects that promoted integration of, and interaction with, the immigrants. The city mayor (who was an attorney) provided free legal advice to the immigrants, while other board members and citizens focused on helping them to understand the community. On five occasions, PACO invited an immigration expert from out of state to assist them with their immigration questions and needs at no cost, and the Mexican consulate from Kansas City was invited to provide Mexican passports and identification cards to them; meeting facilities in a municipal auditorium were provided by the city. The county health department sent nurses to the meetings to screen the immigrants for high blood pressure, HIV, and other health problems as well as to dispense free flu shots. The public schools, library, adult education center, and other social services agencies provided assistance as well. The bilingual woman who co-founded PACO became very involved with translating marriage and birth certificates for the immigrants, which the police chief notarized as necessary.

To date, more than 250 immigrants have benefited from these services, and PACO has sponsored or supported more than 50 community projects. As a result of these efforts, the police chief was recognized by the U.S. Department of Justice and the U.S. attorney general for the department's commitment to community outreach and police-community relations.[51]

FEDERAL AND STATE AGENCIES

Federal Approaches

Several federal agencies are also engaged in COPPS. One example is the U.S. Department of Homeland Security, which has partnered with the Federal Law Enforcement Training Center to offer an intensive, online problem-solving course. Its Advanced Law Enforcement Problem Solving Training Program (ALEPSTP):

> combines the current crime theories with a specific problem identified by the participant which would be relevant to a participating law enforcement agency. The participant will be able to use these crime theories in order to understand how the problem occurred and develop a plan to sustainably prevent the problem from reoccurring. The participants will use web-based tools to develop a custom learning path, collaborate with team members using an on-line discussion forum, and will be evaluated with an online assessment instrument.[52]

This program is designed to be exported to a law enforcement agency-specific worksite, which allows the agency to provide on-site, high quality training at a substantial savings. The agency saves in the budget areas of transportation costs, per diem, and housing costs per student. The courses are three days and 24 hours in length, and the curriculum includes the following:

- Problem Solving as an Operational Strategy
- Scanning to Identify Problems
- Defining Problems through Analysis
- Responding to Law Enforcement Problems
- Assessing Responses

State-level training institutes are a major resource for COPPS courses and exercises. Here, Southern Police Institute instructors conduct a problem solving exercise—translated into Arabic—for Lebanese national police officers as part of a month-long "immersion" program.
Courtesy Southern Police Institute, University of Louisville

- Three Laboratory Exercises
- Practical Exercise[53]

State Police and Universities

Certainly the benefits of engaging in COPPS are not lost on state police/highway patrol or campus police organizations. In this chapter section, we highlight the efforts of a number of them, including the award-winning efforts involving the Washington State Police (see Exhibit 13–2).

Indeed, state colleges and universities across the nation are practicing COPPS. Many of them have focused on improving their planning and technologies toward preventing and responding to such incidents as that which occurred at Virginia Tech in 2007, where 32 people were killed by a shooter. Many college and university police departments—such as those at Harvard, and Tufts Universities[54]—prominently discuss their COPPS approach to public safety on their Web sites, along with their history, philosophy, purpose, goals, and objectives.

In addition to its excellent emergency response program, Tufts University's Web site also showcases its police department's COPPS philosophy, as excerpted in Exhibit 13–3.

Exhibit 13–2   Washington State Patrol's Motorcycle Fatality Problem

In the fall of 2005, the Washington State Patrol (WSP) became concerned with the increasing number of motorcycle fatalities occurring within the state—the year ending with 74 such fatalities, the highest number since Washington reinstated its motorcycle helmet law in 1990. As a Problem Oriented Policing (POP) agency since the late 1990s, the WSP quickly joined forces with other state agencies and citizen groups to form the Governor's Motorcycle Safety Task Force, to determine primary causes for fatal motorcycle crashes, then to provide recommendations for reducing these occurrences.

After performing the scanning and analysis phases of S.A.R.A., the task force learned that in a majority of cases, the most common factors in the fatal motorcycle crashes were lane errors, speeding, impaired driving, and inattention. In addition, it was found that one-third of fatally injured riders did not have a motorcycle endorsement.

As responses, the task force recommended an evaluation of the rider training program—including increased training opportunities, a public education campaign, and increased rider accountability through traffic law enforcement.

Troopers began focusing on serious violations by motorcyclists and significantly increased their enforcement of speeding, impaired driving, and endorsement violations. The WSP also co-sponsored legislation to authorize impoundment of motorcycles operated by unendorsed riders, and issued press releases to educate the public about the problem.

During the initial year following these responses, there were 14 fewer motorcycle fatalities—a 17.5 percent reduction, and the first year showing a drop in motorcycle fatalities for Washington State since 2000. For its efforts, the WSP received a 2008 Herman Goldstein Award for Excellence in Problem-Oriented Policing.

Source: Adapted from the Problem Oriented Policing Center, "Washington State Patrol's Motorcycle Safety Through Licensing, Education, and Enforcement," http://www.popcenter.org/library/awards/goldstein/2008/08-52(F).pdf (Accessed September 11, 2010).

Exhibit 13–3   Community Policing as Described by Tufts University

Tufts University, established in 1852, has three campuses in the Boston area and a European Center campus in southern France; it has 9,200 students. Following is the university police Web site's explanation of its efforts with COPPS:

> Community policing is a direct expression of our mission statement. The goal of the Tufts University Police Department is to consistently work towards providing an environment that is reasonably safe and secure. Community policing is a philosophy of policing in which officers work closely with community residents, developing a sense of the character of the neighborhood through regular, informal contacts with residents and institutions serving the area. Law enforcement officials address not just crimes but their causes; they identify problems and work with community residents to marshal community resources to solve those problems. You are encouraged to contact your local law enforcement agency for additional information about the philosophy of community policing.

Community policing at Tufts University represents a shift from detached, "neutral", reactive policing to close personal involvement between officers and the Tufts community, with an emphasis on proactive problem solving. We ask everyone to take an active role in crime prevention by becoming the "eyes and ears" of the community; it is essential that everyone assert a vested interest in their own security and safety.

Source: Adapted from Tufts University Police, "Community Policing," http://publicsafety.tufts.edu/police/?pid=6 (Accessed September 11, 2010).

Summary

A common thread running through most (if not all) of the COPPS approaches in this chapter is the realization by the police that new strategies were necessary for addressing crime and neighborhood disorder. The cities, counties, and state organizations discussed in this chapter have demonstrated that the path to attaining a full-fledged COPPS initiative involves a complete transformation in ideology and more than mere rhetoric or additional officers on foot or on bicycle patrol. This path may not be an easy one, but it has been shown that the rewards can be substantial.

Items for Review

1. Describe the COPPS efforts that have been undertaken in a large, medium, and small jurisdiction. (Readers might take a comparative approach, looking for similarities and variations between jurisdictions of differing sizes.)

2. Explain how federal and state law enforcement agencies as well as universities are engaging in COPPS activities.

Learn by Doing

1. Assume that your criminal justice "Community Policing" class is engaged in a classroom group project. Each group is to study and make a five-minute report concerning this strategy as it functions in some American city or county. Your group opts to describe how COPPS functions in Hawaii County, Hawaii. What will your group report?

2. Assume the same scenario 1 above. Instead, your groups are to select one large venue as well as one small venue as described in this chapter, and then compare and contrast their COPPS initiatives. Which venues will you select, and what will you report?

Notes

1. Kathleen Woodby and Tess Sherman, "Austin, Texas, Police Department Takes a Bite out of Burglary with GIS," http://www.esri.com/news/arcnews/spring03articles/austin-texas-police.html (Accessed May 28, 2003).

2. U.S. Department of Justice, Office of Community Oriented Policing Services, "Charlotte- Mecklenburg: A Living Lab for Problem-Solving Policing," http://www.cops.usdoj.gov/html/cd_rom/inaction1/pubs/

Organizationalchange/Chapter3CharlotteMecklenburg. pdf(Accessed September 10, 2010).

3. Wesley G. Skogan, *Police and Community in Chicago: A Tale of Three Cities* (New York: Oxford University Press, 2006), p. 57.

4. Sawyer Sylvester, *Law and Politics Book Review*, http:// www.bsos.umd.edu/gvpt/lpbr/subpages/reviews/ skogan0507.htm (Accessed September 10, 2010).

5. Ibid.

6. Ibid.

7. Ibid.

8. Chicago, Illinois, Police Department Web site, http:// www.ci.chi.il.us/CommunityPolicing.htm (Accessed October 20, 2000).

9. City of Chicago, Office of the Mayor, press release (February 15, 2003), http://w6.ci.chi.il.us/mayor/ 2003Press/newspress0215capsrallyaustin.html (Accessed May 28, 2003). Also see the Chicago Community Policing Evaluation Consortium, Community Policing in Chicago, Year Ten (Chicago: Author, April 2004), pp. i–x.

10. Minneapolis/St. Paul Business Journal, "Minneapolis Population Grew Slightly from 2000 to '09; St. Paul's Fell," http://twincities.bizjournals.com/twincities/ stories/2010/09/06/daily36.html (Accessed September 10, 2010).

11. Minneapolis Police Department, "Inside the Minneapolis Police Department," http://www.ci. minneapolis.mn.us/police/about/ (Accessed September 10, 2010).

12. Adapted from Strategic Policy Partnership, "Making Community Policing Real: Taking Minneapolis Policing to the Next Level," http://www.ci.min- neapolis.mn.us/police/news/docs/commpolicing. pdf (Accessed September 10, 2010).

13. Ibid.

14. Ibid.

15. Bob Burgreen and Nancy McPherson, "Implementing POP: The San Diego Experience," The Police Chief (October 1990):50–56.

16. Ibid., p. 17.

17. Steven Bartholow, "Pocket Change: Patrolling San Diego's police force," San Diego News Network, http://www.sdnn.com/sandiego/2010-04-06/politics- city-county-government/pocket-change-politics-city- county-government-news/pocket-change-patrolling- san-diego%E2%80%99s-police-force (Accessed September 10, 2010).

18. San Diego Police Department, "Problem Oriented Policing," http://www.sandiego.gov/police/about/ problem.shtml (Accessed September 10, 2010).

19. San Diego Police Department, "Community Oriented Policing," http://www.sandiego.gov/police/about/ community.shtml (Accessed September 10, 2010).

20. Arlington County, Virginia, Police Department, http://www.co.arlington.va.us/pol/comm/htm (Accessed October 20, 2000); also see Arlington County, Virginia, Police Department "Community Service Officers," http://www.co .arlington.va.us/ pol/comm/htm (Accessed September 10, 2010).

21. Laura M. Hoffmeister, "Best Practices of Community Policing: The Concord Experience," in Best Practices of Community Policing in Collaborative Problem Solving (Washington, D.C.: United States Conference of Mayors, June 2001), pp. 32–36.

22. Hawaii County Police Department, Annual Report, Fiscal Year 2008, http://www.hawaiipolice.com/ pdfDocs/AnnualReport07-08.pdf (Accessed September 10, 2010).

23. Hawaii County Police Department, "Community Policing," http://www.hawaiipolice.com/topPages/ cpo.html (Accessed September 10, 2010).

24. Ibid.

25. David C. Hollister, "In Touch': Neighborhood Stabilizing Data Improving Low Income Citizens Quality of Life," in Best Practices of Community Policing in Collaborative Problem Solving (Washington, D.C.: United States Conference of Mayors, June 2001), pp. 95–99.

26. Lansing Police Department, "Community Policing," http://www.lansingmi.gov/police/community_ policing.jsp (accessed September 10, 2010).

27. Lincoln Police Department, *Five Year Strategic Plan 2007-2012: Lincoln Police Department*, http://lincoln. ne.gov/city/police/pdf/stratplan.pdf (Accessed September 10, 2010).

28. Lincoln Police Department, "What Is Community Policing?" http://lincoln.ne.gov/city/police/cbp.htm (Accessed September 10, 2010).

29. Ibid.

30. Ibid.

31. Ibid.

32. Oxnard Police Department, " History of Oxnard & The Oxnard Police Department," http://www. oxnardpd.org/bureaus/departmenthistory.asp (Accessed September 10, 2010).

33. Adapted from James Q. Wilson, "Oxnard's *Neighborhood Policing Strategy* and Community Policing Model," http://www.oxnardpd.org/docu- ments/james_Q_Wilson_narrative.pdf (Accessed September 10, 2010).

34. Ibid.

35. Ibid.

36. Ibid.

37. Robert C. Van Leuven, Spokane, Washington, Police Department, personal communication, December 14, 1993.

38. Ellen Painter, "Tragedy Sparks Community Policing in Spokane, Washington," Community Policing Exchange (May/June 1995):5.

39. Donald S. Quire, St. Petersburg, Florida, Police Department, personal communication, January 31, 1994.

40. See St. Petersburg Police Department, "Community Service Officers," http://www.stpete.org/police/usb/cso.html (Accessed September 10, 2010).

41. St. Petersburg, Florida, Police Department Web site, http://www.stpete.org/police/commpol.htm (Accessed May 28, 2003).

42. Tempe, Arizona, Police Department, "Overview," http://www.tempe.gov (Accessed November 26, 1997).

43. Tempe, Arizona, Police Department, Geographic Deployment of Patrol (Tempe, Ariz.: Author, 1993).

44. U.S. Department of Justice, National Institute of Justice, Community Policing Beyond the Big Cities, November 2004, p. 1, http://www.ncjrs.gov/pdffiles1/nij/205946.pdf (Accessed September 10, 2010).

45. Arroyo Grande Police Department, "About Us," http://www.agpd.org/about/ (Accessed September 10, 2010).

46. California Commission on Peace Officers Standards and Training, "Arroyo Grande Police Department," http://test-www.post.ca.gov/library/p_ch/flagships/arroyo.asp (Accessed September 10, 2010).

47. Ibid.

48. Elmhurst Police Department, "Message from the Chief of Police," http://www.elmhurst.org/index.aspx?NID=283 (Accessed September 10, 2010).

49. Steve Anzaldi, "Adapting to Needs: Community Policing Around the State," The Compiler (Fall 1993):8.

50. Mike Hall, Chief of Police, Pittsburg, Kansas, personal communication, March 12, 2003.

51. See http://www.northwestern.edu/up/about/services.html (Accessed September 11, 2010).

52. Federal Law Enforcement Training Center, Advanced Law Enforcement Problem Solving Training Program (ALEPSTP)," http://www.fletc.gov/training/programs/counterterrorism-division/advanced-law-enforcement-problem-solving-training-program-alepstp/(Accessed September 11, 2010).

53. Ibid.

54. See Harvard University, http://www.hupd.harvard.edu/faqs.php Aaccessed September 11, 2010); Tufts University, http://publicsafety.tufts.edu/emergency/?pid=34 (Accessed September 11, 2010)

COPPS Abroad
Foreign Venues

KEY TERMS AND CONCEPTS

Australian Capital Territory
  (ACT)
CAPRA (Canada)
Comparative approach

First Nations (Canada)
Koban (Japan)
Nick Tilley Award
  (Great Britain)

Royal Canadian Mounted
  Police (RCMP)

LEARNING OBJECTIVES

As a result of reading this chapter, the student will:

■ Know that COPPS is being practiced around the world

■ Appreciate the value of viewing COPPS from a comparative perspective

■ Be able to compare the practice of community policing in the United States with the manner in which it is practiced in foreign venues

Think globally, act locally.

—RENE DUBOS

The world is but a school of inquiry.

—MICHEL DE MONTAIGNE

INTRODUCTION

The world has become a global village. Through technology, rapid intercontinental travel, and high-technology communications systems, we are virtual neighbors around the planet. Even very disparate countries can learn from, and have shared much with, one another.

It has been said that the **comparative approach** provides the opportunity to "search for order."[1] This chapter does so by comparing the work of community oriented policing and problem solving (COPPS) in foreign venues with that in the United States. It will be seen that COPPS has indeed gone international and is now the operational strategy of many police agencies around the globe.

First we "travel" to Canada, looking at the country generally and then viewing federal, provincial, and municipal policing as they engage in the COPPS strategy. Next we look at some of the earliest community policing efforts in Japan—focusing on the koban system, which is arguably the earliest form of community policing—and then move on to Australia, where COPPS is having a major effect across that country. The next venues studied are three that are located in Europe: Sweden, France, and Great Britain. We conclude this chapter's global travels by briefly looking at Hong Kong, New Zealand, and the Netherlands. Other venues are discussed in five exhibits that are disseminated throughout the chapter. The chapter concludes with "Learn by Doing" scenarios, where you can apply some COPPS approaches that have been taken in the foreign venues discussed in the chapter.

Much can be learned from comparatively examining the activities and approaches that are undertaken in each venue. The reader is encouraged to determine whether there are common elements of COPPS in these countries and to compare each with the American strategy as it is described in earlier chapters.

CANADA

Canada has about 33 million people and is located in the northernmost region of North America. With 3 large territories, 10 provinces, and a total area of 3.8 million square miles, it is one of the largest countries in the world, second only to Russia. The country touches three oceans—the Atlantic, the Arctic, and the Pacific—and its coastline is 151,473 miles long. Despite its vast size, however, 90 percent of the Canadian population is located within 100 miles of the U.S. border, and most of the nation's people live in urban areas.[2]

Federal, Provincial, and Municipal Police

There are about 67,000 sworn police personnel in Canada (a rate of about 2 officers per 1,000 population) as well as 27,000 nonsworn employees. The rate of female officers is high and growing, with about one in five officers being a woman.[3]

The federal government, through the Royal Canadian Mounted Police (RCMP), is responsible for the enforcement of federal statutes in each province and territory, and for providing services such as forensic laboratories, identification services, and the Canadian Police College. The RCMP provides provincial/territorial policing and community policing services in eight provinces and territories (Quebec and Ontario maintain their own provincial police services). Provincial policing involves enforcement of the *Criminal Code* and provincial statutes within areas of a province not served by a municipal police service (i.e., rural areas and small towns). Municipalities have three options when providing municipal policing services: to form their own police force, to join an existing municipal police force, or to enter into an agreement with a provincial police force or the RCMP.[4]

In addition to federal, provincial/territorial, and municipal policing, there are also various types of First Nations policing agreements for Aboriginal communities in place across Canada. The First Nations Policing Policy, announced in June 1991 by the federal government, was introduced in order to provide **First Nations** across Canada (with the exception of Northwest Territories and Nunavut) with access to police services that are professional, effective, culturally appropriate, and accountable to the communities they serve.[5]

COPPS was launched in Canada in the mid-1990s. According to Curtis Clarke, an academic and researcher for many Canadian police organizations:

> There is little question that community policing has become the official philosophy with respect to policing in Canada. Nor is there doubt that it has had a monumental effect on those who have sought to improve police operations, management, or relations with the public. More recently, police policy makers and strategists have begun to build on the foundation of community-based policing and problem solving in an effort to achieve greater levels of efficiency and effectiveness. These operational strategies are based on the concept of proactive police. Examples can be noted in [Toronto's] Crime Management Program, [Edmonton's] Project Archimedes, and in the RCMP's Criminal Intelligence Program.[6]

Exhibit 14–1   Empirical Studies of Best Practices in Ontario

With Ontario having initiated the COPPS strategy in 1996, in 2005 the Community Policing Advisory Council (CPAC) of Ontario decided that enough experience with COPPS projects and initiatives had been obtained that the Council could determine and publish what works. First, CPAC surveyed police leaders, agency directors, community activists, government experts, and others to see what factors they believed were most critical for the success of a local, community-police partnership?" That survey, in turn, launched a project to determine which research factors were critical to the success of any community policing project. CPAC's interviews with experts generated a list of about 50 potential "critical success factors," under five broad headings:

▶ *Infrastructure.* This is composed of values and resources that the program or project needs before it can begin to accomplish its goals.

▶ *Partnerships.* The qualities of the relationships that are needed to stimulate various "partners" to co-operate in the program or project.

▶ *Capacity building.* Decisions, activities, and outcomes of the program or project that are key for partners and beneficiaries to achieve their goals.

▶ *Outcomes.* The desired outcomes of the program or project are clearly specified and monitored.

▶ *Policing.* All activities undertaken by police services, individual officers, or other police representatives—as well as civilian employees—that are related to the initiative.

CPAC initially sought new funding and partners to assist with conducting empirical studies to determine which of the 50 factors actually made a difference in the success of new community problem-solving initiatives.

Source: Adapted from Community Policing Advisory Council, "Best Practices: Community Policing," http://www. communitypolicing.ca/community-mobilization-project (Accessed September 13, 2010).

Royal Canadian Mounted Police

The **Royal Canadian Mounted Police (RCMP)** has its origins in May 1873, when the Parliament of Canada established a central police force; in 1920 the name became the Royal Canadian Mounted Police, and headquarters was moved to Ottawa from Regina.[7] Today the RCMP has 28,000 employees (about 10,000 of whom are civilians and volunteers) who work in 4 regions, 15 divisions, and more than 750 detachments.[8]

As noted above, the RCMP provides community policing services under contract in all provinces and territories of Canada, except Ontario and Quebec. The official view is that the adoption of community policing allows the RCMP to become more responsive to the needs of the communities it serves.[9]

The RCMP's COPPS model is termed **"CAPRA"** (C = Clients, A = Acquire/Analyse Information, P = Partnerships, R = Response, A = Assessment of Action taken). The model emphasizes the importance of:

- developing and maintaining partnerships and trust within communities/the workforce to establish priorities for service delivery and preventive problem solving,
- understanding our clients' perspectives on work-related matters for establishing priorities and potential partnerships in service delivery, and
- encouraging ongoing feedback for continuous improvement.

CAPRA is designed, according to the RCMP Web site, to

> assist the police officer or other members of the work force to anticipate problems and to prevent problems from arising, where appropriate, in consultation with partners, as much as it is to resolve problems through multi-disciplinary, inter-agency and consultative processes. It is a method of service delivery that focuses on providing the best quality service by reflecting an understanding of clients' needs, demands and expectations and, where possible, using partnership approaches.[10]

Through community cooperation, the RCMP pledges to:

- uphold the principles of the Canadian Charter of Rights and Freedoms
- provide a professional standard of service
- ensure all policing services are provided courteously and impartially
- work with the community and other agencies to prevent or resolve problems that affect the community's safety and quality of life
- act within the Canadian justice system to address community problems
- promote a creative and responsive environment to allow all RCMP members to deliver community policing services.[11]

JAPAN

More than 6,850 islands compose Japan, which are spread from the tropical island of Okinawa to the near arctic conditions of Hokkaido. However, the four main islands of Kyushu, Shikoku, Honshu, and Hokkaido contain 98 percent of the land mass. Although only slightly smaller than Canada in overall landmass, about 70 percent of Japan's population (127 million people) reside in a narrow corridor running down the eastern coast of the main islands; with Tokyo's 12 million inhabitants, Japan is one of the most densely populated cities in the world.[12]

Earliest Community-Based Approach

Japan's Showa Constitution contains many articles that are similar to those found in the Fourth, Fifth, Sixth, and Eighth Amendments to the U.S. Constitution[13] and can lay claim to possessing the oldest and best-established community policing system in the world. Japan initiated its system immediately after World War II out of a combination of traditional culture and American democratic ideals. According to Jerome Skolnick and David Bayley, four elements seem to be at the core of this philosophy: (1) community-based crime prevention, (2) reorientation of patrol activities to emphasize nonemergency servicing, (3) increased accountability to the public, and (4) decentralization of command.[14]

Police Organization and Responsibilities

Police responsibilities under the Police Act include "protecting life, person and property; preventing, suppressing and investigating crimes; apprehending suspects; traffic enforcement; and, maintaining public safety and order." Each of Japan's 45 prefectures has its own autonomous police force, and together they employ about 291,000 sworn officers.[15] Also, Japanese neighborhood crime prevention associations (the Japanese tradition of the *gonin-gumi*, a group of five people in a neighborhood) have generally given Japanese culture a much closer relationship between people and their neighbors.

Figure 14–1 is an organizational structure for the National Police Agency, or NPA.

Kobans

The community policing philosophy of Japan is embedded in its long-standing **koban** system. Police boxes (the koban) and residential police boxes (known as chuzaisho-boxes in which police live) are subordinate units of police stations and are located in sub-districts of the station. They are the focal points of community police activities, serve as the "Community Safety Center" for local residents, and play the leading role in the maintenance of the safety of local communities through links with the people and local government bodies. The Japanese koban system consists of about 13,000 total kobans, 6,000 of which are similar to U.S. police substations, and 7,000 residential boxes, or chuzaisho. Each koban is staffed by relatively small number of police officers (3–5 officers is usual); each chuzaisho is usually staffed by a single officer.[16]

The National Police Agency's Web site states that:

> Outside their Koban and Chuzaisho, police officers patrol their beats either on foot, by bicycle or by car. While on patrol, they gain a precise knowledge of the topography and terrain of the area, question suspicious-looking persons, provide traffic guidance and enforcement, instruct juveniles, rescue the injured, warn citizens of imminent dangers and protect lost children and inebriates.[17]

In April 2009, 20 female police officers were stationed at koban (police boxes) in 10 different locations in Tokyo. This was the first time that female officers were stationed at a koban on a full-time basis in the nation's capital (previously, the Tokyo Metropolitan Police department was the only prefectural police unit in the country not allowing women to work full-time in koban).[18] Female officers—who total about 15,000 nationwide, or about 5 percent of the total—have traditionally not been allowed to carry guns, and there was no indication about whether or not that policy would be changed.

There are also mobile police boxes, or wagons, that assist the koban as needed, and temporary kobans are established at times as well.[19] No koban may be less than six-tenths of a mile from

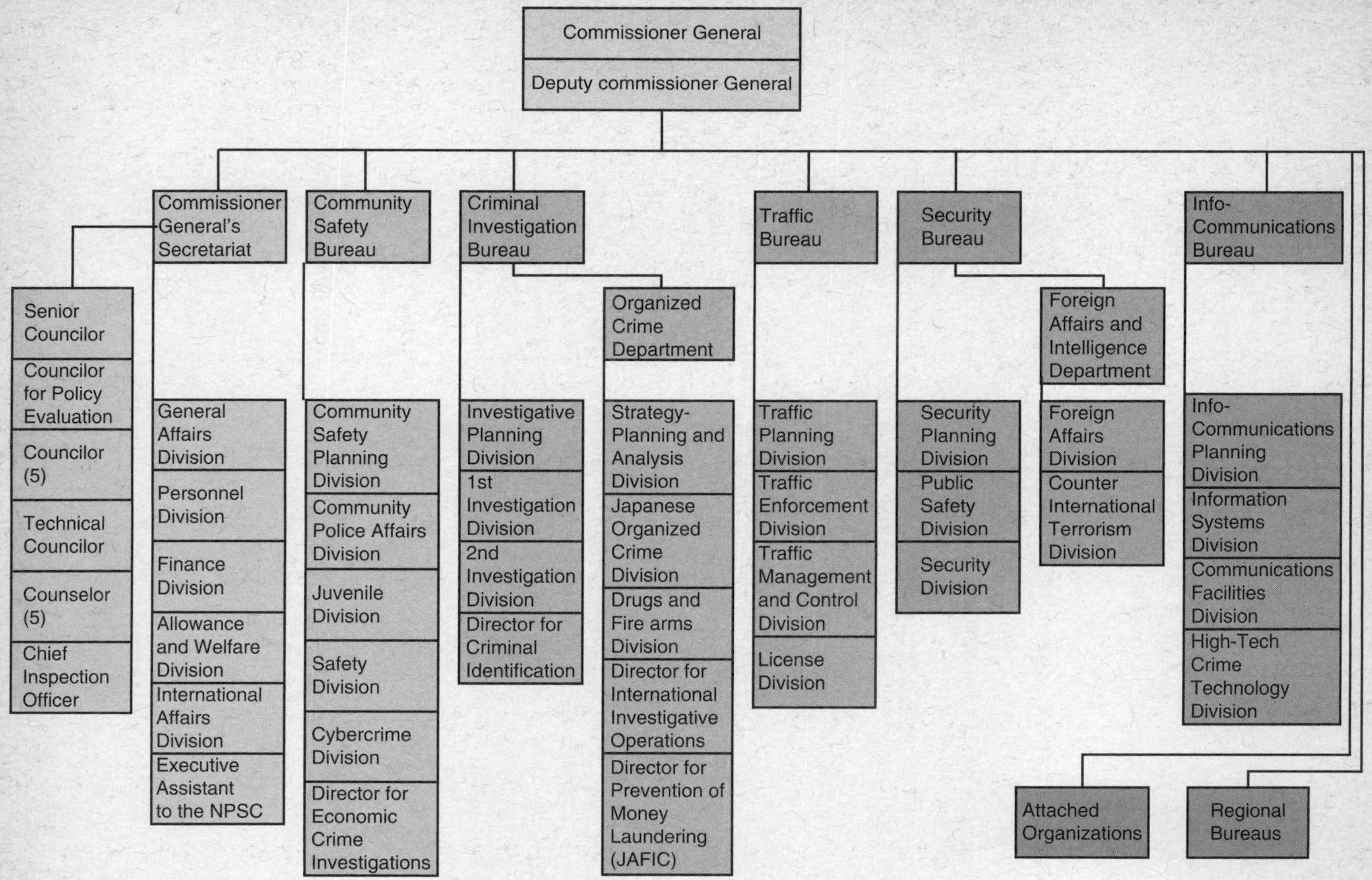

FIGURE 14–1 Organizational Structure, National Police Agency

Source: National Police Agency, *Police of Japan*, p. 3, http://www.npa.go.jp/english/kokusai/POJ_2011.pdf (Accessed May 24, 2011).

Japanese officers in koban
Courtesy of Michael Toppa

another one. They are often put in areas with more than 320 criminal cases per year, more than 45 traffic accidents, and a high volume of pedestrian traffic.[20]

Kobans consist of a reception room with a low counter or desk, telephone, radio, and wall maps; a resting room for personnel, often with a television set; a small kitchen or at least a hot plate and refrigerator; an interview room; a storeroom; and a toilet.[21] The officers' work shifts are long; they spend 24 hours at the koban every 3 days. From a tour of duty in a koban, officers move on to detective work, traffic patrol, riot police, and other specialized assignments.[22] Following is one author's description:

> [The koban officer] has a wealth of . . . data on the jurisdiction . . . such as lists of people working late at night who might be of help as witnesses to crime, of people who are normally cooperative with the police, of people who own guns or swords, of all rented homes and apartments that might serve as hideouts for fugitives of people with criminal records, and of people with mental illness; organizational charts of gangs in the police station jurisdiction (sometimes with photographs of all the gangsters); lists of old people in the area living alone who should be visited periodically . . . and of all bars, restaurants, and amusement facilities in the jurisdiction; a short history of the koban; and a compilation of the total population, area, and number of households in the jurisdiction.[23]

Herein lies a fundamental difference between the Japanese and American police: Whereas American police come to the home only when called by citizens, their Japanese counterparts are constantly watchful of, informed about, and involved with the people in their neighborhoods.

AUSTRALIA

Composed of six states and two territories, Australia has 3 million square miles (about the size of the 48 contiguous United States) and. 22.3 million people.[24] Australia's indigenous inhabitants, a hunting-gathering people collectively referred to today as Aboriginals and Torres Straits Islanders, arrived more than 40,000 years ago, but today only accounts for about 2.5 percent of the population (517,000 of the citizens).[25]

The responsibilities of the Australian Federal Police, headquartered in the nation's capital of Canberra City, include policing the **Australian Capital Territory (ACT)**, or the more remote areas known as the "bush." The ACT is headquartered in Belconnen.[26]

ACT Policing consists of five police stations (patrols), and police constables based at these stations provide general duties, which include community policing. The AFP's organizational structure is shown in Figure 14–2.

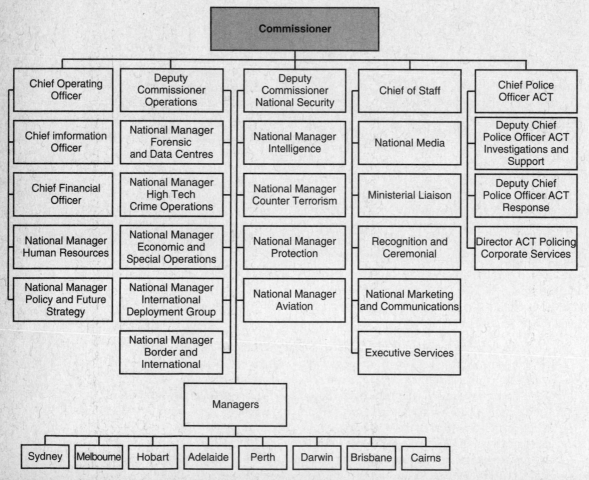

FIGURE 14–2 Australian Federal Police Organizational Structure

Source: Australian Federal Police, *Annual Report, 2008/2009*, p. 12, http://www.afp.gov.au/media-centre/publications/~/media/afp/pdf/a/afp-annual-report-2008-2009.ashx (Accessed September 13, 2010).

As seen at the bottom of the AFP's organizational structure, Figure 14–2, there are eight national divisions where AFP provides national coordination and support to operational areas. The AFP's priorities are:

- Preventing, countering, and investigating terrorism
- Illicit drug trafficking
- Transnational and multi-jurisdictional crime
- Organized people smuggling (including sexual servitude and human exploitation)
- Serious fraud against the Commonwealth
- High-tech crime involving information technology and communications
- Regional peacekeeping and capacity building
- Money laundering[27]

The AFP provides community policing services not only in the more populated areas, but also in the ACT and the external territories. It uses skills from both these areas to support the significant offshore commitments to law and order and peace operations delivered by the International Deployment Group (IDG). The IDG was formally established in 2004 to provide the Australian government with a standing capacity to deploy Australian police domestically and internationally to contribute to stability and capacity development operations.

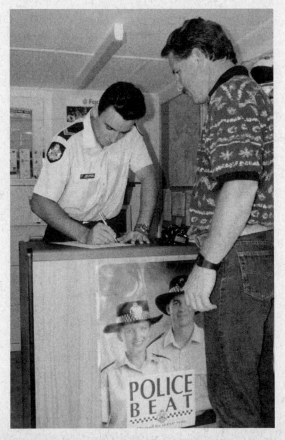

An Australian police officer takes a crime report at a neighborhood station.

According to its 2009 *Annual Report*, recently AFP staff have been developing a community survey to sample 10 percent of the Tongan population, focusing on developing new community policing initiatives, and enhancing aviation security at Australia's 11 major airports (deterring, preventing, and responding to threats of terror; investigating serious and organized crime; performing a community policing role).[28]

Certainly policing the ACT, or bush, requires duties and activities that are quite different from those of most police officers.

COPPS IN EUROPE

Sweden

Located in northern Europe, in the eastern part of the Scandinavian peninsula, Sweden is bordered on the west and northwest by Norway, on the northeast by Finland, and on the east by the Baltic Sea. The fourth largest country in Europe, Sweden has an area of 173,731 square miles), slightly larger than California. Its population is estimated at about 9 million.[29]

Given that Sweden has not participated in any war for almost two centuries (and it maintained an armed neutrality in both World Wars),[30] it is not surprising that COPPS has long formed this nation's perspective on policing policies, structure, and administration.

Sweden began laying its foundation for COPPS in 1972 with the establishment of a national centre for research, development, and coordination of policing; the centre's aim was to educe crime at its social and community roots. A National Council for Crime Prevention was also formed to work with police, social services, and youth groups, and it soon possessed a vast databank of crime prevention techniques and began publishing the "best and brightest" ideas and programs among the local police departments nationwide. Eventually, local crime prevention councils were established in 232 of the country's towns and cities. This Council would also facilitate the introduction of community policing and provide a forum for the community as well as for the police. Police became more user-friendly and accountable for their actions.

Conversely, the Swedish police became quite engaged in situational crime prevention (discussed in Chapter 4), aimed at reducing actual crime rates in each neighborhood by removing persons and opportunities from the area. As a result, they engage in the mapping of crime and the evaluation of their COPPS efforts, based on clear goals.[31]

France

France has the largest land area of any Western European nation and lies between the Mediterranean Sea on the southeast and the Bay of Biscay and English Channel to the north and west. France has a total land area of 211,208 square miles and a coastline of 2,130 miles (being about four-fifths of the size of Texas). France's population is estimated to be about 60 million.[32]

As in Sweden, the development of COPPS over the past 30 years has been marked with tremendous progress in social crime prevention. During the late 1970s and early 1980s, France underwent a number of wrenching social changes, and saw an increase in violence and property crimes, together with local, politically-inspired acts of terrorism. The French national government, sensing that a hard-nosed and repressive police force was making matters worse, published the

Peyrefitte Report that called for a social answer to the crime problem. As a result, the government appointed a committee to study the following factors:

- The psychological aspects of violence
- The effects of improved urban planning on human behavior
- Linkages between economic opportunity and violence[33]

The Peyrefitte Committee, which is similar to the Swedish National Crime Prevention Council discussed above, criticized the traditional structure of French "top-down" police bureaucracy, which had become secretive and unresponsive to public needs and demands. The committee recommended that more power be given to communities to determine their own security programs, and to involve key neighborhood persons and organizations in coming up with workable solutions. This development prompted the national police administration, in partnership with the judiciary (prosecutors, investigating magistrates, parole and probation officers), to form its own council for crime prevention at the most efficient suppression level possible.[34]

Following that, in 1997 the *Local Security Contract* was created to further build partnerships between municipal crime prevention programs and the police. Contracts were signed between police and mayors of cities and towns. Then, in August 2002, the French Parliament enacted legislation that created the *Local Security and Crime Prevention Councils*, to further integrate social crime prevention with security techniques and to leave the important decision-making powers with the local communities.

France also increased the use of local beat officers, who received some special training in community policing skills; these officers developed a number of innovative outreach techniques that proved effective in reducing crime while improving community feelings of safety and participation.

Notwithstanding all of this progress, according to Jones and Wiseman,[35] major problems remain, however, such as the following:

- France is more centralized than most other European countries; therefore, it is more difficult here than in other countries to establish effective policing practices and control them at local level.
- A deep chasm remains between the police and the citizens. Because of their paramilitary history, the police are felt to be overly unilateral in adopting new policies without notifying the public or seeking their input.
- A serious problem exists with minority communities and immigrants, primarily Muslims. As a result, whole neighborhoods turned into "no go" zones for police, controlled by immigrant youth gangs. There is a total lack of police-community interaction and cooperation in those areas, resulting in the spread of local terrorist support cells

It can be fairly said, then, that COPPS in France is still evolving. While it has many enviable crime prevention innovations and has established COPPS permanently, the French police have been seen as slow and tentative in the entire process. As a result, a missing element of COPPS is community participation, which leads to repressive policies being instituted from the top down.[36]

Great Britain

There are 43 police forces in England and Wales: There are 27 county police forces, 8 combined police areas (where 2 or 3 counties have been united for policing purposes), and 6 metropolitan forces.[37] Almost all police forces in this region are introducing or are actively considering the introduction of COPPS in some form.[38]

GUIDING PHILOSOPHY.   The philosophy of community-oriented policing in Britain, as well as several important aspects of its practice (such as neighborhood-based patrols), can be traced to the formation of professional policing in the nineteenth century and the ways in which the police mandate was established and legitimated.[39]

Early architects of British policing established the idea that effective policing can be achieved only with the consent of the community.[40] From the 1970s onward, arguments in favor of greater use of foot patrol have assumed an increasingly important place in public debate about policing in Britain. Community surveys have found that more foot patrol is clearly what most people want, so there has been a return to the bobby on the beat—a virtually unanimously accepted goal of public policy.[41] Foot patrol remains a key feature of community-oriented policing in Britain.

Today, undoubtedly the key issue concerning COPPS in Britain is accountability. Public opinion is especially intense in London, where no local control over the police exists and there are about 31,500 sworn officers. Critics are calling for a greater permeation of the community philosophy throughout the police organization and in its operations. For many, to this point the community approach to policing in Britain has been more rhetoric than reality.

ROLE OF CONSTABLES.   Britain's constables have a mandate to control crime. They are to "penetrate the community in a multitude of ways in order to influence its behavior for illegality and toward legality."[42] The officer's primary role is defined as being concerned with crime and criminals, and the emphasis is largely on crime fighting and law enforcement; contact with the public is to be fostered mainly in terms of its contribution toward meeting these ends.[43]

Almost all of the 41 police authorities in England and Wales now have established formal police-community consultative committees. Some of the issues addressed by the committees are maintaining mutual trust between the police and the public; maintaining community peacefulness and improving quality of life; promoting greater public understanding of policing issues, such as causes of crime and police procedures and policies; examining patterns of complaints against officers; fostering links with local beat officers; and developing victim support services.[44]

A British constable provides a tourist with directions at Parliament Square in London.

Exhibit 14–2	United Kingdom's Nick Tilley Award

The **Nick Tilley Award** is named for Professor Nick Tilley of Nottingham Trent University, who carried out a considerable body of work in community policing in the United Kingdom and was often commissioned by the Home Office to develop problem oriented policing. The award was established in 1999 to recognize excellence in crime reduction using problem-oriented partnership principles. Appropriately, the award is presented at the annual National POP Conference held each fall in the United States and is similar to the prestigious Herman Goldstein Award for Excellence in Problem-Oriented Policing that is conferred by the U.S. Office of Community Oriented Policing Services, Center for Problem-Oriented Policing. The Tilley Award is becoming increasingly valued as a mark of quality, and as such is attracting more and better entries each year. Since 1999, nearly 600 submissions have been made for the award from British police forces.

Source: Metropolitan Police "Tilley Awards." http://www.met.police.uk/saferneighbourhoods/psa/tilley_awards.htm (Accessed September 13, 2010).

For Britain's police, Neighborhood Watch forms the most common and popular form of community-based crime prevention. Neighborhood Watch programs have grown immensely in Britain.[45]

Exhibit 14–2 describes the Nick Tilley Award that has become very prestigious in the United Kingdom for excellence in problem solving.

OTHER SELECTED VENUES

Israel

In the mid-1990s, the police in Israel, providing services to about 6.2 million people, decided to change from a basically reactive form of policing to COPPS, knowing it would not be easy. The national police force had been, for the previous 20 years, engulfed in security duties by virtue of terrorist and other emergency matters. Because of a shifting of police resources to antiterrorist and bomb disposal units, efforts to reduce crime at the local station level had not been successful, and domestic violence and family abuse had become particularly problematic.[46]

A strategic plan was developed to implement COPPS. A new headquarters unit was established to implement the planned change, beginning with a bottom-up approach that would start with the station level and officers in the field because they best knew the communities' problems. In phase one, the local police and mayors of many communities were approached and asked if they were willing to undertake the change to COPPS. Their enthusiasm was usually high. Then the officers and selected community leaders were trained in the working principles of COPPS; such training included explanations of the need for the police and the public to collaborate and of the problem-solving approach to analyzing and addressing problems.

By the second year of its implementation across Israel, more than 50 communities had undergone the shift to COPPS. Cities were "rewarded" by being allowed to send one person abroad to study COPPS in other countries. Furthermore, the shift to COPPS had advanced to such an extent that the decision was made to effect the shift at the senior management (police headquarters) level. Community Policing Centers were set up in neighborhoods to decentralize services, and a major organizational change occurred, resulting in a greater flattening of the force to empower local levels and to provide more efficient and effective police services.[47]

Hong Kong

Hong Kong's population is about 6.9 million, making it one of the most densely populated places in the world—up to 25,000 people per square mile in the urban areas.[48] Hong Kong began practicing some forms of COPPS in the 1960s, with its early policing style being typical of British colonial policing. The result was a series of police-community relations initiatives that were launched in the late 1960s, with a view to improving relations between the police and the public, developing popular trust, and cultivating public support for crime control. During 40 years of evolution of community policing, the Hong Kong police force has undergone six stages, involving five major community policing schemes with different focuses:[49]

1. Police Community Relations Officer (PCRO), a community relations program focusing on the promotion of police-community relations
2. Neighborhoods Police Unit (NPU), a crime control device with the objective of providing convenient locations for the public to report criminal activities to the police and offer support for combating crime
3. Junior Police Call (JPC), centering on the control of juvenile delinquency and including a range of activities and programs for youth
4. Police School Liaison (PSL), dealing with juvenile crimes in school by working with students, authorities, and teachers
5. Neighborhood Watch (NW), which organized local residents' efforts to control and prevent burglaries and sexual offenses

The first stage of community policing for Hong Kong occurred from 1968 to 1973. With the relaxation of police-community tension as the theme, the police established the Police Public Information Bureau. The second stage was the adoption of a community orientation in crime control that signaled Hong Kong's entering the era of community policing. The focus was on two-way communication, and the PCRO marked the first major attempt by the police to reach community members and involve them in crime fighting.

The third stage was the rapid growth of community policing across Hong Kong. The PCRO was quickly expanded to cover every police district, and the NPU, the JPC, and PSL concepts were launched. The fourth stage was the retrenchment of the police-community relations effort briefly from 1983 to 1985. The focus was on the reorganization of tight police resources for effective crime control. NPUs were replaced by a small scale of Neighborhood Police Coordinators (NPCs)—viewed widely as a step backward from the force's previous police strategy.

The fifth stage involved reassessment, during which community policing was under a severe test in a tight resource situation. There was a lack of consensus among police administrators concerning the proper role of community relations activities within the broader context of crime control. The introduction of NW and the restoration of PSL indicated, however, that community policing had remained a preferred strategy for policing the society. The sixth stage was reorientation, with community relations affirmed as the key aspect of the policing strategy. The focus of this stage has been the improvement of the police's public image and collaborative police-community working relationships for crime control.

Today the PCROs have taken an active role in liaisoning with community leaders, and the NPCs have attempted to work with community members. The JPC officers have devoted their full attention to approaching young people, and the PSLs have spent most of their time keeping

| Exhibit 14–3 | India's Homeland Security Initiatives |

Community policing was instrumental for the Kochi City Police in Kerala, India, to change public perceptions of the police from "a necessary evil to a friend and partner." Their philosophy shifted to one of "bringing policing to the doorsteps of the people" and working with citizens to solve public safety problems through community policing. Through a collaborative initiative called "Janamaitri," new committees composed of police officers, citizens, residential associations, and local level leaders have resulted in a 70 percent reduction in the number of fake visa cases, which has helped to reduce the number of individuals entering the country for possible terrorist activities. Kochi City police also initiated Aspirations, a mega campaign utilizing celebrities from all walks of life to portray the ill effects of terrorism in an artistic way, and they created a toll-free Terrorist Reporting Hotline where people can anonymously report suspicious activity 24/7.

Source: Adapted from International Association of Chiefs of Police, "Community Policing," http://www.iacpcommunity-policing.org/about.php#10 (Accessed September 13, 2010).

close contact with schools and schoolchildren. The NW is probably the weakest among all of these programs in terms of communication with the community. Police officers seem more approachable through the NPU and NPC concepts, and the PCRO remains the backbone of the police dedication to COPPS.

Several lessons can be learned from this case study. Hong Kong entered into community policing four decades ago for the primary purpose of obtaining public support for ordering the society. Five major policy schemes have evolved to translate this strategy into action, but they have met with limited success. This lack of progress in the force's COPPS strategy and the limited performance of its policy initiatives are mainly due to the force's pragmatic approach of using COPPS initiatives for the sole purpose of crime control and prevention. Without proper public support, consultation, and participation, COPPS will fall short in attempting to provide a mechanism for addressing crime and disorder.

Exhibit 14–3 discusses a COPPS initiative in India.

Summary

This chapter discussed COPPS as it has developed internationally. Several common themes or practices are identifiable: taking the police from their "mechanized fortresses" and putting them in closer contact with the public (together engaging in the use of problem-solving methods), decentralizing the organization to areas and neighborhoods, developing a sense of community, and sharing decision making (empowerment) with the public. We also saw that some venues initiated a pilot project before implementing the concept department-wide; another common denominator seemed to be the need for sound evaluations of COPPS to determine what works.

Finally, this chapter has shown that the COPPS approach is not that different in foreign venues from what it is in the United States. Perhaps most important, this chapter demonstrated that we are indeed learning from, and sharing with, one another. We are a "global village"; we hope this spirit of scholarly interaction will continue. We should also be mindful, however, that the foreign experience is not necessarily a recipe for Americans to replicate; rather, it can serve as a point of departure in considering what is feasible.[50] These venues offer an opportunity for us to examine issues that might arise as COPPS continues to spread across the United States.

Items for Review

1. Discuss the general system of policing in Canada, including the federal, provincial, and municipal systems.
2. Describe the structure and functions of the Royal Canadian Mounted Police, including its COPPS model, which is termed "CAPRA."
3. Explain the police functions and responsibilities in Japan, with particular emphasis on the koban concept.
4. Review the responsibilities of the Australian Federal Police, to include how it serves the rural (ACT) areas.

5. Explain how crime prevention lies at the root of COPPS in both Sweden and France, as well as other similarities of their approach to, and practice of this philosophy.
6. Review the role of constables in Great Britain.
7. Explain the five stages in the development of community policing in Hong Kong.

Learn by Doing

1. You are an assistant sheriff in your county, where the county manager is a native Canadian. He has developed an interest in further developing the COPPS initiative in your organization, and has a keen interest in: (1) how the Canadians engage in this strategy in general, in such a vast land; and (2) how COPPS functions there under CAPRA as well as the CPAC's emphasis on determining "what works" and evaluating outcomes. You are to draft a report containing such information. What will you report?

2. Your criminal justice professor has undergone emergency surgery, and as her teaching assistant you must fill in and lecture in her "Multiculturalism in Community Policing" course for two weeks. She asks you to prepare and present a lecture on the differences between COPPS in the United States and Japan. What will you say in your lecture?

Notes

1. Mark Kesselman, "Order or Movement? The Literature of Political Development as Ideology," *World Politics* 26 (1973):139–154.
2. Encyclopedia of the Nations, "Canada," http://www.nationsencyclopedia.com/economies/Americas/Canada.html (accessed September 13, 2010).
3. Canadian Centre for Justice Statistics, *Police Resources in Canada 2009*, p. 3, http://dsp-psd.pwgsc.gc.ca/collection_2009/statcan/85-225-X/85-225-x2009000-eng.pdf (Accessed September 13, 2010).
4. Ibid., p. 8
5. Ibid., pp. 8–9.
6. Curtis Clarke, "Democratic Policing: The Canadian Experience," in eds. M. R. Haberfeld and Ibrahim Cerrah, *Comparative Policing: The Struggle for Democratization* (Thousand Oaks, CA: Sage, 2008), pp. 303–321.
7. Royal Canadian Mounted Police, "RCMP's History," http://www.rcmp-grc.gc.ca/hist/index-eng.htm (Accessed September 13, 2010).
8. Royal Canadian Mounted Police, "Organizational Structure," http://www.rcmp-grc.gc.ca/about-ausujet/organi-eng.htm (Accessed September 13, 2010).

9. Royal Canadian Mounted Police, "Contract Policing," http://www.rcmp-grc.gc.ca/ccaps-spcca/contract-eng.htm (Accessed September 13, 2010).
10. Royal Canadian Mounted Police, "Community Policing Problem Solving Model," http://www.rcmp-grc.gc.ca/ccaps-spcca/capra-eng.htm (Accessed September 13, 2010).
11. Royal Canadian Mounted Police, "Community Policing," http://www.rcmp-grc.gc.ca/nb/prog_services/comm_pol-eng.htm (Accessed September 13, 2010).
12. Living in Japan, " Geography and Population," http://www.focusjapan.com/022_16_focus_japan (Accessed September 13, 2010).
13. Richard J. Terrill, *World Criminal Justice Systems: A Survey* (5th ed.) (Cincinnati: Anderson, 2003), p. 373.
14. Jerome H. Skolnick and David H. Bayley, *Community Policing: Issues and Practices Around the World* (Washington, D.C.: National Institute of Justice, 1988).
15. National Police Agency, *Police of Japan*, p. 4, http://www.npa.go.jp/english/kokusai/POJ_2011.pdf (Accessed May 24, 2011).

16. National Police Agency, *Police of Japan*, p. 11, http://www.npa.go.jp/english/kokusai/POJ_2011.pdf (Accessed May 24, 2011).

17. Ibid.

18. *The Japanese Times*, "Tokyo 'Koban' finally get female cops," http://search.japantimes.co.jp/cgi-bin/nn20090402a7.html (Accessed September 13, 2010).

19. Ibid., p. 5.

20. David H. Bayley, *A Model of Community Policing: The Singapore Story* (Washington, D.C.: U.S. Department of Justice, National Institute of Justice, 1989), p. 8.

21. Skolnick and Bayley, *Community Policing*, p. 9.

22. Bayley, *Forces of Order*, p. 47.

23. W. Ames, *Police and the Community in Japan* (Berkeley, Calif.: University of California Press, 1981), p. 39.

24. Countries of the World, "Australian Government 2010," http://www.theodora.com/wfbcurrent/australia/australia_government.html (Accessed September 13, 2010).

25. U.S. Department of State, "Background Notes: Australia," http://www.state.gov/r/pa/ei/bgn/2698.htm#profile (Accessed September 13, 2010).

26. Australian Federal Police, *Annual Report, 2008/2009*, p. iv, http://www.afp.gov.au/media-centre/publications/~/media/afp/pdf/a/afp-annual-report-2008-2009.ashx (Accessed September 13, 2010).

27. Australian Federal Police, "Operational Priorities," http://www.afp.gov.au/about-the-afp/our-organisation.aspx (Accessed September 13, 2010).

28. Australian Federal Police, *Annual Report, 2008/2009*, p. 12, http://www.afp.gov.au/media-centre/publications/~/media/afp/pdf/a/afp-annual-report-2008-2009.ashx (Accessed September 13, 2010), pp. 72, 83–88.

29. Encyclopedia of the Nations, "Sweden," http://www.nationsencyclopedia.com/economies/Europe/Sweden.html (Accessed September 13, 2010).

30. Central Intelligence Agency, "The World Factbook: Sweden," https://www.cia.gov/library/publications/the-world-factbook/geos/sw.html (Accessed September 13, 2010).

31. Adapted from Arthur A. Jones and Robin Wiseman, "Community Policing in Europe: Structure and Best Practices - Sweden, France, Germany," http://www.lacp.org/Articles%20-%20Expert%20-%20Our%20Opinion/060908-CommunityPolicingInEurope-AJ.htm (Accessed September 13, 2010).

32. Encyclopedia of the Nations, "France," http://www.nationsencyclopedia.com/economies/Europe/France.html (Accessed September 13, 2010)/).

33. University of the West of England, "Creating Safer Communities in Europe: A Crime Prevention Sourcebook," http://environment.uwe.ac.uk/commsafe/eufranc.asp (Accessed September 13, 2010).

34. Adapted from Arthur A. Jones and Robin Wiseman, "Community Policing in Europe: Structure and Best Practices—Sweden, France, Germany," http://www.lacp.org/Articles%20-%20Expert%20-%20Our%20Opinion/060908-CommunityPolicingInEurope-AJ.htm (Accessed September 13, 2010).

35. Ibid.

36. Ibid.

37. British Broadcasting Corporation, "Crime Fighters: Policing," http://www.bbc .co.uk/crime/fighters/policeforce.shtml (Accessed September 14, 2006).

38. Adrian Leigh, Tim Read, and Nick Tilley, *Brit POP II: Problem-Oriented Policing in Practice* (London: Home Office Police Research Group, 1998), p. 1.

39. Mollie Weatheritt, "Community Policing: Rhetoric or Reality?" In *Community Policing: Rhetoric or Reality?* Jack R. Greene and Stephen D. Mastrofski (eds.) (New York: Praeger, 1988), pp. 153–174.

40. *Ibid.*, pp. 155–156.

41. *Ibid.*, p. 161.

42. *Ibid.*, p. 165.

43. *Ibid.*, pp. 153–174.

44. *Ibid.*

45. Skolnick and Bayley, *Community Policing*, p. 30.

46. Ruth Geva, "Community Policing in Israel," *The Police Chief* (December 1998):77.

47. *Ibid.*, p. 80. Also, for an excellent discussion of community policing in Israel, which explains the difficulties in encountering resistance of traditional military-style organizational culture as well as a lack of organizational commitment to community policing, see David Weisburd, Orit Shalev, and Menachem Amir, "Community Policing in Israel: Resistance and Change," *Policing: An International Journal of Police Strategies and Management* 15 (1) (2002):80–109.

48. Wikipedia, "Hong Kong," http://en.wikipedia.org/wiki/Hong_Kong#Demo graphics (Accessed September 15, 2006).

49. Hong Kong Police, *Community Policing in Hong Kong: An Institutional Analysis* (Hong Kong: Author, no date).

50. Bayley, *A Model of Community Policing*, p. 29.

The Future
Bright or Bleak?

KEY TERMS AND CONCEPTS

"Accelerators" of crime
Cybercrime
Federalization (of police)
Futures orientation

Intelligence-led Policing
Language of policing
Militarization (of police)
POP *Guides*

Police Futurists International
Predictive policing
Succession planning

LEARNING OBJECTIVES

As a result of reading this chapter, the student will:

- Understand why a futures orientation is important for policing, and be aware of a national organization that has as its sole purpose the study of police futures

- Know how certain "accelerators" of crime—firearms, alcohol, and drug abuse, in particular—will affect society and the police in the future, and why the police must "tool up" in order to deal with cybercrimes

- Comprehend the need for today's police leaders to engage in succession planning, in order to professionally develop police leadership for the future

- Be aware of the views of some police authors and observers who believe that there is a trend of policing to become more federalized and militarized

- Be familiar with the authors' concerns with the language being used in policing in general, as well as the blithe use of labels and creating new eras of policing

Nothing happens unless first a dream.

—CARL SANDBURG

The highest of arts is to affect the quality of the day.

—H. D. THOREAU

INTRODUCTION

As William Tafoya observed, "For 45,000 years humankind huddled in the darkness of caves, afraid to take that first step into the light of day. Police leadership must now be out in front, pointing the way for others to follow, not waiting for someone else to set the pace."[1]

It has been said that the only thing that is permanent is change. Perhaps more than anything else, this book has demonstrated that axiom. Even the historically tradition-bound domain of policing has been shown to be dynamic, as is the general American society in which it exists. But much work remains to be done. The question that should be at the forefront of our minds, and that of the police, is: "What will the future bring?" This question becomes even more poignant and ominous when we consider the world's present state of affairs.

What we hope to do in this chapter is to try and explain why a futures orientation is important for community oriented policing and problem solving (COPPS) and to discuss some areas in which the police must have foresight. In that sense, perhaps this chapter poses more questions than it answers.

We begin by considering why it is important for the police to take a futures orientation, and briefly discuss a national organization that has as its sole purpose the study of police futures. Next, we look at society and the changing nature of crime on the police of the future, including how **"accelerators" of crime**—firearms, alcohol, and drug abuse—will come into play and how the police must "tool up" in order to deal with cybercrimes.

Next is the need for today's police leaders to engage in what is termed succession planning—grooming and providing leadership development for the subordinates of today, so as to have fully capable police leaders for the future. We then review some police authors and observers who believe there is a trend of policing to become more federalized and militarized. Following that, looking backward as well as ahead, we consider the language being used in policing in general, as well as the seeming tendency of some in the field to use labels and creating eras of policing anew. This is now occurring the **intelligence-led policing** and **predictive policing**, and we believe that it is harmful for the police of the future.

After a look at the future challenges facing the police in order to fully embrace COPPS, we conclude the chapter with "Learn by Doing" scenarios, where you can apply your knowledge of the future to hypothetical situations.

WHY A FUTURES ORIENTATION?

Rationale

Because of the reactive nature inherent in their occupation, police officials have tended in the past not to be overly concerned about the future. Even those chief executives who are concerned about the future and futures research usually concentrate on the next budget year rather than on a 5- or 10-year strategic plan for their agencies.[2] But the future is here and probably is changing faster than anyone can envision. As examples, most of us can remember a world without automatic teller machines or cellular phones, but these items as well as computers have changed the world—and the opportunities for crime—in ways that no one could have imagined.[3]

Police chief executives must therefore have a **futures orientation**, anticipating and planning for the future. They must have the capacity to not only manage change but also thrive on it. Boyd et al., point out:

A world exists beyond traditional police exercises of annual budgeting, strategic planning for 3- to 5-year periods, and critical incident debriefings. Futures research

Seal of Police Futurists International.
Courtesy Police Futurists International.

leads to the examination of the probable, possible, and preferable outcomes of the future, and [it] provides a basis for decision making today that will lead to a preferable future.[4]

These administrators also shoulder the responsibility for seeing that the best and brightest individuals are recruited and trained to become the best officers they possibly can be in their performance. They can develop profiles of the skills needed by officers of the future and contemplate how best to integrate testing and recruitment that will attract candidates most likely to fulfill the skill set needed.[5]

A Police Futures Organization

An excellent resource exists for the purpose of planning and forecasting police operations: the Society of **Police Futurists International (PFI)**. PFI was founded in 1991; its members are law enforcement practitioners, educators, researchers, private security specialists, technology experts, and other professionals dedicated to improving criminal and social justice through the professionalization of policing.

PFI focuses on long-range planning and forecasting, as it attempts to more accurately anticipate and prepare for the evolution of law enforcement 10, 20, and even 50 years into the future. Futurists do not view the world as a hodgepodge of unconnected entities acting in arbitrary or random fashion, coincidentally interacting without purpose or meaning. Furthermore, futurists are not preoccupied with immediate concerns, although they do not discount them. Futurists believe that in most organizations, a time lag of three to five years occurs between making a decision and its impact on the organization. Futurists also believe that virtually anything can be changed in society's organizations, given a lead-time of two decades.[6]

MAJOR CHALLENGES AHEAD: THE NATURE AND TYPES OF CRIME

Policing—and therefore COPPS—will be severely challenged in the future by several factors that are both internal and external to the field. In this section, we look at some societal issues that will need to be confronted.

"Accelerators": Firearms, Alcohol, and Drug Abuse

There are about 23 million violent and property crimes each year in this nation.[7] A number of factors contribute to the high number of victimizations: immediate access to firearms, alcohol and substance abuse, drug trafficking, poverty, racial discrimination, and cultural acceptance of violent behavior.[8] While that figure is certainly massive, the good news is that the U.S. crime rate fell from 1992 through 2004 to its lowest point in a generation, although it increased somewhat in 2005 and the first half of 2006. Many people believe that it is because of smarter policing through COPPS as well as tougher sentences on criminals.[9]

Still, there are serious problems with respect to violence in the United States. In both the immediate and distant future, police will continue to deal with the "new violence" that has emerged over the past 10 to 15 years. Today an entire culture has emerged that sees the use of violence as an end in itself. The people who make up this culture (gangs, pseudo-gangs, well-armed young people, and others) are not going to change their way of thinking or reduce their hostility and aggression, and for these people, many of whom are fueled by drugs, the wanton use of violence—aggression for the sake of aggression—is not abhorrent behavior. Taken in combination, these factors present challenges for police leaders. Police will need training and education far beyond what they are given today to understand such violent behavior.[10]

It is well known that substance abuse (including both illicit drugs and alcohol) is a major factor in crime and violence. Nearly 4 in 10 violent crimes involve alcohol, half of convicted jail inmates were under the influence of drugs or alcohol at the time of the offense, and 3 out of every 4 convicted jail inmates were alcohol- or drug-involved at the time of their current offense.[11] Most police agencies remain reactive to the drug trade. They sweep street corners, arrest users and low-level dealers, rely on specialists (narcotics units) to assume primary responsibility for drug-law enforcement, and participate in regional task forces (generally when funded by the federal government). Police leaders will have to "think outside the box" in the future in response to a changing drug market. All agencies will need excellent problem-solving skills and a well-planned strategic approach to deal with the drug trade. More agencies must become involved in teaching employees about market analysis and forecasting in the drug trade.

In addition to drugs and alcohol, another crime accelerator—guns—might still increase the risk of victimization and a general fear of crime. This is a well-armed nation: While estimates vary widely, one source estimated that 250 million guns are legally owned in the United States, and with roughly 83 to 96 guns per 100 people, we are approaching a statistical level of a gun for each person[12] Consequently, gun violence in the United States has become both a criminal justice and a public-health problem; firearms are still the weapons most frequently used for murder and are the weapons of choice in nearly two-thirds of all murders. Strategies and programs to reduce gun violence include interrupting sources of illegal guns, deterring illegal possession and carrying of guns, and responding to illegal gun use.[13]

Cybercrime

Cybercrime will also greatly challenge the police through such activities as data manipulation, software piracy, industrial espionage, bank card counterfeiting, and embezzlement. Hackers of all ages are breaking into computer systems of major corporations and obtaining credit card, telephone, and account information; some entice children for sexual purposes.

We may not have yet seen the worst that can happen: cyberterrorism. Imagine a world where the information superhighway could be used to remotely access the processing control systems of a cereal manufacturer, changing the levels of iron supplement, and thereby sickening and killing children who eat it; disrupt banks, international financial transactions, and stock exchanges, causing our citizens to lose faith in their economic system; or attack air traffic control systems and aircraft in-cockpit sensors, causing large civilian aircraft to collide. These are the domain of the serious, determined cyberterrorist, and the future of terrorism involves much more than planting a relatively harmless virus in a computer system or hacking into a major corporation's voicemail system.[14] These types of crimes require the development of new investigative techniques, specialized training for police investigators, and employment of individuals with specialized, highly technological backgrounds. If the police are not prepared, these crimes could become the Achilles' heel of our society. As Special Agent Edward J. Tully of the FBI sees it, "The specter of a Three Mile Island in the banking industry must cause all of us serious concern."[15]

A "CRISIS STAGE": PREPARING FUTURE LEADERS WITH SUCCESSION PLANNING

Another aspect of the future of policing and COPPS concerns the leadership of police organizations. Soon the administration, management, and supervision of police agencies could be in a crisis stage, at least unless measures are taken in the near future to prepare for what is coming: the current aging, turnover, and retirement of "baby boomers" and other generational employees. Today an essential part of every chief's job is to prepare colleagues in the organization for the next advance in their careers; indeed, today the mark of a good leader is ensuring a ready supply of capable leaders for the future. Thorough preparation of successors can help a chief establish an important legacy—one that will sustain the improvements and progress that have been made, offer opportunities for mentoring, and instill the importance of the organization's history.

Chiefs need to take a long view and look at **succession planning** and leadership development as a continuous process that changes organizational culture. To provide for the ongoing supply of talent needed to meet organizational needs, chiefs should use recruitment, development tools (such as job coaching, mentoring, understudy, job rotation, lateral moves, higher-level exposure, acting assignments, and instructing) and career planning.[16]

Organizations may already have a sufficient pipeline of strong leaders—people who are competent with the ground-level, tactical operations but who are not trained in how to look at the big picture. While not everyone can excel at both levels of execution, there needs to be an effort to help prospective leaders develop a broader vision. As one author put it, "Prepare employees to read as follows: to take on broader roles and 'escape the silos.'"[17]

In addition to attending a police promotional academy or and management institute specializing in developing police leaders, *agencies* can also provide skill development opportunities by having those persons with leadership potential do things, such as oversee a challenging problem-solving initiative, plan an event, write a training bulletin, update policies or procedures, conduct training and research, write a proposal or grant, counsel peers, become a mentor, and write contingency plans. Meanwhile, the *individual* can be laying plans for the future through activities, such as undertaking academic coursework, participating and leading in civic events, attending voluntary conferences and training sessions, reading the relevant literature, studying national and local reports, guest lecturing in college or academy classes, and engaging in research.[18]

DEBATES CONCERNING FEDERALIZATION AND MILITARIZATION

Creeping Federalization?

Some people are also concerned about how some residual effects of 9/11 have affected policing and COPPS, shifting emphases away from the local level of police work and directing available budgets to anti-terrorism rather than to solving problems involving neighborhood crime and disorder.

Certainly September 11, 2001, changed our nation's view of the world, our perception of what is required to maintain a safe existence, and our views of law enforcement and security in major ways. Some observers, however, perceive a trend of the local police being co-opted by federal law enforcement agencies, as well as the police themselves becoming more militarized in this era of community policing. A companion question is whether there is room for a dual role: Certainly the public appreciate having the Officer Friendly type of public servant; however, when they experience a serious problem, danger, or victimization, do they prefer that their officers forcefully and swiftly enforce the law?

Roberg et al. believe a trend toward federalizing local police agencies "seems to be gaining increasing momentum,"[19] while Gaines and Kappeler state that:

> Municipal police are devoting more of their attention and resources to securing the conduits of capital. Whether they are controlling the nation's borders, the Internet, seaports, or enforcing immigration laws, municipal agencies are assuming a more federalized agenda. They are experiencing greater centralization, a loss of jurisdictional integrity, and local political control. Local police are beginning to play a greater role in domestic surveillance, controlling protestors, and are becoming the eyes and ears of Federal enforcement agencies.[20]

Roberg et al.[21] argued that the trend toward **federalization (of police)** undercuts the state and local officers and agencies who are in the best position to deal with most crime, while depleting their resources and creating greater distance between law enforcers and the community, which directly conflicts with the aforementioned community era of policing.

John Baker Jr. a Louisiana State University Law School professor and a former prosecutor, sees increasing federalization of criminal law.

- There has been a proliferation of federal law—now more than 4,000 federal crimes and possibly tens of thousands of jailable regulatory offenses—which means that many people do in fact get charged
- Furthermore, federal crimes typically carry stiffer penalties, leading to alarmingly disparate results for similarly situated defendants depending on prosecutorial venue; Baker cites the case of a Nevada woman who faces up to 20 years in prison and up to $500,000 in fines for cutting down three trees on federal land near her Lake Tahoe home; by contrast, voluntary manslaughter carries a 10-year maximum.[22]

The federalization of national criminal policy is most disturbing, Baker argues, because it leads to a concentration of police power at the national level that is democratically unhealthy and undermines the most basic principles under which the nation was founded.[23]

In light of the above, many believe that it is time to think carefully about the risks of excessive federalization of the criminal law. According to the American Bar Association, Congress should not bring into play the federal government's investigative power, prosecutorial discretion, judicial authority, and sentencing sanctions unless there is a strong reason for making wrongful conduct a federal crime—unless there is a distinct federal interest of some sort involved.[24]

Too Chummy a Military Alliance?

Closely related to the perceived trend of federalization is what many see as the concurrent **militarization** of the local police. Traditionally, the Posse Comitatus Act of 1878 prohibits using the military to execute the laws domestically;[25] the military may be called upon, however, to provide personnel and equipment for certain special support activities, such as domestic terrorist events involving weapons of mass destruction. Certainly this restriction against the use of military power seems warranted in view of how the control and use of military forces in foreign venues has served to enable some foreign dictators to long remain in power, control elections, stifle dissent, trample human rights, and so forth.

Again, however, some viewers have the opinion that the line separating police and military jurisdictions has been blurred and that there has been a heightened level of activity linking the military to the police. For example, in his 2007 testimony before the U.S. House of Representatives Subcommittee on Crime, Radley Balko, senior editor for *Reason* magazine, stated that: "Since the late 1980s, millions of pieces of surplus military equipment have been given to local police departments across the country: military-grade semi-automatic weapons, armored personnel vehicles, tanks, helicopters, and airplanes." Balko noted that these transfers of equipment have caused a dramatic rise in paramilitary SWAT teams over the last quarter century, which, he testified, is troubling because paramilitary police actions are "extremely volatile, necessarily violent, overly confrontational, and leave very little margin for error."[26]

Of course, not all Americans perceive a threat or harm posed by increased collaboration between the police and the military; and, for their part, the police will no doubt welcome military assistance rendered during such crises as hurricanes or terrorist attacks. State national guard units have a nearly 400-year history in the United States, being founded as militias in the earliest English colonies when the colonists organized their able-bodied male citizens for protection against Indian attack, foreign invaders, and to even win the Revolutionary War.[27]

CLICHÉ-ORIENTED POLICING OR COPPS?
A CALL TO "JETTISON—THE JARGON"

"Splitting Eras"

In Chapter 1, we discussed the three eras of policing through which policing has passed, and established that we are now—with the advent of community policing and problem oriented policing—in the *community era*. Today, however, some would believe that we are now in, or that "*the next era* of policing" is intelligence-led or predictive policing (these concepts were discussed in Chapter 5). Still others say that we are in an "information era," or announce that "We're not doing community policing now, we're doing CompStat."

Here, as we examine the future of policing, we wish to address what is perhaps a historical tendency to label everything anew, not talk straight, and use clichés to a fault, and to consider what constitutes—or does not constitute—a new era in policing.

To begin, the following quote is taken from a January 2010 article and made by a high-ranking member of the Los Angeles Police Department concerning predictive policing (discussed in Chapter 5):

> The LAPD has assumed a leadership role in translating these successes into *the next era* of policing: predictive policing. By developing, refining, and successfully executing on the predictive-policing model, the LAPD is leveraging the promise of advanced analytics in the prevention of and response to crime [emphasis added].[28]

At the same time, this official also stated that:

> ILP does not replace the community involvement and problem-solving approaches in the community-policing model; it extends them to include research-based approaches, information and communications technology, and increased information sharing and accountability.[29]

Given its many other challenges to be confronted, policing can ill afford to give the public (and itself) the impression that it is at sea in attempting to define what it is, what it does, where it is in terms of its place in history. However, that is precisely what appears to be happening, particularly concerning COPPS.

The use of jargon, clichés, and "doublespeak" is by no means new or limited to the police, although it has always flourished in government service. Indeed, the use of doublespeak in the Pentagon is said to have its origins back in the Vietnam War, when villages were destroyed in order to "save" them, bombings were "air support," defending against an ambush was "engaging the enemy on all sides," a retreat was actually "tactical redeployment," and a plane crash became a "controlled flight into terrain." In other federal agencies, the homeless were termed "non-goal oriented members of society," and a death in a hospital was deemed a "negative patient-care outcome." Soon the trend caught on in other sectors of society, and garbage haulers became "sanitation engineers" and the person who bagged your groceries was elevated to the status of a "career associate scanning professional."[30] And today, in policing, traffic accidents became "crashes" and "collisions," public roadways are now "surface streets" (aren't all streets on the surface?), and some or most agencies have replaced "racial profiling" with "bias-based policing."

Nor has this phenomenon been limited to the United States: in England, where the roots of modern policing may be found, a Plain English Campaign is underway and recently lambasted police forces there for using "ploddledygook"; they cite police forces who "replaced control rooms with 'citizen focus commands,' rebranded victims of crime as 'customers,' and drew up complex 'mission statements' and job titles such as 'protective services' 'citizen focus,' 'criminal justice change,' and 'director of knowledge architecture.'"[31]

Significantly, in late 2010 H.R. 946, the Plain Writing Act of 2010, was signed into law by President Obama. The law has the general purpose of improving "the effectiveness and accountability of Federal agencies to the public by promoting clear Government communication that the public can understand and use."[32]

Certainly every occupation has its own jargon—which is a body of slang, terminology, codes, and abbreviations that have come to take on certain meaning to its workers and enable them to communicate quickly. But American policing (like the military) probably has more than its share of jargon and cliches. Indeed, even the vaunted and time-honored "ten codes" vary from state to state—so much so that there has even been discussion about doing away with them alto-gether, in favor of with plain verbal communications.

We might add to Braiden's comments those of Mark Twain, who observed in 1888 that "The difference between the almost right word and the right word is really a large matter—it is the difference between the lightning bug and the lightning."[33]

The time has come to seriously question this use of clichés and tendency to label things anew. Why does this happen at all? Is it for political purposes, or for aggrandizement of self, or the work that is done? After all, in most professions emphasis is placed on estab-lishing foundations and then building on them, not on replacing them. In the legal profes-sion, civil law is civil law; in medicine, anesthesiology is anesthesiology; these terms are immutable.

In sum, the language of policing is critical to the field and too often shifting like the sands; this has become particularly acute of late, when some would blithely assign new police strategies and management tools the quality of being a new "era." New concepts such as ILP/PP do not overlay, overshadow, or replace community policing and problem solving or the broader community era in which policing now functions. Rather, ILP/PP are tactics within community policing and problem solving. Information has been the lifeblood of policing for a long while, but it has only been in the past decade or so—under the community era—that the emphasis on partnering with the commu-nity has been reemphasized.

We believe that ILP, PP, and other such concepts are all *management tools* that simply provide a new evolution for better doing the work of community policing and problem solving in an information *age*. Furthermore, the role of the community in addressing and preventing crime and disorder must not be overlooked; it would be sheer folly to revert back to one of the worst aspects of the reform era: when the police were driven and judged primarily by data (i.e., numbers of arrests, response times, calls for service) and primarily seen by citizens as they raced from call to call in their rolling fortresses.

EXPANSION OF THE FIELD: POP *GUIDES*

We would be remiss without mentioning—for the purpose of addressing community crime and neighborhood problems in the future—the ever-growing library resources that exist for determining what works. The Center for Problem Oriented Policing has published to this point more than 60 *Problem-Oriented Guides for Police* covering a wide range of topics; following is a sampling of the topics that are addressed:

Drunk driving	Street prostitution	Stalking
Human Trafficking	Drug dealing	Identity theft
Cruising	Disorderly youth	Bomb threats
Witness Intimidation	Robbery at ATMs	Crimes against tourists
Spectator Violence	Bullying in schools	People with Mental Illness
Stolen Goods Markets	Rave parties	Underage drinking
Street Robbery	Clandestine drug labs	Gun violence
Aggressive Driving	Acquaintance rape	Prescription fraud

The *Guides* are normally 40 to 60 pages in length and include a discussion of the specific problem, some methods for understanding the nature of the problem, and some possible police responses to the problem. Each *Guide* describes what works with the problem, based on experi-ences of police agencies across the nation.

Newly designed "Pocket POP" guides have been developed so that officers can easily access problem-solving information in the field.
Courtesy Office of Community Oriented Policing Services.

The guides are receiving widespread attention and use. This book's co-authors have written three such guides, and have often been contacted for interviews or to author a newspaper column concerning those guide topics. As indicated above, these guides provide a wealth of information for COPPS efforts; all of the **POP guides** are available online at: http://www.popcenter.org/problems/.

IN SUM . . .

More to the point of this book—the practice of community oriented policing and problem solving—we conclude with the acknowledgement that this strategy has not yet become the predominate strategy in and practice in all of this nation's 17,000 law enforcement agencies. Therefore, it must still be said that much work remains to be done:

- Police organizations must come to believe that they alone cannot control crime and must truly enlist the aid of their communities in this endeavor.
- Chief executive officers must realize that the traditional reactive mode of policing is not sufficient for today's challenges and must change the culture of their departments, implement COPPS, flatten the organizational structure of their departments, and ensure the proper evaluations of officers' work.
- Organizations must become learning organizations (discussed in Chapter 9) in order to adapt to change and evolve with the times.
- Chief executives who are competent and worthy must be given the necessary job security to accommodate COPPS because the short-term, at-will employment of chiefs places COPPS at risk.
- Organizations practicing COPPS must work with their communities, other city agencies, businesses, elected officials, and the media in order to sustain COPPS.
- Unions must work with their agency administrators to effect the changes needed for COPPS.

Police must avail themselves of future technologies as they become available, such as this in-car computer with a GPS mounted on the top of the monitor. Computers can add many capabilities to the patrol function; one that is rapidly expanding in use is the automated license plate recognition system, which can read license plates by the thousands and search for wanted vehicles.

- Chief executives and supervisors must develop the necessary policies and support mechanisms for COPPS, including recruitment, selection, training, performance appraisals, and reward and promotional systems.
- Chief executives and supervisors must begin viewing the patrol officer as a problem-solving specialist and give officers enough free time and latitude to engage in proactive policing.
- Chief executives and supervisors must come to view COPPS as a department- and citywide strategy, rather than as a small separate division or appendage, and invest in technology to support problem-oriented policing.
- Chief executives must attempt to bring diversity into their ranks to reflect the changing demographics and cultural customs of our society.

Only time, and the proper effort, will determine whether or not these goals are met.

Summary

Is the cup half full, or is the cup half empty? Should we be optimistic or pessimistic about the nation's future? One thing that is for certain is that our society is changing. This chapter has examined the future, including the need for police to plan for it as well as some prognostications for the COPPS strategy. As noted above, peering into the future raises as many questions as it provides answers. This is obviously a very exciting and challenging time to be serving in police agencies.

The years ahead are not likely to be tranquil, either inside or outside the halls of the police agency. Many dangers and issues now exist that increasingly compel us to "read the tea leaves" with greater trepidation. Today's police leaders must not wait for someone else to set the pace. Bold leadership is essential today to prepare for the future of police reform. More than ever before, police leaders must shoulder the responsibility for seeing that the best and brightest individuals are recruited, trained, and then become the best officers they possibly can be. Police administrators can benefit greatly by anticipating what the future holds so that appropriate resources and methods may be brought to bear on the problems ahead; what is certain is that they can no longer be resistant to change or unmindful of the future. Challenges have always arisen for the men and women of our society who have chosen to wear the badge, but we are confident in their ability to successfully meet anything the future will bring.

Items for Review

1. Discuss why a futures orientation is important for police executives and supervisors, as well as the national organization that exists to foster the study and practice of that orientation.
2. Provide an explanation of the kinds of "accelerators" and challenging crimes that the police must be trained to address in the future.
3. Define succession planning and explain why today's police leaders must engage in that practice.
4. Review the concerns of and reasons for some police observers' beliefs that there is a trend the police to become more federalized and militarized.
5. Explain the authors' concerns with the language of policing in general, particularly the tendency to use new labels and to create new eras of policing; include intelligence-led policing and predictive policing in your response.
6. List a summary of the challenges facing the police in the future in order to fully embrace COPPS.

Learn by Doing

1. As the head of your agency's planning and research division, you have been assigned by your police chief to attend a "Future Leaders Conference" sponsored by your area Chamber of Commerce. Prior to attending, you are to develop a vision of the kinds of challenges that will be facing law enforcement leadership in the year 2020, particularly regarding COPPS, nature of crimes, and the necessary qualities of police officers for performing problem-solving projects. What will be your responses?

2. Your police department has a history of promoting from within, and the popular chief has just announced that he will retire in one year. While guest lecturing to your agency's Citizens' Police Academy, one of the attendees is extremely concerned about what your agency has been doing (i.e., succession planning) and will continue to do in order to ensure that a highly qualified individual will become the next chief. Assuming the agency has been very active and innovaative in doing so, what will be your response?

3. Almost since its inception, the USA Patriot Act has been shrouded in controversy. Critics worry that such powers as roving wiretaps and secret searches of records could lead to invasion of privacy. You have been invited to attend a conference with your criminal justice professor and co-author a scholarly paper setting forth how COPPS can provide even greater assistance in support of homeland security in the future. What will be your basic position?

Notes

1. William L. Tafoya, "The Changing Nature of the Police: Approaching the 21st Century," *Vital Speeches of the Day* 56 (February 1990):244–246.
2. Sandy Boyd, Alberto Melis, and Richard Myers, "Preparing for the Challenges Ahead: Practical Applications for Futures Research," *FBI Law Enforcement Bulletin* 73 (1) (January 2004):2–3.
3. Ibid., p. 3.
4. Ibid., p. 4.
5. Ibid., p. 5.
6. Police Futurists International, "About PFI," http://www.policefuturists.org/about_pfi.htm (Accessed August 8, 2010).
7. Department of Justice, Bureau of Justice Statistics, "Criminal Victimizations, 2005," http://www.ojp.usdoj.gov/bjs/cvictgen.htm (Accessed January 18, 2007).
8. Lee P. Brown, "Violent Crime and Community Involvement," *FBI Law Enforcement Bulletin* (May 1992): 2–5.
9. Ibid., p. 3.
10. Sheldon Greenberg, "Future Issues in Policing," in *Policing Communities: Understanding Crime and Solving Problems*, eds. Ronald W. Glensor, Mark E. Correia, and Kenneth J. Peak, (Los Angeles: Roxbury, 2000), pp. 315–321.
11. U.S. Department of Justice, Bureau of Justice Statistics, "Criminal Offenders Statistics," http://www.ojp.usdoj.gov/bjs/crimoff.htm#inmates (Accessed January 15, 2007).
12. Edith M. Lederer, "Americans Have Far More Guns Than Any Other Population," Associated Press, July 8, 2003.
13. David Sheppard, "Strategies to Reduce Gun Violence" (Fact sheet no. 93) (Washington, DC: U.S. Department of Justice, Office of Juvenile Justice and Delinquency Prevention, February 1999), p. 1.
14. Stanford University, "Computers, Ethics, and Social Responsibility," http://cse.stanford.edu/class/cs201/projects-98-99/computer-crime/future.html (Accessed December 20, 2006).
15. Edward J. Tully, "The Near Future: Implications for Law Enforcement," *FBI Law Enforcement Bulletin*, 55 (July 1986): 1–9.
16. Edward Davis and Ellen Hanson, "Succession Planning: Mentoring Future Leaders." Washington, D.C.: Police Executive Research Forum, *Subject to Debate* (June 2006), p. 5.
17. Douglas A. Ready, "How to Grow Leaders," *Harvard Business Review* (December 2004):93–100.
18. Rick Michelson, "Succession Planning for Police Leadership," *The Police Chief* (June 2006):16–22.
19. Roy Roberg, Kenneth Novak, and Gary Cordner, *Police & Society* (New York: Oxford University Press, 2009), p. 480.
20. Larry K. Gaines and Victor E. Kappeler, *Policing in America* (Cincinnati: Anderson, 2005), p. 579.
21. Roberg et. al., *Police & Society*, p. 481.
22. Samson Habte, "Guest Speaker Warns of Dangers of Federalization of Criminal Law," Virginia Law

Weekly (March 21, 2008), http://www.lawweekly.org/?module=displaystory&story_id=2004&edition_id=86&format=html (Accessed July 6, 2009).

23. Ibid.

24. American Bar Association, "Task Force on the Federalization of Criminal Law 1998," http://www.criminaljustice.org/public.nsf/legislation/overcriminalization/$FILE/fedcrimlaw2.pdf (Accessed July 6, 2009; see also The 2009 Criminal Justice Transition Coalition, "Overcriminalization of Conduct, Federalization of Criminal Law, and the Exercise of Enforcement Discretion" (November 2008), http://www.2009transition.org/criminaljustice/index.php?option=com_content&view=article&id=26&Itemid=86 (Accessed July 6, 2009). Ibid.

25. Codified at 18 U.S.C. § 1385.

26. Radley Balko, "Our Militarized Police Departments," http://www.reason.com/news/show/121169.html (Accessed July 6, 2009).

27. National Guard Bureau, "About the National Guard," http://www.ngb.army.mil/About/default.aspx (Accessed July 6, 2009).

28. Charlie Beck, "Predictive Policing: What Can We Learn from Wal-Mart and Amazon about Fighting Crime in a Recession?" *The Police Chief* (January 2010), http://policechiefmagazine.org/magazine/index.cfm?fuseaction=display&article_id=1942&issue_id=112009 (Accessed February 11, 2010).

29. Ibid.

30. Michael Satchell, "Could you, er, say that again?" U.S. News & World Report, April 20, 1987, p. 71.

31. Chris Greenwood, "Plain English campaigners target police jargon," The Independent, November 10, 2009, http://www.independent.co.uk/news/uk/home-news/plain-english-campaigners-target-police-jargon-1817957.html (accessed June 22, 2011).

32. See Govtrac U.S., "Text of H.R. 946 [111th]: Plain Writing Act of 2010," http://www.govtrack.us/congress/bill.xpd?bill=h111-946 (accessed June 22, 2011).

33. Quoted in Bartleby.com, "Respectfully Quoted: A Dictionary of Quotations, No. 540," http://www.bartleby.com/73/540.html (Accessed September 12, 2010).

APPENDIX

Model Academic Curriculum for Problem-Oriented Policing

Developed in 2006 by the U.S. Department of Justice, Office of Community Oriented Policing Services, Center for Problem-Oriented Policing; available at: http://www.popcenter.org/learning/model_curriculum/files/Model_Academic_Curriculum_Syllabus.pdf.

INTRODUCTION

This curriculum has been designed for undergraduate education, but with minor modifications it can be used for graduate-level education, pre-service police training, in-service police training, and/or community-based training. It is recommended that students complete an undergraduate policing course as a prerequisite to this course.

PROBLEM-ORIENTED POLICING AND PROBLEM-SOLVING

Module 1—The Evolution of Policing

Topics

- Fundamental Objectives of Policing and the Primary Police Functions
- A Brief History of Policing
- Policing Styles and Strategies
  - Types of Patrol
  - Broken Windows Theory
  - One Traditional Police Response—**The Benefits and Consequences of Police Crackdowns**

Module 2—Community Policing

Topics

- The Early History of Community Policing
- Community Policing–An Overview
- Community Oriented Policing versus Problem Oriented Policing (or COP and POP?)

Module 3—Introduction to Problem Oriented Policing

Topics

- POP and the History of POP
- Defining a Problem
- Key Elements of POP
- Why Use POP Today?

Module 4—The SARA Model

Topics

- The SARA Process

CRIME THEORIES & SITUATIONAL CRIME PREVENTION

Module 5—Crime Theories and Crime Opportunity

Topics

- The Problem Analysis Triangle
- Routine Activities Theory
- Crime Pattern Theory
- Rational Choice Theory
- 10 Principles of Crime Opportunity

Module 6—Situational Crime Prevention

Topics

- An Overview of Situational Crime Prevention
- Problem Oriented Policing and Situational Crime Prevention

RESEARCHING/SCANNING AND ANALYZING PROBLEMS

Module 7—Identifying and Researching Problems

Topics

- Identifying and Researching a Problem
- Using Available Research Tools

Module 8—Problem Solving Resources

Topics

- Problem Specific Guides for Police

Module 9—Crime Analysis for Problem Solvers in 60 Small Steps

Topics

- Crime Analysis for Problem Solvers in 60 Small Steps

RETURNING TO THE CRIME TRIANGLE—RESPONDING TO PLACES, OFFENDERS, AND TARGETS/VICTIMS

Module 10—Responding to Crime Places

Topics

- Hot Spots
- Risky Facilities

- Crime Prevention Trough Environmental Design
- Displacement and Displacement Theory
- Closing Streets and Alleys to Reduce Crime

Module 11—Responding to Offenders
Topics

- Thinking and Acting Like an Offender
- Using Offender Interviews to Inform Police Problem Solving
- An Example of an Offender-Based Response—The Boston Gun Project: Operational Cease Fire

Module 12—Responding to Targets/Victims
Topics

- Analyzing Repeat Victimization
- Responding to Repeat Victimization

ASSESSING YOUR PROBLEM SOLVING STRATEGY AND OTHER CHALLENGES TO IMPLEMENTING POP PROJECTS

Module 13—Assessing and Evaluating Responses
Topics

- Assessment and Evaluation—Assessing Responses to Problems
- Conducting Community Surveys

Module 14—Challenges and Future Considerations for Implementing Successful POP Projects
Topics

- Time—The 4th (missing) Dimension of the Problem Analysis Triangle
- Barriers to Implementation
- Shifting and Sharing Responsibility for Public Safety Problems

INDEX